Your Children

Civil War Spain, showing places mentioned in connection with air raids

Your Children Will Be Next

Bombing and Propaganda in the Spanish Civil War 1936–1939

by

ROBERT STRADLING

UNIVERSITY OF WALES PRESS
CARDIFF
2008

British Library Cataloguing-in-Publication Data
A catalogue record for this book is available from the British Library.

ISBN 978–0–7083–2095–2 (hb)
978–0–7083–2094–5 (pb)

Typeset by Columns Design Limited, Reading
Printed in Great Britain by Antony Rowe Ltd, Wiltshire

In Memory of Matthew White
(1988–2007)
A Marvellous Boy
who never knew war and now has peace

Contents

Preface

It goes without saying that everyone who writes of the Spanish war writes as a partisan.[1]

There is nothing more depressing for the historian dedicated to truth than the prolonged prejudice caused by untruths which are supported by the prestige of authority, whether it be intellectual or moral.[2]

This book begins with the killing of children in Madrid during the Spanish Civil War. The incident was identified, described and publicized by the Republican government as a deliberate act of atrocity committed by members of General Franco's air forces at Getafe, a small town lying about ten miles to the south of the actual site of the children's deaths. My task has been to examine the historical circumstances and significance of the various events exposed in these two sentences. This book is my report.

Searching the catalogues of great libraries would turn up nothing of any relevance under the word 'Getafe'. In contrast, the enquirer would discover several dozen references should s/he instead enter the name of another Spanish township – Gernika (aka Guernica). Publication of the present book will not change this state of affairs. I do not refer here to the omission of the word 'Getafe' from my own title, though that decision was certainly a calculated one. Important events, some of them relevant to the task in hand, took place at Getafe during the war. Some of them are related here, in a dedicated chapter. But they do not include the incident that inspired the book – for the simple reason that this story never possessed empirical reality. 'Getafe' was a brilliant propaganda composite, a fictional representation, but one of incalculably greater influence than the overwhelming and obscure majority of 'historical facts'. It has more significance than most real events of the Spanish war in the same way as the *Iliad* is inconceivably more significant than the 'historical facts' of the

Trojan War. (It is, after all, no accident that Clio, with her trumpet and her book, is the muse of both history and epic-heroic poetry.)

The word 'propaganda' is used frequently in what follows, almost invariably in a negative ethical sense, but without conscious definition of its meaning or explanation of authorial intent. Now, supporters and agents of the wartime Spanish Republic were not as a rule amoral cynics for whom the end of winning the war justified any means. On the contrary, at the time they acted, most of them were convinced of the absolute rightness of their cause on the one hand and of the irremediable evil of fascism on the other. Doubtless, even some Comintern operatives can be placed in a similar category. These mostly anonymous protagonists nurtured elemental feelings of the kind encapsulated by Stalin who, in his original declaration for support for the Republic, apostrophized its importance for 'all the freedom-loving peoples of the world', and (in effect) claimed to be acting on their behalf.[3] But just as Stalin's pronouncement itself was the original sin of cynical misrepresentation, which established a template of systematic deceit for the whole campaign of pro-Republican publicity, so even the most well-intentioned word-smith or image-maker was doomed to operate within Stalin's ethically evacuated guidelines. The mission-statement of Stalin's propaganda ringmaster in western Europe, Willi Münzenberg, explained below,[4] can leave little doubt in our minds on this issue.

At the same time, the propaganda work that provides the central intellectual problem here cannot be dismissed as merely and in every respect synonymous with the empire of Stalinist (or Hitlerian) lies. To adapt a Spanish proverb featuring donkeys, not all propaganda is propaganda. At intermediate and lower levels, its creators must often have believed in the ethical purity of their product, whether the raw material was the word of Stalin on the universal matter of 'the cause' or that of some authoritative cadre of the commissariat on specific subjects such as 'the children of Getafe'. As Orwell (again) famously put it, atrocities happened in the Spanish Civil War, even though the British Foreign Secretary said they happened.[5] Thus, to shoot the messenger on sight might entail serious misjudgement. Here we touch, with regrettable but inevitable lightness, upon the issue of individual responsibility for the ideological crimes of the twentieth century that has figured so prominently in the historiography of recent years. We cannot reasonably attach moral blame to the anonymous author(s) of the

'Getafe' poster for the incalculably egregious effect its specific but fundamental untruth had upon contemporary perceptions of the war, and therefore upon its actual course, as well as upon its subsequent media and historical inscription. In the last analysis, the sense of my present argument makes it impossible to say of the editors of the *Daily Worker* (to reverse the blasphemous injunction of their French colleague Louis Delaprée) 'do not forgive them, for they know well what they do'.[6]

Yet it remains true that the knowing *invention of atrocity* not only vitiates the moral veracity of *real atrocity*, an act of desperate nihilism of which propagandists must surely be conscious, but also injects a distorting gene into the bloodstream of subsequent interpretation. Republican propaganda, above all concerning the 'aerial bombing of open cities', was the most palpably effective of any ideologically inspired campaign in modern history. It engendered a censorious scholarly and media orthodoxy that has, arguably more than anything else (I am thinking of Gernika), rendered criticism of the Republic unwelcome and anything short of negative appraisal of its enemies (*tout court*) anathema. Returning, therefore, to authorial intent, it is this discursive process which my book seeks to demonstrate, dissect and even (more ambitiously) to dissolve.

In the course of writing and rewriting, two complex events, one fictional and the other factual, occurred in the general sphere of discourse described above. Both were also specifically meaningful in terms of aerial bombing and 'collateral damage'. On a secondary level, both illustrate how mediation of events by gifted missionaries – the transformation of happening and circumstance into story – are crucial to their survival, at the immediate instance of birth and thence onwards into succeeding generations.

The first event was a feature film released in 2000: *The Devil's Backbone* (*El Espinazo del Diablo*), written and directed by the Mexican cineaste, Guillermo del Toro. The creation of this artefact was deeply imbricated with the subject of the killing of children by aerial bombardment – that is to say, on at least two levels of reference, the subject of my book. Indeed, relevant propaganda imagery issued by Republican sources of the 1930s, both literary and visual, permeates the whole film, to the extent that it becomes both a heroic elegy to dead children who were sacrificed for democracy, and an apostrophe to living children who are the legatees of its future. In del Toro's construction, the

Spanish war has a universal truth, and its sanctions are a warning against tyranny for all times and peoples.[7]

The film is set in a remote region of south-east Spain in the early months of 1939. Most of the action takes place in a residential school for orphaned boys situated in the middle of an empty plain. It later becomes evident that the place is several hours drive away from any town, main road or railway. The film's opening shot reveals the building viewed from above, out of a solid black screen. This act of revelation is identical to and simultaneous with the opening of a bomb-hatch, as if it were a stage-curtain. Next, a bomb falls away from us towards the ground. A deliberate and full-scale bombing attack on the school is taking place, with about six planes participating. In the next scene, a boy of about ten lies on the ground with a gaping wound in his temple and obviously dying. What follows is a ghost story, in which the spirit of the dead boy (Santi) seeks revenge for his murder, but also attempts to forewarn the others of a coming catastrophe.

The bomb we saw falling towards the school lands smack in the middle of the playground – but fails to explode. There it sits for the duration of the subsequent action, an absurdly distended item with unmistakably phallic overtones. It has allegedly been defused, but the boys claim that it is 'still ticking'. Its ominous presence dominates the school and the film. Since most of the school's inmates are refugees whose parents have been killed in the war, the bomb serves as an overarching metaphor for the source of their misery – the enemy, fascism.[8] The narrative is permeated by references to these themes. One of the boys, for no immediately apparent reason, wears a set of flying goggles. Another keeps a sketchbook: the first page shows a plane dropping bombs, presented in the style of a whole archive of similar contemporary drawings.[9] The school physician keeps a collection of foetuses preserved in alcohol solution. These are miscarriages or abortions carried out because of a spinal deformity known as 'the devil's backbone', which results from generations of poverty, ignorance and inbreeding. The Republic seeks to reform Spain, to ameliorate this eternal suffering, against the brutal opposition of Franco's forces.[10] In the last reel, the action is given over to anarchy and blood as the surviving boys struggle for survival

against a gang of murderous criminals. After a series of explosions, culminating in the setting-off of the big bomb, the schoolyard is filled with dead and dying children.[11]

The second significant event mentioned above was the war
between the state of Israel and the Islamic militia (or 'terrorist')
organization Hizbollah, which mainly took place in Lebanon in
the summer of 2006.[12] Like many other armed conflicts since
1936, this raised issues about bombing and civilian deaths that
first became prominent during the Spanish Civil War. The outstanding case was that of the town of Qana, raided by Israeli
bombers on 30 July. First reports stated that fifty-four civilians had
been killed, the majority of them (two-thirds were cited) being
children. These figures were carried (*inter alia*) by the BBC on its
TV news and news website. Their source of origin was not given.
An international outcry against the bombing followed, including
demonstrations in London and elsewhere. Demands for an immediate ceasefire escalated enormously. No less a body than Amnesty
International accused Israel of war crimes. Other sources, including some British MPs, stated or implied the same. The reports of
Robert Fisk (*The Independent*) and other correspondents fostered
this impression.[13] As a result, public opinion in general drew the
conclusion that Israel's response to the *casus belli* had been
'disproportionate'.[14]

Within forty-eight hours, the Israeli government expressed
regret for the action at Qana, stating that it would not have been
ordered had the military known that civilians still occupied the
buildings targetted. At the same time, Israel reiterated its claim
that Hizbollah habitually stored weapons in residential housing in
parts of southern Lebanon. Soon afterwards, the press/BBC
estimate of deaths was reduced from fifty-four to twenty-seven – a
rather neat 50% off. The statistic for children was reduced by a
greater rate. Arguably, without Qana even the miserably inadequate response of the UNO, which eventually engineered a
ceasefire on 10 August, would never have happened. Two weeks
later, the leader of Hizbollah, as well as expressing regret (in
hindsight) for the kidnapping operation which precipitated the
war, also admitted that his organization had stored weapons in
civilian housing. Within Israel, during the war and subsequently,
there was unparalled criticism of government action. Outside
Israel, there was a severe acceleration of popular disillusionment
with its policy, leading to ever-greater questioning of the unique

ethical portfolio – if you like, 'the cause' – which has always sanctioned it. Qana may yet come to play a key role in the working-out of our common destiny in the Middle East.

In producing this book I have been privileged in the willing help of others. Above all, I wish to pay tribute to the staff of the University of Wales Press. Any historian who habitually works in the mode described, often slightingly, as 'revisionism' is likely to face certain difficulties. These include a permanent, exhausting and sometimes dispiriting search for pockets of oxygen in which to air their views. When their interpretations are regarded with distaste – even with detestation – by many dedicated to an often censorious orthodoxy, the atmosphere can become insupportable. The Press has been my main moral lifeline in past years. Especially in the persons of director Ashley Drake and commissioning editor Sarah Lewis it has shown a courageous determination fully in accord with the spirit of its foundation and nurture by the University of Wales.

An explanation is necessary concerning the radically new dimension of scholarly verification represented by the internet. I made occasional use of relevant websites – overwhelmingly of Spanish origin – when writing the early drafts and revisions of my manuscript: that is, roughly from March 2004 to March 2005. During this period I was slow to realize, not only that the presence of specific material at a given website was likely to be ephemeral, but that the website itself might actually disappear permanently and without trace. At times I failed to note the precise date of accessing a site. In these cases I have adopted the procedure noted near the head of the Bibliography (see p. 291) – with apologies to readers and (especially) potentially irritated scholars, and a firm trust in their trust.

My deep appreciation goes to those who have coped with the consequences of my ignorance in some contextual fields of my subject. First of all, to John Scurr, expert on the Spanish war's military (especially aviation) dimensions, who has developed a 'second identity' as author of a compelling trilogy of novels set during and after the conflict. John read and commented – often at length – upon the chapters which comprise Part Two of the book. My thanks go to Roberto Plà and members of the 'Yahoo' e-mail list which he sponsors on the aviation history of the Spanish Civil War. My friends John Lawrence, Ralph Cummins, John Davies, Gerry Harris and Gary Smart, added the excitement of debate and the wonder of nuance to my elementary knowledge of aircraft and tactics. Under the Spanish sky's limitless canopy, my own contribution was merely ground-staff work, fuelling sorties by getting in the occasional round of drinks. I owe much – as usual – to the help and advice of Jim Carmody and Tom Buchanan, who between them seem to have the answer to every question concerning foreign intervention and non-intervention in Spain. I have a particular debt to Alun Hughes, indefatigable idealist and poet of the Spanish War, whose resolutely irenic sensibility was a source of information and moral sustenance. Also within these dimensions, Paddy Kitson, Scott Newton, Chris Norris, John and Gill Mehta, Charles Priestley and George Bernard provided encouragement for one frequently in need thereof. I am grateful for the assistance of Nick Rankin, Elena Gualtieri, Julius Ruiz, José Ramón Pelayo Loscertales, Luis Moa Rodríguez and Rob Stradling (jnr) on various aspects of research. Among so many outstanding librarians and archivists, I recall the help of Peter Keelan at Cardiff University, Eamon Dyas at The Times Archive (News International, London), and the ever-amiable volunteer staff of the Marx Memorial Library. I thank Robin Briggs and the Warden and students of All Souls College, Oxford, the Hearder family, and Meirion Hughes for their continued practical support. Without my wife, Helen, I could never hope to overcome any obstacle, least of all myself.

NOTES

1   Orwell (1938/1998), vol. 11.
2   'No hay nada más deprimente para el historiador amante de la verdad que el perjuicio prolongado que causan las falsedades respaldadas por el prestigio de la autoridad intelectual o moral.' Bennassar (2005), 307.
3   For discursive treatment of Stalin's intervention, see, for example, Howson (1998), Radosh (2001) and Payne (2004).
4   See esp. p. 115ff.
5   Orwell (1943/1966), p. 230.
6   For Delaprée, below, esp. pp. 119–20 and 128–9.
7   See n. 9, below.
8   The words 'fascism' and 'fascist' do not occur in the script, and only one scene is devoted to the atrocities of the victors. Nevertheless, anyone who sees the film, and/or reads this book, would be able to grasp the elemental allegorical message it communicates. Fascism is

still alive and demands our eternal vigilance. The moral is repeated (*mutatis mutandis*) in a more recent del Toro fantasy – this time set in the aftermath of the Civil War – *El laberinto del faun* (2004).

[9] For relevant details and references, see below, esp. pp. 154–5.

[10] A connection may be made between the tumescent nature of the bomb and the well-known cartoons of Franco as priapic centaur made by Picasso in his preliminary work for the painting 'Guernica' – which, of course, is about bombing in Spain.

[11] Review and relevant frame images of this film are available at *http://www.movieforum.com*. See also, Hermann (2002). In an interview included as part of the commercial DVD package (VFC 39017, Optimum Releasing 2002) the director dismissed suggestions that his film was 'about' the Spanish Civil War, adding 'this is just the background to the story ... though it is always present in the activities of the characters'. One of the sources acknowledged in the end-titles is a documentary sound recording: 'Madrid: Cerco y bombardeo de la capital de España', loaned by the Filmoteca de España.

[12] Here I have relied mostly on the online BBC News site (*http://news.bbc.co.uk*) and on the links to various contemporary newspaper stories that this web-page regularly provides.

[13] *The Independent*, especially 6 and 9 August 2006.

[14] The present writer continues to subscribe to this view.

Acknowledgements

The author and publisher gratefully acknowledge the permission granted by the following to reprint extracts from:

Graham Greene, *The Spectator* (September 1939)
  Reproduced by permission of The Spectator Magazine

Robert Colodny, *The Struggle for Madrid* (1958)
  Reproduced by permission of Transaction publishers.

William Soutar, *Upon the Street They Lie*
  Copyright © The Trustees of the National Library of Scotland
  Reproduced by permission of The Trustees of the National Library of Scotland.

Gabriel Jackson, *The Spanish Republic and the Civil War 1936–39* (1993)
  © Princeton University Press 1993
  Reprinted by permission of Princeton University Press

Antonio Candela, from the book *Adventures of an Innocent in the Spanish Civil War* (1989)
  Reproduced by permission of United Writers Publications.

Arturo Barea, *The Forging of a Rebel – The Clash* (1946)
  © Arturo Barea 1946
  Reproduced by Permission of HarperCollins Publishers Ltd

J. Last, *The Spanish Tragedy* (1939)
  Reproduced by permission of Geroge Routledge & Sons Ltd, London

Cary Nelson & Jefferson Hendricks (eds), *Madrid 1937: Letters of the Abraham Lincoln Brigade from the Spanish Civil War* (1996)
  Reproduced by Permission of Routledge (New York)

'Bombers' from C. Day Lewis *The Complete Poems* (Sinclair-Stevenson, 1992)
Copyright © The Estate of C. Day Lewis 1992
Reprinted by permission of The Random House Group Ltd

Herbert Read, 'Bombing Casualties' from *The Last Modern: A Life of Herbert Read* (Weidenfeld & Nicolson, 1990)

John Cornford, *Collected Writings* (1986)
Reproduced by Permission of Carcanet Press

J. Alvarez del Vayo, *Freedom's Battle* (1971)
Reproduced by permission of Heinemann.

Marcel Acier, *From Spanish Trenches* (1980)
Reproduced by permission of Ams Press inc.

E. Fisch, *Guernica by Picasso: A Study of the Picture and its Context* (Lewisburg, Bucknell University Press, 2nd edn, 1988)
Reproduced by permission of Associated University Presses

R. S. Thornberry, *André Malraux et l'Espagne* (1977)
Reproduced by permission of Droz, Geneva.

From *Spain in Arms* (1937)
© Anna Louise Strong 1937
Reprinted by permission of Henry Holt and Company.

M. Wolff, *Another Hill* (1994)
Reproduced by permission of University of Illinois Press

J.-F. Lyotard, trans R. Harvey – Originally published as *Signé Malraux*
© Société des Éditions Grasset & Fasqualle, Paris 1996
© (English translation) Regents of the University of Minnesota 1999
Reprinted with permission from the University of Minnesota Press

N. Monsarrat, *This is the School Room* (Cassell, 1939).
© Nicholas Monsarratt 1939
Reproduced by permission of the estate of Nicholas Monsarrat.

O. Katz, *Nazi Conspiracy in Spain* (Gollancz)

F. Jellinek, *The Civil War in Spain* (Gollancz)

Stephen Spender, *World Within World* (Hamish Hamilton, 1951)
   Permission granted by PFD on behalf of The Estate of Stephen
   Spender

Arthur Koestler, *The Invisible Writing*, being the second volume of
Arrow in the Blue: An Autobiography (Hamish Hamilton, 1954)
   Permission granted by PFD on behalf of The Estate of Arthur
   Koestler

H. Southworth, *Guernica! Guernica!*
   © The Regents of the University of California 1977
   Reproduced by permission of the University of California Press

E. Ambler, *The Mask of Dimitrios* (Fontana/Collins, 1966)
   Reproduced by permission of Hodder Headline

George Orwell, *Looking Back on the Spanish War* (1943)
   © George Orwell 1943

George Orwell, *Book Reviews* (1938)
   © George Orwell 1938
   Reproduced by permission of Bill Hamilton as the Literary
   Executor of the Estate of the late Sonia Brownell Orwell and
   Secker & Warburg Ltd

Every effort has been made to trace the copyright holders of
material reproduced in this volume. In case of any query, please
contact the publisher

Part One

Prelude – Spanish Bombs

Chapter 1

Prologue to an Imaginary Tragedy

Date – 30 October 1936
Place – Getafe, Madrid, Spain
Action – The Atrocity

This book was inspired by a pop song and a poster. On the face of things, neither artefact seems to possess the documentary substance required to inform us about a tragic incident of the Spanish Civil War (1936–9), reported by diplomats and war correspondents seventy years ago. Nonetheless, it was the Manic Street Preachers' smash hit 'If You Tolerate This Your Children Will Be Next', released in October 1998, which sparked off my interest in the poster from which the song's title was taken. The poster was created by the new-minted Propaganda Ministry of the Spanish Republican government in November 1936. It featured a young girl killed by bombing from enemy planes during the onslaught of General Franco's rebel troops upon Spain's capital city. Official government information and contextual news reportage located the event in the small town of Getafe, near Madrid. In what seems to have been a radical genre innovation, the shock tactic was utilized of issuing a photograph of a child's mutilated body in order to convince a mass audience of the horrors of modern warfare; of the potential danger to their own families of remaining indifferent to such atrocities; and (above all) of the urgent need to support the Spanish Republican side in the Civil War. It was the first time that citizens of the western democracies – as Britain, France and the USA were collectively called in that era

– had been brought face to face with any civilian fatality of war, leave alone the face of a child, by definition a being innocent of all but the original sin of humanity.

At the time when the Manics' song went to No. 1 in the charts, I was teaching an undergraduate module about the Spanish Civil War. Suddenly, through none of my own doing, this subject was flavour of the month amongst undergraduates in a city (Cardiff) where the band had an especially dedicated following. In the process of attempting to satisfy students' curiosity about the song's references, my own fascination grew apace. Within a short time I found myself neglecting other research interests in favour of discovering more details about Getafe and its contexts, immediate and longer term. The further I searched, the more dense became the weave of opinion, rumour, exaggeration and contradiction wound around that delicate pole whose opposite ends are fact and fiction. But one can only approach the former by familiarity with the latter: and my subject matter proved to be a puzzling paradigm of the history of the most significant – and therefore, the most lied-about – conflict of the twentieth century. For these two reasons, my appetite grew by what it fed on.

Historians usually prefer to place events at the core of their investigations rather than write about posters, songs or even documents. Events are somehow perceived as hard-edged objects which – once the researcher has barked his shins against them – can be handled, described in words, and subjected to forensic analysis on the laboratory table. This last phrase is intended to be metaphorical, but in practice the processes of exposition and explanation can often be perfectly 'phorical' – that is to say, they may be based upon unique objects that have survived the event and can be 'interrogated' as witnesses. Indeed such verifiable artefacts are often metal rather than 'meta': a necklace from the ruins of Troy, a cannon dredged from a wrecked galleon of the Spanish Armada, a brass token exchanged for beer in a company pub in nineteenth-century Shropshire. In the last analysis, however, objects are little more than accessories to belief, not wholly unlike 'relics' of saints displayed in a medieval chapel. As well as depending on pre-existing personal belief, their potency arises from a testimony that is given both before and after the fact. All the same, historians are (again, usually) more comfortable still if they begin their enquiries with a real event. By 'real', I mean an incident which it is dialectically safe to assume actually happened more or less as represented, rather than being the subject of a fictional invention, or having been disfigured by the processes of mediation. In our present culture, this presumes the presence of a certain amount of verbal (normally written) or visual (normally photographic) evidence. I began research with these minimal presumptions, but also with an open mind. The Spanish Civil War is well-nigh universally considered to be the most profoundly meaningful conflict of modern times. Amongst contemporaries it evoked commitment commensurate with its importance, manifested in a spirit of self-sacrifice and willingness to die for the cause. Outside Spain, this overwhelmingly meant the Republican cause that was ultimately crushed by the forces of General Franco's Nationalists. The war's intellectual heritage, which derives from this commitment and this sacrifice, represents a uniquely valuable store of status and reputation: if you like, of 'eternal values'. Intangible as such assets are, their spiritual influence on attitudes and assumptions concerning (or better, governing) philosophy and politics is beyond computation. It follows that the Spanish Civil War is still to this day a repository of political energy – *in other words, power.* For the seventy years since the Republic fought and lost that war, those who see themselves as in some way its legatees have nurtured and exercised this power. In a variety of manners and circumstances of the world of the here and now, they justify intellectual analyses and policy solutions by invoking the mantra of 'Spain'. The martyrdom of the Republic, the mystical sacrifice of its 'last great cause' became an ark of the covenant, a myth-complex which conveys a benediction of immortality and veracity.

For the whole duration of the dictatorship which Francisco Franco imposed on Spain following his victory in 1939, the consensus of opinion outside that country condemned almost everything about the cause for which he fought. Indeed, apart from publications emanating from kindred regimes in Spanish America, the very existence of any such 'cause' was denied as logically impossible or ignored as irrelevant and pernicious by commentators in all genres of the world's media. The Francoist state became the west's foremost cultural pariah, mindlessly consigned to the moral wasteland of 'fascism'. Since Franco's death, Spain itself has joined the west in this respect as well as every other. In the communications and education structures of its successful democracy the cause of the Republic has been elevated to prescriptive and hegemonic orthodoxy. The 'democratic' Republic's essential virtue and the essential vice of its 'fascist' enemies is – quite simply – a given.[1]

The event investigated in this book took place not in the ancient world or the pre-modern era but within the lifetime of a small but sensible fraction of the second millennium humans who may read these words. In my opening sentences I have described 'the incident', and that it was 'reported', but have carefully not stated that it 'happened'. The truth is that the atrocity of Getafe was a species of composite story, not an historical fact. The *fons et origo* of the story lay with agents of the Republican government, whose actions ensured that the basic narrative details entered the historical mainstream. Though later to be overshadowed to the point of obscurity by the greater atrocity of Gernika, 'Getafe' was of recognisable import and influence in world affairs for something like six months. It left identifiable deposits on many contemporary records, as well as on subsequently published histories. Until now, however, the incident at Getafe, and its significance for deeper understanding of the Spanish Civil War, have attracted little interest from historians. As the reader will discover, the quest for what happened in Getafe is not, and can never be capable of solution via definitive, hard-edged discovery. But as I write the infidel forces, commanded by Generals Scepticism and Suspicion, have the upper hand on my battlefield mindscape.

As profiled in its records, the story has the desired verisimilitude of all true tragedies, deploying the Aristotelian unities of place, time and action. Its scene is the small township of Getafe, situated about twelve kilometres due south of the centre of Madrid, set on 30 October 1936. On this date, Spain was 106 days into a civil war destined to last for a further 881 days. The main army of the rebel generals, commanded overall by Francisco Franco, was advancing on Madrid from the south and south-west. In the capital itself, a sense of panic was beginning to grip ministers of the Republican government. A few days earlier, the President and Head of State, Manuel Azaña, had secretly abandoned his office and fled to refuge in Barcelona. A secure line of defence no longer existed in the rebels' path. Government forces were in retreat or rout in all sectors. The sound of the enemy's artillery, softening up isolated pockets of resistance in the Guadarrama basin to the west, was wafted into the city centre on the early autumn breezes from the Sierra de Gredos. Then, on that

October afternoon – or so *some* histories narrate – this distant tocsin was joined by a more immediate alarm, a steady drone, gradually rising to a tumult that resonated from the city's imposing nineteenth-century apartment buildings and office-blocks. It may be inferred from a good deal of published commentary that what followed represented the first ever deliberate mass attack of bombing aircraft on the population of a largely undefended city.

Some reports of the attack described a massacre of civilians, with a number of children included among the fatalities. That same evening, members of the British diplomatic staff in Madrid were informed by government officials of another air raid on nearby Getafe. This *pueblo* lay directly on the enemy's route into Madrid; indeed, the Nationalist vanguard was no more than twenty kilometres away at the time. It was alleged that a number of people, including children, had been killed in this incident. Photographs were taken of at least eighteen corpses of children, aged between six and twelve years, who had evidently died violently. To be more precise, several of the victims displayed unmistakable signs that the cause of death was flying shrapnel, consistent with the action of an aerial bomb or artillery shell. Twelve days later, at a point when Franco's army seemed to be on the verge of capturing the capital city itself, examples of these photographs, accompanied by relevant reportage from Madrid, were published by communist party newspapers in Great Britain, France and the USA. Here, they were specifically identified by the place, time and action specified above. Soon afterwards, a propaganda poster (hereafter, 'The Poster') was issued which marked a new departure in the field of visual propaganda. It ingeniously combined one of the most moving of these childish death-masks with the dreadful aspect of a sky filled with German Junkers bombers.

I write the above paragraphs with an acute awareness that it will be necessary to revise them many times before the manuscript of this book is sent to the publishers, and even again (perhaps more than once) before it is finally published.[2] For its subject matter is essentially evanescent and elusive. After nearly a decade of research, what happened at Getafe remains essentially unclear to me. As we shall see, the aerodrome situated just outside the town was several times the target of enemy air raids. Yet I have become convinced that nothing *materially related* to the government's accounts, The Poster and the newspaper stories, happened there at all. No eyewitness accounts of such an incident have ever been found, or, at any rate, published.[3] No injured survivors of an enemy air raid ever gave recorded witness to what happened. The most compelling evidence to cast doubt on the established story is a set of copies of the photographs of dead children, supplied to the British press by the Spanish embassy in London. From these it appears beyond question that their subjects lived in a central district of Madrid itself, and not in Getafe.[4]

In contrast to the newspaper treatment mentioned above, no version of The Poster ever carried the name of 'Getafe'. Yet since the end of the Spanish Civil War, The Poster has become one of the most familiar among thousands of its genre produced by the conflict. It constitutes an easily recognisable image of what one contemporary called 'this most photogenic war'.[5] Its tragic portrait of an anonymous, innocent, murdered young girl enjoys a celebrity similar (if not perhaps equal) to generic depictions of Lord Kitchener and Ché Guevara. They are supreme icons of sacrificial commitment in what Eric Hobsbawm has called 'The Age of Extremes', the century *par excellence* of self-imposed human catastrophe, of world wars, revolutions, genocides: a century in which inconceivable cruelty became not simply acceptable but seemingly imperative in the common struggle for survival. Today, most observers appreciate The Poster as an artefact of vivid prophecy, a warning, five years before they happened, of the ghastly consequences of aerial bombardment in the Second World War. It seems to rationalize and epitomize the causative links between the Spanish Civil War and the Second World War: a relationship widely seen as powerful, even inevitable, rather than accidental. At the same time, it retains the immediate partisan character that inspired its creation. It was meant to appeal directly to the individual viewer of 1936, the ubiquitous 'man-in-the-street' so often summoned up by press reporters of that epoch, for assistance and commitment to the cause of the Spanish Republic. It demanded personal intervention, motivated both by human conscience and enlightened self-interest, in order to prevent further atrocity in Spain. Ultimately (it asserts) only such action could preclude the violent destruction of the observer's own family by a dedicated enemy. That enemy is fascism, the predatory and barbaric nature of which it graphically proclaims. 'By their deeds thou shalt know them'. It accuses Franco and his German allies of the mass murder of children as a deliberate act of war. Precisely because so routinely remarked, these things, too, have become an unremarkable aspect of the history of our times. On 23 November 1936, Franco suspended offensive operations against Madrid. Air bombardment of the city on any regular basis ceased, never to be renewed. In failing to capture Madrid, the Nationalist rebels had experienced their first defeat. Conversely, the government had registered its first victory – not just a military triumph, but equally one of propaganda and morale. For the time being, the Republic had survived, and with the build-up of massive military aid from its Soviet allies, the prospects for defence and even for counter-attack began to improve. During the winter of 1936–7, 'Getafe', once presented to the world as an unprecedented massacre, disappeared from government discourse, as though it had never happened. The photo-dossier was occasionally plundered for propaganda use over the issue of 'bombing of open towns', presented for the attention of international agencies, foreign politicians and the world's intellectuals. This book provides an extended interpretative survey of this resonant theme, both as a plural subject worthy of treatment for its own sake, and as dialectical context for the singular concern that lies at its core. But neither this history, nor any of the atrocities it recorded, was now linked to the word 'Getafe'. Only foreign reporters and a few others who had been present in Madrid during the period of concentrated air raids (30 October–23 November, 1936) continued to mention 'Getafe'. These were, in the main, random references confined to material published after the writers had left Spain. By 1939, it seems, hardly anybody remembered either the word or the deed.

Things worked out differently in another case. Quite apart from any consideration of propaganda tactics, the novel tragedy originally represented by 'Getafe' was simply replaced by the authentically unprecedented horror of Gernika.[6] The endless wave of publicity and emotion released by the destruction of a Basque township by the Nazi Condor Legion had the effect of washing away specific memory of the earlier atrocity, or, rather, of subsuming the lesser within the greater. Within a decade, mountains of civilian corpses, victims of air campaigns of the Second World War, effectively obscured any retrospective view of Getafe. Then – as now – select examples of newspaper issues not destined for secondary domestic consumption were consigned to attics or archives, and only The Poster remained. But in any case The

Poster never actually carried the word 'Getafe'. Whilst the Spanish war itself continued, commentators outside Spain even began to confuse the two events of Getafe and Gernika. Today, it is often (understandably) assumed that The Poster refers specifically to Gernika.

In a sense that is beyond dispute The Poster represents an imaginary tragedy, a transmutation of suffering into art. But art by its nature is hermeneutically nebulous or, like history, can even be deliberately misleading. Even the camera can lie; as in the notorious case (as some claim) of Robert Capa's controversial Spanish Civil War photo of 'Death in Action'. If 'Getafe' was an imaginary atrocity, by whom was it imagined, and why? Asking the elemental poststructuralist question of 'who benefits' led me to identify a small lesion of lies, an aborted organism from a belly soon to be pregnant with Gernika, and, in weary succession, with Nanking, with Dresden, and with Hiroshima. In the process, I have tried to illuminate the greater issue of how the Republic came permanently to occupy the moral high ground of the civil war, even though – in the course of a thousand-day struggle – the enemy drove them from every position they ever defended in battle.

Picasso's painting and its tragedy became immortal. Gernika will always remain vivid in the public mind, a lively focus of media discussion and academic debate. But is this not exactly as it should be? Is it appropriate for a non-event to be the subject of history at all? Gernika was physically destroyed, yet in the process passed into a kind of eternal life. In this sense, as in many others, Gernika was undeniably an overture to Hiroshima. The real township of Getafe was not destroyed by aerial bombardment but it nevertheless vanished from sight in a manner that never happened to Gernika or to Hiroshima. On the other hand, because the artefact of 'Getafe' was never fully obliterated, it can be offered as an exhibit in the Museum of Invented Events. If Gernika stands for truth, as firmly stands 'Getafe' for its opposite. The point is, we need both in order to have either.

NOTES

[1]   See Stradling (2007A).
[2]   In the event, they were rewritten in whole or part on seventeen occasions.

[3] But see Appendix B, below, pp. 282–6.
[4] See below, pp. 235–6 for the evidence.
[5] Cockburn (1967), p. 161.
[6] I use the Basque spelling in order to distinguish the historical event from Picasso's painting 'Guernica' that has in effect usurped the Castilian rendering.

Chapter 2

'If You Tolerate This . . .'

The Poster, with its main title 'Madrid – The "Military" Practice of the Rebels', designed and published by the Republican Ministry of Propaganda, was issued in French and English versions in November 1936.[1] In the latter, the rhetorical assertion 'If You Tolerate This – Your Children Will Be Next' appeared underneath the montage portrait of a single victim, a girl aged about ten, tagged with the figures 4–21–35. In the spring of 1937, the British Labour Party issued a pamphlet devoted to Francoist atrocity, using The Poster as front cover, but replacing the original subordinate phrases with the words 'A Record of Massacre, Murder, Mutilation'.[2] Along with other Spanish government propaganda posters of that period that also foregrounded the bombing of civilians, The Poster appeared in the form of a placard on Britain's streets, carried high during dozens of protest marches against 'Non-Intervention in Spain' sponsored by left political parties, 'Spanish Aid' and other activist groupings.[3] Although the general impression it made is now impossible to measure, circumstantial references to its contents can be traced in the correspondence and subsequent recollections of International Brigaders. At any rate, in the course of 1937 the artefact disappeared from public view, being withdrawn from circulation by the Republican authorities as part of a deliberate process of de-emphasizing the Getafe story.[4] Subsequent to 1939, it was occasionally reproduced in publications about the Spanish Civil War, above all in treatment of aerial bombing or pictorial propaganda. Then, quite unexpectedly, in the autumn of 1998, more than sixty years after its creation, The Poster became headline news once again via the curious medium of a rock group from south Wales – the Manic Street Preachers.

All four members of the original band were born and raised in
Blackwood, a Rhymney valley community where political tradition
equals the radical socialism of Labour Party tribune, Aneurin
Bevan.[5] But by the 1980s, local commitment to cooperation and
social progress seemed to have degenerated into terminal torpor
and moral indifference. In their teenage years the boys were
profoundly affected by the decline of their neighbourhood, which
had become little more than a polluted post-industrial desert, and
by the spiritual emptiness evident amongst young and old alike.
As lead singer and lyricist Nicky Wire put things: 'if you built a
museum to represent Blackwood, all you could put in it would be
shit'.[6] Perhaps the group's strong international profile – and even
some of their songs – had an effect in reviving the political
consciousness of the local community. At any rate, it was notable
that in June 2002, Arthur Scargill, venerable war-lord of the
coalminers' last campaign, and by then leader of the Real Socialist
Party, began his campaign for election to the Welsh Assembly with
a meeting in Blackwood.[7]

By the mid 1990s the Manic Street Preachers had already
justified their band title, being recognized as the most prominent
'political' voice in rock music. Just before their song based on The
Poster was released, the group appeared on television to explain
their motivation. The 1984–5 miners' strike had been a traumatic
event in the friends' collective adolescence. Drummer Sean
Moore quoted a famous slogan of the Spanish Civil War: 'it is
better to die on your feet than live on your knees'.[8] This typically
resonant phrase had been coined by the heroine 'La Pasionaria'
in a speech exhorting the people to defend Madrid at all costs. As
it happens, it was made as the 'fascist' enemy approached the
capital in late October 1936 – that is, at the very time of the
incident at Getafe.[9] In a later TV appearance, Wire (one of two
original band members who were history graduates) described
himself as 'trying to be more of a social historian'; further
asserting that 'art and politics can mix, and produce something
good'. The hit song was also acknowledged as the group's tribute
to the artistic-political influence of 1980s New Wave band 'The
Clash', whose repertoire of histrionically pugilistic leftism
included a number called 'Spanish Bombs', devoted to the poetic
heritage of the civil war in Spain.[10] At the dawn of a millennium,
the Manics' radical profile reached an apex with a tour of Cuba,

culminating in a Havana gig attended in person by Fidel Castro, who afterwards gave the boys a private audience.

Yet what actually hit the headlines in October 1998 was not the startling image of The Poster – which, after all, depicts the direct result of Spanish bombs – but its explicatory words. The title of the Manics' hit number, which went straight to the top of the charts, utilized The Poster's original subtitle 'If You Tolerate This – Your Children Will Be Next'; and the lyric made other obvious references to the Spanish Civil War. Victim 4–21–35 and her airborne murderers appeared nowhere in the packaging of or publicity concerning the various recorded versions of the song. Instead, the band created a series of thoughtful correspondences between the theme of The Poster and the sacrifices of the volunteers who went from Wales to fight in Spain with the International Brigades. The cover design for a medium-play remix CD carried a group photograph of the Welsh fighters, members of the legendary 'volunteers for liberty', taken before the battle of the Ebro in July 1938.[11] A detail from this picture also appeared in the CD album insert booklet, opposite the printed lyric, and with the complete subtitle of the poster superimposed.[12] In the lyric itself, Wire not only repeats these words as a catch-phrase in the chorus, but also quotes the remark allegedly made by one of the Welsh volunteers when asked if he wanted to fight in Spain: 'If I can shoot rabbits then I can shoot Fascists'. Finally, the song makes a nostalgic reference to the folk memory of these events which persistently surfaces in the political culture of south Wales: 'And on the street tonight an old man plays / With newspaper cuttings of his glory days'.[13]

All these tropes strive to renew the connection – a connection which for generations had been both politically and emotionally potent – between Wales and the Spanish Civil War. Furthermore, the cause-and-effect link between bombing atrocities and the individual decision to volunteer for the International Brigades was one of the most potent ideas of the propaganda representation of the 'Volunteers for Liberty', who went to Spain prepared to sacrifice their lives to defend 'the Spanish people' against 'fascist invasion'. If the Welsh volunteers had their contemporary 'bard' – a role seen as traditional in Celtic cultures, by which a gifted publicist elevates ethnic heroes to legendary status through poetry and song – it was certainly the manic nonconformist preacher, poet, and committed Stalinist, T. E. Nicholas. In 1938,

Nicholas published an elegiac sonnet in the *Daily Worker*: 'In
Remembrance of a Son of Wales (Who Fell in Spain)'. In this text,
both warrior's inspiration and poet's message seem closely identified with atrocities like that of Getafe – the subject of The Poster:

> Far from the hills he loved, he faced the night,
> Bearing, for freedom's sake, an alien yoke;
> He fell exalting brotherhood and right,
> His bleeding visage scorched by fire and smoke
>
> There, death-charged missiles blazed a trail of woe,
> Leaving each shattered hearth a vain defence
> While flocks of iron eagles, swooping low,
> Clawed out the life of cradled innocence.[14]

Sixty years on, the Manics seemed to claim a role as the new
bards, reviving and celebrating these connections as a deathless
episode in the human struggle for liberal values. When their ideas
are taken together, 'If You Tolerate This' and Nicholas's sonnet
forward the claim that the Welsh volunteers went to Spain
precisely because *they could not tolerate* the literally atrocious threat
of fascism: a doom encapsulated in the sudden and savage
murder of an innocent child.[15] The makers of The Poster
appealed to the conscience of the world to save Spain from
fascism. In Wales, in a somehow unique way – at least the
mythology of my nation teaches – that call was heard. In 1936, we
like to think, Wales *was* the conscience of the world. And, as an
official catalogue of International Brigade memorials proclaimed,
how better to illustrate the eternal realities of that threat and the
need for that conscience, in 1996 as in 1936, than The Poster of
the dead child of Getafe.[16]

As 'If You Tolerate This' rode the No. 1 chart spot for a few
weeks in 1998, the present writer was caught up in the local
enthusiasm for the Manics and their music. My history degree
course module on 'The Spanish Civil War' suddenly became
over-subscribed. A rare experience, especially in the epoch of
mass university entrance, was that students from other courses
came to 'sit in' for a lecture or two. Though, in the nature of
things, the phenomenon was superficial and mockingly transient,
I felt absurdly excited by the fact that students actually seemed to
want to know about the historical and cultural background to the
Manics' hit song. As already explained, questions arising about
the atrocity that inspired The Poster, which I was poorly placed to

answer, planted the seeds of this book. Not long afterwards, I was invited to lecture as part of an exhibition in Cardiff devoted to exploring the political and artistic influences on the art of the Manic Street Preachers. A substantial section of the exhibition was dedicated to the Spanish Civil War and the Welsh role therein. To me it seemed no accident when I discovered that pride of place had been given to The Poster, an original print on loan from the Imperial War Museum.[17] More civil war posters, including a tribute to 'La Gloriosa' – as the air force of the Spanish Republic was known – were on display. Other images included the best-known Spanish Civil War picture of all, the controversial photograph 'Death of a Republican Soldier' by Robert Capa. There were contemporary pamphlets about the conflict, and original letters home from Welsh volunteers in Spain. In general, the Spanish Civil War was presented by the exhibition as an integral part of the history of the working class in south Wales, epitomizing both its progressive tradition and its abundance of compassionate commitment.

Despite all this local enthusiasm, and the Manics' own commitment, the extent to which the message came across to the primary target – even to those who were currently reading university courses in Spanish or Welsh history – is more open to dispute. For a start, the song deliberately makes no attempt at evoking the hearer's empathetic feelings via the usual phononyms of modern war and sudden death. Though the music certainly has something of the elegiac character that some critics have seen as an outstanding feature of 'artistic' representation of the Spanish War, it aims at an ethereal beauty of sound which, if anything, sanitizes and beautifies its subject.[18] The leading online pop review magazine of the time commented:

> 'If You Tolerate This' is a masterpiece ... An emotional and heartfelt rock ballad dealing with the Spanish Civil War, it is successful in sweeping you along in grand passionate style, depositing you at the other end moved and elated, and with remnants of the song's majestic tune still glittering on your face like something angelic just passed your way.[19]

Is this last phrase a reference to the Angel of Death, as represented by the massed Junkers bombers of the Nazi Condor Legion, or the angelic status of an innocent soul, the spiritual condition attained so instantly and unexpectedly by victim 4–21–35? Indeed, the 'some kind of bliss' that HeadCleaner's critic found in the song may have complemented the routine weekend ecstasy of five million teenage punters, but probably failed to evoke interest in its political message among the vast majority.[20]

The Manics' effort of 1998 was not the first time a musical elegy had been inspired by the Getafe incident. In the 1960s, Benjamin Britten, a composer who as a troubled young man had plunged into the heady ideological atmosphere which the Spanish Civil War created amongst British artists and intellectuals, worked on a song-cycle set to poems by an obscure Scottish writer, William Soutar. Designed like so much of his output as a vehicle for the voice of his life-partner, Peter Pears, 'Who Are These Children?' was a reversion to the political passions of Britten's youth. Like Soutar, at the time he had been moved to a state of frustrated fury by the killing of children in Spain. Indeed, not only did Britten compose a funeral march that may have been the earliest non-Spanish artwork inspired by the civil war, but also, a year later, was still considering the possibility of his own enlistment in the International Brigades.[21] In the late 1960s, it seems likely that the war in Vietnam brought the composer back to the turbulent feelings evoked by Spanish bombs. His cycle reaches its climax with an agonized rendering of Soutar's chilling lines – originally written in 1937:

> Upon the street they lie
> Beside the broken stone:
> The blood of children stares from the broken stone.[22]

It was perhaps by deliberate choice that an early version of this work was premiered by Britten and Pears in Cardiff University's music department in 1969. Living in nearby Penarth at that time, and perhaps even present among the audience on the night, was a retired member of the University's teaching staff, Dr Saunders Lewis. One of the founders of Plaid Cymru (the Welsh Nationalist Party) and regarded by many as the lost leader of Welsh independence, Lewis had been president of his party in 1936 when, amongst great excitement and strong public feeling, he and two co-conspirators were tried at the Old Bailey and sent to jail for setting fire to a government establishment on the Llŷn Peninsula in north Wales. Along with many other Welsh people, members of Plaid and otherwise, the men had been outraged by the British War Office's choice of Wales – and a culturally sensitive part of

Wales at that – for the location of a new school for RAF pilots. The government's decision was part of a wider programme of rearmament, but more particularly a reaction to Hitler's announcement of the existence of a substantial German air force (Luftwaffe) the year before. Even before basic preparation of the training site began, the place had already become known colloquially in Wales as 'the bombing school'. Through the intervention of Plaid Cymru, who turned the issue into one of critical national importance, the Welsh people and their media became prematurely familiar with the military imperatives and ethical implications of airborne bombardment.[23]

In February 1936, Plaid's English-language newspaper proclaimed that 'the English Government have already begun to prepare a camp for the official practice of murder . . . for the mangling of the helpless bodies of little children, for the dropping of poison-gas bombs on innocent and helpless people.'[24] This was a powerful and prophetic discourse to employ – five months before the civil war in Spain, eight months before the incident at Getafe, and more than a year before the destruction of Gernika. It was the last of these events which was finally to bring home the bombing issue for virtually every citizen of the western democracies. But meanwhile, in the course of 1936, Plaid organized a campaign of protest, ranging from demonstrations in Bangor and Caernarfon and meetings in every Welsh township, to petitions handed in at 10 Downing Street. Several different strands of opinion coalesced in this movement. It brought together the pacifist temper of middle-class Britain, then at or near the height of its influence, the humanitarian essence of the liberal conscience, and more ethnocentric feelings of outrage at the comprehensive desecration of a place sacred to the language and culture of the Cymru. Though Stanley Baldwin's government had called a retreat on two earlier occasions, when faced with similar objections to proposed sites for the Training School – both of them *in England* – this time they bravely stuck (as it were) to their guns.

That September, as Franco's army was marching on Talavera de la Reina, the last large town that lay in its path to Madrid, Saunders Lewis and his colleagues acted. In so doing – as was certainly their intention – they became martyrs of the modern Welsh independence movement. But as they also recognized, the issues involved reached out far wider than this. As they languished for six months in Wormwood Scrubs, the unparalleled atrocity of Gernika (26 April 1937) turned the emotional debate over the bombing of civilians into much more than a theoretical issue. In May 1937, nearly 4,000 children who had been evacuated from Bilbao arrived in Southampton. These so-called 'orphans of the storm' were part of a total of up to 20,000 children who were sent abroad (to Latin America and the USSR as well as European countries) by Republican authorities in Bilbao and Valencia. The ostensible reason for this exodus was the need to save them from air raids ('the storm'). They travelled to their destinations with numerical tags hanging around their necks – if only inadvertently, a reminder of the Getafe victims to observers' minds. The 'orphans' arrived amidst a welter of publicity and frenetic fund-raising all over Britain.[25] These pathetic refugees were more voluble advocates of the Republican cause than posters and speeches, more effective than statistics and newspaper articles. The Spanish war arrived on Wales's doorstep in July 1937. Of 400 children allocated to the Principality, the majority were accommodated in a old mansion house in Caerleon, rescued by well-wishers from its abandoned state and turned into one of the best-run 'Basque Baby Homes' in Britain. Amongst many other fund-raising enterprises, 'Cambria House' produced a cyclostyled magazine. In the first issue, an essay by one of the older boys was titled 'Aeroplanes'. It describes one sunny afternoon when

> . . . suddenly, Boom, boom, boom! The aeroplanes which were Fascist ones, began to throw out their cargo of death and destruction. Then we heard the banging of the anti-aircraft guns and the sound of the hooters. All the people ran, terrified by this treacherous attack. SCUM! TRAITORS! MURDERERS![26]

Though at least saved from its worst consequences, few doubted that the Spanish children who had come to Wales were victims of war and of its new instrument, the bomber: and millions more would instinctively have added 'fascism' to this devilish list.

One amongst many concerned writers, George Orwell addressed the implications of Gernika with typical incisiveness – and equally typical moral ambiguity:

> The most horrible thought of all is that this blotting-out of an open town was simply the correct and logical use of a modern weapon. For it is precisely to slaughter the civilian population – not to

destroy entrenchments, which are very difficult to hit from the air
– that bombing aeroplanes exist.

Thus far – if Saunders Lewis was reading – he must have felt in
communion with a soulmate. But at this point Orwell's dialectic
took an acutely uncomfortable turn.

You cannot be objective about an aerial torpedo. And the horror
we feel about such things has led to this conclusion: if someone
drops a bomb on your mother, go and drop two bombs on his
mother. The only apparent alternatives are to smash dwelling
houses to powder, blow out human entrails and burn holes in
children with lumps of thermite, or to be enslaved by people who
are more ready to do these things than you are yourself.[27]

This adumbration of the ethical dilemma at the heart of
Nineteen Eighty-Four may (or may not) be taken as a desperate
justification of building 'bombing schools' in principle. Saunders
Lewis's residual objection was that this particular example was
built in Wales, on a unique site of pre-medieval Christian pilgrimage. Not long after Orwell's words were published the Pilot
Officer's Training School was officially opened. This was in July
1938, following several months during which frequent bombing
of Barcelona and Valencia by the Italian air force dominated the
foreign pages of the British press. Hitler had recently swallowed
Austria and was threatening Czechoslovakia. Lord Runciman,
Neville Chamberlain's 'independent mediator' in Prague, belat-
edly realizing that the city was within range of the Luftwaffe,
anxiously enquired as to what circumstances might justify his
returning home.[28] Meanwhile, Mussolini had bombed Abyssinia
into submission. Few could remain indifferent to the apparently
imminent threat of fascism and the bomber. Saunders Lewis,
having been released from gaol, led a deputation of protest to the
opening ceremony at RAF Penyberth. Even if saving the lives of
children had not been his primary motivation, he was still their
defender. He was evidently nonplussed by the change in mood
since he had deliberately sacrificed his liberty (and, as it proved,
his livelihood). Gernika, Bilbao, and now Barcelona, had changed
popular perceptions, bringing Orwell's awful logic home to the
fearful majority. The large crowd that attended the opening –
Lewis unconvincingly but revealingly claimed – 'were much more

impressed by . . . the Welsh Nationalist [protestors] than by the demonstrations of the baby-murderers of the English government'.[29]

But when placed in the contemporary context of international crisis, Lewis seems an equivocal figure. Though never openly, evidence suggests that along with several other Plaid leaders, he sympathized more with the Spanish Nationalists' programme than with the cause of the Republic that moved many compatriots and most younger members of his own party. Even today, Lewis is often described as 'a fascist', or an admirer of Hitler and Franco.[30] Certainly, sixty years later, it was the memory of a rather different hero of Welsh politics that helped inspire the feelings behind the Manic Street Preachers' song 'If You Tolerate This'. The band related intimately to Aneurin Bevan, socialist, idol of the miners, hero of resistance to Baldwin's 'reactionary' government, and outstanding proponent of 'Aid to Spain'. To Saunders Lewis, despite his prophetic vision of bombing atrocities, the Manics related not at all.

NOTES

[1]   For details on the history of The Poster, see below, Chapter 10. In the standard published collection of Spanish Civil War posters (Carulla & Carulla, 1997) examples are reproduced as nos. 1260 and 1261, p. 379; and the full photographic dossier as no. 1245, p. 376.

[2]   See *Madrid* (1937). In the USA, The Poster carried a slightly different wording: 'What Europe Tolerates Or Protects – What Your Children Can Expect'.

[3]   Press photographs show that representation of bombing atrocities soon entered the core of popular responses to the Spanish War. See e.g. Francis (1984), p. 206 and Stradling (2004), front cover illustration. Copies of posters were issued to sympathetic organizations by the propaganda section of the Spanish embassy.

[4]   See below, Chapter 15.

[5]   For biographical information on members of the band, see Middles (1999), pp. 18–39.

[6]   Quoted in 'Manic Street Preachers'; WPP@URL *http://www.manics.co.uk/manics/history/his_ma.htp.* (Accessed November 2002.)

[7]   Despite a typically energetic performance Mr Scargill was not elected.

[8]   'Close-Up', BBC 2, 23 September 1998.

9   Low (1992), p. 29. Dolores Ibárruri (aka 'La Pasionaria') was communist M. P. for Asturias – Spain's most important coalmining region – and a member of the PCE's executive committee.

10 'The Slate', BBC 1 Wales, 12 January 2000; see also The Clash's CD album 'London Calling', Columbia COL 4601142. It seems possible that this influential band actually took their title from that of the civil war volume of Arturo Barea's memoirs (re-issued in 1972), which is also a central source in much of what follows below.

11 'If You Tolerate This Your Children Will be Next', Sony Music/Epic 666 345 5 (1998).

12 'This Is My Truth Tell Me Yours', Sony Music/Epic 491703 2 31–491703–10 LCO199 (1998).

13 This idea may have been suggested by the opening scenes of the Loach/Allen feature film, 'Land and Freedom' (1995) in which a young Liverpudlian discovers a suitcase full of newspaper clippings and other memorabilia in the flat of her deceased uncle, a veteran of the International Brigades. The phrase about rabbits and Fascists is quoted in Francis (1984), p. 215.

14 Cunningham (1980), p. 195.

15 Wire notably explained the song as an expiation of his own lack of moral fibre: 'I wouldn't have joined the [hypothetical] International Brigades to go and fight in Bosnia – the record expresses this inadequacy': 'Design For Life', produced by Darren Broome, BBC Radio 2, 12 October 2002.

16 See Williams (1996), where The Poster adorns the back dust-cover. As I write, there are more memorials to the International Brigades in Wales than in any other country, regardless of size or population: see Lewis & Davies (2005). The 1996 book was published as the Manics were starting work on the material for what became the 'Tell Me Your Truth' CD. For more detailed content and references to illustrate material in this chapter, see my study, *Wales and the Spanish Civil War* (2004) especially chs 2 and 10.

17 'Unconvention' by Jeremy Deller, Cardiff Centre for the Visual Arts, November 1999–January 2000. The Poster also constituted the back cover of the exhibition catalogue.

18 V. Cunningham, 'Aestheticizing Responses to the Spanish Civil War', lecture given at a Continuing Education Day-School in Oxford, 25 January 2003.

19 'HeadCleaner', 24 August 1998: *http://web.ukonline.co.uk/keith.dumble/ 240898.html* (accessed November 2002).

20 All the same, the number later came in at no. 20 in a Channel 4 poll of the 100 greatest pop songs of all time; *South Wales Echo*, 8 January 2001.

21 See Stradling (2003), pp. 74–95.

22 Soutar's lines are quoted from the insert to the LP of the Britten–Pears recording of the final version: Decca SXL 6608 (1973). See also below, pp. 170–1.

23 See Jenkins (1998), and more generally, Davies (1983).

24   *The Welsh Nationalist*, February 1936. These comments were probably
     written by the paper's editor, Saunders Lewis himself.
25   In Britain, evacuees were sent to seventy different 'colonies' in every
     corner of the country: see Legarreta (1984) and Bell (1996).
26   *Cambria House Journal*, No. 1. On the 'Basque Babies', see below.
27   Review of G. Steer's *The Tree of Guernica* (from *Time and Tide*,
     February 1938): Davison (1998), 112–13 (my emphasis).
28   Runciman to Halifax, 10 August 1938, Woodward & Butler (1950),
     Nos 602 and 707.
29   *The Welsh Nationalist*, July 1938. It seems likely that Lewis's vocabulary
     was influenced by memories of the First World War, during which
     German Zeppelin raiders were characterized as 'baby killers' in the
     British press; see Fegan (2002), especially frontispiece and pp. 45,
     65–6.
30   Cf., for example, Black (2000), p. 201.

Part Two

Terror Out Of Spanish Skies

Part Two

Turn Out Of Spanish Shoes

Chapter 3

Collateral Damage, Bilateral Tactics

Everyone believes in the atrocities of the enemy and disbelieves in those of his own side, without ever bothering to examine the evidence.

[Orwell, 'Looking Back on the Spanish War'][1]

Early in 1938, Arthur Hinsley, Archbishop of Westminster, received a letter from a group of Roman Catholic Labour Party members. It protested against the stance adopted by the hierarchy in supporting Franco and the Nationalist cause in Spain. This gesture had been organized by a Catholic layman, Frank O'Hanlon, chairman of Labour's Chichester constituency association. O'Hanlon had assumed that senior party colleagues who were also co-religionists would share his sense of outrage at the clergy's betrayal of democracy. Although the Church's public demeanour over the Spanish war had been remarkably low-profile, O'Hanlon was exasperated that its leaders had so blatantly ignored the feelings of their flocks. Though hardly likely to have been surprised by the shortage of subscribers coming forward in his home constituency, O'Hanlon was surely sadly disappointed to find that only one out of eight Catholic Labour MPs was prepared to sign his letter.[2] Yet this prevarication reflected opinions existing inside Catholic homes more accurately than O'Hanlon suspected. Certainly, family sentiments were often mixed. But whilst in comparatively few cases could they be confidently described as 'pro-Franco', in general they may be fairly reported as 'anti-Republican'.[3] In the end, O'Hanlon managed to collect the autographs of only thirty prominent secular Catholics.

The Cardinal's reply may have further elucidated the reasons for this muted response. The protest letter organized by O'Hanlon had singled out a highly emotional issue, already widely referred to as 'the bombing of open towns'. To its signatories, the absolute moral culpability of the Nationalists in bombing atrocities was beyond peradventure. Indeed, Hinsley had already been the target of a similar one-sided protest, from a Catholic artists' commune and including the influential (if erratic) socialist, Eric Gill. This intervention came when the conflict in Spain was only a month old.[4] At that juncture, no relevant attack of any significance had taken place at all, whilst, in contrast, Republican squadrons were engaged in air raids on nationalist-held cities on an almost daily basis![5] The archbishop's disarming reply to Gill and company was that he had been condemning air attacks for years, having seen their effect on African villages when (by implication) carried out by the RAF.[6] However, by the time of Hinsley's exchange with O'Hanlon, the Nationalist side was embarking on a systematic campaign of aerial bombing of Barcelona and other places on Spain's Mediterranean coast. This was an unprecedented development, to which newspapers understandably gave full coverage. Indeed, only a few weeks later, the Pope (Pius XI) himself was moved to protest to Franco, despite (or in part because of) the fact that the chief instruments of destruction were *Italian* air force machines based in Majorca.[7] For his part, in answering O'Hanlon's letter, Hinsley stoutly defended the British hierarchy's position. He lamented the deaths of civilians in Spain, but argued that Barcelona was a morally legitimate target because of its vital docks and war industries. He pointed out that the nationalist-held city of Oviedo had been attacked by aircraft on no less than 208 occasions during its ten-month siege by Republican forces in 1936–7. Lastly, more in sorrow than anger, Hinsley compiled a hard-hitting paragraph of statistics:

> For eighteen months towns in Nationalist territory have been repeatedly bombed by Government forces. The authority I quote for this is the Barcelona Government organ 'La Vanguardia', 20th July 1937 to the 26th January 1938; in this list a number of towns 100 miles or more behind the lines was bombed (e.g. Seville as late as 25th January 1938, and Salamanca on Jan 22nd 1938). On 12th November 1937 the result of the bombardment of Pamplona was 100 victims, nearly all women and children ... There are other

instances not mentioned [by this source] . . . e.g. Algeciras, Tetuan, Granada, Valladolid, etc.[8]

It may be that O'Hanlon and his supporters were taken aback by this formidable catalogue; perhaps they were even shocked that its source was the Republican government's own official newspaper.[9] Yet though their confidence in the pro-Republican sympathies of the Catholic laity was misplaced, the belief that popular outrage over bombing atrocities was focused exclusively on Franco's side was not in error. Indeed, condemnation of the Nationalists was so fervent, widespread and unilateral at the time, and has been such a routine element of Spanish Civil War studies ever since, that some readers today (seventy years later) may also be shocked to discover the fact that the Republic *ever resorted* to the deliberate 'bombing of open towns', let alone the distressing revelation that it began and for many months alone sustained a tactic that its representatives later ubiquitously condemned as 'barbaric'. The difference, it seems to me, is that an interested person of the twenty-first century would be less inclined to dismiss Hinsley's information out of hand as pure propaganda, a reaction that for most people at the time was not merely possible, but hardly less than certain. Unquestioning faith in the integrity of the Republican cause – perhaps above all on the matter of war crimes – was an instinctual element in the ambience of the vast majority of people in the democracies who were sucked into the emotional and intellectual vortex of 'Spain'. In the propaganda department of the war's conduct, as in any other department, and on both sides, no room for equivocation existed. The virtual war of words may have taken place in a parallel dimension to the bloody reality of battle but it was no less committed, no less ruthless, and no less important to final victory.[10] Nonetheless, the purpose of the present chapter is to establish some parameters of empirical data concerned with what became the central ethical issue, not only of the air campaign, but of the Spanish Civil War as a whole.

Although many historians still find the situation unsettling and problematic, it has long been (tacitly) accepted that civilian casualties were caused by the action of both sides' aircraft during the thirty-two months of military conflict. A generation ago, Ramón Salas Larrazábal, a retired army officer of Nationalist allegiance, estimated that the Franco side was responsible for the deaths of some 11,000 non-combatants in the Republican zone. At the same time, he asserted, they themselves suffered about 4,000 similar mortalities imposed by their enemies.[11] Since then, several experts with loyalties in the opposing camp have accepted this as a plausible guideline.[12] Such a degree of unanimity in any matter concerning the Spanish Civil War – but especially in areas to do with war crimes and atrocities – is striking. But this potentially promising situation is compromised by the fact that until very recently no general history of the war in practice contained even a passing mention, let alone expository treatment, of the relevant Republican activity.[13] Moreover, ideologically driven occlusion of this truth is established throughout the culture of academic 'history', from the grass roots upwards. To give one example: in 1990, a compilation calling itself '*the new historians* and the Spanish Civil War' included a section of local history contributions. One of these dealt with civil defence organization in the Andalusian city of Jaén. Its opening paragraphs stated:

> The phenomenon of bombing open cities . . . became widespread throughout the duration of our last civil war . . . From the very beginning loyal [Republican] Spain suffered crude aerial attacks, which eventually became one of the worst oppressions endured by its civil population.

The essay contains no mention of Republican bombing. In fact, Jaén itself was not attacked by the Nationalists until 1 April 1937, nearly nine months into the war, and after a similar period in which Republican raids were commonplace. So much for the judicious balance of Spain's 'new historians'.[14]

The present section of my book will be largely devoted to a broad survey of the 'bombing of open towns'. As it happens, this aspect of the Spanish Civil War attracted more attention from contemporaries than any other category of its military prosecution. Most survivors of air raids were still able to recall relevant impressions and feelings when other experiences of 1936–9 had faded from memory. Moreover, much of the outside world, stimulated by the voluminous coverage of newspapers, photographs and newsreels, reacted with understandable resonance to this sensational new horror. Outrage was provoked not only on altruistic humanitarian grounds, but also because people perceived a doom of universal extent and imminent potential.[15] It is no exaggeration to claim that without the bombings of Madrid,

Gernika and Barcelona, and the unparalleled media publicity
surrounding these events, interest in the war from the wider
public, and thus its intense inquisition by subsequent schools of
writers, would have been notably more muted, and consequently
of less significance to the culture of the twentieth century. In
these circumstances, it is astonishing that no research study of the
topic appeared until writing of the present book had begun.[16] In
any case, I had never intended to provide a comprehensive and
monographic work of reference. Much of the empirical data
necessary for maturely considered assessment are still not available
in sufficiently full or reliable form. Indeed, on a more
generalized level, and in the spirit of the Orwellian dictum which
stands at the head of this chapter, readers should bear in mind
that, though I have constantly tried to cite corroborative references,
very few of the sources for this history are without some
kind of partisan inspiration or influence. It goes without saying
that the same *caveat* applies to my own procedures and arguments.
My book seeks to establish and interpret the facts on both
sides. Inevitably, this will involve both positive as well as negative
elements. Though in my own view, this book's approach to the
issue is supremely cool and objective, the inclusion of analysis that
does not automatically assume Nationalist guilt and Republican
innocence will be enough in itself to convince many readers
otherwise. I plead guilty here (pleading withal for many previous
cases to be taken into consideration) of presenting an argument
that is not overtly intended to encourage readers to make up their
own minds. However, I must also emphasize that neither is it my
intention to convince those who enter this house by one door and
with closed minds to leave it by another door with minds re-sealed
in the opposite sense.

At the time of the outbreak of military rebellion (17–18 July
1936), Spain's air forces did not constitute a single, autonomous
service – at least officially. For the most part, fighting squadrons
were loosely integrated into the complex command structures of
army and navy respectively.[17] It might be expected that members
of a specialist military category that was weightier in terms of
officer-to-others ratio even than the notoriously top-heavy Spanish
armed services as a whole would reflect the basically anti-
Republican prejudices of the officer class. Curiously, perhaps
uniquely in terms of contemporary air forces, this was not the

case. The fundamental reason for differences in political sympathy is not hard to determine. After gaining power with the coming of the Second Republic in 1931, radical reforming interests had scaled down spending on the army, in the process reducing the size, social status and political influence of its command establishment.[18] In contrast, the air force's element was one area in which investment of scarce national resources had been continued, even increased. As a relatively new addition to the family, cosseted by government and public feeling alike, the aviation services, in return, evolved a markedly (if not uniformly) pro-Republican profile.

In common with other nations of the 1930s, Spanish administrations developed a certain 'air-mindedness'.[19] A fresh impetus came after the centre-right election victory of December 1933. The new war minister, Diego Hidalgo, stated that 'Spain is defenceless', and in 1934, his successor, Gil Robles, adopted a policy of replacing obsolete aircraft.[20] The latter's special intention was to find a suitable strategic bomber type to purchase in numbers from abroad.[21] In the course of his work in the government patent office, Arturo Barea was able to observe attempts to keep abreast of the latest aeronautical developments. Typical of his generation, Barea had been fascinated by aviation since childhood. He made his first passenger flight at an early age and later witnessed the landing of the inaugural flight from Paris to Madrid.[22] Later still, on exactly the same site – the impromptu landing strip at Getafe having meanwhile become Madrid's first civil aerodrome – Barea was shown around a four-engined Junkers transport prototype that was on a world marketing tour. The King was present too, along with officers of the general staff (*Estado Mayor*): An army contract was being considered. For this reason, the Junkers' salesman was keen to display the military potential of his vehicle, which proved easily convertible into a heavily-armed troop carrier and/or bomber. 'It would take only an hour', he boasted, 'for us to modify the planes of a commercial airline somewhere in Germany, in Berlin for example, and come to bomb Madrid.' Barea, Madrileño by birth and socialist by conviction, was appalled. He was already aware of how big German companies were manoeuvring, by ruthlessly corrupt means, for the lion's share of Spain's strategically significant mineral resources, and the extent to which government agencies were prepared to comply in exchange for access to the latest military technology.[23]

Yet for all their status as the darlings of the Republic, the air forces – 'La Gloriosa' as they were later to be tagged – were never able to keep up with developments in other countries. At the outbreak of war in July 1936, the government possessed operational units comprising something over 400 dedicated military aircraft, whilst perhaps another 100 planes were in private hands and/or involved in commercial enterprises. But if not wholly unimpressive in numerical terms, the machines themselves were enormously varied and diverse in terms of age, type and origin.[24] The commitment of the fascist dictatorships to rapid development in this area was proclaimed (even exaggerated) rather than disguised: and this inevitably led to reactive rearmament moves on the part of the democracies. Consequently, Spain's aviation establishment was by current standards already obsolete. Planes were mostly French 1920s production models. There was a handful of multiple-engined bombing machines – Fokker or Junkers monoplanes, but of only marginally younger vintage. One hundred per cent of fighter models owned by the Republic were biplanes from a similar design period. However, in the crisis of summer 1936, these shortcomings were less important to the Republican cause than the benefit it received from the foresight of one official. Following the narrow Popular Front election victory of February 1936, the aeronautical director appointed by the radical left government, Miguel Núñez de Prado, became convinced that a military rising was imminent. He ordered concentration of all the best aircraft in the vicinity of Madrid.[25] The move paid dividends not only in strategic terms, but because of the fact that on the day the uprising began in Spanish home territory (18 July) all the relevant air bases remained loyal to the Republic, with a large majority of officers rejecting the rebellious overtures of their army colleagues.[26]

The immediate result was a series of local confrontations, sometimes (as in the case of Getafe aerodrome) involving pitched battles.[27] The net outcome was that by the end of July 1936, whilst up to 300 assorted aircraft had become available to the government, the rebels had gained the use of barely fifty machines on the Spanish mainland.[28] At the same time, a figure approaching two-thirds of flying officers had declared loyalty to the Republic.[29]

It is notable, for example, that in Tetuán in Spanish Morocco, where the rebellion erupted prematurely on 17 July, airmen were the only corps to oppose it: most were peremptorily 'executed' as a result.[30] It is difficult to overestimate the importance of these developments, if only because many flyers were able to take rapid and effective action in demonstration of their commitment.[31] The dramatic circumstances of its birth sharply illustrate how the conflict that was to reveal the destructive potential of aerial operations actually began, and can only have begun, in the air.

This striking imbalance of air-power in the government's favour is indicated in most textbooks dealing with the Spanish Civil War. The problem is that the student has to infer this elementary (but somehow incongruous) fact by the exercise of converse logic. Few histories fail to relate the urgent demand that General Franco made on his potential German and Italian backers: the provision of planes, a resource without which his crucial enterprise could never (as smart undergraduates put it) 'get off the ground'.[32] It is equally well-known that Franco was only able to reach Morocco and take command of Spain's only full-time professional army via a plane hired in England, which flew to the Canary Islands in order to fetch him. In all this, narrative treatment invariably stresses the significance of the origins of Franco's alliance with the fascist powers, often neglecting to explain that of its immediate strategic explanation. But in any case, as the rebel generals began to gather their forces to north and south, the Republic too looked for aeronautical support from abroad. On 23 July, the day after Franco appealed to Hitler for *ten transport aircraft*, Madrid asked the Popular Front government in Paris for *thirty bombers* and thousands of tons of relevant munitions.[33]

Although these supplies were soon in the pipeline, luckily for the rebels the Madrid government struggled when it came to making effective use of its initial aviation advantage. Having said this, its machines could hardly have been in action more rapidly. *Before the first full day of the war had elapsed,* aircraft operating from Tablada airbase near Seville launched an attack on rebel headquarters in Tetuán, across the straits of Gibraltar in Spanish Morocco. This may have been the first ever inter-continental air raid, but it was also a hastily-improvised sortie which turned into a political disaster. By the time they got back to base, the adventurers found it had fallen into rebel hands. They had caused no damage to military personnel or installations and succeeded only in killing a dozen people in Tetuán's crowded *soudh*. Outrage amongst Arab leaders led many of them to offer their full cooperation to the rebel high command, a change of heart that was to produce crucial supplies of recruits for Franco's colonial regiments.[34]

Over the next ten days, Republican forces bombed the Andalusian cities of Granada and Córdoba as well as the rebel outpost of Huesca in Aragon.[35] This process was more systematic. Córdoba, for several weeks an isolated outpost of rebel power in central Andalusia, was bombed repeatedly from an elevated airstrip at the town of Conquista, some twenty kilometres away.[36] Later, as Madrid prepared a force to recapture the city, a squadron of bombers was relocated from Getafe to Andújar. But in practice, this unit concentrated on the city itself: in order to do so even ignoring, at a crucial juncture, the tactical needs of their own advancing troops! By the end of the summer (that is to say, before any comparable Nationalist operation) some fifteen children had been killed by Republican bombing in Córdoba alone, among a total death toll of around eighty.[37] Granada, first attacked on 29 July, was the target of a further twenty-two raids during August. No fewer than thirty planes took part in one operation. Twenty-six citizens were killed in this period. Two years later, after the 121st such raid, the alleged casualty total (i.e. dead and wounded) had reached 450. With the early sorties, it seems plausible to assume that Granada was being 'softened up' prior to an attempt to recapture it by loyalist militia forces.[38] However, no military installations were damaged, whilst the local newspaper reported hits on two hospitals.[39] During the same initial exchanges of the war, similar attacks were launched against other Nationalist-held towns, either situated close to Republican territory (e.g. Teruel and Saragossa), or in one case (Oviedo) wholly surrounded by it.[40]

That summer, Republican newspapers openly celebrated successful air raids on rebel cities, either oblivious to or careless of the fact that many thousands of Madrileños would have had relatives among the residents thereof. On 1 August, for example, the communist daily, *Mundo Obrero*, declared that 'the bombings of Cádiz and Palma [de Mallorca] have sown panic'. Five days later it reported a similar operation against Valladolid. On

28 August, following the capital's first air raid, the Madrid newspaper *ABC* announced that:

> The rebels are under attack on all sides, as if they were under siege.
> They only have one weapon left – though it is completely useless in
> their hands. Operated with arrogant incompetence, it made its
> appearance over Madrid in the clear skies of early morning. The
> adventure was profitless in its results, and led only to fatal
> consequences for the aerial messenger and his sterile bravado . . .
> Rebel planes, few in number and flown by men of morbid disease
> and inferior mentality, have had no success whatsoever in this war.

On the same front page, two discrete items underlined these
points by boasting of a major attack of 'our heroic aviation'
against Oviedo in which eighty-five bombs were dropped.[41]
Likewise, *El Sol* told readers that 'our aviation, with well-aimed
attacks, has demoralized Huesca'.[42] And all this (the reader is
reminded) was before any serious attempt had been made by the
Nationalist enemy to drop bombs on urban concentrations.

Meanwhile, however, the attentions of 'La Gloriosa' had failed
to prevent Franco's airlift, and the army of Africa soon secured
the Seville–Cádiz area. By the second week of August, the advance
of the *africanistas* into the Andalusian hinterland began.[43] In this
opening land campaign of the war, Franco's field commanders
disposed of perhaps thirty aircraft, which had either been crudely
converted into bombers, or from which bombs could be (even
more crudely) thrown out by hand. These planes now attacked
the militia agglomerations which various pro-Republican
authorities deployed to prevent the rebels' advance.[44] More often
than not, militia forces outnumbered the troops opposite them by
enormous coefficients, not unusually of 10–1 or more. And
though in general poorly armed and worse organized compared
to their enemies, militia units incorporated artillery and motorized transport elements which provided legitimate targets for
bombing. Hundreds of villages lying athwart the roads leading to
Madrid provided potential shelter for ambush. The enemy were
frequently encouraged, by means of air attacks, to abandon them
ahead of the advancing battalions of foreign legionaries and
Moroccan auxiliaries.

It would not be surprising if Nationalist staff officers at times
ordered such strikes as a matter of blanket insurance rather
than because they were acting on concrete information. Franz

Borkenau who, early that September, visiting the front in eastern Andalusia, witnessed episodes of rout and panic amongst civilians and militia troops alike, attests to the dropping of bombs directly upon domestic housing, structures typically so primitive as to be death-traps for anyone caught inside.[45] A few weeks later, during the final phases of Franco's march on the capital, Arturo Barea saw evidence of bombing runs made against various *pueblos* to the south of Madrid. He claimed that even the tiny village of Novés had a family wiped out.[46] There was a dimension of 'terror' to these actions, intended to speed local inhabitants as well as militiamen on their flight to Madrid, choking the roads, spreading fear in front of the advance, and inhibiting the enemy's communications. In this sense, they seem to anticipate the classical Blitzkrieg tactics waiting to be revealed just over the chronological horizon. The issue here is that aerial attack had already become news *and therefore propaganda*. An observer whose trade was the latter more than the former, *Daily Worker* correspondent 'Frank Pitcairn', no sooner arrived at a war zone (in Aragon) than he cabled stories of bombing runs against 'Spanish workers' made by foreign 'fascist' planes.[47] Days after Cockburn filed his story, a Madrid newspaper boasted that in rebel-held Zaragoza, the Aragonese capital, 'both troops and civilians live in fear inspired by the continuous operations of our bombers'.[48] Things were no worse in Aragon than in any other war zone erupting in this fluid and chaotic landscape. No civilians on either side were safe from the deadly (if capricious) attentions of the aeroplane. No pilot ever enquired of peasant or poet with which side he sympathized. One September day, the young Cambridge poet and historian, John Cornford, watched with morbid fascination as Republican planes bombed the Aragonese village of Perdiguera, prior to its assault by the POUM militia company to which he was attached.

> The comrades with me . . . were shouting for delight as each bomb landed. I tried to think of the thing in terms of flesh and blood and the horror of that village, but I also was delighted. Now as I write three enemy planes have passed by and out of sight, but you can hear the thud of their bombs somewhere behind our lines.[49]

Throughout the first summer of the war, Nationalist armies, both northern and southern commands, remained worse off than their opponents in terms of motorized transport of all kinds, as well as in aviation resources. Aircraft were fully stretched in flying sorties which were strictly related to the rapidly developing military situation, and a large fraction of these involved the carriage of supplies to and between the various columns of Franco's advance. During September 1936, the Army of Africa captured both Talavera (about 100 kilometres west of Madrid) and Toledo (a similar distance to the south). At this point the balance of civilian casualties resulting directly from aerial bombing was strongly against the Republic.[50] As we have seen, unlike their enemies, the Republic had resources to spare for such operations. But raids were still carried out by comparatively small numbers of aircraft using relatively low-powered explosives. Death and damage caused by any single operation was light by subsequent standards. Neither side had yet staged an attack by massed squadrons of aircraft to rain large numbers of heavy bombs upon a densely populated town or city.

NOTES

1   Orwell (1938 & 1943/1966), p. 228.
2   O'Hanlon to Middleton (Hinsley's Secretary), 6 February 1938, NMLH, Labour Party, file SCW/12. For background, see Moloney (1985), pp. 63–73; Buchanan (1992) pp. 189–90 and idem (1997), p. 184.
3   See Buchanan (1992), especially p. 167ff.
4   Moloney (1985), pp. 64–5.
5   Cf. Moa (2001), p. 536.
6   Speaight (1966), pp. 273–5.
7   See below, pp. 68 and 71ff.
8   Hinsley to O'Hanlon, 26 February 1938, NMLH, file SCW/9. His information was probably provided by Franco's diplomatic agent in London (the duke of Alba) or perhaps by the pro-Franco lobby calling itself 'Friends of National Spain'.
9   In fact, as early as 12 August 1936 *The Times* reported Republican raids on several rebel-held cities – causing little damage or loss of life.
10 That this prophetic awareness was present amongst Republican leaders is clear from the account given by a main witness to the issues of the present book, Arturo Barea, head of foreign press censorship and radio 'Voice of Madrid'; see Appendix A, pp. 273–9.
11 R. Salas Larrazábal (1980), p. 310. For an important gloss on these figures, see below, pp. 255–6.
12 This is the case, for example, with Pierre Vilar, a French historian of Catalan origins whose outstanding textbook on the war begins with

an anecdote illustrating his personal commitment to the Republic: Vilar (1986), pp. 7–8, 152.

[13] An ideal example is Cortada (1982), pp. 11–13, entries (written by the editor) on the rival air forces. The article on the Nationalists concentrates on its foreign composition and bombing operations. Although twice as long, the entry devoted to the Republican air force fails to mention *even strategic bombing sorties*. Ronald Fraser, alone in this amongst authors of general studies, not only reports the bombing of 'insurgent-held towns (Córdoba, Granada, Segovia, Valladolid, to name only these)', but also adds '*causing civilian casualties*': Fraser (1979), p. 175 and note (my emphasis).

[14] Cobo Romero (1990), pp. 85–6 (my emphasis in superior quotation). The Jaén raid mentioned in the text (155 killed) was in fact a reprisal for one suffered by Córdoba (37) earlier on the same day: Hidalgo Luque (2006), 8 (refers to page number of typescript kindly provided by author).

[15] Just as the war broke out in Spain, communist leader R. Palme Dutt drew attention to an *Observer* report suggesting that a new generation of bombing aircraft would soon be able to attack targets 2,000 miles away from their bases. He noted in particular that Leningrad and Moscow were prioritized in the list of examples given: Dutt (1936), pp. 11–12.

[16] I refer to Sole i Sabaté and Villaroya i Font (2003), treated *passim* below. In 1969, a book on the air war (strongly pro-Nationalist in inclination) meticulously avoided the whole question of civilian casualties: Jesús Salas Larrazábal (1969 & 1974). The author, whose book came out in English in 1974, was a brother and comrade-in-arms of Ramón.

[17] For concise treatment of pre-war Spanish air forces, see Howson (1992), especially pp. 5–10.

[18] Even the centre-right governments of 1933–6 made little attempt to undo the various reforms put through by Manuel Azaña as War Minister and Prime Minister in 1931–2: see Moa (1999), p. 197ff and *passim.*

[19] I employ a phrase coined by Howson (1998), pp. 31–2.

[20] González Betes (1987), p. 33.

[21] Howson (1992), pp. 9–10.

[22] See below, p. 273ff.

[23] Barea (1946/1984), pp. 95–8; see also pp. 37–8, 51–3, 89–91. Barea adds 'I had been very pleased at the time that Junkers did not obtain Spanish army contracts.' But other sources indicate that a number of Junkers machines were later purchased by the Republic.

[24] Information from Sñr Roberto Pla of the Yahoo website, WPP@URL *http://www.aire.org/gce* [accessed 2004–5], to whom I am grateful for private correspondence on the subject.

[25] Howson (1992), pp. 5–6; Alpert (1977), pp. 355 and 403. Núñez was later shot by the Nationalist rebels.

[26] R. Salas (1980), pp. 186–8.

27 WPP@URL *http://www.aire.org/gce/historia/a1936.htm* (accessed 2004–05). For events in Getafe, below p. 79ff.
28 Moa (2001) p. 211 states the government held on to 430 machines out of 549. Cf. Vilar (1986), pp. 59 and 66; R. Salas (1980), pp. 79–80. The Republic's twelve modern bombers 'constituted potentially the strongest bombing unit in Spain'; Salas, p. 188n. Early deliveries of planes from France alone far exceeded foreign supplies to the Nationalists; see Cate (1995), p. 235.
29 The Nationalist aviator José Larios (1968) p. 30 claims the Republic could call on nearly twice the number of trained pilots available to rebel commanders – 155 as against 88.
30 Vilar (1986), p. 51.
31 This contrasted with the plight of other career service personnel in the government zone, where hundreds who remained faithful to their oath of loyalty were nevertheless shot or imprisoned as untrustworthy.
32 In the epoch-making airlift operation which followed, Junkers transports provided by Hitler were supplemented by machines expropriated in rebel-held western Andalusia as well as North Africa itself.
33 Díaz-Plaja (1972), pp. 38–9.
34 Howson (1998), pp. 8–9. Attacks were also mounted against Ceuta, Larache, and Melilla, the other military bases in Morocco; Solé i Sabaté & Villaroya i Font (2003), p. 25ff. (These authors will be hereinafter referred to as 'Solé & Villaroya'.)
35 Moa (2001), p. 214.
36 Bradshaw (1982), p. 7.
37 Hidalgo Luque (2006), 3–5 and 15–17. My estimates here are extrapolated from data offered in this text. See also, however, Martín Rubio (2005), pp. 92–3 and especially photographs on p. xv.
38 Such extenuation is implicitly argued by Gibson (1973/1983), pp. 90–1. He passionately condemns the 'ineptitude' of Republican pilots, but fails to consider (a) whether precision targeting was beyond their technical means, or alternatively (b) whether they were ordered to carry out terrorist killings.
39 Granada data are from Entrala (1996), pp. 240–2, which also carries photographs, allegedly of damaged hospitals. But see Solé & Villaroya (2003), p. 31.
40 Though the case of Oviedo was exceptional (see below pp. 64–6) longer-range raids also took place against Valladolid, Seville, and even Cádiz, all of which caused civilian casualties: see Abella (1973), p. 57; Bridgeman (1989), pp. 107–8, 146, 163. Cate's biography of Malraux (1995), pp. 234–42 has a useful account of early Republican operations which (however) ignores the issue of urban targets.
41 *ABC* (Madrid), 28 August 1936. (I owe this reference to Dr Julius Ruiz.)
42 Jato Miranda (1976), pp. 367–8.
43 The campaign is covered in the detailed monograph by Martínez Bande (1982).
44 For a description of rebel air operations in the south, Larios (1968),

p. 42ff. Nine of the twenty Ju 52s provided by Hitler were dedicated to strategic bombing sorties.

[45] Borkenau (1937/1986), pp. 158–65; Larios, at the time serving as bombardier, describes an attack on 'an enemy-held village close to Seville'; (1968), pp. 42–3.

[46] Barea (1984), 184–90.

[47] *Daily Worker*, 30 July 1936, in Cockburn (1986), pp. 43–9. (In Spain Cockburn was known under his reporting pseudonym of 'Frank Pitcairn'.)

[48] *ABC* 1 August 1936. (I owe this reference to Dr Julius Ruiz.)

[49] Sloan (1938), p. 204.

[50] This statement is couched in the conventional ethical comparative.

Chapter 4

The Ordeal of Madrid

Only three weeks into the war, the first bombs fell on central Madrid. Or, at any rate, this is the story to be found in the memoirs of Arturo Barea, which carefully record that the raid took place on 7 August 1936. In its detail, the incident recalled by Barea closely resembles a dozen others described by writers and reporters living in or visiting the city. It was carried out by a single aircraft. Three bombs were dropped, and the consequence was carnage, with around twenty civilians killed. Barea himself was saved by being indoors when one bomb fell near a friend's home. The busy street outside became a shambles of body parts and viscera, a theatre of screams. Some victims were pregnant mothers and children in destitute circumstances who had been queuing for free milk. The attack, made in broad daylight, seems to have taken everyone by surprise. Yet only a few days earlier, a lone *Republican* airman had carried out the first bombardment of rebel-held Valladolid, killing seven people. If Barea's raid *did* happen – which seems unlikely for several reasons – it may have represented a personal act of retaliation on the part of some enemy vigilante. And, if so, this avenger's victims were not limited to the women and children of loyalist Madrid. That night (Barea goes on to tell us) hundreds of 'fascists' were arrested, and mass 'executions' were carried out with the dawn. Whilst the bodies were still warm they were laid out along the banks of the Manzanares, where a noisy throng of spectators (including women and children) came to admire them.[1]

The unique corroboration of Barea's story – though still inconclusive – comes from an important source. Someone told *The Times'* correspondent Ernest de Caux that 'a black plane' had been spotted over Madrid on 7 August. When he checked with government press officers, de Caux was assured there was no truth in what he had heard. Already upset about censorship, alive to the possibility of deception, he decided to report it nonetheless. In his version, though the plane caused a certain amount of local panic, no bombs were dropped, and no casualties ensued.[2] Coincidence of simultaneous confirmation and contradiction is typical of the historian's difficulties in dealing with the Spanish Civil War, particularly in its earlier days, when official newspapers and government sources were inadequately controlled, and regularly conflicted with oral and printed material emanating from trades union sources and militia units – in addition (of course) to casual rumour.[3]

Potentially, of course, the capital had been within operational range of enemy airfields from the very start of the war. Away to the north, a vast swathe of north-central Spain, stretching from the Atlantic to central Aragon, had been occupied by the rebels in a matter of days rather than weeks. Front lines (which, in contrast, were to stay in place for the rest of hostilities) were soon afterwards drawn in mountain passes some fifty kilometres from the centre of the capital. But approaching Madrid by air was a forbidding as well as a dangerous sortie. The enemy knew that government fighter planes were numerous, and distributed in modern bases around the city's perimeter. A number of artillery batteries possessed anti-aircraft potential. Incoming planes were obliged to navigate the high and gusty sierras of Guadarrama or Gredos, whilst few Nationalist commanders wished to risk losing scarce machines and even scarcer pilots, or to expend valuable fuel in operations of dubious strategic purpose. Whatever the truth about Barea's episode, several more weeks elapsed before the first corroborated deadly raid, on the night of 27–8 August. This was also an isolated and audacious operation, which specifically targeted the Republican Ministry of War, a substantial building situated (then as now) at the junction of Madrid's two grandest boulevards. A bomb fell in the ministry gardens, killing an army sergeant. Again, rumour blamed a single raider. If true, surely his mission was mainly intended to bring home to senior Republicans (and members of the government itself) that they were as vulnerable as the merest mortal Madrileño.[4] Some high-ranking individuals may have been duly affected, but there was no overt public concern and the attack was not officially admitted.[5]

It was well into the autumn before regular activity by enemy aircraft became a feature of daily life in urban Madrid.[6] By then, the vanguard of Franco's army had fought its way north from Seville through Extremadura, and was swinging eastwards into the Tagus valley, highway to Madrid. Now less than 100 kilometres away, Franco's column commanders were able to order up reconnaissance missions towards the capital. Even so, much of October had elapsed before the first concerted attacks by grouped assailant machines took place. By this point, the Republic had lost dozens of planes; indeed, a three-figure estimated total seems probable. Irremediable engine breakdown through exhaustion and lack of replacement parts was almost as important as combat action in this process. In addition, machines had been used and lost with far less caution and to far less effect than on the other side. With the passage of time and the effects of 'non-intervention', replacements from abroad proved more difficult to acquire. The government was now seriously short of fighters (then still generally called 'pursuit aircraft'; in Spain, 'aviones de caza', or hunters). Those which could be mobilized in defence of Madrid were too slow and cumbersome to provide much protection for a large city against the Junkers and Savoias in Franco's armoury, despite the limited numbers of the latter. To this extent – and if only for the time being – the balance of air-power had shifted away from the Republic.

Nationalist aircraft thus began to challenge for occupation of the skies. To the huge entertainment of Madrid's younger citizens, Great-War-style 'dog-fights' became a periodic occurrence. Bombing sorties were linked to preparations for Franco's big push, intended to decide the fate of Madrid, and thus (it was generally assumed) the war as a whole. Following the capture of Toledo on 29 September, Franco paused his armies for recuperation and preparation. Then, in the third week of October, the Nationalists opened a general offensive, committing almost all their reserves of trained shock-troops to a so-called 'final assault' upon Madrid.[7] Whilst others attacked in the west, three columns advanced rapidly from the south towards a line of *pueblos* linked by a single road; Alcorcón–Leganés–Getafe. These places formed the strongpoints of an arc of minor settlements, extending for about 180 degrees across gently undulating river valleys. These approaches to Madrid had now become the decisive theatre of battle.

In this phase of operations, Nationalist aircraft took off from bases near Talavera de la Reina (captured on 3 September) and from improvised airstrips around Toledo.[8] Bombing raids on urban areas were still rare in frequency and low in destructive power. At this juncture, the Nationalists could call upon around fifteen modern aircraft which were suitable for heavy bombing operations: perhaps five survivors of the nine dedicated Savoia bombers provided by Mussolini, and about half of the twenty Junkers 52 transports sent by Hitler which had been roughly converted for use as bombers. These aircraft had been in round-the-clock action ever since arriving in Morocco two months earlier. Several had been repeatedly damaged and repaired, the majority were still flying only because of the determined ingenuity of German mechanics.[9] Problems of range, payload and available fuel supplies continued to limit the range and duration of missions. It made sense to concentrate resources on attempts to disable airbases on the city perimeter, though another priority target was artillery batteries, some of which were established in open spaces (such as the extensive Parque del Buen Retiro) surrounded by residential streets. As far as urban Madrid was concerned, only single reconnaissance missions, or other sorties involving aircraft in very small plural numbers, were observed from the ground, and in a way which made little impression on the population beyond those of novelty and wonder. By 30 October, Franco's land forces had formed a huge crescent, inching menacingly forward. It extended through almost ninety degrees, stretching from due west to due south of the city, with a median distance twenty kilometres from its centre. Even at this stage only a handful of air raids had involved the dropping of bombs on civilian quarters of the capital, whilst casualties had probably not amounted to three figures.[10] But there was another significant outcome. Ominous aerial percussion, in ragged counterpoint with the *basso ostinato* of enemy artillery, wafted into the rooms of his west-facing apartment in the Palacio de Oriente by autumn breezes from the Sierra de Gredos, were enough to persuade President Azaña to seek safer if more modest quarters well away from the capital. The cabinet itself was to follow his example within a week.[11]

Up until this point the government press had resolutely ignored the threat to the capital from General Franco's advance. Every day throughout August and September newspapers were full of upbeat 'news' from the fronts, invariably reported in an elevatingly dramatic and heroic mode. So monotonous and ubiquitous was press triumphalism that newspapers have to be searched carefully for any indication of (what we know by hindsight was) the real situation in the war zones. Until the fall of Toledo on 29 September, the enemy's relentless approach towards the gates of Madrid was never directly mentioned.[12] Within this context it is not surprising that his airborne operations were subject to blanket censorship.[13] Of course, in the circumstances this could be justified on the grounds of maintaining morale alone. But there was another, complementary motive. Now and again, explosions and/or casualties in the streets were opportunistically blamed on 'fascist fifth columnists' who – loyal citizens were repeatedly warned – came out from their hiding-places by night to throw hand-grenades or spray machine-gun bullets from the upper floors of apartment blocks. There were stories about massacres of women in food queues, of children playing in the streets, of frail elders who were unable to gain shelter. Although they were later to be recycled in the altered context of air raids, such tales were originally rehearsed in the context of the struggle against a murderous fifth column. They had the desired effect of inspiring vigilance, hatred and revenge among the people, who were each day hectored to seek out and destroy the traitors in their midst.[14]

As autumn wore on, the increasingly frequent sight of refugees in their streets alerted Madrileños to the true position. From the beginning of Franco's march, people had arrived in the capital in ever-increasing numbers. At first they came from alien Andalusia, later from fairly foreign Extremadura. But now the miserable incomers answered the usual questions with (for example) 'We're from Talavera', often spontaneously adding that 'the Moors are there', and perhaps following up with the equally chilling information that many who escaped the Moors failed to escape the planes.[15] Thus, in October, government press policy was put into reverse almost overnight. From blanket assurances that victory was at hand, the new keynote was 'Evacuate Madrid', a slogan now given saturation distribution on radio, in fly-sheets and posters, and soon to be followed by 'They shall not pass'.[16] On 6 October, a *Comité de Refugiados* was established, which began to evacuate children in large numbers, mostly to places situated east of the capital. Three weeks later it was announced that 200,000 women, children and old men had been successfully transported out of the danger zones using 25,000 cars and 2,500 buses.[17]

What was the nature and extent of the threat faced by the people of the 'besieged' capital? This is an important question, one which is still argued over in today's Spain, and deserves considered treatment. Perhaps not all the reports of raids by aircraft operating alone were invention and/or repetition. Nationalist pilots operating on the Madrid front were a mixture of Spanish, German and Italian officers – even, it seems, one Briton. Though not to the extent that seems palpable on the other side, pilots and crews were capable of capricious departures from specific flying instructions. They were just as much an international assortment as the motley mercenary adventurers who supplemented the much-celebrated champions of the Republican air force.[18] Even if a daily occurrence, a few bombs randomly thrown into Madrid's streets, though they might stimulate waves of rumour and fear, could not have caused the wall-to-wall charnel-house which became the discourse of the world's press. The soon-to-be-notorious Condor Legion of the Luftwaffe did not yet exist. Although spare parts, and even fuselage and engine replacements for German planes, had been arriving in Cádiz and Huelva for some weeks, Franco still lacked an organized strategic air force.[19] At this point, planes were still overwhelmingly being used in a tactical-response capacity, to attack local and specific military targets, as the imperative need of the Madrid offensive dictated. Such objectives, as already suggested, included Republican air bases situated to the west and south of the city; that is, at Cuatro Vientos and Getafe.[20]

But in the late afternoon of Friday 30 October, the targets were apparently changed: and with them, according to some, the course of twentieth-century history. Though accounts differ in detail (and nothing in the following data is established with certainty) it seems that as many as six trimotor bombers came in low over Madrid, dropping a payload of high-explosives apparently at random on streets densely packed with citizens and refugees. According to Koltsov, one bomb detonated near the foyer of a theatre where Largo Caballero was making a speech in praise of the USSR. Another landed on a queue of women waiting to buy milk.[21] Within twenty minutes, the list of total civilian bombing casualties in the war to date may have doubled in length.[22] Several historians record that on the same afternoon (perhaps as part of the same operation) another bomb or bombs fell on the township of Getafe, resulting in the deaths of a large number of children: forty, according to government sources.[23]

Commentators have generally accepted that when Friday 30 October was over, up to one hundred people had lost their lives.[24] But a curiously distinct line was followed by the London *Times* correspondent in Madrid. On 30 October, de Caux filed a report about a single plane, flying north-south at 16.45 hrs, which dropped six bombs, the victims including women in a food queue.[25] Some three months later, in a retrospective summary, he reiterated these facts in detail: and for good measure, added an explosive afterthought:

> On October 30 . . . a single small bomber, flying high, dropped six small bombs in a line in the crowded streets of a populous quarter. Sixteen persons were killed and 60 wounded, mostly women in queues or children playing . . . As it was denied by the insurgents that any machine of theirs had bombed Madrid the rumour arose that a government aeroplane had been told to commit an act of frightfulness, to brace the apathy of Madrid towards the war.[26]

As the stakes went higher, the chips thrown onto the table mounted dizzily. These weeks saw a tremendous increase in the acquisition and deployment of advanced military hardware.[27] In mid-September, a Soviet team had arrived in Madrid with an offer of aid for the Republic. Formally headed by a career diplomat, it was Ambassador Rosenberg's military and intelligence advisers, carefully selected from the Soviet armed services and secret police, who provided the negotiating steel. Discussions were difficult and protracted. Stalin's terms were ruthlessly opportunistic in the sphere of political concessions and harshly exploitative in terms of payment. But the alarming proximity of Franco's armies (and planes) finally overcame the profound reservations of Largo Caballero and his 'government of victory'. The Kremlin's conditions for a programme of military aid were agreed.[28] Less than a week before the first big Madrid raid described above – an event which maybe helped Largo salve his conscience over surrender to Moscow – a convoy docked in Cartagena and Alicante from Odessa, carrying supplies of the latest Soviet fighting machines for both aerial and terrestrial use. More such flotillas were already at sea. Due mainly to the close collaboration of Russian technicians, aircraft were assembled and delivered to the Madrid front with tremendous alacrity.[29] On Thursday 29 October, a squadron of twin-engined Tupolev SB2 ('Katiuska') bombers, flown by Soviet air force pilots, attacked the airfield at Talavera, the Nationalists' main depot and pivotal strategic centre. Severe damage was caused to planes on the ground, as well as aerodrome buildings and nearby military installations.[30]

Just like Largo and his cabinet, Franco and his chief operational commander, Emilio Mola, were faced with a vital dilemma. Urgent negotiations, closely parallel in chronology and very similar in content and significance to the Republican–Soviet talks, were taking place in Salamanca between the *generalísimo* and a team of Hitler's emissaries headed by Admiral Canaris. At this juncture, the Nationalist capacity to carry on operations against Republican airbases and other key defence points had reached a critically insecure point. As it happened, the dreaded Katiuskas were operating from the relative security of Alcalá de Henares, well to the east of the capital, and not from any of the three Madrid bases, seen by the Russians as too close to the enemy for comfort. Since unfamiliar and formidable types of Soviet fighter were also now airborne over Madrid, Mola's field commanders were being denied air cover at a crucial point of their offensive against the capital. In short, a rapid reinforcement of aircraft with greater speed and range was now needed. In practice, this could only mean newer models from Germany. Underneath Franco's preoccupations lay the alarming fact that he now had fewer than 20,000 reliable assault troops available for the forthcoming battles in the streets of Madrid, and very few trained reserves, against defence forces which – at least in crude agglomeration – amounted to over five times that number. It had become the first campaign in European military history to which air supremacy was perceived as decisive.

Franco was therefore under a pressure effectively identical to that simultaneously endured by his opposite number, Largo Caballero, who was war minister as well as head of government. On Friday, 30 October, the former finalized his agreement with Canaris for the stationing in Spain of a (partly autonomous) unit supplied and staffed from Germany: the Condor Legion. Franco now knew that within a matter of weeks he would have at his disposal a dedicated strategic assault corps, equipped with the latest German prototypes in armoured vehicles, artillery and aircraft.[31] The same day – 30 October – he committed his total air force to concentrated assaults upon enemy airfields. The bases at Cuatro Vientos and Getafe were (in any case) vital strongpoints in the defence-system organized by General Miaja's *Junta de Defensa.* Accordingly, they were bombed, at intervals, for over an hour that afternoon. Both targets were adjacent to districts of domestic housing, and there were numbers of civilian casualties, probably the highest experienced from air raids so far in the war.[32] These sorties took place at approximately the same time as the raid on the centre of Madrid described (with an element of conjecture) above, and may well have been carried out by the same pilots.

Some experts leave the reader in no doubt that Franco himself deliberately ordered an all-out 'terror campaign' to break the morale of the population of Madrid.[33] If the guilt of Franco and his closest aides were accepted, it would seem to follow that the decision was linked in some way to the current negotiations with Canaris and company. Gabriel Jackson opined that when General Mola 'attempted to terrorize the city into surrender by indiscriminate bombing', he was 'acting on German theories of war'.[34] This is not the same as asserting that German personnel in Salamanca had even made – far less *insisted on* – the point. However, the extent to which a policy of terror fitted with Franco's own temperament or was rather a pusillanimous surrender to the Nazis is not one calculated to disturb the mindset of those who believe the *Caudillo* to have been capable of any evil .

Much depends on interpretation of Franco's autographed warning delivered by air-drop over the capital on 7 November. The key to this (in turn) is the word 'población' used in the opening sentence below, which can mean 'city' or 'large urban area' as well as 'population'.

> Should resistance persist, the whole *población* will become a military objective and battlefield. Therefore, from this moment, since all objectives of military significance will be bombed without any kind of limitation, we recommend that all non-combatant civilians, especially women and children, should abandon zones of military contest. For this purpose, a section [of the city] has been specially designated as reserved for occupation by women, children, old people, foreigners, and other non-combatants.[35]

It could be argued that, even giving Franco benefit of doubt over *población*, the content of this warning remains disturbing. Indeed, some time earlier, during Madrid's baptismal raid on the night of 27–8 August, the warning was more clear-cut. Crudely-typed and cyclostyled 'leaflets' were showered on the streets. One was picked up by a member of the British embassy in the morning. It was, in effect, a proclamation addressed and couched in patriarchal terms to 'Madrileños'.

> Today we begin air operations in preparation for the occupation of Madrid, which will shortly take place. This first bombardment is directed only against military airbases and weapons factories, as well as fighting troops, but should you continue with this sightless suicide, if you do not force your leaders to surrender the capital without conditions, we will take no responsibility for the grave damage which we will be obliged to inflict on you in order to overcome your resistance. Be warned, Madrileños, that the greater your obstinacy the greater must our action be against you.[36]

The sequence of events here suggests that, if anything, Franco's intentions were reined in, rather than exacerbated, by his dealings with Hitler's representatives.[37] This conjecture may be supported by the Caudillo's careful insertion of the following justification for his threats, in sentences placed immediately before those just quoted.

> [Red air forces have made] barbarous and cowardly bombardments of open cities . . . causing death to women and children . . . These are the only victories scored by the Reds in this war, criminal and cowardly acts against human rights and peace-loving citizens.[38]

Though conventionally regarded as a warlord who was crippled by excessive caution in decision-making, if Franco had one unmasterable passion it was the code of honour and the atavistic instinct to strike back.

Yet there is all the difference in the world between a threat and its execution. The former – if at that time unprecedented in nature – was in itself a legitimate tactical move.[39] In the world war to come, Germany and Britain both made and carried out similar threats. The allies issued ample warning to Japan before obliterating Hiroshima and Nagasaki in August 1945. The evidence of 1936 (as will be argued later) simply does not support the proposition that the Nationalists mounted a campaign of indiscriminate destruction against Madrid. This may be explained more by insufficiency of resources than by lack of desire. Yet even when the fresh aeronautical supplies promised by Hitler actually arrived on site and organized – a matter of days rather than weeks after the warning message of 7 November – no systematic terror campaign was initiated.

Given this complex scenario, it is difficult to be sure whether the crucial sortie of 30 October was a planned manoeuvre at all, let alone an initiative representing a change of tactics, and far less a fundamental shift of policy on the aerial front. Attacks on urban concentrations certainly continued and even increased after that 'Black Friday', a feature that aids the impression that 'terror raids' were somehow related to the discussions being held with German military specialists.[40] In this context, the bad news from Talavera may have been a vital catalyst in Franco's mind, hastening conclusion of his agreement with Canaris.[41] Here, too, the culture of *pundonor* (the military honour-code) and propaganda requirements, imposed upon the *Caudillo* an imperative need to demonstrate to his supporters that he was not merely a helpless supplicant, the passive and deferential client of German power. But before extending the rule of momentary revenge, so prevalent amongst the mass of his own and his enemies' supporters, to embrace Franco himself, we must consider a further development. Nearly all military observers were expecting Madrid to fall. In these days of assumed endgame in both negotiations and military contest, there had been another twist of fortune's wheel, and one which far exceeded the losses at Talavera in importance.

During the last week of October the Republic's leaders were planning its first major counter-attack since the war began.[42] In the wake of the arrival of substantial cargoes of Soviet tanks and planes, Largo's cabinet accepted communist demands for radical changes in the organisation and command of Madrid's defence.[43] On the night of Wednesday 28 October, a section of the communist Fifth Regiment, actually comprising just a single fully-trained and equipped brigade (some 3,000 men) and representing the only reliable assault regiment at the government's disposal, was sent into positions south of Getafe. Doubtless because protection of the town's well-equipped airbase from capture or destruction was itself a powerful *desideratum*, Getafe had been selected as the focal command-point of the offensive. Modern concrete fortifications had been constructed during the summer to defend the airfield.[44] Now, new lines of trenches were hurriedly excavated in a wide area surrounding the military installations, and hurriedly occupied by reserve militia units transported to the front in double-decker buses. The main priority of Enrique Líster, in command of the Republican vanguard, was to liaise with a group of fifteen tanks, which had only just arrived on the scene after a forced drive from distant Cartagena, and was now manoeuvring around Chinchón.[45] In an operation which some see as adumbrating Wehrmacht tactics in 1939–40, the Republicans aimed to push forward and encircle enemy-held strongpoints on a front of about 30 kilometres (Torrejón–Esquivia–Seseña). The ultimate objective was to decapitate the right wing of the advancing army. It was hoped the threat to the enemy's rearguard and logistics, particularly the shock effect of the manner it which it was achieved, with hitherto unsuspected state-of-the art resources in both aviation and armour, would inspire his general demoralization and retreat.

Perhaps because it was tightly concentrated upon the new priority target of urban Madrid, Nationalist reconnaissance failed to detect the Republican build-up. On Thursday 29 October, Líster's forces advanced a distance of over twenty kilometres, and went some way towards isolating enemy pockets. The most bizarre of the day's dramatic scenarios was that of General Monasterio's cavalry brigade, dominating the Nationalist right, being confronted by the unannounced appearance of T-26 tank squadrons around Seseña. But Líster's offensive quickly ran out of steam. In an outcome destined to be repeated endlessly throughout the history of the war's pitched battles – Seseña being arguably the first – superior command initiative, combined with general levels of experience and professional training in the Nationalist ranks, enabled them to resist and recover. On this occasion their survival was also due to understandable errors and communications problems among their adversaries, above all between Spanish (infantry) and Russian (tank) commanders. The Republican army was simply not ready for the task demanded of it. Lacking sufficient numbers of trained men, its leaders also experienced paralysing problems with the direction of aviation and even artillery support. Indeed during the thirty-odd daylight hours that the counter-offensive lasted, Republican aviation was largely absent from the critical zones of action.[46] On the other side, by 30 October the seriousness of the situation on the ground had dawned upon Mola and his staff. As soon as they could be gathered and primed, all available Junkers and Savoias were sent to plaster the airbase at Getafe. As enemy aircraft took off, some of Líster's units were already in helter-skelter flight, streaming back in the direction from which they had come.[47]

The alleged bombing of Getafe town, and attacks on the centre of Madrid, occurring between 4 and 5 p.m. on 30 October, were incidents promiscuously mixed into the frantic and confused events of that Friday. Though it seems possible they were not intended as the opening of a 'blitz', heavy air raids on the capital were subsequently to continue over a period of three weeks, during which hundreds of civilians lost their lives. In the first week of November, both Getafe and Cuatro Vientos fell to Franco's forces. It now seemed that Nationalist pilots had the capital city, chaotically crowded with thousands of helpless refugees, at their mercy. On 8 November, Franco's assault columns, consisting mainly of Legionary *banderas* and Moorish units, began the battle for Madrid. By now, however, Republican resistance had stiffened, and once the Nationalists entered built-up areas their advance was slowed to a crawl. So severe was the haemorrhaging of irreplaceable units in street-fighting (notably in the working-class *barrio* of Carabanchel) that Mola and Franco were driven to use planes in any way that might reduce losses. Furious assaults across the Manzanares river and battles in the relatively open spaces of the University City (15–23 November) were accompanied by bombing sorties of an unprecedented weight and ferocity. A Welsh volunteer with a legionary battalion waiting to cross the river witnessed 'a week's aerial bombardment of the enemy positions' as part of preparations for this attack.

> Zero-hour came, and to the screams of artillery and trench mortar shells, and the heavy concussions of the bombs dropped by the twenty-three German three-engined Junkers overhead – the first time we had ever seen them – Madrid awoke from a dreamy dawn into vigilance.[48]

At this stage, it becomes difficult to avoid the conclusion that deliberate terrorism against civilians had indeed become part of the Nationalists' tactical equation. On 19 November, for example, no fewer than fifty planes were used to drop forty tons of bombs.[49] The lists of victims included proportions of women and children which – given circumstances which at the time were entirely novel – might nowadays be accepted as 'normal' in terms of demographics.

These operations were periodically intense, but the campaign as a whole was sporadic rather than continuous. It was not sustained on a regular daily basis, in the routine ordeal that was to characterize civilian life in major domestic theatres (Britain, Germany, Japan) during the Second World War.[50] Nonetheless, during approximately six weeks of what might be called the 'active' Madrid campaign (that is, from about 12 October until 23 November) the city endured damage to life and property which represented a departure from anything previously experienced in war; terrifying to inhabitants; to newspapermen and their readers, horrifying and sensational. Civilian survivors recall those days vividly, but often with feelings that had become mixed with the passage of time, in the same ways as so many cockney witnesses to the winter of 1940–1 later spoke with ironic humour and a kind of collective pride of events that at the time were unrelentingly grim and miserable.[51] Though casualties may have exceeded a thousand dead and wounded, there was no hecatomb, and no shambles in Madrid's hospitals.[52]

On 11 January 1937, *The Times* correspondent asserted that 'Madrid has suffered 33 aerial bombardments in 10 weeks', adding that only nine attacks had occurred since the beginning of December.[53] The reports of other foreign journalists, most firmly anti-fascist, present in Madrid that winter illustrate (if inadvertently) that by December bombing was no longer a regular factor in the ordeal of Madrid.[54] One correspondent went further, attesting specifically that death and destruction was caused mainly by artillery rather than planes. The Canadian reporter Frank Griffin, who spent most of December inside 'besieged' Madrid on behalf of the *Toronto Star,* also estimated the vulnerable districts to constitute no more than one-fifth of the city. He later told a distinguished audience back home that the only area of Madrid actually reduced to ruins was the dense 'wall' of major private and public buildings in the select district of Argüelles, along its western perimeter. From these extended positions, overlooking the parkland zones of the Casa de Campo, Parque del Oeste and Ciudad Universitaría, the besiegers' frontline trenches could be easily observed and targetted. This, therefore, was an obvious battle-zone, accordingly emptied of inhabitants at an early stage to make room for heavy machine guns and similar emplacements.[55] Elsewhere, according to Griffin's observations, damage to buildings was scattered and slight. For good measure he added some rather unusual sentiments:

> Maybe Franco showed restraint. Maybe, much more likely, he did not have the guns, shells, aeroplanes and bombs in sufficient quantity really to plaster Madrid. I believe he did not, in spite of all you have heard about the amount of German and Italian help he has received. At no time since the siege of Madrid really settled down has Franco shown a big superiority of armaments or aeroplanes. In the air over Madrid the government planes in December, and I think since, had a decided edge and bombings were scarce. In the main, these planes of the government were, I believe, Russian, and they were largely manned by foreign airmen, a number of them French, with some English and some Americans, but many of the pilots were Russian. It may interest you to know that these Russian machines, especially when piloted by young ardent Soviet pilots were generally credited with out-flying and out-fighting the German and Italian machines and pilots of Franco.

> I will merely add this: If Franco had had the guns, the aeroplanes and the will, in a week of merciless, unrelenting bombardment he could have made Madrid at once a shambles and a hell in which the surviving civilian population, yes, even these stoic Spanish people, accustomed to suffering, inured to fate, would have gone mad. No such continuous bombardment of the city at large for days or even for hours was at any time practised, except in the deliberately devastated zone of the west side.

Griffin's audience may have been surprised by this, all the more so since he had opened with a strong statement of pro-Republican sympathies.[56]

On 23 November 1936, Franco called a halt to his assault on Madrid. He had not exactly admitted defeat: but he could hardly have been surprised that the Republic lost little time in proclaiming victory. Thereafter, until the surrender of Madrid on 29 March 1939, the city was only rarely attacked from the air, terror raids ceasing abruptly and for good. In practice this afforded little relief for the population, which was tormented with artillery bombardment, ranging from precisely targeted buildings to more or less indiscriminate barrages – though again on a sporadic rather than continuous basis – for the rest of the war. But our cultural conventions dictate that this should be regarded, in ethical as well as ballistic terms, as another story.

NOTES

1   Barea (1946/1984), pp. 154–6. For discussion of Barea's testimony in general, see Appendix A. pp. 273–9. For the raid on Valladolid, see Martín Jiménez (2000), p. 295. For 'reprisal' killings, see below, pp. 255–60.

2   'Uncensored report', *The Times*, 12 August 1936. For his resentment of censorship; see, for example, De Caux's letter to Deakin, 14 August 1936, TNL Archive, Ralph Deakin Correspondence. (This incident happened before Barea himself had become a press censorship official.)

3   'Disinformation was the only rule' as a recent compilation states: Figueres (2004), pp. 19–20.

4   Koltsov (1963), p. 60; Cate (1995), p. 241. This sortie probably originated from Avila, some 90 kilometres distant; see Bernecker in Serrano (1991), p. 146. Montoliu Camps (1999), I, p. 170 states that this was the first raid on the capital, and this is followed in the recent monograph by Solé & Villaroya (2003), p. 45.

5   Graham (1999), p. 126 follows Koltsov's diary (1963), pp. 59–60 in claiming this raid as 'the first of [its] kind anywhere in Europe' – and as the opening of *a designated blitz on Madrid's civilians*. Others subscribe enthusiastically to the 'epic of Madrid' construct. They range from second-hand montages by Méndez Luengo (1977), p. 130ff. and Kurzman (1980), p. 213ff to studies of an ostensibly scholarly nature, e.g. Reig Tapía (1999), pp. 189–234. In contrast, the revisionist writer Moa (2002), p. 338 argues that credit for the epithet 'epic' should be reversed, given that attackers were vastly outnumbered both in men and materials. A compilation edited by C. Serrano (1991), *passim* is more detached.

6   Barea (1946/1984), p. 178, claims 'many casualties' resulted from a raid *c.*20 September. But accounts of 'the siege of Madrid' differ sharply on the extent of bombing before enemy infantry reached Madrid's outskirts (7 November). The most recent believes that no serious raids occurred before 27 September; Reverte (2004), p. 5. Another states that despite official silence 'lo cierto es que en la última semana de octubre Madrid sufrió un continuo y masivo bombardeo'; Montoliu Camps (1999), I, p. 173 and cf. Alcocer Badenas (1978), p. 169.

7   For details of the Madrid offensive and its constituent operations, see Martínez Bande (1982) and idem (1976). A useful account in English, based largely on Colonel Martínez's works, can be found in Hills (1976).

8   A chronicle of aerial exchanges during these weeks, set in the context of the overall campaign, is given by Cate (1995), pp. 228–52.

9   A British volunteer with Asensio's column to the south-west attests that during October Nationalist aviation constantly attacked defensive positions in the path of its advance: (Navalcarnero, Brunete,

Alcorcón, Cuatro Vientos); Thomas (1998), p. 58ff; see also Larios (1968), pp. 54–5.

10 On 30 October, Ogilvie-Forbes, *chargé d'affaires* at the British Embassy, reported that 'since October 28, Madrid has been constantly raided by rebel aircraft attacking working class quarters and populous centres', adding that 'bombs do considerable damage amongst food queues'; BNA, FO 371/20546/W15040.

11 Barea (1946/1984), p. 191 states that artillery was first heard on 13 October.

12 A generalization based on files of various Madrid newspapers. *El Socialista*, for example, maintained an exclusive diet of morale-boosting news well into October. A faithful summary of Madrid press coverage was made by the French Communist daily *L'Humanité*. A memoir by a Nationalist supporter in Madrid includes *résumés* of newspaper content; Alcocer (1978), pp. 170–3, 186.

13 Jato Miranda (1976), p. 368ff. Following the 28 August raid, written regulations for 'civil defence' were published, but the government reassured Madrileños that 'subterranean shelters are already in existence with capacity for four million persons – four times the present population' (ibid., p. 377). This (in any case wildly optimistic) presumably referred to the Metro subways.

14 See, for example, Barea (1946/1984), pp. 131–266 *passim*, and cf. the scenarios painted by *Daily Worker* correspondent 'Frank Pitcairn' [Claud Cockburn], below, pp. 101–2 and 120–1.

15 See Koltsov (1963), p. 147ff; Barea (1946/1984), pp. 182–6; Jato Miranda (1976), 513–14.

16 The government itself chose to obey the first of these orders rather than the second, and abandoned Madrid on the night of 6–7 November.

17 Vázquez & Valero (1978), pp. 182 and 211–12. All figures were hugely exaggerated, but the operation continued well into 1937; see Barea (1946/1984), pp. 229–30, 238–9, 246–8.

18 Bridgeman (1989), pp. 27–41 and 47–8.

19 For years it was incorrectly asserted that systematic air assault on Madrid began much earlier than is indicated above, and was spear-headed from the first by 'Nazi bombers' or even 'The Condor Legion'. See, for example, the communist writer Arthur London (1965), p. 164; the monograph on newsreel coverage by Aldgate (1979), p. 142; and even one account published by the pro-Nationalist Editorial, San Martín–Elstob (1973), p. 121. In fact the Condor Legion took no part in the Madrid campaign. See Proctor (1983), p. 65; Garriga (1978), p. 73; Ries & Ring (1992), p. 35ff.

20 Stalin's personal emissary, Mikhail Koltsov, heard explosions from raids on these airfields, both about 15 km distant from his city-centre apartment, on 2 October: Koltsov (1963), p. 119.

21 Koltsov (1963), p. 165, cf. Cockburn, Koltsov's close friend and collaborator (1986), pp. 111–12).

22 R. Salas (1977) prints an appendix (page unnumbered) reproducing the death registration of Carmen Sánchez Delgado, killed in Calle

Fuencarral (city centre) at 17.00 hrs on 30 October. But reliable data on casualties are rare, and even this one has been strenuously challenged – see idem (1983), p. 18. (I owe this reference to John Scurr.)

23 For detailed discussion, see below, Chapter 7.

24 Ogilvie-Forbes cabled the Foreign Office that 'total casualties on October 30th *apart from Getafe* were 150 killed and injured'; 1 and 2 November 1936, BNA FO. 371/20545/W14861. (Note my emphasis.) However, the loudest denouncer of bombing atrocities, French correspondent Louis Delaprée, stated that Madrid's first heavy raid took place on 4 November, and that 'la matanza metódica de la población civil no fue emprendida hasta el 16 de noviembre'; q. by Solé & Villaroya (2003), p. 47.

25 *The Times*, 31 October 1936. This report, which mentions Getafe in passing and without detail, was telephoned directly to Printing House Square, indicating de Caux enjoyed the cooperation of the British Embassy: TNL Archive, De Caux File.

26 'The Bombing of Madrid – An Uncensored Account', *The Times*, 23 January 1937.

27 R. Salas (1980), pp. 206–7.

28 Howson (1998), especially p. 120ff. Abramson (1994), p. 183ff.

29 Hidalgo de Cisneros (1986), p. 71; Yakushin (1986), pp. 347–9.

30 Gárate Córdoba (1977–8) II, p. 98; Hills (1980) p. 83.

31 Elstob (1973/1980), pp. 107–8; Garriga (1978), p. 70.

32 Jato Miranda surely errs in placing the time of the raids at *4.30 a.m.*; (1976), p. 610.

33 For example Trythall (1970), p. 111; Reig Tapia (1999), p. 216; Graham (2005), pp. 70–2.

34 Jackson (1965), p. 320. In fact, radical new theories came from Italy, not Germany: Garriga (1979), p. 138, Lindqvist (2000), *passim.*

35 Q by Martínez Bande (1976), p. 235.

36 BNA FO 371/20537/W10729/209–12. The document bears Franco's name, but in the circumstances this cannot be taken as definitive. In remitting it to London, an embassy official noted 'possession of it means death' to any citizen caught with a copy. (I am most grateful to Dr Julius Ruiz for sight of this file.)

37 Considering their negative experience in battle with Soviet armour on the ground around Madrid, German commanders may have been wise to resist proposals inevitably involving a similar and all-out contest in the air: especially, perhaps, one fought in the glare of attendant international newspaper searchlights.

38 Reference as n. 36.

39 It might equally be considered that Franco was seeking the same end as the Madrid authorities – evacuation of the city by those unfitted or unwilling to fight.

40 The direct link is asserted by Thomas (1977), p. 470.

41 Only five days before the Soviet attack (see above p. 50) Malraux's 'international' squadron had also raided Talavera, destroying several Fiat 32 fighters on the tarmac. Within forty-eight hours, 'a crushing

riposte . . . smothered Barajas under an avalanche of bombs': Cate (1995), p. 249, see also *Partes* I (1977), p. 58, and Larios (1968), p. 77. Proctor (1983), p. 56 makes a retaliatory link between the raids on Talavera and Getafe on 29–30 October, but this inference is not present in the source he cites, namely Hills (1980).

[42] Martínez Bande (1976), pp. 64–70.

[43] Koltsov (1963), p. 151. This event was the origin of the new professional army, the *Ejército Popular.*

[44] *Daily Mail,* 3 November 1936, information from Nationalist source at nearby Fuenlabrada.

[45] Koltsov (1963), pp. 158–9.

[46] A Soviet pilot present in Getafe 'shortly before it was captured . . . stared in disbelief at uncamouflaged Republican aircraft neatly lined up as if waiting to be bombed'; Wyden (1983), p. 176

[47] At this point, the strategic narrative context of this chapter becomes intertwined with the experience of war in Getafe; continuation of the latter will be found in Chapter 6.

[48] Thomas (1998), pp. 67–8.

[49] Ries & Ring (1992), p. 37. However, 19 November marked the end, rather than the beginning of intense air bombardment.

[50] On 1 November, Koltsov noted that raids were now taking place at the rate of three or four a day – 'en mis telegramas he dejado de describir y referirme a todos los bombardeos; son demasiados'; Koltsov (1963), p. 168.

[51] See, for example, Vidal (1996), p. 141ff.

[52] One scholar estimates fewer than fifty deaths per day during 25 days of regular aerial bombardment; Jackson (1965), p. 321; (and see below, pp. 242–3). This accords neatly with the 1,150 total claimed by Republican authorities. But a total of 312 deaths was arrived at from Republican reports found in Madrid's military archive: J. Salas (1969) I, pp. 214–15. An eminent research physician who worked in Madrid throughout this period, with many colleagues caring for war-wounded, mentioned air raids just twice in his diary, and then only in passing; Baquero Gil (1997), pp. 160 and 173.

[53] *The Times,* 23 January 1937. The breakdown given was: October = 1 raid, that of 30th; November = 23; December = 7; January (to date) = 2. Yet on 28 October the same reporter had remarked 'the usual air raid on Madrid did not take place today'; ibid., 29 October 1936.

[54] See Solé & Villaroya (2003), pp. 56–8. Detailed treatment of the press's role is offered in Chapter 8.

[55] According to Vázquez and Valero (1978), pp. 210–11 this operation began on 7 November.

[56] F. Griffin 'The Tragedy of Spain', 25 March 1937. Full text in *The Empire Club of Canada Speeches, 1936–37* (Toronto, Empire Club of Canada, 1937), pp. 289–307; see *http://www.empireclubfoundation.com* (accessed 10 January 2004). Alexander Werth later confirmed that the zones Griffin stipulated were the only parts of Madrid dramatically affected by bomb and shell damage: *The Manchester Guardian,* 31 December 1937, q. (in Spanish) by Armero (1976), p. 197. Revisions

of A. Beevor's well-known study, originally appearing in 1982, are instructive. In the 1999 edition he continued to insist (p. 201) that 'air raids destroyed thousands of buildings in Madrid'. In his 2006 version (p. 181), this datum is reduced by 90% to 'hundreds'.

Chapter 5

From Bilbao to Barcelona

The winter of 1936–7, a period often referred to as 'the siege of Madrid', was dominated by Franco's attempts to attack the city directly, or when these failed, to isolate it from its supply hinterland. Operational freedom for the Nationalist air force was severely restricted by the arrival of several squadrons of Soviet fighter planes, including the state-of-the-art Polikarpov 1–16 – nicknamed, with typical Spanish ambiguity as 'Mosca', The Fly. Indeed, even during the November battles, it became evident that the pendulum balance of air-power had swung back in the Republicans' favour. For the time being, at least, Franco had to fall back on his over-extended infantry battalions, largely made up of volunteer recruits, and with ever-decreasing numbers of veteran 'africanistas' in their ranks. In the early months of the new year, a sequence of hard-fought offensives extended the Nationalist reach around to the north-west of the city (Pozuelo, Majadahonda, Las Rozas); they were followed by pitched battles to the south and the north-east (Jarama and Guadalajara). These campaigns absorbed the attention of aviation units on both sides. During the latter two, which were prolonged and almost joined-up engagements (lasting from 5 February to 21 March, with a short break) it was again the Republicans who established control of the skies. Indeed, this factor was probably decisive at Guadalajara, their only outright, uncomplicated field victory of the whole war.[1]

Finally giving up the notion of a decisive breakthrough on the Madrid front, Franco turned north, beginning a well-prepared campaign to reduce the great Republican pocket comprising (going from east to west) the provinces of Vizcaya, Cantabria and Asturias. In these mountainous regions, naturally favourable to defence on the ground, the tactical role of the aeroplane was to prove fundamental. Only by harassing enemy troop concentrations, destroying depots in the rear, damaging arms factories, disrupting transport infrastructure, and taking out battery emplacements at key elevated positions, could the progress of the Nationalist army be ensured.[2] A series of attacks on the village of Durango – in late March and early April, only days after the campaign had opened – was justified on several of these criteria. Likewise, the vastly more notorious raid (nearly four weeks later) on Gernika, a town with vital strategic significance, in which both a vital bridge and a small-arms factory were situated, was on paper a legitimate action. Nevertheless, these events brought a new dimension to the aerial war's toll of civilian casualties, involving over 500 deaths and twice that number of injured. Though figures were high when compared to those experienced in densely populated cities like Madrid and Granada during more sustained operations, they were not surprising when smaller settlements were targetted by more and more modern aircraft. Gernika itself fell to Francoist forces only three days after the raid, and soon Bilbao, capital of the autonomous Basque Republic, and the central government's main centre of war-related industrial production, came under regular attack from the air.[3]

The fall of Bilbao on 19 June 1937 by no means brought the northern campaign, and its mounting total of civilian casualties, to an end. Almost by definition indiscriminate, killing from the air went on through the prolonged subsequent offensives aimed at reducing and occupying a series of large Republican enclaves further to the west. The whole process was completed only by the fall of the Asturian port of Gijón in late October 1937. A little earlier, the Nationalists had reached Oviedo, capital city of Asturias, thus at last deciding the outcome of a siege that in effect (if not quite according to the strictest terms of definition) was one of the longest of modern times. Captured for the rebels by the local garrison commander, Colonel Antonio Aranda, in the first days of the war – with the aid of an audacious ruse – Oviedo was thereafter completely surrounded by loyalist forces. With only about a thousand defenders (regular troops and volunteers), situated in a narrow valley dominated by mountain peaks, and nearly a hundred kilometres distant from the nearest rebel-held territory, Aranda's position seemed hopeless. Among other things, the besiegers were led from the front by Asturian coal-miners, men who were not only Spain's most fanatical opponents of the military but also professional experts in the range of sapping techniques traditionally important to siege warfare. Whilst countless sticks of dynamite as well as bombs were tossed upon them from the air, the rebels were forced back from street to street as seemingly impregnable nineteenth-century buildings were blown out beneath their feet. Meanwhile the loyalists, mobilizing every mule and lorry in the region to haul their big guns into position on nearby heights, proceeded to pound the city below them into dust.[4]

Oviedo's long agony was the Nationalist equivalent of the 'epic of Madrid'. Indeed, at first, Madrileños rejoiced in the progress of the siege. On 27 August, for example, the newspaper *La Voz* told them with relish that 'eighty-five powerful bombs' had been dropped on the city the previous day. Two days later, the government claimed that 'eight tons of bombs were ... dropped on Oviedo, the rebel stronghold in Asturias'.[5] By October 1936, most of the 70,000-strong civilian population were living in the cellars. According to Aranda himself,

> 10,000 shells, 5,000 air bombs, millions of rifle bullets and several hundred bottles of inflammable fluid fell into the city ... in one day, September 24, during the 111 and 112 air raids, a total of 1,910 bombs were dropped in one day. On another day, 500 fell. The entire Santo Domingo and San Lazaro quarters [are] heaps of ruins.[6]

Aranda was speaking to an American reporter, Webb Miller, shortly after a volunteer column of Mola's army had fought its way through to Oviedo at the cost of many casualties. Miller's description of what he saw and heard would surely be taken unhesitatingly, by any reader unaware of its actual location, for a story about Madrid or Barcelona under 'the barbarous fascist bombers'.

> Children, some still wearing bandages covering wounds, played in the safer streets ... [one] game was called 'bombing'. A boy lay on the ground while his companion held a half-brick above, then dropped it. The excitement lay in rolling over before the brick hit him ... When the bombing was at its worst, tens of thousands lived day and night in cellars ... On October 6 [1936], a heavy bomb cut clean through a six-story apartment building, killing forty-four

people living in the basement. Another bomb went through a
five-story house and killed fourteen. They said that seven hundred
women and children had been killed and wounded in the
bombings . . . as we talked, a Government plane appeared. People
in the streets scurried for cover in the public shelters and cellars
. . .[7]

As a result of the relieving action by which Miller reached
Oviedo, a secure corridor, albeit one permanently under artillery
and small-arms fire, was established to run in military, medical
and food supplies. But it was by no means the end of the siege.
Typhus already had a grip on a starving population which had
been literally decimated by enemy action, not to mention the
defenders themselves, who (admittedly in desperate circumstances) murdered hundreds of the loyalist prisoners they had
taken in July.[8] Although its worst ordeals were over, Oviedo's daily
struggle for survival hardly abated until Asturias as a whole finally
fell to the Francoists almost a year later.

For the whole duration of the successive Nationalist offensives
in what might be called 'Biscay Spain', their domination of the air
was rarely less than complete.[9] Very few fighting aircraft had been
based in these regions before the war, and although reinforcements arrived in Bilbao from French and Russian sources during
its first winter, they were soon driven from the skies by the
combined strength of their enemies (Spanish, Italian and German). In addition, the geographical circumstances that developed
during 1936, the factor of sheer physical isolation, meant that air
communication between the Basque-led coalition and their regular Republican allies to south and east was never less than
hazardous. As the line of battle moved further west, hope of direct
assistance from the main Republican zone faded to zero. From
their (slightly discrete) point of view on this front, the Valencia
government was contemplating a massive setback, Franco's con-
quest of Spain's most important regions of mineral resources and
strategic industry. The only chance of averting this disaster was to
create diversionary and disruptive attacks on other fronts. Such
was one of the two main reasons for the Republic's first great
offensive, at Brunete (5–25 July 1937). A rather less well-known
secondary response was a large-scale and sustained bombing

campaign against Nationalist-held cities. This operation was initiated shortly after the start of Franco's northern campaign, and before the enemies' notorious raids on Durango and Gernika had occurred.

The first Republican target was the relatively vulnerable city of Saragossa, which suffered eight attacks in March. The Aragonese capital, within relatively comfortable reach of Republican bases, was hit on a further twenty-two occasions over the following two months. Nationalist authorities claimed a loss of sixty-seven civilian lives, plus nearly 300 wounded. In the first week of April, a further seventy citizens were killed by a series of raids on more distant Valladolid.[10] The first of these targets was undoubtedly a major centre of Nationalist military activity and war-related installations. Both cities were important focuses for recruitment and training. The next target of 'La Gloriosa' was Burgos. Some time after the fall of Bilbao, and only a few days before the launching of the Brunete offensive, a lone Republican plane flew over the Nationalist capital. According to the local press, the pilot deliberately dropped his bombs in the streets of the city, killing nineteen people, including eight children.[11] Though it seems unlikely that these operations had much effect on the course of the northern campaign, we may at least presume they made committed Republicans feel that something was being done to help the Basques.

During the battle of Brunete (which took place in the Guadarrama plain, west of Madrid) a big raid was mounted against the provincial capital of Cáceres, in Extremadura (23 July). This city was an important training and recuperation centre for Nationalist soldiers, at the same time being equipped with a strategically important airfield. Official sources recorded that the bombing killed thirty-one non-combatants, including five children.[12] Whatever the consequences, it can hardly be questioned that the Republican objective in these attacks was to disrupt the enemy's air support and logistics at a crucial point in the Brunete battle.[13] The same intention explains the Nationalist raids carried out in February against the town of Albacete, a provincial capital in La Mancha, which happened to be the HQ and supply base of the International Brigades. These coincided with a series of counter-offensives against Franco's army during the battle of Jarama, in which most units of the International Brigades were mobilized.[14] Likewise, during the Republican offensives in Aragon later that year, a heavy Nationalist air raid was made against the provincial capital of Lérida (Lleída) in the western marches of Catalonia. The town was a key centre for the marshalling of transport, as well as a depot for supplies and troop reserves. On this occasion it was claimed that 225 civilians lost their lives.[15]

A year before the final collapse of the Republic, in April 1938, a British RAF officer made an official visit to the Nationalist zone in order to reconnoitre the situation in the air war. He engaged in conversation with some liaison officers:

> When I pointed out that most Nationalist towns are legitimate bombing targets, it was freely agreed that this is so, and certainly no town I have visited has not been bombed by Government bombers, the bombs generally falling in the centre of the town and causing loss of life to civilians. And it must be admitted that there has been no outcry or propaganda against these attacks. The view is taken that in modern war all must share the risks. It was, however, stated on several occasions that there is now comparatively little bombing by the Government side.[16]

By the time this report was made to the British government, the city of Barcelona had been the subject of a number of heavy Nationalist raids. Indeed, claims have been made that it was the Catalan capital and not Madrid or Bilbao (or Shanghai) that became the first city to endure what is now commonly referred to as a 'blitz'. Such exaggerated scenarios were created by propaganda, as well as the large number of eyewitness reports.[17] Though it is true that persistent attacks by small numbers of planes did become a feature of weekly (if not daily) life, the serious damage was done in two highly concentrated periods in January and March, 1938. In the first phase, bombs fell mainly on docks facilities and railway yards, though at the same time it seems certain that civilian casualties reached into the hundreds.[18] It coincided with the Nationalist counter-offensive against Teruel, which had been captured by the Republic after a surprise initiative in the last week of 1937.

A British nurse serving with the Nationalist army – an aviation 'groupie' who was fascinated by planes and (especially) their pilots – spent one of her days off observing the action close to the front line of the battle for Teruel. She was thrilled to witness wave after wave of Condor Legion bombers passing directly overhead on the way to plaster the enemy's defences.[19] At Teruel, arguably the crucial turning point of the war, the Republic committed and lost immense reserves of men and material that were by now irreplaceable. Having winkled out the last resistance, recaptured the city itself, and now determined to exploit his enemy's exhaustion, Franco launched a general counter-offensive to the north of the Teruel sector in early March 1938. The front of Republican resistance in Aragon was shattered into fragments. After some five weeks of panic and headlong flight, accompanied by further huge losses of men and supplies, loyalist forces withdrew across the Ebro in disarray.

Thus the second phase of the Nationalists' air campaign in Catalonia was also linked to the progress of their armies on the ground. But in practice things were different: this time, the evidence available tends to suggest a deliberate terror tactic intended to destroy the morale of the civilian population. It must be remembered that Franco and his advisers fully expected a stiff rearguard campaign, based around the towns where anarchist revolution had been so thoroughgoing in 1936–7, and orchestrated from Barcelona itself. In particular, they feared that the Catalan capital, identified with class war and social revolution on the one hand and the historical struggle for regional autonomy on the other, would become another 'Madrid' – or worse – holding up final victory and immeasurably adding to its human and material costs.

During the bombing campaign that ensued, according to official figures, nearly 1,000 civilians died, including 112 children. Apart from hearsay and propaganda, there is little evidence to connect the Condor Legion with these operations. All the large-scale raids on the city of Barcelona itself were mounted by Italian air forces operating from Mallorca. In particular, the dreadful onslaught of March 1938 seems to have been ordered personally by Mussolini in an attempt to compete with (and impress) his Nazi allies. Both Franco, whose own aviation contributed little or nothing to the Barcelona raids, and the German ambassador, still attempting to deal with the international backlash over Gernika, far from being impressed, displayed serious concern. The former, in particular, was stung by what amounted to an open letter of rebuke from Pope Pius XI published in the *Osservatore Romano*.[20] Nonetheless, within a short lapse of time both the Condor Legion and the main Nationalist air force were flying regular operations against selected strategic targets along the Mediterranean coastline. At least as often as not, these raids led to the killing of civilians in 'collateral damage'.[21]

Until this late and critical juncture in its fight for survival, the Republican government's official position was never to admit ordering air raids on enemy-held towns.[22] In June 1937, for example, International Brigaders were assured that the 'Government Refuses to Bomb Open Towns'. It was emphasized that this policy was voluntary, and did not arise from any military inability to use the same evil tactics as the fascists. 'If up to this moment we have not taken reprisals of a similar nature, it is through scruple of conscience.' However, as this Valencia spokesman added, at once ominously and anomalously, 'perhaps our scrupulousness may be excessive'.[23] As late as January 1938, an official communiqué claimed that 'the systematic bombardment of open towns, with no military objective, is the sole preserve of our enemy'.[24] So morally repugnant was the idea of retaliation in kind that (we are led to believe) Republican troops on the ground spontaneously protested when they heard that towns had been raided – even when the town in question was the objective of their own forthcoming offensive and such action might lessen the risk of falling casualty![25]

Nevertheless, the line issued for foreign consumption was (as we have seen) frequently contradicted in the domestic Republican press, which had the different objective of maintaining public morale. Although stout denials were accepted with enthusiastic relief by many supporters of 'the cause', others were inclined to be more realistic. After leading an Oxbridge delegation to Barcelona, the communist student Philip Toynbee rejected allegations that prisoners-of-war were being shot 'because this would be directly contrary to government policy in other matters: its refusal, for example, ever to bombard open towns'.[26] But another undergraduate felt obliged to reassure a meeting of the Cambridge Socialist Club that any government actions which might have had to be undertaken in this respect 'were the *most humane* you can imagine'.[27] The American reporter Virginia Cowles asserted (wrongly) that 'Franco's chief headquarters, Burgos, was never bombed during the entire war', but also (equally wrongly) that 'Salamanca, Valladolid, Seville and other Nationalist cities *only suffered a few attacks*'.[28] Even the Italian communist and International Brigade commissar, Pietro Nenni, somewhat equivocally asserted that 'Republican aviators have *more often* flown over [enemy] towns in order to drop leaflets than to carry out bombing'.[29] When the *News Chronicle*'s Geoffrey Cox flew out of Spain in late 1936, he saw 'at Alicante, bombers with their noses pointed towards Madrid . . . a hint of what the rebels might expect if they ever captured Madrid'.[30] Many years later, the poet and essayist Stephen Spender, on this occasion more honest and resolute than most members of his guild, reflected that

> our indignation at the death of a child killed in an air raid was deeply suspect unless we were opposed to all air raids. Unless we spoke out against the murder of children by both sides, were we not really utilizing as propaganda the horror and sympathy we imagined ourselves to feel?[31]

In January 1938, following the first big raids on Barcelona, the Republic launched a new initiative aimed at pressurizing the democracies to broker a moratorium on strategic bombing of cities.[32] As the Spanish ambassador, Azcárate, wrote to the British Foreign Office, 'Republican aviation will completely abstain from bombing urban areas in the enemy's rearguard if for his part he makes the same renunciation'.[33] Faced with the implacable attitude of Burgos, prime minister Juan Negrín announced:

> The crimes committed by the fascists in bombing cities in the rear without any military objective, slaughtering with impunity defenceless citizens, women and children, have deserved the condemnation of the whole world . . . Several times the Minister of National Defence has announced his readiness to renounce any warlike action against the towns of the rear on a basis of guaranteed reciprocity. Until this is achieved – painful as it may be – the Government declares that it will be compelled to answer enemy aggressions by similar methods.[34]

Negrín's words represented little more than a desperate and empty threat. By this time, the Republic had hardly enough planes left with which to defend itself, leave alone to indulge in serious retaliation. In any case, with the sudden and unfavourable shift of the war-fronts towards the east, major enemy cities were now beyond reach. Valladolid, for example, experienced its last raid on 25 January 1938, with a toll of twelve killed and thirty-nine injured.[35] Government planes attacked Salamanca three days earlier, 'killing, according to their own account, two hundred

persons, but, according to that of the Nationalists, only eight.' In
the spring, a major Republican attack on Ceuta (Spanish
Morocco) apparently killed outright no fewer than 165 citizens.[36]

During roughly the same period, the Republican air force was
hitting back against the island of Mallorca, which the Italians
controlled and were using as a kind of vast, stationary aircraft
carrier, base for their onslaughts on Barcelona and Valencia.[37] In
fact, long before this campaign began the Republican government was worried that its occasional raids on Palma de Mallorca
(which reached back well into 1936) might not go down well
amongst an extensive empathetic constituency in London.
Ambassador Azcárate, asked to report back on the reactions of the
English press, assured Valencia that only one newspaper (*The
Daily Telegraph*) had ventured critical comments, and public opinion had not been adversely affected.[38] A year later, Palma came
under sustained assault, to the dismay of the British consul,
Hillgarth. The consul and his staff felt obliged to resort to the
cellars of the consulate for much of their office-hours. As raids
persisted, the security of this refuge gave Hillgarth cause for
concern, and he brought in local workers to construct a bomb-
proof shelter. This was a move to which even the embassy in
Madrid had never been forced to resort.[39]

Meanwhile the industries of Barcelona, and the dockyards
there and in other Mediterranean towns (Tarragona, Sagunto,
Valencia), via which the Republic imported essential supplies of
fuel and food as well as military hardware, came under frequent
attack. As with Lérida, in most of these places, districts of domestic housing, vulnerable streets over-filled with refugee families,
inevitably lay adjacent to specific strategic targets. The trial and
triumph of 'Madrid 1936' had given the cities of Spain's Mediterranean littoral an early and ample warning of what they might
expect. Accordingly, by 1938 most of them were equipped with
anti-aircraft batteries and purpose-built public air-raid shelters
(*refugios*).[40] Though ultimately inadequate to prevent terrible loss
of life (as in Britain in 1940–1) these defences considerably
ameliorated the overall toll of casualties. Nevertheless, as the raids
continued – sporadically rather than relentlessly – throughout the
year, the bomber gradually ground down the general will to resist.
Franco persisted with bombing well into the period of his final
and successful military thrust into Catalonia in December, though

raids were eased off as it became clear that, in terms of backs-to-the-wall resistance, 'Barcelona' would not be another 'Madrid'.[41] In his address to the legendary last meeting of the Cortes, held during a pause in the Republican leadership's flight to the French border, Negrín repeatedly referred to the enemy's war against children and their mothers.[42] Meanwhile, once Catalonia had fallen, at the end of January, the Nationalists were able to return their attention to the Teruel front. During the war's final phase (February–March, 1939), as the enemy's armies advanced inexorably towards them, it was the port-towns of the south, from Castellón to Cartagena, which suffered the calamity of destruction out of the skies.

All that was left to the Republic now was a threadbare hope to stop the enemy, 'whose crimes of mass executions and civilian bombings have outraged the whole world', by enlisting that world in its salvation.[43] Mounting concern in the British Foreign Office was to lead to the despatch of an official commission to Spain in the summer of 1938. Earlier, the British and French governments made a joint protest to Burgos about the Barcelona bombings. Franco had replied with a brusque rebuttal. Now Halifax agreed to the appointment of Group-Captain Smith-Piggott as leader of an investigative delegation to be invited by the Barcelona government. The nomination itself failed to convey an impression of strict objectivity, since Smith-Piggott was, in his own words, 'an ardent Catholic (distressed at the excesses committed against Mother Church in Spain)'. Yet once his mission was over, he confessed to Halifax that he had been equally distressed by the terror-bombing of Valencian ports by knights of the air ostensibly acting on behalf of a Catholic Crusade. He now deeply craved to point out to 'my fellow-Catholic, General Franco ... that the continued slaughter of helpless civilians by his foreign pilots will do more to kill it [sc. the Catholic Faith] than the devil himself'.[44] At the same time, Smith-Piggott was anxious to explain the inherent technical difficulties of accurate detection and targetting of specific strategic targets from machines operating at a height of several thousand feet. Having investigated forty-six incidents involving the important strategic town of Alicante he concluded that 'at least 41 raids were deliberate attempts to hit the port area or the railway stations'. Two others, however (including one in which 273 people were alleged to have died) 'were deliberate attacks on a civilian area of the city'; whilst one or two others were terror-inspired operations representing cold-blooded 'attacks on a defenceless civilian population'.[45]

In the summer of 1938, both sides were asked by the League of Nations to submit a report about enemy air attacks on 'open towns', and the resultant human losses, since the start of hostilities. The result was like a macabre card game, since neither could even remotely guess what figures the other would call. In the event, the results must have seemed plausible at the time, especially to distant and detached office-bound bureaucrats, and when no statistical benchmarks could have been available for the unprecedented phenomenon being assessed. The Republican government alleged a total of 1,054 enemy raids, which had caused *over 26,000 infant casualties alone.*[46] For their part, the Nationalists entered 2,091 attacks on 373 different targets, accounting for 18,985 non-combatant victims. Burgos did not fail to claim that loyalist bombers had made a speciality of killing children. According to their report, between the start of the war and the end of June 1937 (that is, not quite a year later) only one day had been free of air raids on one or other of the towns in 'National Spain'.[47]

The Italian attacks on Barcelona were so obviously indiscriminate and bloodthirsty that Franco was appalled. As a rigorously unsympathetic biographer writes: 'Although it is clear that Franco previously and subsequently permitted the bombing of industrial and military targets in Barcelona, as well as of other Republican cities, in this case he was outraged.'[48] Celebrations in Rome over what was arguably Italian fascism's worst-ever war atrocity were dampened by an official request from Burgos to desist.[49] On the other hand, Franco was never prepared to accept any foreign intervention that might limit his own strategic freedom of action. The Barcelona raids had presented the Republican government at close quarters, for the first time since its evacuation from Madrid, with the awful damage caused by the bomber. Since the Catalan capital was now its actual location, this experience was perhaps too close to home for ministers and civil servants. Many accounts of this issue have too tamely accepted Republican 'positive' propaganda, which continued (*a fortiori*) to announce that bombing produced the reverse effect on morale than that assumed by the enemy. In fact it was becoming obvious that the spirit of Catalan resistance was being undermined. If we may be allowed to desist from offering homage to Catalonia on this one occasion, it was mainly because resistance had never been all that firm in the first place.[50] The tame surrender of the capital to Franco in late January, 1939 was perhaps one of the most important gifts which patron Mussolini bestowed upon his (less than sincerely) grateful client. But Barcelona's fall did not mean the end of the war. For another sixty days, to paraphrase the chilling encapsulation of the issue patented by Stanley Baldwin and adapted by George Orwell, both sides continued to drop bombs on each other's mothers.[51]

NOTES

[1] For detailed narratives, see relevant monographs in the epic series by Martinez Bande (1976 and 1984). In English, treatment of military campaigns in the revised general survey by Beevor (2006) is a great improvement on any predecessor. Only the presence of fighters could guarantee air dominance during key battles. As it happened, the importance of defending Madrid meant that Soviet aviation supplies to the Republic concentrated to a large degree on fighters; see Howson (1998), pp. 278–303.

[2] In particular, the difficult topography provided opportunities for the Condor Legion in the matter of training for precision attacks, with (usually) modest anti-aircraft resistance; Garriga (1978), pp. 133ff. On the northern campaign, see also García Volta (1975) and González Portilla & Garmendía (1988).

[3] It should be pointed out that Bilbao and the towns of its hinterland had been a significant centre of high-quality ordnance and firearms production since the sixteenth century. These and other issues arising from the Basque dimension are discussed below, pp. 213ff and 268–71.

[4] No general history of the war in English I have seen mentions the aerial bombardment of Oviedo. It is ignored by the two most widely read accounts, Thomas (1961/1977) and Beevor (1982/1999 & 2006, the latter merely noting 'carpet bombing' *of the besiegers*) and also by a leading work of reference – Cortada (1982). See, therefore, Cabezas (1984), a narrative survey; and earlier treatment by Cañete (1975) and Muñiz Martín (1976). Photographic evidence, apparently of destruction at least as extensive as that in Madrid, appears in the (pro-Nationalist) work of Aznar (1958), I, pp. 358–412.

[5] Q. in Jato Miranda (1976), p. 367; syndicated item in *The Cork Examiner*, 29 August 1936.

[6] Miller (n.d. 1937), p. 340. Cf. the relevant figure given by Archbishop Hinley, above, p. 28.

[7] Miller (n.d. 1937), pp. 341–2. Like reporters in the opposing zone,

Miller was fed spurious statistics (and probably, stories). Much damage was caused by shelling and mining rather than bombing. Yet another American journalist, Virginia Cowles, less vulnerable to Aranda's charm, gave a description strikingly reminiscent of Madrid: Cowles (1941), esp. pp. 94–5.

8 Abella (1973), pp. 146–9, and the recent monograph by Solé & Villaroya (2003), p. 34ff.
9 See the recent study by Fusi Aizpuru (2002).
10 Abella (1973), p. 256; *Ataques Aereos* (1937), pp. 32–3 and *passim*.
11 Rilova Pérez (2001), pp. 348–9. Curiously, in Valladolid the local paper (*El Norte de Castilla*) later claimed that fifteen children had died in a raid by one bomber on 12 April – two weeks before Gernika; see Martín Jiménez (2000), p. 298.
12 'Relación nominal de las bajas . . .' AGM Rollo 250, EM 1a/5/1/7.
13 Cortada (1982), p. 96.
14 Martínez Amutio (1974), pp. 98–102; see also Serrano (1989), pp. 395–6.
15 *The Volunteer for Liberty*, 8 November 1937; Romero (2001), p. 348.
16 'Report on a visit made to National Spain by Group-Captain Douglas Colyer, Air Attaché, Paris, April 13–24 1938', BNA FO/371/22626/W5627/41–2.
17 See Solé & Villaroya (1986), *passim*.
18 Raguer (1980), pp. 22–35.
19 Scott-Ellis (1995), p. 40.
20 Raguer (1980), pp. 28–9. The document was almost certainly drafted by Papal Secretary of State Pacelli, soon to be Pope Pius XII. In an earlier study of relations between the wartime Republic and the Holy See, the nationalist writer V. Palacio Atard divagates on the former's persecution of the Church but contrives to overlook the bombing issue: see (1973), 79–120.
21 The volumes by Infiesta Perez (2000–1), provide comprehensive details of these operations.
22 For example, Cockburn (1936), p. 80; *The Volunteer for Liberty*, 24 May 1937, 2. The Nationalists also insisted that their planes only ever attacked military objectives: e.g. in *Bombardeos* (?1938), 6.
23 International Brigade News Bulletin, No. 155 (5 June 1937); IBA Box 22 file A.
24 *Episode* (?1938), p. 8.
25 As in the case of Zaragoza in August, 1937; Fyrth (1986), p. 101.
26 Toynbee (1976), p. 159.
27 Howarth (1978), pp. 216–17.
28 Cowles (1941), p. 81.
29 Nenni (1977), p. 268. My emphases in nn. 27–9.
30 Cox (1937), p. 210. He was referring to the air base at La Rabasa.
31 Spender (1951), pp. 225–6.
32 Avilés Farré (1994), pp. 157–9. For more extensive treatment of British and other foreign reactions see below, ch. 12.
33 *Episode* (?1938), pp. 9–11. This claims that 'La Gloriosa' was ordered to desist from such attacks even after Franco had rejected an

international *démarche;* but failed to notice the clearly implied confession in Azcárate's words that Barcelona had been acting in a similar manner to Burgos all along!

34 'Premier Negrín Speaks to the Cortes', *The Volunteer for Liberty,* 13 February 1938.
35 *Documentos Inéditos para la Historia del General Franco,* I (1992), pp. 177–82.
36 Allison Peers (1943), p. 40, for these raids and the quotation. This authority accepts the Nationalist claim that an orphanage was hit during the Salamanca raid.
37 One research study is typically silent about Republican raids on Mallorca whilst devoting two chapters to the Italian operations from the island: Massot i Muntaner (1976), p. 260.
38 Communication of 1 June 1937, MAE Archivo de Barcelona 894/62. In July 1938 Negrín's cabinet discussed direct bombing reprisals *against Italian cities.* The premier insisted that Genoa, or even Turin, could be attacked; Zugazagoitia (1940), pp. 433–44.
39 BNA FO/369/2513/K6154/337. In this extended correspondence (May–August, 1938) the consul offered no information about casualties. Hillgarth's immediate superiors were reluctant to pay for the shelter, and eventually Foreign Secretary Halifax himself authorized the expenditure. The harbour was a legitimate target, but it seems that both airfields used by the Italians were situated well outside urban Palma. See also, ibid. 371/22626/W5627, stuffed with reports solicited by the government about raids on townships of the Mediterranean coast.
40 See Vera Deleito (2000), *passim.* Raguer, however, states that Barcelona was 'prácticamente indefensa'; (1980), p. 24. For descriptions of local experiences, see, for example, Piqué Padró & Sánchez Cervelló (2000), 195–205 and Arxer i Bussalleu & Torres (1999), pp. 69–78.
41 The last raid to cause large-scale civilian losses was that of 31 December 1938, with 44 dead and 66 wounded. A British commission was invited to inspect the bodies: IWM 70/9/1 (Smith-Piggott Papers).
42 'Diario de Sesiones del Congreso', 1 February, 1939; Diaz-Plaja (1972), especially pp. 577–9.
43 *El Socialista,* 6 April 1938, Diaz-Plaja (1972), 494.
44 Smith-Piggott to Halifax, 10 September 1938, IWM 70/9/1.
45 'Commission for the Investigation of Air Bombardment in Spain. Report No. 1: Alicante', 19–20 August 1938, MAE Archivo de Barcelona R1057/6. The Commission remained in being until early 1939. In most cases, official Republican casualty figures were accepted, since sites could not be inspected without specific invitation. See also, below, pp. 242–3 and 255–6.
46 *Bombardements* (1938), 6 and 52; *The Volunteer for Liberty,* 13 April 1938.
47 Republican Report dated 14 September 1938, MAE Archivo de Barcelona R1058/14. The Nationalist equivalent was reproduced as *Bombardeos de la aviación nacional a la retaguardia republicana* (?1939).

[48]   Preston (1993), p. 302.

[49]   Coverdale (1975), p. 349. Both Franco and the Pope acted long
        before hearing the appeals of their co-religionist, Smith-Piggott.

[50]   At least – that is to say – since the original heroic actions against the
        military uprising in July 1936. See Seidman (1990) and *idem.* (2002),
        both *passim.*

[51]   As early as 1932 Stanley Baldwin proclaimed that 'in the next war you
        will have to kill more women and children more quickly than the
        enemy if you want to save yourselves'; q. in Linqvist (2001), p. 61.

Chapter 6

The War in Getafe

At the coming of war in July 1936, Getafe was a small suburban town of around 8,000 inhabitants. Located twelve kilometres due south of Madrid's city centre, then (as now) it was a rapidly growing settlement, its development owing to expansion in Spain's industrial and military infrastructure. During the Great War, Spain had been able to benefit from its neutral status in supplying both sides with a range of products, demand that gave a unique (if ephemeral) impetus to the nation's generally torpid industrial revolution. Almost by accident, Getafe became the main centre of the brand new aeronautical sector, a matrix industry that brought with it considerable ancillary investment.

In recent generations, the town's prosperity had depended on a rather different category of extra-terrestrial obsession. Not far away from Getafe rises Cerro de Los Angeles, an isolated conical hill reputed to be the exact geographical centre of the Iberian peninsula. In the last decades of the nineteenth century, the site came to be associated with the Catholic cult of the Sacred Heart of Jesus. During the early part of the new century a huge monument and basilica were constructed on the hill's summit, and an annual pilgrimage – sponsored by the royal family – was inaugurated.[1] For many years this and other associated liturgical events provided many business people of Getafe with a reliable income. In 1911, however, the Spanish winner of an air race from Paris to Madrid, wishing to express his gratitude and homage to The Sacred Heart, landed his machine near the township, and a new era began. A school of aviation was set up in Getafe two years later, and in 1915 a propeller factory was established. In the 1920s, a spate of aeronautical-related concerns, led by the manufacturing company Construcciones Aeronáuticas (CASA), sprang up in the town and its environs. Under the Republic, as part of its prestige aviation policy, a military aerodrome was laid out to the south-east of the town. It was opened in the presence of the government aviation adviser, Commander Ramón Franco Bahamonde, in 1935.[2]

A year later, during the crisis of 18–20 July, Getafe's experience was typical of many other communities in Spain, at least in that it witnessed a bloody struggle between 'rebels' and 'loyalists'. The new airbase, constructed a short distance from the town's outskirts, was staffed (in addition to aviation personnel) by an infantry company serving as garrison guard. Between aerodrome and township stood a barracks where an artillery regiment, additional protection for the airfield, was billetted. On 18 July, the commander of the latter force brought his men out in support of the army coup, only to find that his officer-colleagues at the airbase remained loyal to the Republic. We may presume that negotiations between the rival commanders took place by telephone, whilst both used the same medium to seek instructions from like-minded authorities in the capital. During the night, now assured of assistance from rebellious units which were reasonably near-at-hand, the artillery commander moved his batteries into position to attack the airfield. At dawn on 19 July the barrage began. But if the rebels had counted on an element of surprise they were themselves surprised by the speed with which their adversaries got planes into the air. In short order the batteries were silenced by ruthless strafing, and their gunners sent fleeing in panic back to the barracks. The loyal garrison troops, quickly reinforced by proto-militia forces from the township, quickly surrounded the artillery compound. In the event, no help arrived, and long before nightfall the battle was decided in the loyalists' favour.[3]

The saving of its showpiece airfield, along with the planes, stores of parts and equipment – not to mention the relevant factory sites – was vital to the Republic in strategic terms, as well as providing a boost to morale. Over the following weeks and months, Getafe was to prove an indispensable asset in the government's resistance to the military coup. Meanwhile, their victorious planes soon took to the air again in order to attack rebel-held points within the capital itself. Similarly, hundreds of Getafeños, members of scratch militia units who had taken part in the attack on the artillery barracks, and were now flushed with the fever of struggle and success, headed for Madrid, hoping to repeat their performance. As things worked out, over the following forty-eight hours both elements played an important role in Madrid's most celebrated access of popular revolutionary action, the capture of the Montaña barracks, the insurgents' main bastion.[4] In addition, planes taking off from Getafe repeatedly bombed another barracks at Campamento, an important centre of rebellion on Madrid's outskirts, where the garrison was bludgeoned into panic and capitulation by this tactic alone. However, in the course of these operations, the total munitions supply stored at Getafe airbase were exhausted![5] In the immediate circumstances of popular triumph – and triumphalism – it hardly seemed to matter. Within a week of the uprising, except for Avila and Segovia, over ninety kilometres to the north-west (and on the further side of a dense range of mountains) the only rebel troops that remained in arms within three hundred kilometres of Getafe were a small group of army training staff and Civil Guards besieged inside the ancient citadel (Alcázar) of Toledo.

But despite the rejoicing, this apparently comprehensive victory was an illusion, and security proved shortlived. On 23 August, five weeks into the war, the Nationalists mounted a major air attack on the Getafe airbase. Only the modern German and Italian 'trimotores', with their greater range and higher altitude capacity, were suitable for such an operation. Accordingly, no fewer than eight of Franco's twelve Junkers 52 were assembled in Salamanca with a squadron of fighters in attendance. During the raid 'an estimated nineteen aircraft on the ground were destroyed or damaged'.[6] A few days later, the government admitted an attack had been made, but again claimed a single aircraft had been responsible. A Ministry of War spokesman in Madrid announced that 'the bombing was ineffectual as the machine was at once driven off by anti-aircraft defence'.[7]

In the meantime, like most other local communities in the wider province of Madrid, Getafe was gripped by the fever of revolution. Its factories were occupied by trades union organizations on behalf of the people, and local businessmen were rounded up as suspected 'fascists'. Prominent members of rightist political parties were also arrested. The town seemed to abjure its devotional past with a cathartic and violent emphasis. Heads of well-known Catholic families were dragged off to jail. The churches were burned and several priests murdered. The vicar of

the main parish church, Padre José-Ignacio, was taken to Madrid
and thrown into prison at Las Ventas. In a celebrated incident, he
gave absolution to the distinguished right-wing political scientist,
Ramiro Maeztú, before the latter was taken to his 'execution' in
the cemetery of Aravaca.[8] In Getafe itself, at least fifty-five 'fascists'
were shot over the course of the next four months. Victims
included shop- and landowners, businessmen and priests, along
with teachers and students of a local theological institute. The
socialist *alcalde* of Getafe, Daniel Ovalle Gómez, seems to have
taken little part in these events. Presumably a working man with
considerable experience and knowledge of aviation technology,
he was sent to Belgium in search of suitable sources of weapons
supply, including, perhaps, replacement stocks for the base
armoury.[9]

These latter were certainly in urgent demand. Citizens of
Getafe, most of whom might reasonably have assumed themselves
to be far behind the front lines, in fact lived cheek-by-jowl with an
outstanding target of the enemy air force. Indeed, the crucial
importance of the airbase to the defence of Madrid was a byword
inside government circles. When President Azaña called upon the
left-wing socialist leader, Francisco Largo Caballero, to form the
first genuine 'Popular Front' government in early September,
Largo's PSOE colleague and rival, Juan Negrín, was overheard to
remark that his promotion represented a worse setback to the
Republican cause than if the rebels had taken Getafe.[10] Meanwhile, the airfield was being improved and extended. Getafeños
were informed by the authorities that 'if this is not done we will
fail in an urgent duty to the cause of defending the Republic'.[11]
Alongside this, civil defence was also emphasized. 'From the start
of the military rebellion', as the town's governing committee
claimed, 'either the street lighting has been kept off altogether, or
it has been extinguished before ten at night.'[12] Despite such
precautions, when caught in the side-blast of the airfield's many
poundings, the local population seems to have experienced the
same fury of revenge that can be observed elsewhere.[13]

Getafe was a community whose living derived mainly from the
air forces, with thousands of families directly or indirectly dependent on the airbase and its associated aeronautical and technological infrastructure. Moreover, as must have been generally
known, the airfield was being used regularly for bombing sorties
against rebel-held townships, especially in the provinces of Teruel

(to the east) and Cáceres (west). These facts made little difference to the mood of violent outrage produced – here as in so
many other places – by 'collateral damage'. Soon after the end of
the war, Francoist military tribunals held in Getafe condemned
two men to death for reprisal murders of 'fascist' civilian prisoners in 1936. Justo Bizoso Butragueño, a labourer, was condemned
for taking part in the killing of Miguel García García. According
to witnesses, whilst hiding in a cave during an enemy air raid the
defendant exclaimed that 'we have to get those bastards'; early
the next day he carried out his threat by leading a group to the
jail, where 'numerous murders' took place. Marcelino Zapatero
Jiménez, another labourer described as a 'dangerous marxist',
and a member of the local Popular Front committee, was also
condemned for taking part in 'revenge' murders of civilian
prisoners.[14] The worst massacre, accounting for nineteen victims,
took place on 7 October, following a period when the airfield
came under sustained attack from enemy squadrons. One of these
raids was made at night, in this case a moonlit night, but hardly
conducive to accuracy all the same. Forty-eight bombs were
dropped. The assailants destroyed four Republican aircraft on the
tarmac, but, not surprisingly, they also accounted for several
non-combatants in the town.[15]

Meetings of the local 'superintendence committee' (*Comisión
Gestora*), a revolutionary substitute for the traditional town council, were suspended by the Madrid government in late September.
One of its last acts was to rename the town centre as 'El Barrio
Rojo', and its streets were accordingly re-titled as Avenida de la
República, Calle Azaña, and so on. They also ordered that
women, children and old men should be evacuated to Madrid,
though the extent to which this was actually achieved is uncertain.[16] Matters were confused since by this time a fresh influx of
refugees was moving into the town from the south. At first, these
wretched masses were deliberately kept *in situ*, but later it became
imperative that they too should be moved on to Madrid.[17] The
whole town had to be cleared, not just for humanitarian reasons,
but to help facilitate the Republic's upcoming frontline military
plans. On 16 October a new mayor, appointed by the military
authorities, proclaimed that all food supplies to non-combatants
would cease within five days.[18]

The town's death-agony was played out in early November
1936, as a result of its selection by General Miaja and Colonel

Rojo as the tactical pivot for the Seseña counter-offensive.[19] As we
have seen, the operation faltered before the end of its second day,
and on Saturday 31 October, frustrated and repulsed all along the
line, Líster's men fell back precipitately upon Getafe.[20] As they
approached the town, they found that most of the reserve militia
companies had already disintegrated. Thousands had abandoned
their weapons and poured back towards the shelter of Madrid.
Likewise, Republican planes now began to abandon the base. It
was reported that several of these were shot down by enemy
fighters and crashed in flames onto nearby houses.[21] Utter confusion prevailed amongst those who remained in the surrounding
trenches. By now, enemy aviation was busily provoking the widespread panic and rout of the Republican army.

An English reporter, Geoffrey Cox (*News Chronicle*), spent some
hours observing the chaos inside Getafe. Indeed, his book opens
with a dramatic description of the town on 31 October, in
passages reminiscent of the American Civil War epic *Gone With
The Wind*, with its broken army retreating amid scenes of despera-
tion, disorder, death and destruction.[22] Cox noted that the
schoolroom in the main street was acting as a dressing station for
wounded men, whilst in the cellar 'three nuns watched over a
group of children. Their lips were moving in prayer'. He spoke to
several people he found in the town, including a member of the
Scottish Ambulance Unit and 'an Englishman fighting with the
militia'.[23] Nearby, a well-known Spanish journalist, Ramón
Sender, was tenuously in command of a militia company. Jeff Last,
a Dutch writer and communist, was acting commissar of another
such company, whose men broke and fled along the road to
Madrid. On the same day, the Communist Party sent Dolores
Ibárruri – 'La Pasionaria' herself – to help staunch the flow of
desertion. In a scene described apocalyptically by several writers,
she stood on the parapet of a river bridge in order to question the
loyalty and virility of retreating troops. A young Extremaduran
refugee who had been pressed into the 5th Regiment was among
those who retreated from Seseña. On the night of 29 October (he
recalled):

> We were to occupy new positions in some trenches which had
> already been dug outside the small town of Getafe. We passed the
> night and the whole morning expecting the arrival of the enemy
> infantry. They were preceded by enemy Junkers, throwing more

bombs upon us. The planes came at the very time that La Pasionaria, accompanied by a group of high-ranking officers and civilians, appeared on top of our trenches, but she, and her companions, remained standing on top of the trenches while the bombs were falling all around us. She was calling for courage, and determination, and she went on and on talking to us in a loud voice so as to be heard by as many soldiers as possible... [24]

But it seems that just like this soldier, neither Cox, nor Líster, nor any other of the powerful and celebrated figures who spent time in or near Getafe in the last three days of October 1936, heard anything about a massacre of children by enemy bombers.[25]

In the first days of November, General Varela's column closed in on Getafe. The Lincoln Battalion veteran, Robert Colodny, has described what followed:

Militia units bombed out of Parla attempted to re-form at Getafe whilst buses from Madrid rushed up reinforcements, but a lack of officers did not permit of any reorganization of the demoralized groups of hungry men who were being herded ever closer to Madrid by the rebel air force. The roads, choked with refugees, were rendered impassable, and with the breakdown of communications, the disposition of the rebel forces was unknown.[26]

Both town and airfield came under heavy artillery fire. Despite the atmosphere of defeat inspired by the unlooked-for setback of Seseña, Republican officers were ordered to defend the airfield at all costs. They attempted to pour fresh resources into the town, including, according to (mistaken) rumour, elements of the First International Brigade, which was now marching to the aid of Madrid. On 2 November, *Daily Mail* correspondent Harold Cardozo, travelling with Varela's staff, claimed that they were only two and a half miles from Getafe, 'the Croydon of Madrid'.[27] As fighting continued around the town, a vehicle of the Scottish Ambulance Unit arrived to help ferry wounded to safety. William Forest, Madrid correspondent of the *Daily Express,* reported:

When the hospital had been vacated a few nuns, who had acted as nurses, went down into the cellars to await the coming of the insurgents ... Three old women of the village begged to be taken to Madrid. There was no room for them in the ambulance. The old women stood in the doorway, watching the ambulance drive away.[28]

On Wednesday 4 November, attacking at dawn, the Nationalists fought their way into the town centre, street by street. This time, a much stiffer resistance was offered by militia units, holed up in their favoured combat-points, behind barricades and occupying public buildings. For almost the first time Varela's veteran shock-troops of legionaries and Moroccan auxiliaries took heavy casualties. A young telephone operator kept a line to the Madrid Ministry of War open, describing the approach of the yelling Moors towards the building and up the stairs towards his work station.[29] As night fell, Varela's troops occupied airfield and township. Both were smoking shambles of destruction. Next day, the *Daily Express* devoted its cover headline story to the event.

Franco Captures Madrid Airport

General Varela, insurgent leader under General Franco, marched into Madrid's great airport centre of Getafe last evening after a day-long battle ... Varela entered Getafe to find it a mass of smouldering ruins. He summoned newspapermen and told them 'You can announce to the world that Madrid will be captured this week.'[30]

In fact, the experience of that day's fighting was a foretaste of the bitter frustration which was to come for Franco's generals during the assault upon Madrid itself. In some ways, Getafe was to mark the beginning of 'the epic of Madrid'.

Three days after Varela's victory, he nominated a new *Comisión Gestora* for Getafe, which duly held its first meeting. It was ordered that 'the bodies lying in the cemetery should be buried forthwith, along with those of combatants left on the battlefield. Likewise, the cadavers of horses must be buried or cremated as soon as possible.'[31] In addition to this grim work, probably allotted to prisoners of war or army punishment units, restoration of the airstrip was undertaken immediately. Getafe was now to play its part in the 'final assault' on Madrid. A few months later, the Jesuit chaplain at the base wrote to Cardinal Gomá to rejoice in the inspiring religious feeling among the men. During a recent visit, General Kindelán, head of the Nationalist air force, had remarked to him that 'because of the supremely Christian spirit we have in our ranks, God has given us the victory'. Despite being under constant attack from the 'Reds' (for in fact 'final assault' had not quite resulted in victory) morale was high.[32] As the Nationalist poet Jose Pemán was soon to express it:

Golden pilots of the New Spain,
Lift up your oars in the sight of God![33]

In 1941, in accordance with a general resolution of the Falang-
ist aid organization *Auxilio Social,* the Franco government ordered
local councils in Madrid province to take measures to protect 'the
orphans of the revolution and the war'. Lists of children eligible
to receive succour and education in Getafe were drawn up. The
priority list (and at fifty-nine names the longest) was of those
orphans whose parents 'have been murdered by the Reds'. Next
came seven children whose pro-Franco parents (*'de frente
nacional'*) had died during bombardment of the town. These were
followed by abandoned children of 'Red parentage' (twenty-
three); and last of all were placed nineteen unfortunates whose
parents had been executed following the capture of the town; in
other words, the victims of summary reprisals.[34]

NOTES

1   Devotion to the Sacred Heart, originating in France, reached its
apogee following defeat by Germany in 1871. At a later stage,
Spanish Navarre became its most fanatical centre.
2   The growth of Getafe's population in the 1920s is matched by its
more recent expansion. It now boasts 160,000 denizens: see *El Pais,*
20 February 2004. Getafe's history was recently chronicled at
WPP@URL *getafe.net/ciudad/historia/index.phb.* and WPP@URL *ayto-
getafe.org/paginas/asp/pagina.asp?p=82.* (Accessed 2004–05.) See also
interciudad.com/historia.html. The sole reference of these sites to
the civil war is the undecorated (if at least correct) information that
the town fell to the Nationalists on 4 November 1936.
3   Romero (2001), 114–16; Casas de la Vega (1994), 63–4. For a slightly
differing version of events, Tagüeña (1978), 76–7.
4   One historian reckons that accurate air-bombing of the barracks was
crucial in undermining defenders' morale; Vilar (1986), 55.
5   Cortada (1982), p. 310. Also WPP@URL *aire.org/gce/historia/a1936.
html.*
6   Larios (1968), p. 47. See also Katz, (1937), p. 243; Jato Miranda
(1976), p. 349.
7   Syndicated report, *The Cork Examiner,* 29 August 1936.
8   See MAE Archivo de Burgos R1060/17, undated note of Burgos
foreign ministry. The priest later gained refuge in a Madrid embassy,
thence escaping to France. His curate, Guillermo Huellín, also
escaped, joined the rebels and became a chaplain in the Foreign
Legion; Manuela de Cora (1984), p. 66; Casas de la Vega (1994), pp.
163ff and 360.

9   Casas de la Vega (1994), pp. 286–7 and 311–98 *passim;* Howson (1998), pp. 85–6.
10 Q. Graham (1999), p. 132; see also Jato Miranda (1976), p. 394.
11 Minute of public notice, 9 September 1936, AHMG Secretaría, leg. 50/4/2.
12 Report on anti-aircraft protective measures, 10 October 1936, ibid.
13 Vázquez y Valero (1978), p. 185.
14 I owe this information (from the Central Administration Archive in Alcalá de Henares) to Dr Julius Ruiz. The killing of Miguel García took place on 11 October 1936; Casas de la Vega (1994), p. 346. The issue of reprisal killings is discussed below, pp. 256–60.
15 The final reprisal victim, Indalecio Fernández García, was shot following a raid of 23 October; Casas de la Vega (1994), pp. 287 and 311–85, *passim*; Bridgeman (1989), pp. 121–2 and 127. See also BNA FO371/20547/W15491, 28 October 1936. Earlier, the authorities noted the death of 'Eustaquio Tejero Magán, muerto por metralla de aeroplano [killed by strafing fire]', Minutes of 4 October, AHMG Libros de Actas, 1936.
16 Minutes of 4 October, AHMG Libros de Actas, 1936. This meeting was the last held in Getafe, which in effect passed under martial law. Soon afterwards the commission removed to Madrid. On 4 December it met to dissolve itself pending the end of the war
17 On one occasion, the deaths of seven unknown people (presumably refugees) from bombing or strafing were reported to the Committee; Minutes, 4 October, AHMG Libros de Actas, 1936.
18 Minutes of notices, 18 September and 16 October, 1936, AHMG Secretaría, leg. 50/4/3 and 50/4/1.
19 Aznar (1958), pp. 452–6. See above, pp. 53–5.
20 Koltsov (1963), p. 166.
21 *Daily Mail,* 6 November 1936.
22 Margaret Mitchell's novel was published in 1936; Darryl Zanuck's film followed in 1939.
23 Cox (1937), pp. 13–15.
24 Candela (1989), pp. 56–7. The author was a PCE member, though this fact is obfuscated in the text.
25 Accounts of events in and around Getafe by other participants and broadly corroborated by Candela and each other, are: Líster (1978), pp. 164–8; Last (1939), pp. 88 and 98–101; Cox (1937), pp. 11–35 *passim*; Sender (1937), pp. 213–33. Last's unit was sent towards Getafe, in a vain attempt to stiffen resistance, in the early morning of 2 November. Sender's text is a novel in which his personal experiences and those of others are intermixed. All allocate priority to describing the effects of air power. 'La Pasionaria's' published memoirs (Ibarruri [1976]) reveal virtually nothing about her activities during the war which gave her immortal fame.
26 Colodny (1958), p. 34.
27 *Daily Mail,* 3 November 1936. See also *The Times,* 2 November 1936.
28 *Daily Express,* 6 November 1936. Forrest's reports were generally of a high quality, but he was not present at the events he describes here.

29 This story, widely circulated for propaganda/martyrological purposes, was noted by Koltsov, amongst others.

30 *Daily Express*, 5 November 1936. The *Express* adopted a broadly
   pro-Republican stance, but its actual coverage of the war was normally downbeat and intermittent.

31 AHMG Libros de Actas 1936, f. 2. A correspondent based in Lisbon
   reported that 2,000 Republicans were killed in the defence of the
   airfield and town; *The Times*, 6 November 1936.

32 Enrique Asunce S. J. to Cardinal Goma, 29 January 1937, Andrés-
   Gallego & Pazos (2002), pp. 477–8.

33 The closing lines of the epic *Poema de la Bestia y el Angel* (1938), q. in
   Monteath (1994), p. 59. The awkwardly mixed metaphor refers to the
   crusading oarsmen of the Christian galleys at Lepanto (1571).

34 Report of 12 April 1941, AHMG Secretaría, leg. 50.

Part Three

Suffer, Little Children

Chapter Three

Suffer Little Children

Chapter 7

Getafe in the Headlines

Few subjects are more urgent to human society today than that together constituted by war crime, military atrocity, and other tragic outcomes of organized violence between peoples. Within an intense and widespread public consideration of this emotional issue, the predicament of children has come to occupy a central ethical place. Deliberate massacre of the innocents has been a recurrent cultural image for western society at least since the Christian evangelists recorded the crimes of King Herod. Equally deliberate re-enactments of mass martyrological sacrifice, such as the Children's Crusade, occasionally refreshed the collective cultural memory. In recent decades, the horrors of Rwanda and Darfur, Bosnia, and Beslan, stemming from elemental causes that despite all the efforts of international politics and modern media remain largely beyond positive intervention and common comprehension, have stunned popular feeling. This most recent phase of concern, like some other profound preoccupations of pan-democratic capitalist culture, has its origins in the Spanish Civil War. From 1936 onwards we sometimes saw the victims' faces and frequently the means of their destruction. Child 4–21–35 was the forerunner of Ann Frank; of the naked Vietnamese girl fleeing towards the camera from a village incinerated by napalm; of the murdered baby in the forest of Srebenica; of twelve-year-old Ali Abbas, whose arms were blown off in the bombing of Baghdad. Perhaps most disturbing of all, the dead children of Madrid adumbrated the killing of eighty-five German schoolchildren in the village of Esens in 1944 – 'a target of opportunity' for allied bomb-crews frustrated by weather conditions from an attack on nearby Emden.[1]

Despite the occasional appearance of The Poster in books and articles, the Getafe incident has – of course – nothing like the universal prominence that the destruction of Gernika has attained in terms of popular appreciation of war's disasters.[2] All the same, its factual reality was conveyed into the public domain by a number of (broadly) contemporary journalistic accounts, often published as books; and as a result the story can still be found in monographs and textbooks produced by professional historians and other writers. Sources in the former category had a pronounced pro-Republican (if not Soviet) profile.[3] Perhaps surprisingly, however, the latter group contains no preponderance of authors to whom one might (subjectively) allocate a residual loyalty to either side.[4] It is also important to stress, at the outset, that 'Getafe' – the incident which is the *fons et origo* of this book – was never at any time headline news *within Spain*. Nowhere in the contemporary Republican press have I been able to discover an explicit reference to bombs falling on this township, nor were any reliable details given about the larger operation against Madrid on that day, of which it had apparently formed part. Indeed, things were almost to the contrary. On 30 October itself, Prime Minister Largo Caballero's party organ, *El Socialista*, foregrounded the (entirely fictional) exploits of the *Republican* air force in supporting the Seseña offensive, whilst carefully emphasizing the absolute moral contrast of enemy raids on a hospital and an old people's home; which, however, caused no casualties! The following day, *El Socialista*'s headline pointed out that

> While Fascist Aviators Bombard the Civil Population, the Republicans Hit Only Enemy Airfields[5]

Republican officials were well aware that nothing aided morale on the ground better than triumphant news of punishment meted out to the opposition by 'our glorious aviation'. But it seems doubtful that anyone in Madrid government circles appreciated the Barcelona edition of *Solidaridad Obrera*, which on 30 October chose to tell readers about a massive aerial operation by Republican forces on 'rebel Valladolid', an action demonstrably intended to terrorize the population:

> From a secure source [we hear] that a great number of bombs were dropped. This produced panic in the city, which sent urgent messages for help to Burgos in order to resist a powerful enemy – an adversary whose strength had been previously unsuspected.[6]

Two days later the same newspaper acknowledged 'new enemy incursions over Madrid' – adding immediately that 'no damage has been caused'. This reassurance was repeated *a fortiori* later in the same report:

> Investigations by our informants in police headquarters, and amongst the emergency wards in the hospitals, have not revealed any indication that these raids have produced serious casualties.[7]

On Saturday 31 October, the Madrid press wrote of the previous day's air raids in terms that were deliberately vague. Of course, the main intention was to preserve morale and preclude panic among Madrid's population. Such reticence was consistent with the policy that (with rare and outstanding exceptions) imposed strict censorship on reporting of air raids and especially of relevant casualties.[8] In a manoeuvre which had already been used several times to explain away damaging enemy air operations, it was claimed that the bombs had been dropped by a single aircraft. The intruder, they reassured readers, had only managed to evade the capital's normally reliable defence system by flying at a great height. At the same time, these abortive Nationalist raids (*El Socialista* explained) were 'una crueldad inhumana', the result of 'una desesperación demente' in the enemy camp.[9] In roughly the same period, *El Sol* devoted many pages to the heroic deeds of Republican airmen, with only a single report of enemy action, the bombing of a hospital near Bilbao.[10] However, that same weekend, the evening paper *Claridad* murmured darkly that following 30 October 'non-intervention equals Spanish women and children being bombarded by foreign aircraft'.[11] A few days later, and once squadrons of new Soviet fighters had taken to the air, *El Socialista* suddenly changed its tone (and, implicitly, its facts): 'Now at last we can destroy and put to flight the murderers of women and children'![12]

The domestic reasons for government press policy within Spain are easily understandable. What calls for exploration is what was happening on a different plane of propaganda action, though perhaps one that is equally to be explained by 'the exigencies of war'. The blanket of *public* silence about 'Getafe' contrasts sharply with the squealing litter of concrete details about the incident which was made *privately* available to various foreigners in Madrid, above all to senior members of the British embassy staff and key agents of the Comintern. This conduces to the impression that

'Getafe' was *a story intended exclusively for distribution outside Spain.* That is to say, it was part of the discrete propaganda campaign aimed specifically, and for specific strategic purposes, at public opinion in 'the democracies'. The arrival in Madrid in early September of the Soviet 'embassy staff' and Mikhail Koltsov was a turning point. Koltsov and Goriev headed a team of experienced intelligence agents and press experts (the journalist Ilya Ehrenburg, the film cameraman 'Karmen', the American writer Louis Fischer, amongst others). In collaboration with PCE colleagues – including writers and artists – they brought new intensity, focus, and resources, along with an international extension of logistical reach, to the propaganda effort.[13]

Germane to the issue here is evidence indicating that a propaganda ruse involving Nazi bombers and Spanish children had been exercising minds for some days or weeks before 30 October, and that at least one earlier attempt had been made to 'launch' it. I was alerted to this by a curious confusion of dates and events in the coverage given by the latest study of 'The Siege of Madrid'. José María Reverte's *La batalla de Madrid* belongs to a sub-genre of books on its subject, for which a ready market exists in Spain and in which, accordingly, contributions periodically appear. Reverte's treatment of the last week of October is marked by strange interventions in the previously accepted sequence of events. It's a tale of two Fridays, 23 and 30 of that month. Reverte recounts that on Friday 23 October, Madrid was the target of a heavy raid on military targets, whilst Getafe was hit by the first-ever 'terror' attack on residential districts from the air. The latter information is used to illustrate an alleged decision in favour of an air-terror campaign taken in principle by General Franco.[14] Arriving at 30 October, Reverte enters the killing of sixty children in a Getafe school by bombing from Ju 52 aircraft, but says nothing about a raid on Madrid proper.[15] It might be argued that these are merely understandable and inconsequent confusions, arising from contemporary press reports, which (after all) were full of tactically purposeful lies and their subsequent, contingent contradictions; that is, were it not for *The Times.* On Saturday 24 October a report appeared in the newspaper that during the previous day insurgent planes overflew the city at various hours, mainly taking reconnaissance photographs and doing 'aerobatics'. However,

A few bombs were dropped and several persons were injured, none, it would seem, fatally. Another report says that a bomb dropped on a school and killed several children. Móstoles, the village now nearest the front, has been heavily bombed.[16]

The confluence of dates and details observable here makes it plausible to suspect that a propaganda trope along the lines later made palpable over 'Getafe' had emerged from the minds of Koltsov and company for some time before the show actually hit the road. With the enemy almost at the gate, the need to sting the democracies into action was an end which justified any means.

So it is time to ask: where did the basic details, by now familiar to the reader, come from? There are only three extant, unambiguous claims to direct 'eyewitness' observation of bombs falling from aircraft *on Getafe township itself* – as opposed to the airbase, its extended installations and peripheral defences – on 30 October. The version cabled by de Caux to *The Times* before the day was out conveys a (somewhat equivocal) impression of being the result of direct observation. The headline 'Bombs on Madrid – Many Killed' was followed by an editorial summary highlighting the 'Air-raids yesterday ... on Madrid and Getafe ... at least 55 persons reported killed.' The story itself, datelined 'From Our Own Correspondent, Madrid October 30', continued:

> One plane dropped six bombs on the populous centre of Madrid. A still more destructive raid on Getafe, a village near the aerodrome ... has caused excitement and indignation. At Getafe the death-roll is reported to exceed forty and the wounded one hundred. Many of the dead and injured were children who were outside in the streets. A convoy of lorries was drawn up not far away. The bombs were of a highly explosive kind and turned the streets into a shambles.[17]

An apparently more substantial claim was made indirectly on behalf of an anonymous English reporter, whose account was later utilized by British newspapers in compiling their own stories. There is – however – no original text, nor any by-line or other personal ascription. Contemporary Communist Party sources refer to 'English newspaper correspondents' being present when the bodies of the dead children were photographed and/or loaded into a van belonging to a local shopkeeper.[18] In addition, George Ogilvie-Forbes, British *chargé d'affaires* in the Madrid

embassy, reported to the Foreign Office that a 'Reuters correspondent was a witness' at the scene in Getafe itself.[19] If this were
true, the person concerned must have been John Allwork, who
alone fits Ogilvie-Forbes's description.[20] The *Daily Worker* quoted
'a British reporter' as attesting in writing that 'I saw parents
searching for bodies. The bodies had been placed in a small
delivery lorry belonging to local grocers. I tried to look in but the
sight was too gruesome.'[21] Frustratingly, no account of the incident by Allwork himself of any kind, direct or indirect, written or
spoken, however provisional or incomplete – *in short, not even one
word* – seems to be extant. It is now impossible to trace the
original eyewitness sources upon which the editors of *The Times*
and the *Daily Worker* amongst other British, French and American
newspapers, presumably based versions of the Getafe story.[22]

The second personal testament, in marked contrast to every
other source, provides several pages of detail. It was written by an
English volunteer, James Albrighton, who years later claimed to
have been serving with an anarchist militia group, one of several
reserve units stationed just outside the town. On 30 October 1936,
according to his own account, Albrighton had been despatched to
fetch supplies, and happened to have reached the outskirts of
Getafe in a lorry when aeroplanes were heard approaching. In a
text which he claimed was extracted from a diary kept at the time,
he goes on to describe a deliberate and sustained attack by a
number of 'fascist planes' (the context suggests at least six) on an
open space in which a large group of children were at play. The
bombers circled above the spot, flying 'so low that their black
shadows swept the ground'. They first of all blew the children to
bits, then waited until the parents (along with the witness himself)
rushed forward to help before targetting them also. 'Many
children' died in the arms of Albrighton and his comrades.
Visceral details of the carnage are provided in plenty. Not surprisingly, the volunteer's horror knew no bounds:

> This action taken by the murderous scum will for ever disgrace the
> name of man. It should be sufficient in itself to show the free world
> what the future holds in store for all humanity under a Fascist
> regime ... I wonder if the so-called press who stay in Madrid will
> give full coverage to this day's work, I have my doubts if any of
> them will publish a true account of this outrage.[23]

Despite the curious circumstance of being wholly unknown before 1982, Albrighton's 'diary' closely reflects the contemporary media version of 'Getafe'. To a greater extent than any other contemporary account, this apocalyptic description combines all the chilling elements recorded in published sources about the bombing of Madrid – but, above all, it reflects the specific images to be found in the The Poster. If taken at face value, it would not only justify but materially enhance the general publicity case on bombing which the Republic built upon the foundations of 'Getafe'. With the same insistent proviso (if now intended ironically), it can be observed that Albrighton's worries about the capacity of the newspaper press to 'publish a true account of this outrage' proved to be uncannily prescient.

The third eyewitness report defies belief to a degree well beyond any other version. Joe Boyd was a Belfast man who went to Glasgow in the summer of 1936 in response to appeals for volunteers to man the Scottish Ambulance Unit. Several sources attest to the presence of this Unit in the vicinity of Getafe on 29–31 October. A week later, Boyd and a colleague were captured by the Nationalists, and soon afterwards repatriated.[24] When speaking of his experiences privately to a daughter, he was always emphatic that during his time in Spain he saw terrible atrocities *on both sides.* But in particular the daughter recalled the following tale, in which the presence of certain dissociated particles of the 'Getafe' story can unquestionably be detected.

> He was near some village just after it had been bombed by the Luftwaffe. The children had been in the school and as soon as the siren sounded the nuns who were looking after them opened the doors and sent the children out, but there were machine guns set up across the square and the children were mowed down. My father's people were in retreat at the time and he was ordered to drive on over the bodies of the children in the road, and they didn't know which children were already dead.[25]

How can any historian make sense of this nightmare scenario, a phantasmagorical episode emitted *viva voce* nearly seventy years after the original experience, having been through countless filters of change, emphasis, subtraction and accretion? It may tell us something about the nature of memory and the myriad metamorphoses of chronology, but as it stands it cannot represent a source for history, which is by prior definition a logocentric enterprise.

In the last analysis both newspaper reports and any other subsequent witness must (that is, can only) derive from details provided to carefully selected persons by senior officials in the days following the incident. In the days when *The Times* was regarded as a major player in its own right on the stage of international relations, correspondents like Ernest de Caux could command special treatment. De Caux started the war as a covert supporter of the rebels, a sort of fifth columnist *avant la lettre*. But as Franco's army got nearer to Madrid, his attitude changed, at least partly because of the airborne atrocity issue.[26] Indeed, by mid-November 1936 William Stirling, Printing House Square's 'envoy' with Franco, warned that 'it would be unwise of [de Caux] to remain in Madrid when the Nationalists enter . . . he could not vouch for de Caux's safety in view of Franco's displeasure'.[27] In the Madrid embassy itself, George Ogilvie-Forbes experienced a similar sea-change. A Catholic conservative, his initial repugnance towards the Republican cause was gradually overcome in the weeks preceding 'Getafe'. Though concerns persisted about the promiscuous violence of revolutionary Madrid, Ogilvie-Forbes established a positive relationship with the Republican foreign minister, Julio Alvarez del Vayo. In a touching testament, the politician later recalled:

> [Ogilvie-Forbes was endowed] with great human kindliness. I shall never forget his emotion when the Getafe hospital was destroyed by German planes and a number of children met a most horrible death. He arrived in the hospital almost before the authorities and made personal arrangements for assistance.[28]

However, the diplomat himself made no reference to this incident either in his official or private correspondence and we can only conclude that whatever the impressions left on the minister, *it never happened*. What *did* happen was that Don Julio asked his assistant, Margarita Nelken, to escort the diplomat to another village (Leganés, a few miles away from Getafe) 'to view [the] bodies of adults and children killed by bombs from an aeroplane flying low'. In this despatch, Ogilvie-Forbes meticulously pointed out that the deaths of children in Leganés *and Getafe* were additional to casualties incurred in Madrid proper.[29] It seems no coincidence that Nelken (who worked in her spare time as a reporter for the Parisian magazine, *Regards*) had earlier disseminated a story that the rebels had bombed a hospital in Irún, burning many mothers and babies to death. In fact the town was torched by retreating anarchist militias.[30]

On the day after the alleged Getafe raid, the French communist daily *L'Humanité* carried on its front page a sub-heading asserting 'Barbarie Fasciste'. The story, datelined 'Madrid, 30 Octobre' presented readers not only with the crime but also with a plausible motive:

> La colère fasciste devant l'offensive républicaine s'est traduite cet après-midi par un crime qui indignera le monde. Une escuadrille rebelle a survolé Getafe, dans le banlieu de Madrid: une bombe a détruit l'école, ou 70 enfants ont été tués.[31]

In contrast to its Parisian comrade, it was not until nearly two weeks after the event that the *Daily Worker* brought 'Getafe' to readers' attention. However, once a dossier of photographic evidence was received from Madrid, this exercise was carried out in a manner so sensational as to mark a radical departure in the nature of war coverage in the British press. In a set of inside page features, full of font- and print-size contrasts, and surrounded by photographs of dead children, the editorial staff made a series of key factual assertions.

What Happened

> when death fell among 100 schoolchildren, playing in a sunlit street in Getafe, near Madrid, on October 30. Three of Franco's Nazi Junker planes flew over the little town. They dropped a bomb on the street where the children played. That bomb killed 72 schoolchildren ... Photos show the broken bodies of Fascism's little victims and the dead children lying in the school which they had attended.[32]

Curiously, the initial *Daily Worker* coverage of 'Getafe' carries no authorial by-line, and makes no reference to its own staff reporter, Claud Cockburn (aka 'Frank Pitcairn'), who was working in Madrid at this time. Yet Cockburn was certainly describing the alleged events of Friday 30 October when on the following Sunday he filed a story written in such graphic, technicolour terminology that the addition of monochrome photographs would almost have detracted from the net effect:

> Without being low enough to aim at anything in particular, the
> raiders opened fire with machine-guns on streets where children
> were playing and women standing in milk-queues . . . The number
> of dead in Friday's massacre has now risen to between 140 and 160
> . . . One place which I saw where a bomb fell near a milk-shop
> there were bits of flesh and brains plastered against walls many
> yards from the actual scene of the explosion.

Cockburn went on to describe a new type of bomb used by the
enemy, 'designed not for the destruction of buildings – far less of
any military objective – but for killing the maximum number of
people':

> These are the types being used by the Fascists on the streets of
> Madrid. One was thrown into a children's school, where those
> among the little boys and girls who were not literally torn to rags
> were perforated and chopped by the bullets.[33]

Like Koltsov, who was in effect the media supremo of Madrid's
Junta de Defensa, and with whom he enjoyed a close working
relationship, Cockburn failed to identify Getafe as the site of this
outrage. Rather, the immediate context of the events it portrays
indicates a location in Madrid itself. Over three weeks later,
however, Cockburn compiled a feature article in which he
claimed that the massacre of children had occurred during the
battle in which Getafe fell to the enemy – *that is, on Wednesday, 4
November*:

> The main body of Government troops left the village under
> appalling bomb and shell attack which killed in half a day a third of
> all the young children of the place. They were blown to pieces
> while they played in the street. The German Fascist aviators went
> on throwing bombs on them as they tried to run for shelter. That
> any of those wounded were saved from slow and agonising death is
> due to the Scottish Ambulance whose members, as usual, faced
> daily and hourly as a matter of course risks as great as great, and
> often greater, as any front line soldier faces.[34]

The dichotomy here with the specific information being supplied
to Madrid's diplomats by the Foreign Ministry, and retailed in the
dispatches of Ogilvie-Forbes, is not easy to explain.

An even keener note of discord was sounded in the relationship between the London *Daily Worker*'s treatment and that of its
New York cousin and namesake. The CPUSA mouthpiece began
to work readers up over bombing in its first October issue, and a

week later brought on a 'sky blackened with fascist bombers'.[35] By the last third of the month, ever-increasing space was given over to the Junkers, and on 24 October, in what soon became its standard metaphor, 'fascist planes rained death' on the people of Madrid.[36] Then, on 31 October, under the heading 'Madrid Children Die in Air Raids', the front page announced that 'in nearby Getafe, where one of the capital's aerodromes is situated, 70 were estimated dead, mostly children'.[37] But follow-up stories entirely failed to corroborate the central 'facts' about Getafe set out by London on 11 November. Not until 20 November did the New York paper utilize pictures selected from the photographic dossier, and although they gave them similar full-page treatment, the keyword of 'Getafe' is conspicuous by its absence.

Let the Civilized World be the Judge!

Fascism Spares Neither Women Nor Children Nor Aged

What Happened . . .

On the 6th of November the fascist air force, flying low over Madrid in full daylight, deliberately dropped bombs over a square where numerous children were playing. Many of them were killed, as well as some of their mothers, who, when they realised from the movement of the aeroplanes that a bombardment was intended, had come to fetch their children away. A bomb which failed to explode bore the trademark of a fascist country.[38]

In the immediate aftermath of the bombing of Madrid, the London press as a whole was predictably reticent. Although most newspapers noted the large civilian casualty list of 30 October (some commenting the ominous change in the nature of warfare that this development represented), only *The Times*, the *Daily Mail* and the *News Chronicle* were confident enough to name the precise site of the atrocity. The treatment accorded to the Getafe incident by the first of these is still puzzling. In the issue of Saturday 31 October, de Caux casually allowed the inference that he was physically present at the crime-scene.[39] Yet a day later, in a story datelined 'Madrid, November 1', all trace of personal observation is removed:

The death-toll in Friday's air-raid has increased to 43, many injured having died. In the raid on Getafe, the airport near Madrid, the casualties are given as 73 dead and 175 wounded. The population has been evacuated, as the village has again been severely bombed, being on the direct line of the insurgent advance.[40]

The *Daily Mail*, noting the existence of 'conflicting reports', revealed that 'some agencies stated that at Getafe, the "Croydon" of Madrid, as many as 70 people – including many children – were killed'. A certain lack of consistency then crept in: 'One bomb apparently aimed at a convoy of lorries used to take troops to the front, fell among 100 schoolchildren who were playing in the sunlit street of Getafe and 70 were killed'.[41] To its extensive coverage of the bombing of Madrid and its consequences, the *News Chronicle* added with intimate detail, apparently the product of Superman-type X-ray vision, that,

> In the town of Getafe . . . there were even more ghastly scenes . . . In one ruined house stood a dark, ringletted-haired woman looking down at the body of a little boy whose right side was a mass of bloody flesh. Over twenty people, mostly children, were killed or wounded.[42]

On the evening of Wednesday 4 November, just as Getafe was being occupied by the Nationalists, a messenger entered Mikhail Koltsov's office in Madrid. He handed over a portfolio of photographs taken of some of the infant victims of the air raids, including that of a young girl, labelled '4–21–35'. The complete file (Koltsov is precise on this detail) comprised twenty pictures. His relevant diary entry reads:

> Today alone there have been a further four aerial bombardments. Many children have died. Twenty photographs have just been brought in and placed on my table. They are **large and beautiful photographs** of children who appear like dolls. They are broken dolls, with great black holes in their faces, in their necks and around their ears. If these black holes of death were not present, the children would seem to be alive. Some of them even have their eyes wide open, as if in surprise. Their hair is disordered, their lips smiling, showing little white teeth. The children died because they spend all day in the streets . . . [43]

Notably, Koltsov does not state that the photographs were of the 30 October casualties. Indeed, if anything, the context more readily permits the inference that they were the results of that same day's events; that is, 4 November. Furthermore (as we have seen) Koltsov did not link the pictures with Getafe, nor with any other specific part of Madrid and its extended war-front.[44]

Almost certainly on the same night as Koltsov examined it, the portfolio was also seen by Luis Rubio Hidalgo, head of the Press Bureau at the Ministry of Foreign Affairs, and his immediate subordinate, Arturo Barea, who was acting as censor of despatches filed by foreign correspondents. Some years later, by this time an exile in wartime Britain, Barea composed a remarkable autobiographical work, which has since become a standard text in university courses both inside and outside Spain. In the book, he recalled in vivid detail the dramatic circumstances in which he rescued the photographs from destruction.[45]

Barea tells us that on the evening of Saturday 7 November, he was called to Rubio Hidalgo's office. Barea found his boss busily burning documents in the grate. Without interrupting his task, Hidalgo revealed that Franco's armies were poised to enter Madrid: that nothing could prevent them: and that the government, accompanied by most of the senior staff of its ministries, was to abandon the capital that very night in order to establish secure headquarters in Valencia. Unfortunately there was no place in the convoy for Barea, who would have to fend for himself when the marauding Moroccans arrived on his doorstep the next morning. Hidalgo handed him a compensatory packet containing two months' advance wages, in a currency which he presumably expected would soon be not only worthless but positively dangerous. As he did so, Barea noticed the file of photographs of dead children lying on his boss's desk, awaiting its turn for the fire. Evidently convinced that his miserable assistant was as good as dead already, Hidalgo agreed to Barea's request to take the portfolio away. Despite his sickening confusion and fear, the latter was conscious of the unique potential value of the photographs as propaganda. He took them home and hid them under his bed. Within a few days, it became evident that the immediate military crisis had passed, and that the fall of Madrid, if still on balance likely, was at least not imminent. On Monday 9 November, Barea handed the photographs over to the Communist Party, satisfied that he had saved the children from a second and much more definitive 'death'.[46] In the following selective passage I quote only what Barea states about 'the facts' of the event:

I knew the pictures. They had been taken in the mortuary in which the school children of Getafe, killed by bombs from a low-flying Junkers a week before, had been lined up, each with a serial number on its chest . . .[47]

The seminal account of his own role in the genesis of 'Getafe' by Arturo Barea completes this summary presentation of evidence from contemporary witnesses who were present in Madrid at the time. But we cannot finish with this chapter without reference to a group of texts composed subsequently, most or all of them crucially influenced by the source-texts already described. Rather than quote interminably and often repetitively from all existing sources which refer to 'Getafe', I have tried to present the salient factual content of each one in tabular form (see Appendix C). From this medium it can be seen that on critical matters of detail, qualitative and quantitative differences exist, to such an extent that fundamental doubt is cast upon the reality of a bombing tragedy having taken place in Getafe at all.[48]

In total, only four of these sources neglect to identity the town of Getafe: but even these seem to refer to the incident of 'Getafe' – rather than, say, to the Nationalist raid on Lérida (Catalonia) a year later, an event that was also reported as claiming the lives of a large number of children in a school.[49] Variations in numerical data illustrate contemporary uncertainty of report and the domination of rumour, both of which are to be expected; but above all they reflect the imperative demands of propaganda. Indeed, the political calculations involved in 1936 are depressingly familiar to twenty-first-century sensibilities: the numbers of aircraft involved in the raid (one, three, six, or more?); the number of bombs dropped (only one, or a veritable carpet?); the numbers of infant victims (twelve, twenty-five; say, in some cases where a mixed toll of adults and children are reported, fifty; and so on up to 363). A similar emotional function is performed by the precise scene of the slaughter – a school, or a hospital, places which resonate an almost tangible discourse of communal goodness and peace, have a higher impact margin than any old shop or square or street.

The majority of Section A texts emanate from pro-Republican sources, no fewer than six out of nine having either explicitly communist origins or having background links with the Soviet network in Spain. (The cases of *The Times*, and especially the *Daily Mail*, provide curious exceptions.) In Section B, all examples are from pro-Republican authors. In Section C only one, or possibly two, of the sources may be regarded as neutral. Also remarkable is that fourteen of these twenty-eight texts were composed within a year of the event. It follows that from 1937 to the present time nearly seventy years later, *relatively* few published sources contain any reference to 'Getafe'. Though this has still been sufficient for the event to achieve an imperishable historical profile, it demonstrates a widespread avoidance (or ignorance) of the subject to be found in the relevant work of modern historians. The Spanish Civil War is a topic that has had more scholarly investigation, and produced more textbook and other media-educational coverage, than any other event in the history of any single nation during the last century. Yet on the evidence of the indexes of nearly 100 separate publications, the great majority produced by professional historians, that I have been able to check, *'Getafe' figures in only five*. On a hypothetical level, it may be conceded that many other events of the Spanish war, potentially of equal or greater significance, have met with equal or greater lack of attention. Doubtless too, this is the case with most major conflicts of the past. Yet if there was any substance in the story of Getafe other than its propaganda manufacture for reasons of ephemeral moral advantage and political gain, surely this singular atrocity and the unique dossier of photographs of its little victims would never have faded from history? For reasons which will become increasingly evident in the course of this book, I find the treatment of 'Getafe' in subsequent commentary to be uniquely revealing of ideologically-driven hermeneutic procedures in the realm of orthodox liberal scholarship.

NOTES

[1]   'Blitz – Bombing and Total War', prod. (for NDR Hamburg) K. Weinrich, dir. F. Huber, broadcast Channel 4, 15 January 2005.

[2]   To remind the reader: no version of The Poster itself carries the word 'Getafe'.

[3]   In the 1930s a fundamental public consensus assumed the veracity of media report. Indeed, as I write these lines (14 February 2005) a speaker on BBC Radio's 'Today' programme has just stated that without journalists we should be entirely at the mercy of propaganda.

[4]   'Getafe' figures in books by Thomas (all editions); Jato Miranda (1976); Hills (1976); Reig Tapía (1990 & 1999); and Montoliú Camps

(1999). In addition, a recent monograph again confirms the traditional median figure of sixty dead children; Sole & Villaroya (2003), p. 46. See also WPP@URL *aire.org/gce/historia/a1936.htm*. Thomas originally wrote of a 'particularly severe' raid, with 'sixty children being counted amongst the deaths'; (1961), p. 317 and (1965), p. 403. No source reference was entered. In a later edition (1977), p. 470 mention of victims was suppressed, also without explanation. Like Jato Miranda, Hills insisted the target was the airbase but that (unintentionally) some 'bombs fell on a nearby school killing sixty children' (1980), p. 85. Reig Tapía agrees the figure of 60 but (expressly) *not* the matter of intention: (1990), p. 95–7, and cf. (1999), p. 217.

5   *El Socialista*, 30 and 31 October 1936.

6   *Solidaridad Obrera*, 30 October 1936. Double standards were underlined by the appearance soon afterwards of a cartoon titled 'COBARDES' [Cowards]. It pictured Nazi bombs falling and dead children scattered among toys and school-books, with the comment: 'World opinion will have to take note of the crimes committed by the fascist dogs'; ibid., 8 November, 1936.

7   *Solidaridad Obrera*, 2 November 1936. Cf. Koltsov, who recorded on the previous day that 'the morgues are full [of air-raid victims]'; Koltsov (1963), 168.

8   Statement based on files of five daily newspapers, plus several news flysheets of individual military units, published in October–November 1936.

9   *El Socialista*, 31 October 1936. Despite minimal to zero damage allegedly caused, readers were exhorted that 'our style of war is the iron fist against combatants, but a correct attitude to prisoners. The Republic does not shoot prisoners.'

10   *El Sol*, 29 October 1936.

11   *Claridad*, 1 November 1936. The article was accompanied by a mordant cartoon by 'Robledano', 'Worse Than The Beasts' – an early example of the *Pietà* type examined in Chapter 10.

12   *El Socialista*, 4 November 1936.

13   A fully-equipped newsreel team arrived in Madrid on 23 August. The first consignment of rushes arrived back in the USSR as early as 3 September. Within weeks edited versions had been shown in cinemas all over USSR; Kowalsky (2006). One later example was devoted to the 'refugee' children sent to Russia, and begins with spliced scenes of dead children, planes and bombs – probably from Madrid, November 1936.

14   'En Madrid pretenden dañar instalaciones importantes como la estación del Norte y la Compañía del Gas. Pero en Getafe quieron solo sembrar el terror. Las bombas caen en el centro del pueblo'; Reverte (2004), pp. 117–18. The book is organized by chapters as a 'journal'.

15   Ibid., p. 142. The author's only citation in support of this detail is four lines of a poem by Herbert Read in Spanish translation. On p. 169, the story is repeated, with no citation at all. Later (p. 171) we

are told that no bombs fell on private houses until 4 November. For the poem, see below, p. 168.

16 *The Times*, 24 October 1936. Codes and conventions seem inscrutable here: e.g. is de Caux suggesting that the bombed school was in Madrid or Móstoles? In any case, some of this must have come from official press briefings.

17 *The Times*, 31 October 1936. This follows the official *El Socialista* line on the Madrid bombs. But Getafe is wrongly identified as part of 'the populous centre of Madrid'!

18 See, for example, [P. Merin] *Erlebnisse in Spanien* (n.p. 1938), 4; used from WPP@URL *felix2.2v.net/english/spain/sp3e.html* (accessed 5 November 2003).

19 Madrid Telegram No. 430, 30 October 1936, BNA FO 371/20545/ W14737.

20 Read (1999), pp. 237–8; Desmond (1984), p. 43; Armero (1976), p. 409.

21 *Daily Worker*, 11 November 1936. The source of these details is unknown.

22 Nonetheless, Ogilvie-Forbes was in touch with the British press corps, and was anxious to bring HMG's attention to the bombing. On 4 November he passed on the government's claim (via a radio message to HMS *Resource* off the Spanish coast) of 'many women and children being killed' by a raid two days previously: BNA FO/371/20546/ W15032.

23 IBA Box 50/Al/10. See full transcript in Appendix B.

24 *Belfast Telegraph*, 19 November 1936. See also Cox above, p. 84 and Cockburn below n.34.

25 'In the Fields of Spain', BBC Radio Ulster, broadcast 18 March 2006. Programme produced by Anna-Marie McPhail, presented by Diarmid Fleming. This anecdote obviously refers to the Getafe incident. But who killed the children, and why? And – even in Spain 1936 – can ambulance men really have driven over children's dying bodies?

26 See the perceptible change of tone in letters to Deakin, 14 and 28 August, 4 and 18 September 1936, TNL Archive, Deakin Correspondence.

27 Stirling to Deakin, 18 November 1936, ibid., Stirling File.

28 Alvarez del Vayo (1940), pp. 231–2. (There is no other reference to Getafe Hospital being hit.)

29 Transcript of embassy wireless report, 4 November 1936, BNA FO/371/20546/W15040. For an assessment of Ogilvie-Forbes's mission in Madrid see Buchanan (2003). Dr Buchanan has kindly provided the negative information from his private papers which I state in the text.

30 Brothers (1997), pp. 112–15, 128, and sources cited.

31 *L'Humanité*, 31 October 1936.

32 *Daily Worker*, 11 November 1936. The same day, *L'Humanité* carried a front-page photo of one of the victims, arguing that all supporters of

non-intervention were complicit in the 'victims destroyed by Italian and German bombs that fell on Getafe'; *L'Humanité*, 11 November 1936.

33   'Women and Children Blown to Pieces', *Daily Worker*, 2 November, 1936; see also Cockburn (1986), pp. 111–12.

34   'Frank Pitcairn Tells of Spain's Great Fight', *Daily Worker*, 21 November 1936. Though some Scottish Ambulance unit members later gave accounts of their experiences, none (including J. Boyd, see above p. 99 & n. 25) mentions any Getafe bombing. Cf. however, Cockburn's account with that of Albrighton, below, pp. 282–4.

35   [New York] *Daily Worker*, 1 & 8 October 1936.

36   Ibid., 20 October 1936 et seq.

37   Ibid., 31 October 1936.

38   Ibid., 20 November 1936 (my emphasis). Eight days later the deluxe Sunday edition carried a front page consisting solely of the photograph of child 4–21–35 with a reprint of the 'WHAT HAPPENED. . . ' story. But again, with no reference to 'Getafe'.

39   See above, p. 97.

40   *The Times*, 2 November 1936. The correspondent was a French national who had lived in Madrid for two decades. Some years earlier, foreign editor Ralph Deakin expressed serious concerns about his linguistic ability: 'it has been almost impossible to put some of his recent articles into English': to Dawson, 10 June 1931, TNL Archive, Personal Files, E. de Caux.

41   *Daily Mail*, 31 October 1936. This seems to draw on the same source as *The Times*, and was itself later to be plundered (oddly, given their diametrical opposition over the Spanish War) by the *Daily Worker*. However, subtle differences suggest that Lord Northcliffe's man wanted readers to believe the victims were 'collateral damage' from a military operation.

42   *News Chronicle*, 31 October 1936; q. in *Madrid – The Military Atrocities* (1937), p. 10. As we have seen, the paper's own correspondent Geoffrey Cox, was present in Getafe on the day after the alleged bombing: above, p. 84.

43   Koltsov (1963), p. 179 (my emphasis).

44   The published edition of Koltsov's diary, which reached Paris clandestinely from a Russian source in the early 1960s, carries nearly 150 photographs, most of them previously unknown in the west. They include (on one page) 12 individual portraits of children, fitting the descriptions given in the quoted text. Several other photographs also attributed to 'Getafe' and published during the war, showed bodies allegedly placed in the local schoolroom and/or morgue, including those of adults. Koltsov's entry seems to suggest all 20 pictures were of children. But Koestler (see below p. 115) refers to 'twelve unrecognisable little corpses'.

45   At this point, readers might find it useful to look in advance at the Appendix analysis of Barea's memoirs; below, pp. 273–9.

46   'The faces of those murdered children had to reach the eyes of the world . . . I went home, fetched the photographs of the murdered

children of Getafe, and took them to the Communist Party office, to be used for propaganda posters.'; Barea (1946/1984), pp. 191–4, 207. [The portfolio included the negatives.] The author does not give the actual date of this action, which I have deduced from the fact of the photographs' publication in the *Daily Worker* of Wednesday, 11 November. But see also below, p. 279.

47 Barea (1946/1984A), p. 193.

48 See Appendix C. This form of presentation is adopted mainly to provide completeness of reference: it cannot hope to represent, far less to analyse, the myriad cells of intertextuality, inconsistency and contradiction in the various accounts.

49 On Lérida, see below, *passim* and esp. p. 221.

Chapter 8

Hitting them Hard

No event is ever correctly reported in a newspaper, but in Spain, for the first time, I saw newspaper reports which did not bear any relation to the facts.

[George Orwell, 'Looking Back on the Spanish War'][1]

It would be a mistake to think that the Spanish Civil War provided front-page news on a daily basis to the foreign press. In Britain, certainly, several national newspapers employed staff correspondents permanently on the ground (and on both sides), whilst others preferred to engage reporters on a more casual basis. In general, however, it was the politically committed press that struggled to keep the subject prominently before readers' eyes, and whose reporters were accordingly given space and prominence on a regular basis.[2] Though the fact was a surprise to the present author when originally encountered (as it would be to most of his generation), the *Daily Express*'s line was consistently anti-Franco. But in practice, this did the Republican cause little good, because for most of the time the war's events were either ignored altogether or firmly relegated to the paper's introspective interior.[3]

Ironically, by the time its editor felt obliged to promote events in Spain to the front page, the *Express* was already looking forward to the end of a messy business, which its owner and spiritual mentor, Lord Beaverbrook, believed was a mere distraction from Britain's true (imperial) concerns. Indeed, he and his staff were becoming increasingly unsettled by the very nature of 'news from Spain'. In the same issue that reported General Varela's capture of Getafe and his announcement of the imminent fall of Madrid, the newspaper gave voice to these concerns. A leading article, full of scepticism about the veracity of news material emanating from the Spanish front, began gently to warn readers that both sides in Spain, along with their supporters in Britain, *were capable of systematic lying*.[4] The motives for this regrettable desertion of liberal values were elemental: to improve their own morale and damage that of their enemies; to improve their prospects of actual success in battle; and (above all) to improve their image in the outside world. The potential rewards for successful propaganda reached as far as victory itself.[5] Though the *Express* was correct that both sides were committed to publicity in preference to honesty, the Republicans were well ahead of their enemies in terms of awareness of propaganda as an indispensable instrument of war. This was an advantage they were never to relinquish. Almost from the start, all manner of writers and artists were mobilized in huge numbers, and provided with the resources for their task. The summer months of 1936 accordingly witnessed a steady development and sophistication of media techniques, in tandem with increased management of all forms of public expression.[6] In comparison, Nationalist publicity men seem almost as backward as readers of the *Daily Express*, blithely knitting or pipe-smoking in their suburban armchairs.

Meanwhile, during the critical battle for Madrid (November, 1936) beleaguered Republicans resorted to the strategic use of propaganda on a scale hitherto unimagined. Both expertise and intensity had been increased by the arrival of Soviet and Comintern agents. The former had experience of mass psychological manipulation during the ruthless and relentless sequence of Stalin's domestic programmes – collectivisation, urbanization, industrialization and militarization, not to mention extermination. Comintern operatives, often from central and eastern European communist backgrounds, were veteran anti-fascist campaigners, well used to clandestine operations. Stalin's most trusted and powerful representative in Spain, Mikhail Koltsov, was a senior editor of *Pravda,* but in addition skilful wordsmiths like Ilya Ehrenburg and the American communist Louis Fischer were despatched to Spain There they were joined by gifted colleagues from every party organization in the 'western democracies'; including, from Britain, Bill Rust and Claud Cockburn, who were at once *Daily Worker* correspondents and Comintern agents.[7] Within the extended Soviet 'diplomatic' team which gathered in Madrid during September, the interface between intelligence and communication components was intimate. Both elements had an unreserved acceptance of propaganda as perhaps the fundamental, 'spiritual' element of successful resistance to Franco. Thus, it is not surprising that almost the last act of Largo's government before it abandoned Madrid was to create a Ministry of Propaganda.[8]

Arthur Koestler, a Hungarian communist and professional propagandist, arrived in Madrid in October. He was a brilliant product of the Comintern's heavily subsidized agit-prop department, established in Paris under the inspired leadership of the German exile, Willi Münzenberg. Though not taking a direct role in the Soviet team's media programme, Koestler became one of the most influential advocates of the Republican cause, above all in Britain, his adopted home. At the time (like other dubious agents) accepted as a *bona fide* journalist, he was accredited as a correspondent by the *News Chronicle*, and commissioned by the Left Book Club to compile a detailed indictment of the Nationalists' criminal conduct.[9] Over 100,000 copies of Koestler's *Spanish Testament* were sold in Britain alone, and its world readership, extending into the latter reaches of the last century, was vast. This great audience was provided with a detailed narrative of Franco's bombing campaign against the population of Madrid. The butchery is vividly evoked. Indeed, the book's pages are so saturated with violent death that readers must have feared any remotely dubious response would cause blood to ooze out onto their hands. The drama begins on 30 October 1936, the day of the raids that included the supposed attack on Getafe, with a passage that is both germane and representative:

> It was shortly before dusk . . . In the Plaza del Progreso, a square situated in one of the oldest districts of Madrid, at ten minutes past five, three children were playing at soldiers in a deserted building site opposite an infants' creche. They saw something black fall from the sky; and one of them shouted in fun, 'A bomb . . . a bomb!' and all three threw themselves on the ground. They were the only surviving eyewitnesses of the destruction of the infants' home . . . a few minutes later twelve unrecognisable little corpses were dug up out of the ruins. Franco's squadron, consisting of six three-engined Junker bombers, had silently and almost noiselessly approached the town at a very great height. The bombs were dropped on the unsuspecting city out of a clear sky. **In the streets of Getafe sixty children lay dead**, blown to pieces.[10]

Many years later, Koestler was to reveal some interesting details about the 'creative' aspects of his Parisian education. His chief, Münzenberg, and his mentor, Otto Katz, were dedicated exponents of the creed that any lie, however extreme or absurd, was justified in the struggle against Fascism and counter-revolution. When the apprentice handed up a first draft about fascist atrocities in Spain, Münzenberg exploded:

> Too weak. Too objective. **Hit them! Hit them hard!** Tell the world how they run over their prisoners with tanks, how they pour petrol over them and burn them alive. Make the world gasp with horror. Hammer it into their heads. Make them wake up . . .[11]

Koestler was an apt student, and took careful notes. Soon enough, a relevant paragraph appeared in *Nazi Conspiracy in Spain*, a book produced by Münzenberg's outfit and also published by the Left Book Club in Britain:

> The German tanks which ploughed their furrows through the Spanish streets and buried brave militiamen under their caterpillar bodies, the German aviators who sent **a hundred children to their deaths in Getafe**, the Krupps guns which bombarded Irun, these were emissaries of German Imperialism which was stretching out its hand to Spain . . .[12]

In *Spanish Testament,* Koestler writes as though he had personally interviewed the surviving children of the Plaza del Progreso, and makes other references to the evidence of 'eyewitnesses'. Yet – as he was later to reveal – his purpose in Madrid had been to carry out research for Otto Katz's celebrated polemic, *Nazi Conspiracy*. Indeed his focus on this assignment was so complete that (as he implicitly admits) he never personally witnessed a single air raid, nor any other salient event of frontline Madrid. Despite his defection from Communism in the 1940s and a corpus of widely appreciated writing about the evils of Stalinism, Koestler's memoirs fell short of retracting the 'facts' he himself had published about 'fascist' atrocities. On the contrary, they not only repeat but (if anything) embellish the original story:

> The bombardment of Madrid, **the dead children of Getafe**, the razing of Guernica, were public events to which the public reacted with a spontaneous convulsion of horror . . . The shadows of the Middle Ages seemed to have come alive, the gargoyles were spouting blood . . . the air smelt of incense and burning flesh.[13]

Indeed, Spanish war propagandists were to go so far beyond the paradigms of vocabulary set by Münzenberg as to transport its discourse to a level of hypertrophic horror-fantasy its godfather could hardly have imagined. Soon, burning prisoners alive was to seem almost a sideshow in the shambolic circus of 'fascist atrocity'. And after all, Münzenberg's disciple, Koestler, was only one amongst a host of publicists whose business it was to evoke the 'spontaneous convulsion' of the man in the British, French, or American street. Many of them were communists, a large number being professional Comintern agents. The material they distributed was exclusively drawn from Party sources: especially from 'advisers' with fingers on the pulse of Republican government.

Pressmen who operated outside the Soviet network were obliged to rely on official briefings, local newspapers, and (of course) street-level stories – that is, rumour. Depending on their connections and comportment, they might be able to garnish this diet with occasional (supervised) interviews with participants or 'eyewitnesses'. The Ministry of State under Julio Alvarez del Vayo was in charge of the propaganda machinery, in which department Luis Rubio Hidalgo, Margarita Nelken, and Constancia de La Mora played important roles. The wickedly unfavourable portrait of Rubio Hidalgo, given by his long-suffering underling, Arturo Barea, should not obscure his dedication to the cause of news-management. Rubio Hidalgo concentrated with determination on .the censorship of foreign correspondents' files. The direct reports of British newspapermen in Madrid provide mute but voluble evidence of the success of his (and Barea's) labours. Though censorship is, in essence, the negative face of propaganda, in this case it obliged reporters, on a routine basis, to telephone home the government version of events (usually accompanied by accessory detail) or to remain silent.[14] On the 'creative' side of the campaign, Nelken and La Mora, both of whom were closer to the Soviet team, were prominent.[15]

In autumn 1936, as Franco's army marched into the Tagus valley, with its eyes fixed upon Madrid, a concrete political objective assumed urgent priority. The world had to be convinced that the Republic, guardian of democracy and protector of the people, was threatened by an international alliance of vicious dictators bent on crushing it to death. There was only one way to save Madrid, and 'Spain', from this 'fascist barbarism': intervention. At this stage, both the Kremlin and Largo Caballero's government believed a reasonable chance still existed that 'the democracies' might intervene on their side, even to the extent of directly providing military supplies.[16] In this interest it was necessary to persuade voters, in their millions, of two principles, one general and the other specific: first, that the struggle was not so much a civil war as an outright invasion of Spain by Germany and Italy, at the invitation of the indigenous 'fascist' generals; and second, that these allies were dedicated to the wholesale massacre of the Spanish people. The latter objective (the official line ran) was being advanced by ruthless employment of modern methods of warfare, in particular by aerial bombardment of populous cities. This point, in turn, spawned a host of powerful ideas. The enemy – who, after all, were 'fascist reactionaries' as well as 'fascist barbarians' – picked out women and children in the packed working-class districts of Madrid (later, Barcelona and Valencia) for their attention. They made a speciality of destroying hospitals and art galleries. In the process, Spain's cities were being reduced to ruins.[17]

The Republic's enemies outside Spain soon became aware of the strident emphasis being placed upon civilian casualties caused by bombing. Anyone involved in politics in 1936 knew that nothing was more likely to evoke a *grand peur de nos jours,* moral outrage, mass emotion, even mass panic, than the shadow of the bomber. On 4 November – the day Getafe fell – a meeting of the Non-Intervention Committee was held in London.[18] Normally dominated by shouting matches between the contending parties, at this session (according to Ivan Maisky, the Soviet delegate) 'the temperature of the political passions aroused reached its peak'. During a vitriolic exchange, Maisky's Italian counterpart, Count Grandi, launched a deeply sardonic assault on the 'bombing' front:

> Every time that an appeal is made to the public opinion of civilised countries by those who, for one reason or another, are interested in distorting truth, this appeal is always made in the name of women and children. If the aircraft of the Spanish Nationalists carry out war operations, it is straightaway said that the harmless women and children of democratic Spain are the only victims of such operations. If Soviet Russia starts subscriptions and sends goods to Spain, these funds and these goods are sent to the women and children of Spain. On reading the Soviet statements one really wonders whether the Spanish civil war is not after all a strife

between the men under General Franco and the women and
children that Soviet Russia has taken under her motherly wing.[19]

Despite the disgust of the Committee's neutral members at his
outrageous cynicism, Grandi had accurately exposed the concentration of the Soviet–Republican alliance on the theme of suffering women and children. Although (it begins to go without
saying) Grandi's side was simultaneously engaged in similar exer-
cises, he highlighted, in particular, the special moral righteousness paraded by the Republic. A fellow-Hungarian has recently
noticed that: '[for example] in Koestler's account, only women
and children, hospitals and proletarian homes are bombed'.[20] But
even at the time, at least one reporter pointed out that in his
colleagues' despatches 'the enemy planes, almost always manned
by foreign pilots, always killed "mostly women and children",
while the Loyalists planes never dropped bombs on anything but
"military objectives"'.[21]

In the spring of 1937, the American writer John Dos Passos was
making his way towards Madrid from Valencia. Favourable impressions of life in the loyalist zone disseminated abroad by influential
foreign writers were of prime interest to the Republican authorities. Ignoring the pedestrian indications of the author's name
(which means 'two steps' in Spanish) they supplied a car, a
chauffeur, *and* an interpreter. Dos Passos's group stopped for
recuperation and restoration at a wayside village. People gathered
round them in what seemed a naturally curious throng. 'When we
asked the little boys what the sores on their faces came from the
woman said it was because they'd been scared by the Fascist
bombers flying over the village'.[22] Not long before, John Stein-
beck, in one of a series of articles publicizing the desperate
conditions of 'dustbowl migrants' in California, used Spain as a
point of reference that would be familiar to his readers. 'There
has been no war here, no bombing of open cities . . . but all the
same, children are dying of starvation'.[23] Such stories indicate the
intricate elaboration and universal reach of the Republic's main
propaganda trope.[24]

A leading exponent, perhaps even progenitor, of the discourse
was the French journalist, Louis Delaprée. Despite (or rather,
because of) his covert communist affiliation, Delaprée went to
Madrid for the centre-right paper *Paris-Soir*.[25] With a series of

reports that form the literary equivalent of his compatriot,Gustave Doré's, nineteenth-century illustrations to Dante's *Inferno,* he chronicled the daily agony of the people trapped under Franco's German bombers. His speciality was prose-pictures of dead or dying children, parts of whose bodies are often distributed around the devastated streets of the poverty-stricken slums in which they had been playing.[26] Delaprée proselytized widely amongst fellow-journalists, and in November he provided details to a delegation of British MPs who had arrived in Madrid to report on the condition of its people.[27] One of his last files provided 'evidence', allegedly corroborated by doctors, of Francoist gas attacks on the city.[28] After some months, however, he discovered that only heavily-subedited versions of his reports – or, more often, no version at all – had actually appeared in the newspaper. After wiring his editor to accuse him of finding 'the massacre of a hundred Spanish children less interesting than a Mrs Simpson's sigh', he boarded a plane for Paris.[29] The flight was intercepted in error by a Republican fighter, and Delaprée was fatally wounded.[30]

Claud Cockburn took up the fountain-pen baton of his dead colleague. Having served briefly with a militia unit at the front, Cockburn claimed personal experience of attack from the air. His *Daily Worker* files were fully competitive in the hyperbole stakes when it came to the Republic's favourite propaganda trope.

Hospitals Ring with Children's Screams

For 48 hours crowded wards of the Madrid hospitals have resounded unceasingly with terrible screams of children who do not even know why they are dying. . . [31]

Rebels Bomb Children – Shopping women killed

The shrieks of wounded children were as terrifying as the sight of small bodies lying silent and still. Water from a burst main racing through the square became a crimson flood . . .[32]

On another occasion, Cockburn and Katz collaborated on concocting an entirely fictional battle in convincing detail, with the specific purpose of putting pressure on the French government to release munitions supplies.[33] (Continuing from where I left him off at the head of this chapter, Orwell writes: 'I saw great battles reported where there had been no fighting. . .') The awkward fact that Cockburn's reports appeared in a newspaper that, like the Madrid press itself, exclusively proclaimed victories on all fronts until the moment Franco's army arrived on the city's doorstep, perhaps limited his impact on the British public. More important to the cause were numerous conversions among the reporters of the 'capitalist press'. Since the pews of oddly denominated press 'chapels' were notoriously occupied by congregations of weary cynics, the transformation of so many hard-bitten hacks into delirious advocates of the Republic is an amazing testament to their propagandists' skills.[34] This is strikingly so with the dazzling array of American writers who came to Spain. Of course, some (like Anna Louise Strong and Abe North) were already stalwarts of the CPUSA. But in addition, Vincent Sheean, Herbert Matthews, Virginia Cowles, and Ernest Hemingway, writers surely not susceptible by temperament or training, were recuperated by the cause. These soloists added their voices to the chorus of left-liberal writers, working (to mention only British examples) for the *Manchester Guardian*, the *News Chronicle* and the *Daily Herald*.[35]

None of them plugged the 'massacre of the innocents' theme as obsessively as Matthews (*New York Times*). 'Why is it', he asked a policeman in a Madrid street (Signor Grandi not being on hand) 'that all the casualties today were women and children?' The occasion was an air attack which took place in the *barrio* of Tetuán, near the city centre, in January 1937. Matthews reached the scene some twenty minutes after the bombs fell. No evidence of the atrocity, not so much as a bloodstained cobblestone, was left on view, but the helpful policeman attested that

> an Insurgent pursuit plane swooped down low over a main street where there was a long queue of women before a grocer's shop. At a cruelly precise moment the machine gunner let go full blast straight into a petrified group of housekeepers. Some twelve or fourteen were killed or wounded.[36]

The same month, and in the same supercharged style, Matthews reported raids on the Argüelles district. He 'counted twenty-two Junkers sailing by, though there were supposed to be as many as thirty that day'. As a result, he saw fourteen bodies of women and children excavated from the ruins and piled into an ambulance.[37] Many of these scenes, like others from different incidents and periods, take place in densely packed working-class streets. Matthews was prepared to admit that 'not all' victims of bombing were women and children, and did not explicitly endorse the claim that the enemy deliberately targeted them. But these reservations had more to do with the credibility limits of his readers (or his editor) than with his own feelings and beliefs.[38]

Of course, it cannot be confidently (let alone unreservedly) stated that attacks similar to those Matthews described never took place. We know from other places and events well-corroborated, that Nationalist pilots and machine-gunners were capable of deliberately killing civilians. The same is true of personnel who flew for the Republic. The two texts examined here were rendered more plausible to a remote readership by a careful blend of detail and imprecision. No dates are given for the raids. Matthews arrived in Madrid on 2 December 1936, but his reports refer to a month or more later. The report 'Under the Death-Spurting Skies' is datelined 21 February 1937, and describes events happening 'a few weeks ago'. Some detail (food queue of working-class mothers, children playing nearby, planes flying so low that pilots can be seen, piles of bodies) repeats material already threadbare through over-use.[39] They were ubiquitous props of propaganda, rolled out for a belated New York revival of 'Getafe'. Matthews himself states (a fact amply backed by press colleagues) that 'the worst of the bombing was over' by the time he got to Madrid.[40] No twenty- or thirty-bomber raids took place thereafter, though sporadic air activity certainly continued into January 1937.[41]

More significantly, the Argüelles district had been an intense war zone since the beginning of the 'siege'. Its long, imposing lines of apartment blocks were once the preserve of wealthy citizens. Doubtless, during the summer, after expropriation from 'fascist' owners, they had been filled by working-class families and/or refugees. However, as things turned out, the buildings stood immediately adjacent to the route of Franco's army into Madrid. Situated on a west-facing ridge overlooking the Manzanares, they offered a convenient fortress to the defenders. More for military than humanitarian reasons, its recent immigrants were removed in October, making room for observation posts and emplacement-points for light artillery and heavy machine-guns.[42] In the course of the following month, the 'wall' was pounded incessantly by enemy bombers and artillery. Though never wholly demolished, Argüelles became the one area of the city about which comparisons with standards of war-devastation soon to be set elsewhere would not be out of order. On the other hand, it seems unlikely that communities of civilians could have been wiped out there in January 1937, especially not families consisting only of women and children.

Yet Matthews was by no means the only reporter to re-cycle the horror in order to revive the outrage. Arriving in Madrid at the same time as Matthews, and following the identical story trail, Anna Strong

> visited a section in the north of Madrid near the edge of the city where a score of workers' flats had been destroyed the previous week. The foreign bombers in Franco's service had poured half-ton bombs all over this district ... Four hundred bodies had already been found, chiefly women and children. Even a layman like myself could see the totally unmilitary character of this bombing, which was intended to terrorize civilians. Everyone in Madrid tells you that bombers attack especially the long lines of women waiting at food stores.[43]

Witnessing or (preferably) surviving air raids became an expected badge of honour not only amongst war correspondents, but by a long list of international celebrities, the so-called 'tourists', who were effusively welcomed to Spain by the Republican publicity machine. Amongst this category were the celebrated American essayist Dorothy Parker and the popular English art critic, Hannen Swaffer. Parker, for her part

> saw a woman who lives in the poorest quarter of Madrid. It has been bombed twice by the fascists; her house is one of the few left standing ... One [orphan] colony was in a seaside resort near Valencia. There were sixty children from Madrid ... The fascist planes had bombed their school ... They drew planes and bursting bombs and houses in flames. You could see by the dreadful perfection of detail how well they knew their subjects ...[44]

Swaffer noted, less ambitiously, that 'they drop bombs on [Madrid] from the air in darkness. Brutal and desperate, they turn their guns on wounded in hospitals, women working in their homes, children playing in the streets'.[45] The famous Hollywood writer, Lillian Hellman, was later caught out in an extended untruth by her compatriot, Martha Gellhorn.[46] Gellhorn herself came to Spain having already been converted from pacifism to anti-fascism by travelling in Germany and France. She had no Spanish and no previous journalistic experience, but became on the instant determined to write as 'the only way I could serve the Causa, as the Spaniards solemnly and lovingly called the war'.[47] With this firm aim in view, but (as bad luck would have it) having got to Madrid after the bombing campaign was over, she made the best of her circumstances. Her book describes how she observed the ghastly death of a little boy killed in the street, whilst still holding his mother's hand, during an artillery bombardment. 'A small piece of twisted steel, hot and very sharp sprays off from the shell; it takes the little boy in the throat.'[48] But one Madrileña told her that 'the bombing in November was far worse'; 'in November there were black Junker planes flying over and dropping bombs' added another; still others said that 'the bombing had been very bad . . . the children couldn't go to school because the school had been bombed'.[49] Nearly forty years later, during a return visit to the city, Gellhorn recalled that in 1936, 'Madrid was half-destroyed'.[50]

One ostensibly neutral journalist obtained a writing commission for Spain after being appalled by a wave of *anti-Republican* atrocity propaganda in the London press. His insiders' insight into the damage such work might cause to democracy and truth was advanced and perceptive:

> Propaganda is a very powerful force, possibly more effective than the strongest armament. It is more potent than the deadliest gas-bomb, for that of necessity can kill only a certain number, while this hidden armament can mass killers by hundreds of thousands. It can turn the most peaceful into the most warlike; it can incite hatred where there was friendship; it can breed intolerance and blood-lust; it can divide a whole population. . .[51]

Yet once this writer, Jerome Willis, arrived in Madrid, whether or not on a genuinely 'spontaneous' mission, he was sucked into the government propaganda machine. His subsequent treatment of the war was a faithful reflection of ministerial attitudes and the party (if not the Party) line. This experience was identical with that of a clear majority of foreign correspondents. There was a strange but persistent descant to the dominant 'bombing' theme of mass human agony and misery. A notion that appealed to some Republican copywriters was that of a reckless popular contempt for the enemy aviator. It responded to a perceived need to let the enemy know that Madrid was not downhearted, and to avoid damaging in advance the morale of still-unscathed populations in

Barcelona and Valencia.[52] Some reports speak of citizens making light of their ordeal with jokes; of grown-ups as well as children enjoying the spectacle of bombers and dog-fights. One story, more mischievous than others, was lucky to escape the censor. A man was asked why he hadn't bothered to take cover during a raid. He replied that since everyone knew that only women and children were attacked by bombers, he couldn't see the point.[53] Of course – it remains necessary to reiterate – children were killed, both alone and in small groups. The innocents died under the bombs of autumn 1936, and in the sporadic artillery fusillades which featured in the siege of Madrid almost until the end of the war. Yet despite several explicit claims, and other less explicit indications to the same effect, no reporter ever witnessed an air raid on a city at close quarters. This applies to the relevant tragedies of the whole war, not just to the alleged incident at Getafe.[54]

Meanwhile, the Nationalists also exercised an 'absolutely iron' control of foreign war correspondents, who generally operated under conditions even less conducive to honest reporting.[55] The *Daily Mail*, whose correspondents were (in today's parlance) 'embedded' in the Army of Africa, ignored the bombing of Madrid until a very late stage, attributing civilian casualties exclusively to strategic shelling. Then, after printing a photograph of an alleged aviation raid on the city, they followed up with the story that victims were 'mostly workers erecting barricades', a claim as patently absurd, in its perverse, converse way, as the shibboleth of women and children in shopping queues.[56] For their part, Nationalist sources made no reference to victims of aviation, unless we count a growing concern to respond to Republican propaganda. Sympathetic English observers took their cue from Grandi's mordant exposure of the Republic's tactics. In a chapter neatly titled 'The Fiction Factory', the *Daily Mail* reporting team of William Foss and Cecil Gerahty asserted that the Republicans

> know exactly the right moment to pull out the vox humana of 'bombed [Red] babies' ... In communiqué after communiqué they announced the bombing of hospitals ... at a time when Franco had a great inferiority in aircraft. ... The next great Red 'wail' was the bombing or bombardment of 'open towns'. Before we give examples, we will mention a few facts about their own work in that direction ... They bombed sixteen towns before General Queipo de Llano retaliated ... Granada ... was bombed practically

daily [for] six weeks. The town had no anti-aircraft guns, and
certainly presented no huge factories or stores like Barcelona ...
nor was it in the front line like Madrid ... Cordoba suffered the
same fate ... There was, in fact hardly a town in Nationalist
territory which was not bombed. At Valladolid one Red machine,
disguised as Nationalist, bombed the centre of the town in the
afternoon ... and had a fine haul of children. None of this stirred
our Press. Curious. Why?

The real reason for this intensive 'plugging', this propaganda
about women and babies, was to make the word 'Madrid', by sheer
weight of publicity and repetition, stand for a symbol of 'Fascist
aggression' ... Looking back, does it not seems strange that the
Reds, according to their communiqués, bombed and hit only
military targets, whilst the Nationalists never hit any military
objectives, but only, and deliberately, priests saying Mass in Vizcaya,
nuns in their convents, waiters in cafés, queues of starving women,
girls' schools and babies?[57]

But to expose, however powerfully, the enemy's propaganda
tactics is never fully effective as counter-propaganda. *In extremis*
(and the Nationalist situation in this contest was a desperate one)
what is needed is creative copy of one's own. The woeful standard
they actually achieved can be illustrated by the ponderous prose
and dubious allegations of the English Catholic writer, Sir Arnold
Lunn:

I can understand all those who denounce bombing from the air as
inhuman, but I cannot understand the position of those who are
indignant when Guernica is bombed and who raise no protest
against the bombing of Saragossa, Talavera, Seville, Avila or
Granada ... The most disagreeable form of Red propaganda is the
deliberate policy of using women and children as a shield for their
retreating troops.[58]

Most authorities agree that this aspect of the Francoist war
effort never matched the creative (even 'artistic') standards set by
their opponents, and fell miserably short of achieving the same
audience figures.[59] Indeed, much as any weary cynic might hesitate
to offer stricture on this score, these assessments seem to put
things mildly. By summer 1937, the sobering experience of the
world's backlash over Gernika had alerted Burgos to the urgent
importance of atrocity propaganda, above all in the context of
bombing. Yet the Nationalist response to the expert practitioners
on the other side was feeble, naive and incompetent. In the case

of Córdoba, a city which had been raided on a frequent basis since the beginning of the war, they astonishingly managed to issue *a serious underestimate* of civilian casualties![60] The best they could manage in the field of propaganda – in stark contrast to most other aspects of the war effort – was to offer their enemy the flattery of imitation.[61] How they managed to win the war nonetheless may be wondered at. One is less surprised that they did so at the cost of losing their moral case continuously 'at the bar of history' ever since.[62]

NOTES

[1]   Orwell (1938 & 1943/1966), p. 234.
[2]   For example, in terms of readership figures, *Daily Mail* and *Daily Telegraph* (pro-Nationalist); *News Chronicle* and *Daily Herald* (pro-Republican). Regional and local press tended to ignore the war, though several papers carried lively correspondents' debates; see e.g. Stradling (2004), *passim* but especially pp. 86–94.
[3]   Beaverbrook's attitude can hardly be described as pro-Republican, being a function of fears over Franco's attitude to Gibraltar, and his own powerful anti-Catholic prejudice. He simultaneously, and much more actively, supported non-intervention; see Taylor (1972/74), pp. 477, 487, 495–6.
[4]   *Daily Express*, 5 November 1936.
[5]   There is no dedicated study of the British press and the Spanish Civil War. Nor is there a scholarly study of propaganda; we know little about its internal politics, bureaucratic structure or technical stratagems. Approaching sixty years after Orwell's death, and in the present phase of media-soaked intellectual culture, these lacunae may be described as surprising. The most important study yet to appear concentrates on activities in the USA; (Rey García, 1997). Also useful are Armero (1976); Desmond (1984); and a discursive chapter in Knightley (1975/2000), pp. 207–35.
[6]   See, for example, Montoliu Camps (2000), I, pp. 148–51 and 164–9.
[7]   Beckett (1995), p. 50.
[8]   Abramson (1996), especially pp. 101–12, 161–72 and 251–60.
[9]   Koestler (1937). Under Münzenberg, who was entrusted with the external direction of pro-republican propaganda, Koestler worked on a pamphlet about Francoist atrocities, published in Paris as *L'Espagne Ensanglantée* (1936). *Spanish Testament* is still to be found on the shelves of university libraries and even educational booklists. In my view, both Rey García (1997), pp. 202ff and Knightley (2000), pp. 208ff. fail to grasp the extent to which western journalism was suborned by Sovietism during the Spanish War.

[10] Koestler (1937), pp. 166–7 *et seq*. Like some other foreign observers, Koestler believed Getafe to be a district of Madrid.

[11] Koestler (1954), p. 333.

[12] [Katz (1937)], 21. This production was intended to convince public opinion (and through it, the Non-Intervention Committee) that the Third Reich had masterminded the rebellion and war in Spain. (My emphases in this and preceding quotes.)

[13] Koestler (1954), pp. 325–6; and cf. Knightley (1975/2000), pp. 211–12. (My emphasis in this and the previous three quotations.)

[14] The odd exceptions to this rule were those who enjoyed access to secure telegraph or radio transmitters, usually within foreign embassies.

[15] Rey García (1997), pp. 203–4.

[16] Armero (1986), p. 25.

[17] For a short account presenting as regular events virtually every atrocity story employed by Republican 'bombing' propaganda, see Fisera (?1937). This material was largely drawn from the files of *El Socialista*, October–November 1936. But see also *L'Humanité*, for example, 16–18 November 1936: 'Dans les quartiers ouvriers les torpilles italiennes et allemandes tuent les femmes et les enfants ...' On the role of art galleries, see Stradling (2003), *passim*.

[18] The British and French governments set up the Non-Intervention Committee to provide international legal sanction for their determination not to get involved in Spain. The dictatorships, whose agenda was to prosecute intervention for all it was worth, agreed to join. The Committee brokered an agreement which only its sponsors had any intention of honouring. Thereafter it supervised an elaborate and increasingly fraudulent quarantine operation which ignored systematic infractions and sought to punish only the private entrepreneur. In effect, though not intention, this affected Spain's legitimate government more seriously than it did the Nationalists.

[19] Maisky (1966), p. 68. The writer's position was vulnerable because of evidence of huge Soviet military supplies arriving in Republican Spain.

[20] Barta (1990), p. 78.

[21] Q. by Rey García (1997), p. 213, from E. Knoblaugh's *Correspondent in Spain* (1937).

[22] Q. by Sperber (1974), p. 195. Dos Passos, who had a bad experience in Spain, probably realized later that his interpreter had deceived: the sores were certainly related to malnutrition.

[23] 'The Dustbowl Migrants', BBC Radio 4, 7 February 2004.

[24] See also below, Chapter 12

[25] Cf. the achievement of Kim Philby in representing *The Times* in the Franco zone.

[26] Delaprée (1936), see esp. pp. 14, 19–20, 24, 27, 36, 38, 46.

[27] Delaprée was interpreting for Nelken, minister in charge of entertaining the delegation. Its leader was the Labour M. P. Seymour Cocks, whose 'eyes drowned in tears' when told of the children killed by bombs; Delaprée (1936), pp. 35–6.

28   Delaprée (1936), pp. 45–6. The claim was echoed by the *Daily Worker*,
      14 and 19 November and re-echoed by the *Daily Herald*, 16 and 21
      November 1936. There were never any such attacks.
29   Delaprée (1936), p. 47. The specific massacre mentioned here seems
      inspired by 'Getafe'. To the frustration of the Republican publicity
      network, for much of December 1936 Madrid was driven off the front
      pages in the democracies by the abdication crisis in London.
30   The damaged plane landed safely but Delaprée died in hospital. His
      death was presented as another heroic sacrifice (like those of Dur-
      ruti, Beimler *et al.*) but was the result of genuine (i.e. accidental)
      'friendly fire'. Republican (mercenary) flyers were often drunk in
      charge of their machines. It was claimed Delaprée had been assassi-
      nated by 'fascist aviators' whilst on a mercy mission to save Spanish
      children, which placed a benediction of perfect verisimilitude upon
      the event: see Koltsov (1963), p. 265ff; Torriente Brau (1938), p. 78.
      His reports were soon published in Spanish, English and French. His
      anti-fascist epitaph was the injunction 'do not forgive them, for they
      know what they are doing'; Delaprée (1936), p. 28.
31   *Daily Worker*, 2 November 1936.
32   *Daily Worker*, 16 November 1936.
33   See Knightley (1975/2000), p. 212.
34   Credit for many such conquests was claimed by the beautiful Con-
      stancia de la Mora, a Lorelei with an irresistible song. How could
      victims, including representatives of antipathetic organizations like
      Hearst Newspapers Inc., be able to tell the dancer from the dance?
      See Armero (1976), pp. 36–8.
35   A compilation of British newspaper reports on the bombing of
      Madrid was made in the Labour Party pamphlet *Madrid – The Military
      Atrocities of the Rebels* (1937), especially pp. 10–13. Space and copy-
      right considerations inhibit a fully-documented analysis of news-
      papers or reporters here. My cursory assessments can be audited by
      recourse to the bibliography, especially books by Langdon-Davies,
      Cox, Jellinek, Merin, and others not named here.
36   'Under the Death-Spurting Skies of War-Torn Madrid', *New York
      Times Magazine*, 21 February 1937; see Jackson (1972), p. 56.
37   Matthews (1938), pp. 196–7, see also 186.
38   Matthews remained a lifelong advocate of the Republic, though later
      coming to suspect that 'loyalist Spain did not exemplify all the desires
      and ideals we harboured in those years'; Matthews (1957), p. 28.
39   See (e.g.) files of the *Daily Worker* and *l'Humanité*, November 1936,
      passim. Like Koestler, the *News Chronicle*'s Geoffrey Cox recorded
      bomb-by-bomb descriptions; see (e.g.) Cox (1937), pp. 35, 73–4,
      113–17. And like Matthews, he posed the rhetorical (and surely
      disingenuous) question, 'why in many raids have machines dived and
      machine-gunned women and children rushing for refuge . . .?'; ibid.,
      p. 130.
40   Matthews (1938), p. 200; cf. Willis (?1938), p. 213 and Strong (1937),
      p. 39.
41   Matthews was confused about whether the fourteen bodies he saw (or
      glimpsed) were victims of a 'pursuit plane' (i.e., a fighter) or a Junkers.

42   Persons not of an age deemed useful for defence purposes were evacuated from Madrid in large numbers in 1936. See also above, pp. 56–7; and on child evacuation, *El Socialista*, 30 October 1936.

43   Strong (1937), pp. 38–9, see also p. 33. Strong's 'workers' flats' were actually the same streets in Argüelles described by Matthews, and she probably refers to the same raid(s). Her treatment is a perfect encapsulation of officially required content.

44   'No Axe to Grind', reprinted in *The Volunteer for Liberty*, 15 November 1937. On the children's drawings, see below, pp. 154–5.

45   *The Volunteer for Liberty*, 29 January 1938.

46   'Hellman's harrowing description of a bombing raid on Valencia belonged, Gellhorn proved, to the realm of imaginative fiction. Valencia suffered no attack during Hellman's stay'; see Carey (1987).

47   Since then, 'I have praised the Causa of the Republic of Spain on the slightest provocation for twenty years'; Gellhorn (1959/86), p. 20. An extended obituary of Gellhorn derived its title from memories of stoical Madrid women in food-queues being attacked by fascist planes: 'No-one leaves her place in line': Harding (1998).

48   Gellhorn (1959/86), p. 26. Evidently she happened to be staring intently at the victim at the very moment of his death, and saw the fatal missile fly towards him – as it were, in slow motion. Capa's camera could not have done better.

49   Ibid., pp. 23–5. Children are foregrounded in Gellhorn's account of the bombing in Barcelona a year later; ibid., pp. 46–9. Her book, which opens with a powerful affirmation of the ethical contract between the journalist and absolute, fundamentalist truth, is a widely-used text in courses of media studies in higher and further education.

50   'When Franco Died', reproduced in Gellhorn (1989), p. 338.

51   Willis (?1938), p. 168.

52   Yet similar tropes were later used about these cities too; see 'Raids on Civilians', *The Volunteer for Liberty*, 5 February 1938.

53   Montoliú Camps (1999), I, p. 173.

54   See e.g. Cox (1937), pp. 73–4. See also J. Stubbs-Walker in the *Daily Herald*, 2–18 November 1936, esp. the last of these dates. The book by Frank Jellinek of the *Manchester Guardian*, whose author was not in Madrid at the time, nevertheless includes a substantial section on the bombings, and claims that 'most of the events I saw personally'; (1937), pp. 12 and cf. 509ff.

55   Armero (1976), pp. 21–6.

56   *Daily Mail*, 9 November 1936.

57   Foss & Gerahty (n.d. ?1938), pp. 432 and 445.

58   Lunn (1937/74), pp. 142 & 146.

59   For example, Republican supporters even managed to exploit the mistreatment of pressmen by the other side as propaganda for themselves; see A. Journalist (?1936).

60   See Hidalgo Luque (2006), 1 & 16–17.

61   See e.g. *Ataques* (1937); *Bombardeos* (?1938).

62   Rey Garcia (1997), *passim*.

Chapter 9

Views from Ground Level

Common sense suggests that there are people alive today who were present when civilians were bombed to death during the Spanish Civil War. Logically, too, such witnesses must be numbered at least in dozens, if not hundreds. Though, of course, these anonymous citizens would have been very young at the time, such survivors by definition observed the consequences of air raids with their own eyes, and/or felt it with their bodily senses.[1] Whether or not any given event constituted a deliberate war crime or (conversely) was the result of unintended 'collateral damage' was immaterial to them at the time, and probably remains so. It goes without saying that we empathize with such feelings. These were the first European victims of a universal phenomenon which, more so even than the First World War, the Stalinist Terror and the Nazi Holocaust, represents the ultimate political and moral rationalization of the nation-state. They may be regarded, to some degree (and without pejorative intent), as the guinea-pigs of postmodernism, prototype citizens of a world city which, three generations later, finds itself trapped in a global war against terrorism, its people involuntary if only potential victims in a civil war that is both universal and eternal. Descendants of non-combatants killed and injured by enemy bombs in Madrid in the autumn of 1936 may well have been among the 192 persons killed and injured by terrorist bombs in Madrid on 11 March 2004. And, precisely because of the keen edge that living in this new millennial dystopia gives to our fraternal emotions, it seems important (once more) to recall that the hypothetical witnesses with whom I began this paragraph must include survivors from both sides of the conflict in Spain.

Historians (generally) may neglect to mention the Republic's
record in 'bombing of open towns': but it seems that none has
actively questioned the resulting toll of 4,000 deaths in Nationalist
territory. However, as might be expected, most witnesses who have
left testaments to their experiences have come forward from the
Republican side. In the prevailing cultural climate, the average
reader of any relevant book, magazine or newspaper article, the
viewer of any TV documentary, is almost certain to be presented
with the Republican perspective on the issue of bombing
atrocities. Only a handful of victims from the Francoist wartime
territories have ever spoken about the effects of bombing.[2]
No-one (to my knowledge) has ever been able to view newsreel
footage of ruined streets and shops, of broken little bodies, of
distraught friends and relatives, originating from any Nationalist
town. The unspoken but all-pervading assumption in any medium
or context that presents the smouldering issue is that the details
of death and destruction have been suffered exclusively by the
people of the Republic, and was imposed on them by Franco's
Italian and Nazi allies, ruthless mercenary adventurers determined to win the war for 'international fascism'. As we shall see,
Gernika provides the ubiquitous template, an all-pervasive pattern for any treatment of the general subject of aerial bombing.

Yet a peculiar anomaly pervades the oral evidence if only by a
sense of absence – something is missing. In the course of ten
years' work on this book, I never encountered a post-war interview
with any survivor who – from his or her own experience – was able
to communicate verifiable details of any specific air attack anywhere in Spain, to supplement the usual generalities about noise,
horror, damage and death.[3] This chapter will (therefore) examine contemporary testimonies; and perforce, it will deal mainly
with the Republican perspective. By 'testimonies', I mean
recorded accounts *that give the reader to understand* that their
author was present at the scene of the crime and speaks directly
about events experienced in person. Since the previous chapter
analysed contemporary media reports, the present one concentrates on personal accounts by known individuals.[4] Leaving aside
Gernika – which was not the most typical *but precisely a wholly
atypical* bombing atrocity – the bulk of the documentary residue
was provided by persons actively involved in the struggle on the
Republican side, and was distributed to the world accordingly.
Equally striking is that comparatively little of the *corpus* derives

from indigenous civilian sources; the bulk of it comes rather from foreign military volunteers present in Spain on behalf of the Republic. *Prima facie*, and in terms of contextual evidence, there is little to connect these testimonies with the policy-making and publicity-seeking machinery foregrounded in the previous chapter. However, since a great majority of the authors were members of the Communist Party, the impression of casual, honest observation is largely an illusion. Apart from newspaper journalism, the most common source of information is the contemporary correspondence and later recollections of hundreds of volunteers of the International Brigades.

In the summer of 1937, Fred Copeman, commander of the British Battalion of the XV (International) Brigade of the Spanish Popular Army, was sent home for a furlough after the terrible battle of Brunete. He was soon pressed into service as a speaker at 'Aid Spain' meetings, drumming up public support for the Republic. Since recruiting for the Brigades was illegal, and Copeman was a known agent of Bolshevik revolution, he was shadowed by a Special Branch officer. In one place (this agent informed his superiors) Copeman addressed an audience 1,000 strong. He shocked his hearers to the core with 'an account of what he had seen in Tortosa in the Aragon':

> Not a wall in that town has been left standing as a result of the dastardly work of the Franco bombers. Every woman and child in the town has been killed. I walked along one street and I counted seven hundred and thirty dead bodies, all were those of women and kids. You could smell the town from miles away as the ruins were full of dead bodies which had lain there for days.[5]

The historian who discovered this document, James Hopkins, comments that Copeman 'offered *a powerful narrative* to accompany all the still photographs of the staring eyes of dead children . . . shown at Aid Spain rallies'. Hopkins adds that the speaker was '*almost unbearably moving*' and all the more convincing for being '*not fictional*, but a real working class hero'.[6]

Though we must bear in mind that the quoted text comes from a (presumably) *unsympathetic* hand, Copeman's story amounts to a lunatic caricature of any situation that would normally be taken for 'reality' by any audience, however *sympathetic*. It seems relatively unimportant that his audience were unaware that Tortosa was not 'in the Aragon', and not a little town suitably similar to

Gernika, but rather a substantial settlement in the Catalan province of Tarragona, almost on the Mediterranean coast; or that its
approximately 25,000 inhabitants would have offered the preda-
tors somewhat richer pickings in terms of women and children
than a mere 730 body count. Rather more telling, Tortosa had not
been heavily bombed at this juncture of the war, and Copeman
had never been there at the time of his speech. Ten years later,
when he came to write his memoirs, he had all but forgotten his
Aid Spain speeches.[7] In contrast, some of his audience doubtless
carried these words in their hearts and perhaps passed them on to
their children. After all, as they listened to Copeman, the horrors
of Gernika were fresh in their minds. Yet surely Count Grandi
could not have confected a more diverting spoof of Republican
propaganda than the script some Party hack provided for Fred
Copeman. The twentieth century's two greatest exponents of
propaganda, Willi Münzenberg and Josef Goebbels, apparently
believed that the most effective stories are those which observe
the golden rule of plausibility. It seems possible that both were
wrong.

Fred Copeman was an amateur propagandist, pressed into
service because of his fame as a fighter for the working class.
Many of his fellow officers were professionals, or at least semi-
professionals. A virtual corps of skilled wordsmiths from all over
Europe and America served 'the cause' in Spain as officers in the
International Brigades (IBs). Frequently enough they were brave
soldiers whose courage in battle was exemplary. But the Party also
'encouraged' them to compile accounts of their experiences, to
be sent out via communist-controlled avenues, often to their
countries of origin, where they were duly published. For readers,
the epic heroism James Hopkins emphasizes in the case of Fred
Copeman gave their words the ultimate *imprimatur* of veracity. It
was not generally known in Britain, France and America that the
IBs were created and controlled by the Comintern, far less that
their principal *raison d'être* was the interests of Stalin rather than
'Spain'. As far as most public were concerned, these writers were
altruistic warriors whose impressive personal sacrifices were made
precisely in order to preserve democracy and truth.[8]

Oracular examples are many. Jef Last, a writer well-known in
his native Netherlands, and now active in the defence of Madrid,
provided regular horror-copy to Amsterdam:

I have seen how bombs were dropped on the slum quarter where the women brought us their last chunk of bread and the last of their wine . . . I have seen the corpses of little children being taken away in lorries . . . The proletariat of Madrid realize that they are defending not only themselves but also the peoples of Europe. It is obvious that the enemy concentrates the greater portion of his bombs and shells almost exclusively and with the greatest refinement of cruelty, not upon points of strategic importance, but on working-class districts . . . The enemy bombarded their poverty-stricken hovels with sadistic delight. In our trench we could hear the fearful shrieks of the victims. When it was all over, we carried away from the crumbling ruins the little bodies of children who had sat upon our knees, and the mangled bodies of women who had taken care of us.[9]

The Irishman Frank Ryan, the IRA's leading propagandist, was mostly employed in Spain on work of a similar category. A practising Catholic and non-communist, Ryan was nonetheless not above lying in the service of 'the cause'. He sent reports to Fenian contacts in the US, aimed at countering the effect of Nationalist propaganda upon Irish Catholics. Among them we find the claim 'I have seen how Franco and his Italian and German masters "Fight for the Faith". The bodies of babies cluttered in a schoolyard after an air raid, breadlines of women blown to bits, working class houses razed.'[10] In contrast, Cuban communist Pablo Torriente was more honest in despatches to Party associates in Havana. Hearing on the morning of 31 October about the previous day's Madrid raid, he wrote: 'I shall go and see what has happened. They say that there were many women and children wounded and some of them killed.' A few days later Torriente went to visit Louis Delaprée on his deathbed in Alcalá de Henares. Whilst there he witnessed an attack on the airfield, but unlike other foreign communists present, who laid on details of civilian carnage and destruction quickly and thickly, the Cuban described a non-event. 'The bombers flew so high that no anti-aircraft guns were used. Naturally, the bombs . . . fell far away, setting fire to fields of stubble.'[11]

Torriente was a month dead, killed fighting in the defence of Madrid, when the German communist, Alfred Kantorowicz, apparently witnessed an air raid in the city.

Straight above were twenty-three Junkers and Capronis. Women picked up their children and fled . . . The raid had taken a toll of over 300 lives according to figures available late this afternoon. On their return flight . . . these flyers directed their machine gun fire at women and children . . . dropping to within 200 feet of the earth in order to mow down rows of women and children who had been standing in line to get some food. That is 'Fascism'. The bodies of women and children laid out in rows on the streets of Madrid: such is the picture by which history will identify this human scourge.[12]

Kantorowicz's letter was dated 5 January 1937, a month or more after the last serious raid on Madrid. Days later, the same correspondent reported in detail on fresh air raids, again including the strafing of women and children.[13] Yet the American communist Mildred Rackley, present in Madrid for most of January, wrote home that 'there was no air raid while we were there'; whilst the American doctor Edward Barsky, writing at the same time, stated that Madrid had suffered 'nowhere near the amount of destruction the N[ew] Y[ork] papers would lead you to believe'.[14]

All over the world, newspapers carried reports and correspondence from the Spanish front sent by men of the IBs. The newspapers concerned were in many cases pre-biased towards the cause of 'Spain'. But oftentimes, editors who did not fit this description, and/or were not normally in search of cheap sensationalism, were moved to publish horrific allegations of 'fascist' war crimes *because submitted by a local man* fighting for democracy in Spain. In fact, these letters were (rather more often than not) the work of the censorship office in Albacete, where a staff of scribes would append their own or other names (plausibly selected from muster-lists) to hundreds of template letters addressed to a range of destinations, from *The Aberdare Leader* in the south Wales valleys to the *Chicago Tribune* on the shores of Lake Michigan. Even authentic, holograph examples of such propaganda were usually scissor-and-paste jobs, loyally compiled from a ready-made store of details and phraseology provided by the CP commissars in the trenches.

As it happened, Albacete itself became the target of enemy bombers. On the night of 19 February 1937, it was raided by at least fifteen aircraft arriving in waves of three at a time. The ordeal lasted intermittently from 8.30 p.m. until 2.30 a.m., 250 bombs being dropped. The town had no anti-aircraft defences, and civilian deaths were inevitable.[15] An American witness claimed 'one hundred civilians, women and children, were killed and three hundred wounded'.[16] The operation was carried out at the height of the battle of Jarama, at a time when the IBs were in action to frustrate the Nationalist army's plan to encircle Madrid from the south. The city was a hive of military activity, location of the administrative, training, supply and recuperation infrastructure of the IBs, and represented an important communications apex. (It contained no war-related industries.) An American intellectual, Leon Davis, working in the press department, later wrote home that

> When one has seen German planes, piloted by German aviators, bomb a defenceless city which was not in any sense military and then machine-gun the civilians who were fleeing through the streets to safety, the hateful reality of Fascism is no longer merely words . . .[17]

Words, a product for which he receives little credit by men who fought with him in Spain, apparently did not fail the Dublin Communist Bill Scott when it really mattered. He (or more likely his commissar-ghost) wrote to alert readers about 'the screen of foul lies' disseminated in the clericalist newspaper *The Irish Independent*:

> Having witnessed some of the horrifying acts of terrorism committed on the Spanish People and the wholesale massacre of innocent women and children in Madrid . . . Franco, with the aid of Hitler's and Mussolini's modern weapons of war, having failed to break through the lines of the unconquerable defenders of Madrid, has now resorted to the use of gas, and many of our men are in hospital as a result of this new idea of the 'Christians' . . .
>
> I was free for a few days and decided to see Madrid. Here is what I saw: On December 4, thirty low flying Fascist planes loomed over the city as if considering where to release their loads of death. Suddenly a succession of terrific explosions shook the city, and dense volumes of smoke were seen rising about a mile from the centre. I went to the scene of the raid. I saw firemen and militiamen endeavouring to rescue dying men, women and children from the burning pile, which half an hour before had been a block of tenement flats. I saw heaps of bricks and mortar mingled with human flesh and blood. I saw the mutilated bodies of children wedged between heavy beams. In the middle of the street I saw, what on examination proved to be a child's cot containing a

mangled body. People in adjoining streets, not fortunate enough to be killed outright, were blinded and shell-shocked by the explosions.[18]

It would have been possible to observe *at least some* of the details provided in Scott's text had he been present in an appropriate district of Madrid on various dates between 30 October and 23 November. As it happens, Scott was indeed in Madrid for some of that period, but was rather preoccupied – being engaged in the thick of fighting in the University City![19] Quite aside from this lapse of memory, his account lacks fundamental authenticity or credibility; it represents another parroted version of the model artefact patented by Delaprée and others. Yet Scott's objections to the dissemination of horror stories by the other side (a genre to which the *Irish Independent* contributed generously) was well-founded enough. Hailing from a community dominated by the Catholic church and outraged by its persecution in Spain, it was simply that Scott's desire to provide some antidote to the daily litany of tortured priests and violated nuns overcame, temporarily, his commitment to truth.

Though Scott himself never joined the British Battalion, dozens of Free State citizens served alongside other English-speaking volunteers in Spain. Part of the Welsh heritage of the Spanish Civil War, a cultural monument that has formed the portal of introduction to this book, is a hallowed scripture of 'fascist war crimes and oppression', of which 'bombing' forms an essential part. The Irish-Welshman Bob Condon was sure that the righteousness of his cause would bring victory against the 'German or Italian trained troops' he was fighting – 'with all their bombing of women and children':

> Back home in Aberdare when an aeroplane flies over, everyone comes out to look at it. Here the reverse is the case. I have seen women faint at the sound of aeroplane engines, and I shall never forget the cries of some little children of about two or three years of age, when the bells rung out their warning of enemy planes.[20]

Despite its austere moderation of detail, this text cannot withstand critical attention. To see one woman faint at the sound of aeroplanes would be extraordinary enough, but to claim repeated such collapses suggests hyperbole. Yet later, a compatriot writing to his local paper confirmed the nub of Condon's point. 'I have seen a crowd of women and children begging for crusts on the

quays by the ships, deliberately bombed and blown to atoms.'[21]
Stories recounted by American *brigadistas* (already sampled
above) are less reticent than those of the Welsh, even when
dealing with a strikingly similar incident. Harry Fisher was visiting
a beach on leave from Albacete when suddenly

> four huge bombers were roaring by . . . as they got near the town
> they dropped their bombs . . . what shook me up was the effect of
> the bombing on the women and children . . . After it was all over I
> saw a group of women and children come out of a tunnel . . . They
> were all wet and most of them were sobbing hysterically. . . . This
> incident brings home clearly the methods of fascism – terrorizing
> women and children.[22]

It seems strange that the bomber crews chose to release their
deadly cargoes 'as they got near' rather than over the town itself.
Did the inhabitants, the 'fascist's' presumed targets, live outside
the town rather than in it? Or were the pilots actually engaged in
targeting the docks and/or railway sidings, generally (if grudg-
ingly) accepted as a legitimate military objective?

Most of the glowingly lurid accounts quoted above are eclipsed
by those from the pen of Canute Frankson, an American who
reported experiences of air raids in Barcelona in 1938. By the
time Frankson came to write his letters home, the framework
elements of his narratology were established in newspapers, fly-
sheets, political 'discussions', radio broadcasts, and (not least)
posters. The subject of bombing had already spawned a discrete
'discourse', one which is still frequently encountered today:

> Hundreds of women and children have been killed while they
> slept, by the bombs from the planes of German and Italian Fascists
> . . . Most of the bombs during these raids fell in the section where
> the working people live . . . [I saw] the blood which stains the walls
> from which human flesh has been scraped . . .

> The blood of its women and children run on the streets of
> Barcelona . . . Hundreds of women and children have been
> needlessly slaughtered. Spain is being bathed in the blood of her
> children.

> Several of the bodies were blown to bits. Here a leg; there an arm;
> a few feet away, a head; and against one of the remaining walls the
> mangled trunk of what was a human being. I watched the men
> shovel the small pieces of human flesh into baskets then throw

them in the truck. And as they scraped flesh from a broken door
. . . I felt my stomach coming out of me.

These people have been slaughtered because the democratic
governments have chosen to refuse selling the government of
Spain the airplanes she needs . . . The blood literally flowed on the
streets. Everywhere the marble slabs are stained with the blood of
mostly women and children.[23]

Frankson's letters were composed at a time when the IBs were
being urged to ever greater efforts of determination on and off
the battlefield. Careful monitoring of their correspondence was
part of an all-pervasive system of internal intelligence. Hundreds
of men were arrested and punished for 'political' reasons, often
on the strength of 'evidence' (provided by their own words) of
lack of resolution, a failure of nerve which might be passively
contagious or was being actively disseminated amongst their
comrades.[24] Like many others, Frankson's missives end with
scenes of defiance and indomitability, a stoical anticipation of
final triumph. He claims to have been in 'many air attacks' and
includes for good measure a reminder of the destructions of
Durango and Gernika which '*of course* killed hundreds of women
and children, *as usual.*' By now, the reader may have come to
detect a whiff of *deliberate* overstatement in Frankson's prose. This
was aimed at the censor; perhaps it was an act of defiant disin-
genuousness, perhaps he was merely laying it on in order to be
excused further dangerous assignments, or (even worse) being
sent to the front. Either way, how eagerly his family back home in
the States must have looked forward to his letters![25]

The chief internal publicity organ of the IBs was a professionally
produced and well-financed magazine, *The Volunteer for Liberty*,
which appeared in the five main languages of the Brigades approximately every fortnight from April 1937. Apart from an emphasis on
political correctness and good discipline, its main purpose was to
encourage morale by promoting good feelings about 'Spain' and
its heroic people; and conversely to evoke derision and contempt
for the enemy. The hostile in question was frequently presented as
being Franco himself and his satrap generals, along with the
persons of Hitler and Mussolini, and the mercenary adventurers
(Condor Legion and Italian troops) they sent to kill Spaniards.
Franco's Moroccans came in for similar treatment. Little or no
distinction was made between any of these elements on the one

1. The Poster.

2. 'What are you doing to prevent this?' A self-explanatory appeal to
the conscience of the world.

3. 'Murderers! On seeing this, who would fail to take a rifle
and resist the Fascist destroyer?'
This poster presents eight of the victims originally attributed to
'Getafe' in an attempt to stimulate volunteering – or at least to counter
shirking conscription – in the Republican rearguard.

4. 'Spain today – tomorrow the world'. A similar message to The Poster:
act now to save the Republic – or the Fascists will get you too!

5. 'The barbarians arrived, their arms blessed by the Pope' – a curt but
dramatically effective 'explanation' of the enemy's tactics.

6. 'Bombardment of my street in Madrid', by Manuel Arías. From a postcard booklet of schoolchildren's drawings published by International Red Aid to raise money for 'the orphans of war' (see pp. 154–5).

7. 'Fascism has passed this way', by Manuel Pérez.
From the same collection as no. 6.

From SPAIN.

Decode.   Mr. Ogilvie Forbes. (Madrid).
                                    October 30th. 1936.

        D. 9.55.p.m. October 30th. 1936.

        R. 9.30.a.m. October 31st. 1936.

No. 430. (R).

------oOo------

My telegram No. 429.

Rebels have been heavily counter-attacking Government lines and bombed Madrid this afternoon in several places. Fifteen people killed and about seventy injured. In Getafe about thirty small children were killed or horribly maimed. On this Reuters correspondent was a witness.

2. Today the press advocates proper treatment of prisoners and [gr.omit.] I have no doubt that official answer to the note on this subject was disappointing your remarks have gone home. But if the rebels continue killing innocent people especially children as above popular indignation cannot be contained.

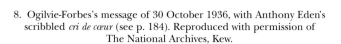

8. Ogilvie-Forbes's message of 30 October 1936, with Anthony Eden's scribbled *cri de cœur* (see p. 184). Reproduced with permission of The National Archives, Kew.

On hundreds of children like these, once names, now numbers, death dropped from the sky.

9. A characteristic contemporary magazine montage, compiled from newspaper photographs of (real or alleged) bombing victims in Madrid or Barcelona.

10. A photograph of Getafe airbase, taken not long before the Civil War. In the distance is the Cerro de Los Angeles with its basilica of The Sacred Heart (see pp. 79–80). Reproduced from Jorge M. Reverte, *La Batalla de Madrid* (Crítica, 2004).

11. The Puerta del Sol, Madrid's main commercial and transport nexus. As the poster dominating the scene reveals, this photograph was taken during the campaign to clear the city of useless mouths in autumn 1936 (see pp. 47–8).

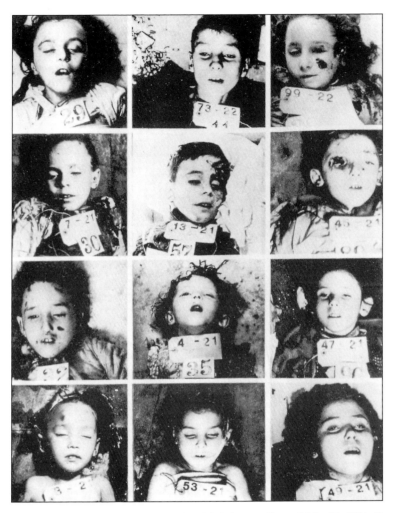

12. This gallery collection of twelve 'Getafe' victims was first published in Mikhail Koltsov's *Diary of the Spanish War*, published in 1963. The originals were probably found amongst his papers after he was 'purged' by Stalin in 1938 (see p. 104). Reproduced with permission of TopFoto.

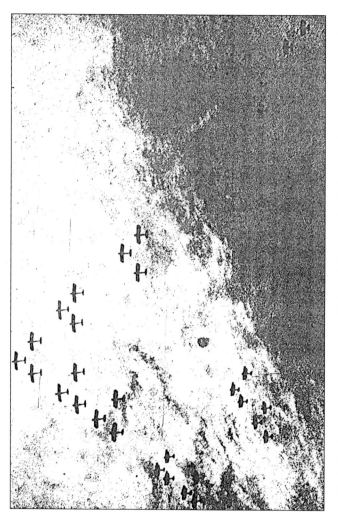

13. In this image, a camera negative of (at most) three overhead planes has been crudely tampered with in order to demonstrate 'a sky black with bombers'. A rare example of amateurish, counter-productive Republican propaganda; which may have provided light relief for officials of the Non-Intervention Committee.

hand and 'International Fascism' on the other, any more than the Nationalists, for their part, observed nice differences amongst the conglomerate 'Red Hordes of Moscow'. In the pages of *The Volunteer*, quite simply, there were no ordinary Spaniards fighting on the other side. Regular items referred to the policy of terror-bombing that summed up the nature of Fascism. A regular contributor was the communist physician Dr Busch, whose stories about the deliberate bombing and strafing of medical installations aimed to stiffen comrades' sinews. *Inter alia*, he described an attack by 'six fascist bombers' on a village near a field hospital: 'one half-hour later we are busy treating women and children that our ambulances bring in from the village. . . ' During another air raid on another village, Busch was able to observe that

> many a mother has a babe in arms and some drag other children behind them. Here and there one sees an old woman being hurried along by a younger person, or a fear-stricken mother running through the streets calling frantically for a child she is unable to find. . . This time the bomb destroys the hospital in the village. . . [26]

In the spring of 1938, Republican forces were involved in a series of catastrophic retreats in Aragon. One soldier found himself only a stone's throw from an appalling enemy atrocity.

> The avion was up again. This time six of them, and soon we saw six more following and then a tail-group of three . . . we saw them shoot downward behind the nearest hill, heard their machine-guns going full blast. Strafing the road, we thought. Only afterward we found out they were strafing the people, the streets and houses in Gandesa. They were sore; they had dropped their bombs, but had evidently miscalculated. Most of the eggs had had landed in the empty football field. So they strafed the town, and its women and kids.[27]

Well might any reader conclude from such writing that no woman or child, even in the smallest, remotest communities, was safe from Fascism. Its agents of death single them out; in the cases 'witnessed' by Busch, near a hospital, where victims can be succoured and saved from death by persons certain to bear detailed testimony to their crimes; then – as seen by 'W.T' – in the streets of a market town, in preference to an attack on enemy troops in the open country nearby.[28]

In 1943, as part of preparation for D-Day, the US government sponsored a research project about combatant morale. No less than 300 veterans of the Abraham Lincoln Battalion agreed to fill in questionnaires about their experiences in Spain. The results urged Americans about to go into battle in the European theatre to prioritize a political view of their endeavours, that is, 'the cause'. 'The soldier must have the war aims within his skin ... The enemy soldier should be hated as a representative of the Fascist system.' By far the most effective stimulant to such motivation was the thought of fascist war crimes, above all the 'damage inflicted by the enemy on helpless civilians or the bombing of cities.'[29] At this point, it might be observed, Germany was already well on the way to its return figure of over half-a-million civilians killed as a result of allied bombing.

Nothing to be read and pondered in this chapter should obscure the fact that bombing of civilians in Spain was a frequent experience, frequent enough to enable some foreign visitors to share. However, testimony to air raids given by indigenous civilians has normally been derived from oral interviews. Most of these were recorded years, in some cases decades, after the event, and transcriptions differ markedly in tone and content from the foreign genre examined above. Memories of those who were children during the war tend to stress the excitement of being in the 'refugios', an atmosphere of sociability and togetherness. Some stressed the unique privilege of not having to go to school; one actually stating in this connection that 'I always loved to hear the sound of the sirens'. Others recalled the fun of collecting bits of shrapnel and fragments of downed enemy aircraft. Above all, the fascination of watching the dog-fights, better entertainment than any film show. Much worse than the fear of bombing was the prospect of 'evacuation', especially of being sent abroad, perhaps leaving their families for ever.[30] In contrast, one subject recalls 'the Junkers coming down to machine-gun the people'.[31] A young Madrileño later to become a celebrated writer and dramatist recalled many torments, including bombing by the enemy, arbitrary arrests and 'executions' by his own side: 'But the worst of all these was acne. My teenage face was like a lunar landscape'.[32] It seems that nobody, even in Barcelona, was able to recall the goriness of it all, the dismembering, the headless children, the crushing of mothers with babes-in-arms, or any other line from the litany of Münzenbergian horror that saturates the official literature.[33] Perhaps we should see this as anomalous. Or perhaps, in the last analysis, the detail was just too painful for them to bring to mind.[34]

And what of the men directly responsible for these brutal and sometimes murderous events? Nothing, if you please, your honour. We hear or read nothing from them relevant to the subject of this book. Silence. Absence. A very muted (and apparently unique) exception is José Larios, later an acclaimed fighter ace of Franco's air force who during the attack on Madrid was an acting bombardier. Larios admits that 'a sector of the capital was included in our strategic bombing, and although we did our best to hit only military objectives, this did not always work out'.[35] But on the whole, the knights of the air have remained exalted Olympian heroes, floating ethereally above the moral melée. From a dedicated Spanish-run website, the Last Post swells out around the visitor, whilst a perpetual flame burns in cyberspace to honour their memory, and virtual vignettes record their glorious deeds in defence of the Republic or of 'Traditional Spain'.[36] One frequently-encountered cliché of our subject literature is the claim that 'fascist planes' often flew so low that those on the ground about to die could actually see the pilots in their cockpits, even being able thereby to detect their Italian or German nationality. Yet today (unless we count one or two proud veterans of the Condor Legion's triumph in Gernika) they are still 100% anonymous; robotic drones who may have jumped from the pages of a futuristic novel about airborne Armageddons – a genre which pullulated in this epoch.[37] In any case, no veteran flyer of the Spanish Civil War has ever described a sortie against 'open towns', far less taking part in the bombing of civilians. These are memories which are now well past the point of any 'recuperation'.

NOTES

[1] It may be presumed that in order to recall any incident in detail, a witness would need to have been born no later than 1930.

[2] To judge from Abella (1973) and Díaz-Plaja (1994).

[3] Under the dictatorship it was impossible to publish material about the *Republican* experience inside Spain, whilst the authorities also wished to avoid encouraging relevant *Nationalist* testimony. Yet this still represents an odd lacuna in the (unilateral) campaign of present-day Spain to evoke 'historical memory'.

4   Both publisher and readerly patience are necessarily finite: here, sample quotations are selected from a file of relevant sources many times larger.
5   Q. by Hopkins (1998), p. 243, from a document in the BNA FO files.
6   My emphases in this paragraph. Hopkins (1998), pp. 413–14 states that Will Paynter also witnessed this scene. But the two stories fail to coincide in most details except the place-name of what Paynter calls 'the little town of Tortosa'; for the latter version see Cook (1979), pp. 57–8. (The 'visuals' used at Copeman's rally seem to have been taken from the 'Getafe dossier'.)
7   See Copeman (1948), p. 138. This and similar police reports influenced Copeman's future in an unexpected manner. On the strength of his 'experience' of air raids he was appointed as a senior manager of the London civil defence set-up in 1940!
8   Not until long after 1939 was the relationship between the IBs and the Soviet Union properly understood. Indeed, it is not uncommon today to see it obfuscated or even denied.
9   Last (1939), pp. 92–4 and 106–7. (This material dates from November 1936.)
10   Letter of 17 February 1937, Acier (1937), p. 115, see also p. 117. The details refer to alleged incidents which occurred before Ryan arrived in Spain, doubtless extracted from an appropriate file in his office.
11   Torriente Brau (1938), pp. 73 and 78; however, Acier (1937), pp. 65–6 includes a letter dated later than any printed in the 1938 collection. This complies in full detail with Party line and standard vocabulary over bombing atrocities.
12   Acier (1937), pp. 77–8, see also 73. (This is an atrocity anthology largely comprising letters from Party commissars or office-workers at the IB HQ in Albacete, a place some distance from the 'trenches' of its title.)
13   Ibid., pp. 80–1.
14   These letters appeared – presumably as a result of poor liaison between editors and censors – in ibid., 10–11. The compilation includes a chapter (pp. 9–33) of letters from foreign medical personnel, mostly communists, who had recently been incorporated into the IBs. At that time, no correspondent referred to treatment of civilian bombing victims in the Madrid zone. However, a few months later, the commandant of the medical unit told a vastly different story; see 'American Hospitals in Spain', *The Volunteer for Liberty*, 30 August 1937.
15   Serrano (1989), pp. 395–6.
16   Acier (1937), p. 171. Among the dead were 26 Brigaders, including members of a medical team at work amongst civilian victims; Martínez Amutio (1974), p. 315.
17   Acier (1937), pp. 165–6. Though a full moon may have assisted observation of the flying formation and the number of projectiles dropped, strafing of crowded streets seems an inherently unlikely manoeuvre. Davis fails to specify victims as women and children; cf., however, ibid., pp. 144, 146, 148. The first of these refers (more

truthfully than he knew) to the 'attempt to destroy our factory' – i.e., the IBs administration offices.

18 *The Worker* (Dublin), 9 January 1937.
19 See Romilly (1937/1971), p. 93ff. None of Bill Scott's comrades seems to have noticed the raid he describes, though Romilly's book includes several other bombing stories.
20 *Aberdare Leader*, 17 April 1937, q. in Francis (1984), p. 271.
21 Q. by Stradling (2004), 57. The writer was a communist seaman who crewed supply ships to Republican Spain. Another Welsh volunteer repeated the image of 'women and kids' targeted by 'Fascist planes' four times in the same letter: Francis (1984), 279–80.
22 *Madrid 1937* (1996), 114–15. The target here was probably Alicante. As Fisher admits, most of the bombs fell in the sea and little damage ensued. For comment on the frontispiece chosen by the editors to illustrate this compilation, see below, ch. 10.
23 Letters of 28 February and 18 March 1938, in *Madrid 1937* (1996), pp. 425 and 430. At this very time, President Roosevelt was moved to action by the bombing of Barcelona. In a unique lapse from his own policy of neutrality, he became involved in a clandestine (and abortive) project to supply the Republic with American fighter planes in considerable numbers: see Tierney (2004), esp. pp. 308–10. A Welsh volunteer, Robert Peters, recalled that 'in Barcelona they were bombing all the time . . . They particularly bombed the working class areas . . . They didn't touch the upper class areas': Lewis (2006), p. 46. But on the same page Peters states that bombers were 'high-flying'. But not only was it impossible to select specific districts for attack, it seems equally inaccurate to speak of 'upper class areas' in post-revolution Barcelona
24 Detailed illustration of this system in operation is provided by a full muster of the British Battalion in August 1938, endorsed 'with comments of censorship', in which names carry manuscript marginal remarks such as 'good letters' or 'bad letters': RAPH, Comintern Papers (International Brigades Section) 545/6/39, ff. 65–98.
25 My emphasis in the last quotation.
26 *Volunteer for Liberty*, 6 December 1937, 6–7; see also ibid., 30 August 1937, 4–5.
27 'Avion!' by W.T., *Volunteer for Liberty*, 13 April 1938, 6.
28 Cf. the memoirs of P. Gillan (1937) who, when stationed between Franco's soldiers and their Madrid objective, saw planes ignore his trenches and fly 'on to the city to kill women and children'. 'Later we heard the muffled roar of explosions and fancied we could hear the shrieks and moans of the dying kiddies' (p. 6). For similar IB material not quoted here, see (e.g.) Acier (1937), pp. 65–6, 80, 144–8 *passim*; *Madrid 1937* (1996), pp. 114, 421, 427, 434, 445; *Volunteer for Liberty*, 8 November 1937, 3, 20 December 1937, 10, 3 January 1938, 9, 5 February 1938, 6, 13 April, 1938, 1, 6 October 1938, 7.
29 Dollard (1944), esp. pp. 41–8.
30 Bullón de Mendoza & De Diego (2000), pp. 101–10. The editors

point out that a high proportion of subjects lived in areas close to armaments factories.

31   Vidal (1996), pp. 142–4.
32   Fernán-Gómez (1986).
33   Serra & Serra (2003), pp. 147–82 *passim.*
34   A rare civilian account which describes being in an air raid includes embellishments of the routine detail. A young woman living in the Catalan town of Rosas 'heard the sound of aeroplanes. People started to run. They rushed into a shelter which had been built next to my house. I never liked the shelters and instead threw myself into a small hole in the ground outside.' The *refugio* was hit and everyone in it died. Later, 'on the road I saw horrors: a dismembered child, and a young girl whose head was caught in a tree, whilst other bits of her were scrambled with those of her nearby bicycle'; Pérez Couto (1988), pp. 40–3. This memoir, by a Cuban communist, was published by a Party press in Havana
35   Larios (1966), p. 77.
36   'En Memoria...' (*http://www.aire.org/gce/portada/inicio.htm*). This provides pen-pictures of a total of sixteen bomber pilots from both sides. All save one are Spanish. All are hailed as 'Caballeros del Aire' – 'Knights of the Sky'. Thus, on the Republican side, only one entry (from nine) even so much as mentions a raid on a town (in passing). On the nationalist side, one pilot flew over 300 missions without (apparently) ever bombing a town; another was only an observer when shot down during an attack on the village of Leganés; yet another, a Ju52 pilot in 1936, (apparently) only flew over Madrid once – in order to drop loaves of bread to the people! See also, 'Cazas en los cielos de España', (*http://usuarios.lycos.es/henrisb/index.htm*), which commemorates fighter pilots and ignores bombing altogether, though normally, flyers performed both roles during their war service.
37   See Lindqvist (2001), sections 76–129 *passim.*

Chapter 10

Masks for Murdered Innocents

I have always before my eyes a poster which bears a photograph of one of the many lovely children of Madrid, whose face still shows the horrors he [sic] has experienced. Behind him is a sky full of aeroplanes, and the words – 'Madrid: the "military" action of the rebels. What Europe tolerates or protects. What your children can expect'.

The writer of these lines, Joseph Fisera, was a Spanish student, appointed as chaperone to an international student delegation visiting Republican Spain in the last days of 1936. The Poster's image of child 4–21–35, appearing as a symbolic death-mask, was burned onto his mind's eye, inspired him to compile an essay that is a digest of fascist bombing atrocities.[1] The outside world saw the first photographs of the 'Getafe' victims in mid-November, 1936. The Poster itself had probably already been born. It was one of the earliest examples of the genre produced by the Ministry of Propaganda, set up (under Carlos Esplà) only two days before Largo Caballero's government abandoned Madrid for Valencia.[2] Towards the end of January 1937, W. H. Auden was walking the streets of the new Republican capital when he spotted examples of The Poster displayed on public buildings and dedicated propaganda hoardings. Like the young propagandist just cited, he was impressed – though not quite in the same way. In an article seemingly written for the British socialist dinner-party set, Auden noted that 'altogether it is a great time for the poster artist and there are some very good ones . . . in photomontage, a bombed baby lies couchant upon a field of aeroplanes'.[3] It is doubtful that

the otherwise invincibly cynical Claud Cockburn, who was
Auden's sightseeing companion in Valencia, would have appreciated this sally. Cockburn himself had earlier met 'a complacent
ass who was temporarily Propaganda Minister of Catalonia'. This
official (probably the Catalan writer Jaume Miravitlles) was
troubled enough by the media's salacious obsession with deathly
images to remark that the conflict in Spain was 'the most photogenic war that anyone has ever seen'.[4]

The young Auden's breathtaking command of the apt word
and phrase was at once perfectly attuned to the expression of his
own era and that of preceding ones (cf. 'photomontage' and
'couchant'). But on this occasion his own cleverness betrayed
him, or so it seems at first dash. We are probably misled. It is not
that he was immune – even in non-poetic mode – to compassion
itself, but rather, proof against the stimulus to knee-jerk emotion
which The Poster crudely demands. The few indications we have
suggest that Auden reacted against the blatant propaganda culture of the government he had come to support, particularly in
the light of its persecution of the Catholic Church, evidence for
which the poet saw all around him. In contrast, nonetheless,
others who had not been privileged to witness the 'reality' in
Spain were moved to much stronger action than Auden's. Such
men and women unreservedly offered themselves and their lives
to 'the cause'. For example, Bill Alexander, future commander
and historian of the British Battalion, and Alvah Bessie, future
senior officer of the Lincoln Battalion and Hollywood screenplay-
writer, were alike inspired to join the International Brigades by
images like that of The Poster. Bessie, for example, 'cringed
watching newsreels of German bombers and screaming civilians
. . . and dead babies lying in the streets, their name tags fluttering
in the wind.'[5]

These and similar reactions present the analyst with a
procedural problematic. The Poster is obviously both photograph
and montage (thus 'painting'); but also, less obviously, it is
cinema and literary text. A poster which features in a documentary or feature film remains a poster, but simultaneously becomes
part of the film's larger, more complex, narrative panorama. To
the critical sensibility currently prevailing amongst us, these
genres should not be isolated as if each had a self-contained,
autonomous meaning, but rather treated holistically as a single
hermeneutic wave of impact. The impact, worthier of study (says

the critical theorist) than the artefact, is necessarily upon all the faculties of human comprehension. But this (I would argue) was not the case in the pre-computer age, when the spaces, both generic and chronological, between the various communications media created by advancing technology were still open enough to occupy the frontal lobes of the observer's brain. In any case, the modern textual critic might detect a certain element of discourse-slippage in the present chapter. (And perhaps elsewhere too.)

We should bear in mind that the Republic's propagandists had to address the need of communicating in some dramatic modality with an imperfectly literate population. This objective fortuitously overlapped with the importance of placing images in the mind of an international public that did not understand Spanish. And of course, by its very nature, the image encounters less resistance than the written word, even amongst a fully-modernized citizenry. As it happens, the subject of atrocity in war lends itself to dramatic image-making, tending to convince and convert upon the instant – nothing more so than aerial bombardment. In the interests of 'The Cause' and its final victory, it was necessary to persuade responsible individuals outside Spain (and ignorant of its circum-stances) *to visualize for themselves* the situations on the ground which air attacks created.

This agenda can be seen vividly at work in an issue of the *Daily Herald*, dated 2 November 1936, that is, three days after 'Getafe'. On the front page the reader is told that 'Bombers showered death on Madrid in nine raids yesterday and Saturday . . . and as the raiders pass, women and children are left dying, terribly mutilated.' Under an inside page headline ('RAIN OF DEATH ON MADRID'), the *Herald*'s correspondent, J. Stubbs Walker, who by his own admission had been unable to observe a single military action of any kind at close quarters, reported that

> In the city morgues at least 160 corpses are lying torn and shattered . . . The actual centre of the city has been machine-gunned from the air . . . machine gunned from the air! The real tragedy of the bombing is the enormous percentage of women and children who have been killed.

By struggling so palpably to summon up images that he himself needed to absorb, the reporter hoped to stimulate the same visual horrors in the minds of his readers.[6] On the same page of this issue, the recently-retired leader of the Labour Party, George

Lansbury, pointed out that 'it is the little babies, and women, the
sick and the aged who are being brought into the firing line'.
Lansbury, an avuncular figure of venerable moral influence,
'implored [British] mothers *to try to visualize what was happening* in
Spain.' The editorial column took up this plea, exhorting readers
to 'try to imagine, *try to see with the mind's eye* . . . try to hear the
roar of the explosion, the cries of the maimed, the weeping of the
bereaved. *Try to picture the bodies of those children*'.[7] With this
insistent assistance, *Daily Herald* readers (as many as five million
Britons) were required to construct the images for themselves –
just as Stubbs Walker had done in Madrid. *Manchester Guardian*
correspondent Frank Jellinek was thinking along the same
pictorial lines. Government officials he interviewed in Valencia
believed and hoped that

> The lolling grins of the children of Getafe had shocked the whole
> of Europe . . . The mangled children, the quartered airman, the
> heroism of Madrid, should be having their effect upon English
> public opinion, *which could still decide the issue.*[8]

Caroline Brothers, in an accomplished analysis of the photographic gallery presented to newspaper readers in Britain and
France, claims that the Republican government re-tuned its
propaganda priorities towards aerial bombardment and the killing of children in the immediate aftermath of the Getafe incident. Likewise, foreign press photography that previously had
implied the extent of killing but without actually showing death,
began to alter this perspective. Picture features illustrating 'The
Air Raid' became an editorial obsession.[9] Brothers comments that
such images are invariably, even inevitably, propaganda. Photographs are a medium of persuasion for a public increasingly
demanding of 'reality' in their daily news. They 'can be understood as weapons rather than as simple illustrations.' Above all
(Brothers concludes) they provided 'the cornerstones of today's
civil war myth.'[10] In both countries the alleged Fascist air campaign against art galleries and museums is a prominent feature. At
times, damaged or destroyed masterpieces of architecture and
painting threatened to compete with women and children for
attention. Possibly, too, the increasingly dominant deployment of
the artistic trope of the *Pietà*, which perfectly united the themes of

Fascist barbarism and the massacre of innocents, owed something
to the influence of Republican art-scholars in Madrid's famous
Prado gallery.[11]

The *Pietà* is a quintessentially Catholic convention of religious
painting which presents the suffering mother (*Mater Dolorosa*),
Mary, cradling Christ's body in her arms following His crucifixion.
Examples of its use in the propaganda imagery of the Spanish
Civil War are legion, though no-one has commented the paradox
of an explicitly anti-Catholic regime resorting to a stratagem so
obviously aimed at evoking quasi-religious passions. In the immediate aftermath of 30 October 1936, the Madrid evening paper
Claridad carried a cartoon by 'Robledano' that hinted strongly at
the *Pietà* idea.[12] As it firmed up, the generic image became
irresistible to propagandists, because the emotions it aimed to
evoke were so deeply rooted in Spanish popular culture. Indeed,
the murderously *anti*-Catholic Marxist party POUM – familar
(even beloved) to students of the war through Orwell's advocacy –
issued a poster that is one of the genre's outstanding examples![13]
On another occasion a companion series was issued of three such
Pietà posters, derived from some routinely pious original even
down to conventional details of the mother's/Blessed Virgin's
apparel. A similar image appeared on a postage stamp issued to
raise money for an orphanage for bombed-out children.[14] More
recently, the editors of a volume of Lincoln Battalion letters
rather incongruously chose a frontispiece presenting the mother
and child in a pile of rubble, surrounded by a halo-like penumbra
of immortal glory.[15] A recent study of exiled German photo-
journalists of the 1930s has noted that

> dead children, desperate women, *again and again mothers with
> children amid the ruins*, still alive or dead; photos of refugees and
> homeless children . . . helpless children and women, endangered
> or killed by enemy bombs, predominate strikingly in the selection
> of subject-matter.[16]

Even where the creators, in this case photographers like Hans
Namuth and Gerda Taro, may have overlooked the point, the
distributors of these images rarely failed to characterize their
subject as the result of 'Fascist Barbarism'. Though by no means
'embedded' in the pro-Republican publicity network, Pablo
Picasso was a regular reader of the French communist daily
L'Humanité, which (as we have seen) had printed front-page

images of the 'Getafe' children, amongst others. In May 1937, as
he was working on his commission for the Paris International
Exhibition, the artist became aware of the plight of the 'Basque
children under Nazi bombs', and immediately added to his
sketches a transfixing version of the traditional *Pietà*. The mother
and child are the first image one sees in the final version of
'Guernica', as the viewer's eye enters the charnel-house and
travels from left to right. Picasso's reference to the source of the
mother's distress is fixed unmistakably by her representation,
pointing her screaming face geometrically skywards.[17] As a critic
on the staff of *World Film News* commented when reviewing a
newsreel campaign, 'one shot of a weeping mother with her
children conveys all the horror of the Spanish Civil War'.[18] The
referential scope of the *Pietà* also embraces The Poster itself,
despite the absence of a grieving madonna – a 'structured
absence' if ever there was one, since every adult observer is
emotionally projected into the required role, *in loco parentis*.
Innumerable observers must have come to apprehend the threat
of fascism via the thought of their own children being attacked by
bombers. Moreover, the reason child 4–21–35 was chosen for The
Poster may well be that she bears a certain resemblance and was
of a similar age to the ubiquitous Hollywood child star, Shirley
Temple.[19] Overhead, the massed Junkers in profile appear like a
plague of deadly winged insects, almost like pernicious flying
crosses. Down below, the little victim has been crucified by these
Teutonic missionaries of Franco's barbaric 'crusade'; the numbers
on her breast suggesting the New Testament acronymic 'INRI'.[20]

Though (ironically) no *Pietà*-related image seems to have
appeared on the Nationalist side, in most other respects their
image makers, like their prose publicists, again slavishly followed
the enemy's successful techniques. Piles of children's bodies
appear in photographs allegedly taken following a Republican
raid in Aragon. Sliced-apart buildings are presented (again, indis-
tinguishably from shots taken in Madrid) showing beds, chairs,
and other domestic props about to tumble into the street.[21] But
the most remarkable example was the inspired notion of labelling
individual victims by number. This enemy ploy was taken up in
one of Burgos's most important propaganda projects, issued
under the rubric of 'The General Cause'. The volume, which was
distributed *gratis* and unsolicited to hundreds of foreign libraries
and educational institutions, carries a series of photographs of

murdered victims of 'Red Terror', mostly taken during the Nationalist occupation of Andalusia. Mutilated corpses are tagged with the identical tripartite numbering system used for the 'children of Getafe'.[22] Produced during the 'Great Antifascist War', this dossier of indictment was circulated in 1946, a time when international feeling against the Franco regime was strong enough to cause serious apprehension in Madrid. It was forlornly hoped that its images would counter, even cancel out, residual popular visualizations of the bombing of children by the Nationalists and their allies.

In 1938, a contributor to *The Volunteer for Liberty* was moved to an outburst of self-fulfilling prophecy:

> The posters are helping to light the way to victory . . . they tell, teach and inspire . . . The Spanish people's genius has taken it and raised it to perhaps the most brilliant height of expression and effectiveness ever reached . . . Perhaps these posters are works of art . . . The museums of victorious Spain and the archives of the international working class will give these posters a place of highest honor.[23]

The poster (he added) elevates atrocity into art, transmuting the bitter into the beautiful. From the very beginning of the war the Republic's supporters grasped the importance of the poster as a medium of communication. Before long it was of great value not only as a weapon against the enemy, and as a vehicle for the re-imposition of order and discipline upon society, *but also as an art-form in itself.*[24] As we have seen, the Ministry of Propaganda was created on 4 November 1936. Not long after birth the bawling Hercules was taken to Valencia along with all the rest of the government apparatus which was being 're-allocated' away from Franco's immediate reach. It was there that workshops were established and teams of artists employed. They were to produce designs on an industrial scale that put earlier prototypes of Peter Paul Rubens and William Morris in the shade.[25] In Valencia, Barcelona and Madrid perhaps as many as 2,000 different posters were produced by the Republican government and its constituent Popular Front organizations. In the standard Carulla (published) collection, around fifty assorted images of aerial bombardment are distributed in various sections. In contrast to the invariably sinister aspect imparted by Republican drawings to the enemy's aircraft, their own machines are consistently presented as 'La Gloriosa' in images suffused with an aura of selfless heroism.[26]

Children, the innocent victims (and targets) of enemy barbarism, were also obliged to suffer the pressures of friendly propaganda. The Catalan government (*Generalitat*) in Barcelona, aware of the approaching storm, issued a comic strip depicting the epic resistance of Madrid. An air raid is placed at the narrative's central point. *Scene One:* Swastika-daubed bombers drop their missiles on a street where little girls and boys are at play. *Scene Two:* bodies disintegrate in the explosions. *Scene Three:* as the bombers pass, the street is littered with the dead and dying.[27] But the Republic needed to do more than exercise a bounden duty to inculcate notions of civil defence – if, indeed, such was the main motive of scaring its children. The critical *desiderata* of defence and survival remained the enlistment of foreign opinion. Here, as elsewhere, the Republic (like its enemies) did not flinch from turning infants into infantry.[28]

In a number of institutions dedicated to orphaned or displaced children, as well as regular schools, pupils were set to draw pictures that ostensibly illustrated their own direct experience of air raids. Thousands of crayoned images were produced by these methods, apparently spontaneously committed to paper by young artists, some of whom came from tiny and remote villages. There is a remarkable verisimilitude of style as well as subject about the large majority, but perhaps this is to be expected from such immature hands. Over 600 originals were sent to America, whilst a typical selection adorned a booklet of picture-postcards which sold widely, especially among foreign visitors to Barcelona and Valencia.[29] The Welsh journalist John Williams-Hughes was able to bring several originals home when he returned from service in Spain with the ambulance corps.[30] So great was the interest created that in California Aldous Huxley introduced a celebrated volume, *They Still Draw Pictures*, issued to raise money for Spanish children – at least ostensibly, on both sides. This artefact was recently revived in a new edition, and is now fully and freely available on the internet.[31] A high proportion of extant examples show Nationalist aircraft directly attacking residential buildings, hospitals and/or ambulances.[32] Huxley's chosen title also proved to be a self-fulfilling prophecy, for on several occasions since 1938 the phenomenon has repeated itself almost as a necessary by-product of war. The 2002 volume included various examples stretching down to the war in Kosovo (1995). Even as I write the British press reproduces examples of a fresh crop of such pictures: a familiar by-product of media intervention in the long-running civil war in Sudan.[33]

Such images partake of the generic essence of Tragedy. Strangely, however it never seems to have occurred to the modern distributors of such images, whether those of Spain in 1937 or of Sudan in 2004, that they (or at any rate, some of them) might perhaps represent the results of a managed propaganda operation. During researches for the reissued edition of *They Still Draw Pictures*, a number of surviving artists were tracked down and interviewed. The only one of these quoted at length, Alfonso Ortuño, had been evacuated from Madrid before any serious (far less sustained) air raids had taken place: in his case, on 1 October 1936. Recalling the actual circumstances in which he executed his drawing, he felt that 'probably someone told me to draw what I had seen in Madrid.' The elderly subject went on to recall his mother's terror as the German bombers attacked their street.[34]

The poster legacy of the Spanish Civil War has in recent decades become one of its most popularized aspects. A stream of articles, books, and TV documentaries, along with regular exhibitions of its artefacts in museums and galleries all over the world, have brought the events of 1936–9 vividly to life, especially for those of a relevantly creative disposition.[35] Dramatic innovations of artists in the fields of representational and abstract art have embellished the subject with a golden thread of art appreciation. It occupies a privileged cultural category, which has transformed its original, ephemeral propaganda purpose into an eternally active one, working forever to boost the reputation of the Spanish Republic whilst simultaneously depreciating that of its enemy. Through art, above all, the one is reified, the other demonized. This particular verdict of history, in a case which reflects an outstanding victory won at the time, now seems quite simply impervious to the action of historical research.[36]

In addition to posters, postcards, stamps, comic-books and conventional newspapers, the image-making propagandists of 1936 eagerly embraced the newest and most promising medium of all, the movie camera. The Soviet Union, as well as several of its dependent organizations, had camera teams on the spot around Madrid by the time of the Getafe incident.[37] But private enterprise was first in the field, with the French Pathé, American

Movietone and British Gaumont newsreel companies (*inter alia*)
operating with the armies of both sides from early August. In the
first week of December 1936, the weekly Gaumont edition concentrated on bombing havoc in Madrid, but featured the damage
caused to great architecture and art galleries rather than the
human suffering. The standard authority comments (aptly
enough) on the bourgeois attitudes thus revealed; lamenting the
while that 'there is no mention of the fact that most of the
bombing of Madrid was being carried out by the German Condor
Legion [that] systematically bombed the city both by day and
night.'[38] These deep-seated misconceptions are typically instructive of the irremediable half-life of Republican mythology and its
favoured narratives. An outstanding example of contemporary
film work is 'Heart of Spain', a propaganda essay of tremendous
emotional power.[39] Filmed in the early months of 1937, it focuses
on children at play, in distress, and – their bodies broken and
dirtied – being dug out of rubble, in scenes which would move
any average viewer to visceral hatred of 'fascist barbarism'. The
victims are intercut with pictures of bombers and explosions and
scenes of Hitler and Mussolini in jubilant self-congratulation. The
voice-over informs, in sequence:

> This is Madrid. One-third of the city is in ruins . . .

> We must give them credit. This is the kind of thing the fascist
> dictators do very well. . .

> Germany and Italy want Spanish steel for guns, Spanish coal for
> warships. . .

In the present day, viewers experience the considerable filmic
archive of the Spanish Civil War mainly through footage selected
from newsreels by the makers of TV and video/DVD documentaries. Here, extant film-images of bombing damage and casualties
derive exclusively from Republican cities. If only for this reason,
such documentaries, frequently (in any case) dominated by the
theme of this book, present it in a version monopolized by the
Republican side.[40]

Contemporary cinema audiences, for whom newsreels were
still a dramatically novel medium of news presentation, were able
to witness scenes of dead children and weeping mothers in
Spanish cities during the intervals between the A and B feature
films they had primarily come to enjoy. But, at times, even the

serious entertainment transported the audience to suffering
Spain. Films like *Last Train from Madrid* (though politically
neutral) illustrated the panic of ordinary Madrileños trapped in
an 'inferno' of enemy bombs.[41] The Hollywood producer Walter
Wanger was rather more determined than President Roosevelt to
protect and project the Republic. His film *Blockade,* released in
1938 and starring Henry Fonda, was originally designed to apos-
trophize Madrid's stoical agony under the bombers' assault. The
project was harassed by pressure from the US Catholic (pro-
Franco) lobby, and many alterations were enforced. Nevertheless,
considerable expense and persistent effort were invested, above
all in the scene showing aerial bombing of a civilian crowd.
Fonda's closing peroration jostled the viewer out of apathy and
towards empathy:

> Our country has been turned into a battlefield. There's no safety
> for old people and children. Women can't keep their families safe
> in their houses. They can't be safe in their own fields. Churches,
> schools and hospitals are targets. It's not war – war is between
> soldiers. It's murder. Murder of innocent people. There's no sense
> to it. The world can stop it. Where's the conscience of the world?[42]

A sub-category of feature films set in the Spanish Civil War has
continued to accrete since the end of the war in 1939: a relatively
small one, perhaps, but almost invariably pro-Republican in mood
and tone.[43] Most of them, for example, the Hollywood version of
Hemingway's *For Whom the Bell Tolls* (1943), include scenes of air
raids on cities. *The Angel Wore Red* (1960) was arguably the only
American movie ever to lean towards the Nationalist side. Yet its
scenario still managed to open with an air raid on a Republican-
held town, complete with shots of slaughtered women and children; later scenes included the strafing of civilian refugees by
Nationalist fighters.[44]

A substantial minority of people in the developed world do not
need to leave their homes in order to absorb a grand narrative of
the Spanish Civil War that inevitably inspires a pro-Republican
sympathy. The narrative's core elements comprise a series of war
crimes and atrocities committed by the Nationalist side, with a
central role allocated to the aerial bombing of civilians. This
theme is invariably linked to the role of Nazi Germany, thus
highlighting Franco's alliance with Hitler, which in turn tends to
implicate the Nationalist side in the supreme atrocity of the

Jewish Holocaust. Constant supplements to the domestic diet can be found in the high streets of our cities. Indeed, images from all the genres of pro-Republican image-making discussed in this chapter are on permanent display in dozens of museums and galleries, as well as forming part of regular temporary exhibitions.[45] With the advent of the internet they have become accessible instantly, and almost costlessly, on a universal basis.[46]

NOTES

1   'The Bombardment of Madrid', by J. Fisera in *Spain Assailed* (1937), pp. 41–2. The quoted description refers to the version of The Poster made for US distribution.

2   The main work of reference suggests it may have been issued as early as 5 November 1936; Carulla & Carulla (1997), p. 379. The Imperial War Museum holds an original example (actual size 670 x 495 mm); IWM PST15348.

3   'Impressions of Valencia', *New Statesman*, 30 January 1937, in Cunningham (1980), pp. 100–2. This remains the only reference I've found to what presumably was a Spanish (or Catalan) language version of The Poster.

4   Cockburn (1967), pp. 161–2. For Auden and Cockburn in Valencia, see Stradling (2003), p. 85ff. and sources cited.

5   Wyden (1983), p. 24 (abstracted from Bessie's book *Men in Battle*); for Alexander, see Low (1992), p. 62. It seems no coincidence that The Poster is reproduced on the dust-jacket of the official book of IB Memorials edited by Alexander *et al.* (1996).

6   See also this correspondent's by-lines in *Daily Herald*, 6, 9, 10, 16 and November 1936.

7   (My emphases.) These words inspire the suspicion that a copy of the Koltsov photo dossier was lying on the editor's desk as he wrote, even though the date seems too early for this to have been possible. (See Appendix A, below, pp. 273–9.) A recent textbook, in describing the dossier's subjects as 'young victims of nationalist bombing', also acknowledges the objectives of Republican propaganda in its distribution; Lannon (2002), pp. 58–9.

8   Jellinek (1938), p. 511 (my emphasis). One historian states 'the moving faces of those little ones served for the confection of millions of posters'; Jato Miranda (1976), p. 611. Another writes that The Poster was 'un cartel que causó gran impresión internacional'; Raguer (1980), 27. Jellinek's other reference is to the captured Republican flyer Antonio Galarza whose dismembered body was dropped over Madrid. Photographs sent to the FO by Ogilvie-Forbes were never made public: see BNA FO/371/21287/141 and 159.

9   Brothers (1997), pp. 60–1, 102–5, 135ff.

¹⁰ Brothers (1997), pp. 3–5 which also gives print-runs of her main sources of study. It is not possible to assess readership levels or the *political results* of the phenomenon.
¹¹ See Stradling (2003), *passim.* The fount of wisdom on anti-art 'atrocities' is Alvarez Lopera (1982); but see also Moa (2003), pp. 447–72.
¹² 'Peor que las Fieras' ('Worse than Beasts'), *Claridad,* 1 November 1936, p. 3.
¹³ 'Criminales', which shows a mother and dead child in a ruined townscape on which the bombs are still falling; Anderson (2003), between pp. 98 and 99. Almost any illustrated volume on the Spanish Civil War could be cited here. But for examples from camera, brush and pen, see Grimau (1979), p. 216; Díaz-Plaja (1994), p. 61; Carr (1986), pp. 22 & 155; Morris (1986), p. 43; Cope (2007), p. 136; and, of course, Carulla & Carulla (1997), pp. 228 and *passim.*
¹⁴ Carulla & Carulla (1997), pp. 66 and 300. These appeared, it seems, partly in order to satisfy the average Spaniard's 'coleccionista' needs, which even civil war failed to quench.
¹⁵ 'Fruits of Fascism' by Maria M. Schroetter in *Madrid, 1937* (1996).
¹⁶ Schneider (1992), p. 189 (my emphasis). See also Brothers (1997), pp. 144–5. A Spanish expert argues that the many posters through which the government urged mothers to evacuate Madrid, or to allow the evacuation of their children, were the most terrifying of the whole war; Grimau (1979), 215–17 and 222, see also Carulla & Carulla (1997), especially p. 301.
¹⁷ Martin (2002), p. 89. In 1938, after seeing the painting in London, Herbert Read made the first reference to the *Pietà* template; see ibid., pp. 136–7 and King (1990), pp. 171–2.
¹⁸ Q. by Aldgate (1979), p. 146.
¹⁹ The seven-year-old cherished all over the western world had stoutly declared her support for the Republic; see Carr (1971), p. 125; Coma (2002), p. 145. Her latest celluloid romp, 'Dimples', set in the *American* Civil War was premiered in New York on 9 October 1936; [New York] *Daily Worker,* 10 October.
²⁰ Cf. the poster by 'Raga' (UGT, Valencia), 'Como ha sembrado la iglesia su religión en España'. Here, tiny barbed crosses are seeds which a Nazi priest sows in the field of Spain. Spain becomes a cemetery and the seeds sprout into lines of sepulchral crosses; Grimau (1979), p. 84.
²¹ *Ataques Aereos* (1938), no page numbers.
²² *The General Cause* (1946), especially 76–81 and 197–201. Most victims are also identified by name.
²³ 'What's in a Poster?', *The Volunteer for Liberty,* 5 February 1938, 4–5.
²⁴ Much of the supervision and subvention of poster artists was undertaken down to September 1936 by the Fine Arts section of the Ministry of Public Instruction.
²⁵ See Vergara (2001) for a short history of studios and artists, based on the memoirs of Carles Fontseré. Josep Renau, senior communist involved in arts administration, and a pioneer of photomontage, may have had a leading input into The Poster. Not all examples were so

skilful. One attempt to show the world a Spanish sky dark with bombers was a crude forgery resembling nothing so much as an entry in a 'spot the ball' competion; see 'Junkers partant pour un bombardement des villes ouverts', *Bombardements* (1938), 12; see also the similar style cover of Romero (2001).

26   Carulla & Carulla (1997), *passim.*
27   'Aleluyas de la Defensa de Madrid', Carulla & Carulla (1997), p. 515.
28   Figuratively speaking; see (e.g.) Carr (1986), p. 151; Díaz-Plaja (1994), p. 267.
29   A set was received from a contact in Albacete by Sylvia Taylor, wife of the International Brigader, Gilbert, who died in Spain: Private Collection. I am grateful to John Mehta for the opportunity to copy it. All six examples show bombing scenes; two are reproduced here.
30   These eight pictures are now in the Museum of Gwynedd, Bangor, North Wales, Accession no. 73/16.
31   Huxley (1938); Geist & Carroll (2002); *orpheus.ucsd.edu/speccoll/tsdp/index.html*. The full NYC collection is catalogued at *columbia.edu/cu/lweb/eresources/exhibitions/children*. The Huxley item was produced under the auspices of the Quakers, who were dedicated to aiding both sides in Spain. It is dominated by the theme of air raids. Curiously, Huxley had addressed the inaugural Conference of Anti-Fascist Writers in Paris (1935) on the subject of 'Children and Propaganda'; 'The Meeting of Minds', prod. F. Stonor-Saunders, BBC Radio 3, broadcast 28 November 2004.
32   Another common theme is that of children and their guardians sheltering in *refugios*, more often than not railway tunnels – that is, legitimate military-logistical targets.
33   *The Guardian* (G2 Supplement), 29 July 2004, pp. 12–13.
34   Geist & Carroll (2002), p. 76. (Sñr Ortuño was interviewed on 8 March 2001.) See also above p. xiv. The 11-year-old Manuel Arias, one of whose sketches I reproduce, also contributed to the same artefact a technically accomplished image, *seen from a point above* the Junkers squadron attacking 'my street in Madrid'.
35   For example, the influence of Republican posters lauding the achievements of its air force can be seen in the most famous British sculpture of recent decades, Antony Gormley's 'Angel of the North'.
36   See Stradling (2003), ch. 1. Typical exhibition catalogues are Morris *et al.* (1986); Ades *et al.* (1995); Becker & Caiger-Smith (1995); *Spanish* (2001). Authorities cited here are unanimous on the quantitative and qualitative superiority of Republican posters (as of 'art' generally); some publications and exhibitions have no space for Nationalist examples.
37   See e.g. the book version of the famous documentary film by Frédéric Rossif, *Mourir a Madrid* (1963), esp. pp. 54–62.
38   Aldgate (1979), p. 142.
39   Made by 'Frontier Films, USA', unmistakably a Comintern outfit. Directed by Herbert Kline, photography by Geza Karpathi.
40   For example, see *La Guerra Cotidiana* (DVD, Planeta, Barcelona, 2000) where the script misinforms (for example) that 'the first aerial

bombardment in history on a defenceless city took place in Barcelona. The victims were overwhelmingly old men, women and children'; *The Spanish Civil War* (Vision 7/Gaumont Productions, 1986, Video AVE 7005); and *The Spanish Civil War – The Last Great Cause* (W. H. Smith/Castle Communications, Video, 1995). The nearest approach to a balanced treament is *The Spanish Civil War* (Granada/TVE, Channel 4, 1983), especially episodes 3 and 6.

41 Rey García (1997), p. 341.
42 Coma (2002), pp. 101–9 and 209, who comments that contributors represented 'an impressive list of communists and fellow-travellers' (I. Ehrenburg, V. Sheean, C. Odets, E. Kazan, K. Weill, L. Milestone). See also Rey García (1997), pp. 343–4.
43 One authority finds only two examples of films with pro-Nationalist elements made outside Spain: see Valleau (1982), pp. 56–8 and 65–6, and as a bonus, the author's personal indictment of Nationalist bombing policy, p. 40. For films made in wartime Spain, see Caparrós Lera (1981), especially pp. 38–45 and 169–202.
44 *The Angel Wore Red*, starring Ava Gardner, Dirk Bogarde and Joseph Cotton, director/screenplay N. Johnson (MGM, 1960). For extended discussion of a more recent example, Guillermo del Toro's *The Devil's Backbone* (2002), see above pp. xiii–xv.
45 See, for example, from exhibition catalogues of recent years: Morris (1986), pp. 43, 45, 56; *Spanish* (2001), pp. 30, 32, 35, 41. In Salamanca, a 2001 exhibition on *Los Niños, Las Primeras Víctimas (Educación y Cultura en la Colleción de Carteles del Archivo General de la Guerra Civil)*, opened with a section dedicated to 'Los Bombardeos'. In Barcelona, the *Museu de Catalunya* has a multi-media display devoted to the bombing of the city in 1938.
46 Of course, there remains the comforting thought that cyberspace is less vulnerable to hegemonic ideological appropriation than any previous space, including space itself.

Chapter 11

The Blood in the Streets

Come and see the blood in the streets.
Come and see
the blood in the streets.
Come and see the blood
in the streets.

[P. Neruda]

At an early point in the Spanish Civil War, the poet Luis de Tapía appealed to the world to 'Send aeroplanes / So that they may give wings to the people'.[1] Of all the world's nation-states, only the Republic of Mexico and the Union of Soviet Socialist Republics responded energetically to this plangent appeal. But the Spanish Republic had a third ally. This was a Great Power over which the Non-Intervention Committee had no jurisdiction, and that it was not even equipped to recognize. Throughout the conflict's course, the International Republic of Letters stood at the side of the Spanish Republic. And (though that's another story) it has faithfully remained there ever since.

Thus, all over the world, intellectuals expressed support, not least in their writings and artworks. This was the case even – indeed especially – for Germans, Italians, and other artists/writers forced into exile by hostile regimes in their native countries. In their adopted homelands, be they in Europe or America, the commitment of intellectual exiles, just like that of their host fraternities, was expressed against a background of broad public indifference and frequent official disincentive. The European, antipodean and American democracies, with Britain in the van, adopted (and, on the whole, maintained) a policy of strict neutrality. The cry of 'Planes for Spain' fell on intermittently

impaired ears in Paris, on the hard of hearing in Washington, and
on the invincibly deaf in London. Still, if the chancellories were
not biddable through secular channels of diplomacy and legal
plaint, the Spanish Republic continued to hope that the Republic
of Letters, its great spiritual ally, could effect the longed-for
miracle of moral persuasion: the conversion of the consensual
masses, if necessary one by one in the manner of Paul on the road
to Damascus. Thus the Republic cultivated and represented the
'creative artist' and his/her institutions even more assiduously
than its enemies paid court to the forces of Catholic Rome.
Though neither ally was ever to be enlisted unequivocally, in
practice both sides achieved a monopoly of support, and conse-
quent public influence, from these universal corporations.[2]

As St Paul was overwhelmed by God's light whilst engaged in
activities hostile to His word, so now hundreds of writers on the
selfish, cynical road to some artistic Damascus were suddenly
subjugated and mobilized by the power of a humanitarian message. In an impressive number of individual cases, the compelling
motive was a gut reaction to the aerial bombing of innocent
civilians, above all, children. The death of children was a ragged
wound carried, always in the heart, sometimes on the sleeve, by
many politically thoughtful citizens.[3] Their response to 'If You
Tolerate This' was to scream out from the rooftops that it was not
to be tolerated for an instant. And so that the protest should
continue even while the writer slept, so that the world should
know where s/he stood, so that history should note – even if
posthumously – the record of rectitude, it was duly encapsulated
in the work of art. 'Veni, creator spiritus' was Valencia's mantra:
and as the black Junkers quitted the sky, the Unholy Ghost of
propaganda extended its velvet wings over the dead children
below. As in our own day the noisy intervention of rock bands like
the Manic Street Preachers moves and shakes those otherwise
careless of 'world issues', in the 1930s poetry was the most
seductive form of predication. The Chilean writer Pablo Neruda
sounded its siren theme.

> Bandits with planes and Moors,
> Bandits with finger-rings and duchesses,
> Bandits with black friars spattering blessings
> Came through the sky to kill children
> And the blood of children ran through the streets
> Without fuss, like children's blood.[4]

When the war broke out Neruda was an assistant on the staff of the Chilean embassy in Madrid. Like many colleagues of the diplomatic corps, he lived in the fashionable Argüelles district, near the University City. As we have seen, when Franco's army arrived 'at the gates of Madrid', this area became a primary line of defence, and was gradually reduced to ruins, mainly by concentrated artillery fire.[5] Neruda's poem looks back at the recent summer of revolution, with the *barrio* wonderfully transformed into a working-class quarter, teeming with refugees, suffused with the sounds and smells of their daily congress. In this place, it seems, he witnessed the bombs falling.[6] A fellow-bard, who hailed from a background as socially distinct from Neruda's as could be imagined, out-shouted him in relevant hyperbole.

> Beneath those implacable aeroplanes
> That snatch terribly
> Terribly, ignominiously, daily
> Children from the hands of their mothers
> . . .
> Spain is not Spain; it's an immense grave
> A vast cemetery, red and bombarded.[7]

Miguel Hernández had been a shepherd boy in his native Murcia, whose first poetic stirrings had been those of an elementally believing Catholic, but who now became a communist, and commissar in the Republic's cultural militia. Traumatized by the sufferings of the '*pueblo*' to which he belonged, he openly preached the atavistic need for revenge on the fascist murderers. In this, however, he was at one with the more 'civilized' Neruda, who warned the 'treacherous generals' that

> From every dead child sprouts a rifle with eyes,
> And from every crime bullets are born
> That one day will find
> Their way into your hearts.[8]

Of course, there was a softer, more humanist line too. Complementing (rather than contradicting) a spirit of violent reprisal not normally associated with poets, we are given the parallel notion that Madrileños, the *pueblo*, steadfast in humanity, indomitable in democracy, made light of fascist barbarity. A mood of communal stoicism was widely commented by foreign newspaper reporters; and may have provided the precedent for the cockneys' rhetorical watchword 'Are We Downhearted' in the blitzed London of only four years later. Here too, General Miaja's communist advisers, the brains and discipline behind the Madrid Defence Junta, drew on the manifold experience of building the Soviet state by turning laughter and song into propaganda for resistance. During the great enemy assault of November 1936, Andalusian folksongs arranged by the 'martyred' poet Federico García Lorca were enlisted as part of the anti-fascist hymn-book:

Madrid, que bien resiste,
mamita mía, los bombardeos.
De las bombas se ríen,
mamita mía, los madrileños.[9]

On the other hand, Antonio Machado, by acknowledged repute Spain's greatest twentieth-century poet, was not inclined to the comic muse. Machado was among a group of senior intellectuals evacuated by units of the communist 5th Regiment from besieged Madrid. This exercise, attended by much publicity, took place some days before the period of heavy bombing which formed part of the attempt to conquer the city during 7–22 November. Nevertheless, Machado was almost certainly still present in Madrid at the time of the alleged 'Getafe' incident and the killing of children by bombs in Madrid. Curiously, he was not amongst the signatories of a letter published on 31 October, in which some academics and artists appealed to the outside world to put a stop to 'the barbarism represented by the aerial bombing of our city'. 'We cannot remain silent (they continued) at the shocking spectacle of women, children and old men torn apart by aircraft fire in the streets.'[10] At any rate, on his arrival in Valencia, Machado too denounced the fascist barbarians to reporters. It was obvious (he remarked) from the wanton attack on the Prado and other repositories of national art treasures, that the enemy intended to destroy Spain's cultural heritage. Eighteen months later, in March 1938, now a wiser man struggling painfully towards empathy with *el pueblo* as distinct from *La Cultura*, he was in Valencia when it came under air attack. During the long, sleepless night he wrote a sequence of four sonnets, of which no fewer than three concerned the sufferings of civilians caught under the bombs. In one poem a mother and child are huddled together in a garret room. The boy is already dying, his fever the symptom of an earlier bombing injury. The noise of approaching planes thunders in the air, its waves hammering on the window pane, resonating with those of the child's pain. The cold moon obligingly illuminates the hapless city; agonized mother weeps over delirious son. Machado's lines represent another version of the *Pietà*:

'Sleep, my child.' And the clock's ticking oppresses
the mother, crouching at the bed. 'Oh, flower of fire!
who could ever wound you, bloody flower, tell me?'[11]

Machado's suffering family in one room is of course already universal, but the subject was explicitly universalized by another poet, Inocente López:

Black planes fly by
slashing the clear sky.
The drone of their engines
is made of moans.
. . .
In the stricken houses
children scream and weep,
women driven to madness.[12]

Little or none of this indigenous production could have been familiar to British or American poets moved to intervene in the Spanish Civil War. At the same time, however, some who were Party members were privy to a certain variety of 'inside knowledge'. In poems published in 1939, the young scientist Jacob Bronowski reflected various propaganda images from the desired agenda of the Republic. He praised it for attempting to build a new Athens. Its enemies, the barbarians, murder the poet Lorca in a darkening landscape. Meanwhile, 'The bomber leaves a wilderness / to those who tried to make it Greece'. Bronowski adopts a similar line to that of Hernández and Neruda in warning that the children of the dead will one day take revenge on the criminals.[13] To judge from the general content of poems about bombers and their infant victims, many of Bronowski's contemporaries saw photographs of dead children in the *Daily Worker*. Even though some relevant texts were apparently composed months or years after the actual time of the 'Getafe' story, the event-specific references they contain are often striking. Cecil Day-Lewis, for example, seems to provide a supplementary response to The Poster's rhetorical declaration that 'If You Tolerate This, Your Children Will be Next':

Choose between your child and this fatal embryo.
Shall your guilt bear arms, and the children you want
Be condemned to die by the powers you paid for . . .?[14]

According to his biographer, the prominent art critic Herbert Read, enthusiastic anarchist, friend of Picasso and Dali, emoted to 'a grainy newspaper photo of the corpses of children slaughtered by the fascists'. His poem 'Bombing Casualties' is unmistakably (and nothing other than) a literary transmutation of the photo dossier:

Dolls' faces are rosier but these were children
their eyes not glass but gleaming gristle
dark lenses in whose quicksilvery glances
the sunlight quivered. These blenched lips
were warm once and bright with blood
but blood
held in a moist bleb of flesh
not spilt and spatter'd in tousled hair.[15]

Similar considerations apply to poems by Stephen Spender and George Barker, amongst others. Spender's 'The Bombed Happiness', first published in February 1939, was intimately influenced by picture images of dead children, as well (perhaps) as the metaphorical language of Machado.[16] Barker's 'Elegy on Spain' carries a 'Dedication to the photograph of a child killed in an air raid on Barcelona'. It was, perhaps, the first artwork ever dedicated to a cameraman's creation. But closer inspection reveals that memory had mistaken the city. It was the *Daily Worker*'s notorious page that had generated Barker's poetic processes:

O ecstatic is this head of five-year joy –
Captured its butterfly rapture on a paper:
And not the rupture of the right eye may
Make any less this prettier than a picture.[17]

If Barker was writing merely about the wrong photograph, other poets actually apostrophized the wrong event. In a well-aired satire aimed at 'The Wife of any Non-Intervention Statesman', Edgell Rickword indicted Mussolini for a crime which sprang from the propagandist's artifice:

On Barcelona slums he rains
German bombs from Fiat planes,
Five hundred dead in ninety seconds
Is a world record so far reckoned;
A hundred children in one street,
Their little hands and guts and feet,
Like offal round a butcher's stall,
Scattered where they'd been playing ball.[18]

The American Norman Rosten was not alone in confusing the
'Getafe' story with the Condor Legion destruction of Gernika
which occurred nearly six months later.

In Guernica the dead children
were laid out in order upon the sidewalk,
. . .
On their foreheads and breasts
are the little holes where death came in.[19]

In the whole period of the Popular Front movement (1934–
49), and nowhere more than over 'Spain', a writer's emotional
response to any general and/or given injustice was usually conditioned by politics – at any rate, in the published expression
thereof. Of course, even where raw humanity was not the main
motivating force of any given poem, it would be unreasonable to
assume that common human feelings were not germane to its
inspiration. But two British poets in particular seem to have
reacted to the Getafe photo dossier in ways which penetrate to the
authentic core of the case. To demonstrate this, their poems must
be quoted in full. The affective lines of F. L. Lucas, with their
meticulously painted and subtly ironic nuances, succeed in tran-
scending both vicarious rant and propaganda rhetoric, and in
establishing the real:

Jose's an imp of three,
Dolores' pride.
'One day', she dreamed, 'he'll be
Known far and wide'.

Kind Providence fulfills
Dolores' guess:
Her darling's portrait thrills
The foreign press.

Though that's no wreath of bay
About his hair:
That's just the curious way
Bomb-splinters tear.[20]

More obscure even than Lucas to the present-day anthologist,
the Scottish poet William Soutar was viscerally moved, beyond
both art and politics, by the faces of the Spanish children:

Upon the street they lie
Beside the broken stone:
The blood of children stares from the broken stone.

Death came out of the sky
In the bright afternoon:
Darkness slanted over the bright afternoon.

Again the sky is clear
But upon the earth a stain:
The earth is darkened with a darkening stain:

A wound which everywhere
Corrupts the hearts of men:
The blood of children corrupts the hearts of men.

Silence is in the air:
The stars move to their places:
Silent and serene the stars move to their places:

But from the earth the children stare
With blind and fearful faces:
And our charity is in the children's faces.

As we have seen, over thirty years later, Benjamin Britten set this
poem to music as part of his Soutar song-cycle, 'Who Are These
Children?'[21] The composer himself, as a young man, had been
caught up in the emotional storm over the killing of Spanish
children. His diary entry for 5 November 1936, for example,
strongly suggests a familiarity with the *Daily Worker*'s coverage of
the war in Spain. 'Madrid bombed by air for the umpteenth time.
No. of children killed not specified. *70 were killed in one go the other
day*. What price Fascism?'[22]

At this point, Britten had probably not seen the photographs,
which were not published until a week later. The future Lord
Britten did not yet count amongst the category of selected *maîtres
á penser* of national life to whom, around this time, the Spanish

embassy posted copies of the 'Getafe' dossier. The mailing list seems likely to have embraced several writers treated in this chapter, and with the results already presented. Nonetheless, Virginia Woolf is the only recipient of whose experience we have positive knowledge. In her celebrated tract, *Three Guineas*, Woolf describes how

> The Spanish Government sends [the photographs] with patient pertinacity about twice a week. They are not pleasant photographs to look upon. They are photographs of dead bodies for the most part. This morning's collection contains the photograph of a man's body, or a woman's; it is so mutilated that it might, on the other hand, be the body of a pig. But those [others] certainly are dead children . . .[23]

Woolf evidently shared the universal belief of that era that 'the camera cannot lie'; that is, she clearly did not believe the pictures of the dead man were in reality those of a pig. We can assume, therefore, that she accepted the pictures of the children were indeed from Getafe. Nevertheless, in her case, the results of their 'patient pertinacity' must have been disappointing to the staff of the embassy. Woolf was not a 'natural' militant of the Popular Front. Somewhat to the contrary, she was painfully disorientated by the crisis of the late 1930s and distressed by the persistent canvassing of friends and colleagues to which she was subjected.[24] Her reaction to 'Getafe' occupied two opposite poles of mental engagement, neither of which proved at all helpful to herself or for 'the cause'. On the one hand, she immediately wrote to her beloved nephew, Julian Bell, hoping that her description of the chaotic nightmare of Spain would deter him from his (incipient) desire to enlist in the International Brigades. In the event, her intervention had exactly the opposite effect, and one of unbearable *hubris*. Bell left his academic post in China in order to join the British Medical Unit in Spain, and was killed by bomb shrapnel during the battle of Brunete only a few weeks later.[25] His death was the indirect result of a sequence of events begun by the anonymous Getafe propagandists: but Woolf blamed herself, and, given an opportunity, Bell's comrades of the International Brigades.[26] On the other, she composed *Three Guineas*, a foundation document of modern feminism, in which she analysed the nature

of subjective reaction to war-horror images, in the process expos-
ing the motives and procedures of those who produced Tragedy
from atrocity.[27]

For many communists and fellow-travellers, the tribes of scribes
who harassed Virginia Woolf, the essential subject of Tragedy was
the 'children of Getafe'. At this time Eric Ambler, now considered
the greatest exponent of thriller-writing, in the decade that
witnessed its pinnacle, was working on his masterpiece, *The Mask
of Dimitrios*. No mere creature of Marx or Moscow, Ambler was
nonetheless keen to make the analogy between fascist-inspired
war crime and greed-motivated organized crime, ascribing both to
the evils of Finance Capitalism:

> Good Business and Bad Business were the elements of the new
> theology. Dimitrios was not evil. He was logical and consistent: as
> logical and consistent in the European jungle as the poison gas
> called Lewisite and the shattered bodies of children killed in the
> bombardment of an open town. The logic of Michaelangelo's
> *David*, Beethoven's quartets and Einstein's physics had been
> replaced by that of the *Stock Exchange Year Book* and Hitler's *Mein
> Kampf*.[28]

Ambler's rival and fellow fellow-traveller, Graham Greene, was
of the same mind in this moral zone. In Greene's thriller *The
Confidential Agent*, a Spanish academic, 'D', is sent to England on
an undercover mission to secure coal contracts for the Republic.
In his London digs he befriends a little girl who, as a result, is
murdered by evil agents working for the pro-Franco interest. The
body of 'Little Else' is found broken on the pavement beneath D's
window. The hero stoically reflects that 'there have been four
raids [in Spain] today. I dare say they've killed fifty children
besides her . . .'[29] To give a last example of this fictional category,
it seems that an infernal shambles described in one of his novels
by Nicholas Monserrat was also produced by readings of the *Daily
Worker*, along with other reports from bombed Madrid. In Monserrat's scenario, Madrid's main thoroughfare, the Gran Via, is
'literally a ruin from end to end':

> In that one day's raiding upwards of 400 people [were] killed . . .
> there were corpses everywhere . . . and children being carried out
> and added to the pile . . . It was the same all over Madrid. Blocks of
> working-class houses had been smashed to bits by huge bombs and
> aerial torpedoes, great fires were started whose flames served as

torches to light the work a loading shattered humans, or scraps of humanity, on to lorries.[30]

As dust settled and temperatures cooled in the post-Popular Front decades, writers of fiction were able – more so than historians – to look beyond the horizon of fear and hatred. John Masters, a popular author of adventure novels (usually with a British army setting) worked out his conclusions in the form of a domestic dispute, thus:

Wife of Franco volunteer: How could you wear that uniform when you knew about Guernica . . . prisoners being shot . . . women and children massacred . . . ?

Franco volunteer: Prisoners were shot on both sides . . .Guernica wasn't the only city bombed nor the Germans the only bombers . . .[31]

At the time merely a minor clerk in the Order of Fellow Travellers, Cyril Worsley joined Norman Béthune's famous medical team, and observed the bodies of refugee children killed by Nationalist air action during the flight from Málaga (February, 1937). Decades later, he put dialectical flesh on Masters' bare bones in a novelistic recreation of the London literary set's responses to the Spanish Civil War. The book's main characters belong to a circle of friends and lovers who are curiously coalesced by the war and by Stephen Spender's boyfriend, Tony Hyndman, a volunteer in the International Brigades. Worsley's reflections were inspired by the poet's description of his sudden (and typically confusing) realization that it took two sides to make a war and that perhaps not all the murdered children were buried behind Popular Front lines. Worsley makes his Spender character, 'Martin Murray', remark that

If we are fully human we must accept that the other side too, has its heroes . . . that they too have a Cause that they are prepared to die for – they are not all conscripts; that they, too, suffer and die in pain. If Madrid was 'martyred' by the Fascist bombs, no doubt was Seville by ours. We are fiercely indignant when children are blown to pieces in the streets of Almeria, but children are blown in pieces in their streets, too.[32]

Fiction and criticism, if only at one remove, are a necessary documentation of the historic past. Here, at any rate, they demonstrate in detail the influence of the propaganda representation of 'Getafe', and to a secondary degree of the general issue of 'the bombing of open towns' in Spain, on the thought-processes of numberless citizens of the democracies.

NOTES

1　'Workers of the World' (9 September 1936); Kenwood (1993), p. 149. Here and in the next two quoted cases, the poems are translated by the editor.

2　On the one alliance see Raguer (2001); on the other, Stradling (2003).

3　See Guttmann (1962), esp. pp. 175–85, pages which vividly (if perhaps unwittingly) illustrate the specific impact of 'Getafe' on intellectual life in the USA.

4　These and the lines under the chapter heading are from Neruda's 'I'm going to explain a few things', in his *España en el Corazón – Himno a las glorias del pueblo en la guerra* (1937); Kenwood (1993), p. 133.

5　See above, pp. 56–7.

6　'Face to face with you I have seen the blood / of Spain rise up like a tide'; Kenwood (1993), p. 133. As someone once put it, 'the poet cannot lie in the exercise of his calling'. But by the time the bombs began to fall, Neruda had long since left for Paris, where he doubtless read about 'Getafe' in the pages of *L'Humanité*; cf. Reverte (2004), p. 236.

7　'Gather This Voice' – dated 'Madrid, 15 January 1937'; Kenwood (1993), p. 151.

8　Kenwood (1993), p. 151; see also Rosenthal (1975), pp. 83–4.

9　'So happily we make our fight / oh mama dear, against the bombers. / We laugh at every bomb in sight / oh mama dear, we stout Madriders.' (My English rendition from Llarch (1978), p. 72.)

10　*Claridad*, 31 October 1936. It carried sixteen names, including those of cultural historian Menéndez Pidal and art scholar Moreno Villa. It illustrates the influence of both 30 October's events and the Communist Party. Cf. Vázquez & Valero (1978), p. 187. The appeal was reported (of all places) in the *Daily Mail* on 2 November. (Machado had signed an earlier declaration of support for the Republic which had a more distinguished cast.)

11　See the excellent analysis and holograph reproduction in Whiston (1996), pp. 162–7 (my English version). Machado also wrote prose articles condemning the bombing.

12　'Los Negros Aviones', translated by Alun Hughes (whom I thank for permission to quote) from the *Romancero General* (1937).

13　Bronowski (1939), especially pp. 3, 5–6, 8.

14　'Bombers', in Cunningham (1981), pp. 170–1.

15　King (1990), pp. 172–5. King reveals that Read's friend, Robert

Payne, 'provided him with vivid bulletins' of atrocities in Spain: but dates the poem to late 1937 at the earliest.

16 Cunningham (1981), p. 163.

17 Cunningham (1981), p. 157. These lines surely refer to child 46–21–89 (José Pomar Montes), featured in one of five such photoportraits shown in the *Daily Worker* on 11 November 1936.

18 Cunningham (1981), p. 375, published in *Left Review*, March 1938. (This fact does not acquit the Italian dictator of his crime in bombing Barcelona.)

19 'Spanish Sequence, No. IV', in Alvarez Rodríguez & López Ortega (1986), p. 228. (My emphases in the last four quotes.) Though we may presume a number of children were among Gernika's dead, no photographs have ever come to light.

20 'Proud Motherhood: Madrid AD 1937', ibid., p. 154.

21 See above, p. 18. A holograph copy of 'The Children' is signed and dated '21 November 1937'. This was possibly a revision of an original draft made a year earlier. The poem (still unpublished) remained unknown until Britten's later discovery of Soutar. The holographs were published as part of a booklet produced for the LP recording (DECCA SXL6608, December 1973).

22 Mitchell and Reed (1991), I, p. 439, and see Stradling (2003), especially pp. 74–81 (my emphasis). The *Daily Worker* was the only paper to give the figure of seventy.

23 Woolf (2001), p. 65. See also her letter to Julian Bell, written a few days after the *Daily Worker* story: idem (1980), p. 85. The dismembered corpse was that of the pilot Antonio Galarza (see above, p. 158).

24 As chronicled in Bradshaw (1997–8), *passim.*

25 Stansky & Abrahams (1966), especially p. 391ff., which, though without mentioning the original miscalculation, trace Woolf's attempts to cancel the impact of the photographs on her nephew.

26 Returning from six months' service with the British Medical Unit in Spain, Archie Cochrane was invited to dinner at Tavistock Square. He was astonished to find himself more part of the Wolves' menu than an honoured guest, victim of a savage attack by the whole den over the circumstances surrounding Bell's death; Cochrane (1989), p. 45. Perhaps Bell was the only verifiable victim of 'Getafe'.

27 See Gualtieri (1998), especially pp. 167–70.

28 Ambler (1939/1966), p. 185.

29 Greene (1939/1958), p. 97, see also p. 35.

30 Monserrat (1939), pp. 313–17. The novel's title 'This is the Schoolroom' is surely a specific reference to 'Getafe', intended to use the atrocity as a metaphor for life and death in suffering Madrid. (It is dedicated to the communist writer Lewis Clive, killed in Spain with the International Brigade.) Also in 1939, James Barke published a novel (*Land of the Leal*) in which a vicar sermonizes about the 'paths of fascist glory paved with the mangled bodies of little children'; q. in Cunningham (1986), pp. 344–5.

31 Masters (1983), p. 111.

32 Worsley (1971), p. 240. See also idem (1939).

Chapter 12

A Horrified World

All the stale old phrases! And the unimaginative callousness of it!
The sang-froid with which London faced the bombing of Madrid![1]

In 1944, Graham Greene's thriller *The Confidential Agent*, a
story loosely derived from the war in Spain, was made into a
feature film.[2] By this time, the Great Anti-Fascist World War had
entered its final phases. An appropriate closing line for its
Spanish Republican hero (apparently not written by Greene) was
introduced into the film's screenplay: 'One day, I know, we must
win'. The statement resonates with a sentiment that had become
common amongst people of the Allied states during the endgame
of the war against the Axis powers. Such resolute feelings had not
necessarily been predominant in 1937 – when the action of the film
is set – nor at any time down to 1944 itself. But during the Spanish
Civil War, in the form of '¡Vencerémos!' ('We shall overcome!') it
had been a rallying-cry of the Popular Front. The imperative
notion was ceaselessly imposed, for example, on the minds of
members of the International Brigades. With a not-unusual
tendency to ignore a certain catastrophic continuity break –
known to history as the Nazi–Soviet Pact – those who brought *The
Confidential Agent* to the silver screen used their very public forum
to suggest that the war in Spain and the Second World War were a
single, unbroken, epic narrative, involving the same fundamental
concerns and the same protagonists. In this story, supporters of
the Spanish Republic were 'premature antifascists'; by virtue of
which they later came to be hailed as prophetic and self-
sacrificing champions of the unexampled victory finally achieved
in 1945. The 'we' of Charles Boyer's soulful remark to his screen

partner, Lauren Bacall, are the Soviet Union and 'all the freedom-loving peoples of the world' – as Stalin, who clearly felt himself qualified to speak for them, put it in a celebrated declaration of support of the Republic. But no credit was due to the pusillanimous governments of 'the democracies'. By their very nature the latter were at best morally neutered by pro-Nationalist class instincts and material interests, or at worst acted in secret complicity with the Fascist dictatorships that they saw as the necessary bulwark against Bolshevism.

The original text of *The Confidential Agent* is certainly no anti-fascist rant. Indeed, in contrast to the film version, the word 'fascist' does not occur, whilst several references are made to the rampant moral evils practised *by both sides* in Spain.[3] All the same, the makers of the screen version did not seriously misrepresent his message. In the film, as in the novel, the hero 'D', sent clandestinely to secure British coal supplies for the Republic, is befriended in London by a precocious little girl. In the novel she asks, why is someone trying to kill him? When he answers 'because I am a soldier', she objects 'but the war is in Spain, not here': 'Not yet' comes the reply. Later, in the Midlands mining village of 'Benditch', one man, whose son is with the International Brigades, speaks up for 'D':

> When [my boy] sees those German planes it makes him think that maybe it's the beginning of summat else. That maybe he's fighting to keep those bombs from being dropped here in Benditch.

Of course, in 1945, these exchanges represented political point-scoring based on selective hindsight and the bitter clashes over 'appeasement', more than active propaganda. But even more telling, in terms of the Spanish Republic's predicament in 1937, is the screen exchange between 'D' and a London character he meets in passing. The latter commiserates routinely that 'The Civil War in your country upsets us greatly': 'D' replies (in a tone of suppressed bitterness) 'Yes, it upsets us too'. At the opening of Parliament in November 1936, King Edward VIII's speech from the throne on which he was so uncomfortably seated referred to his government's intention 'while maintaining their determination to support the international agreement for non-intervention in Spain ... to take every opportunity to mitigate human suffering and loss of life in that unhappy country.'[4] The Madrid newspaper *ABC* commented with brusque acidity on this high-toned intervention, and Whitehall's attitude in general, in a headline: 'Madrid Bombed, London Sorry.'[5]

Perhaps not as pusillanimous as often claimed either then or now, His Majesty's Government was deeply concerned and divided over the Spanish war.[6] Nothing reflected this more than the bombing issue, which erupted in the London press with sudden emotive force (and coincidentally with the opening of Parliament) in autumn 1936. Of course, factors other than sheer human sympathy for 'suffering Madrid' were present in the complex hothouse of diplomatic considerations that Whitehall had to manage. One was public opinion: another, closely linked to that elusive phenomenon, was apprehension over what might soon happen to Britain's cities. For the British government the latter was far more demanding in terms of ethical priority than the fate of Madrid. For one thing, the empirical fact of civilians being killed in unprecedented numbers by aerial bombing during the Spanish war now seemed incontestable. For another, underneath each bowler hat was emblazoned the primary principle of government, ethnocentric, perhaps, but inescapable: *sallus populi suprema lex*. All the same, it was not the FO's practice to believe everything found in the papers, far less to respond in policy matters to the lobbying of pressure-group or personality.

It seems important to recall that during the first three months of the war (mid-July to mid-October 1936) British newspaper comment on Spain was divided more or less equally in its affiliation. Indeed, in some respects, the relative indifference to be found in certain quarters (like the *Daily Express*) was taken as another indicator that the underlying mood was one of effective neutrality. It was during this period that the British government committed itself to the non-intervention project initially proposed by France; and, in an undertaking that was both thankless and expensive, proceeded to set up the huge national and international machinery required to manage it. The legal and ethical principles underpinning this policy were recognized by the multipartisan nature of Parliamentary support.[7] In the second half of October, however, the rules of engagement were radically altered by events on the ground in Spain. A small but highly motivated and professional army, which had been consistently victorious against a rag-tag opposition, was advancing inexorably upon an

apparently defenceless Madrid crowded with demoralized refugees. The campaign was carefully charted in newspapers and
newsreels. Coverage in the right-wing press presented the fall of
the capital city as inevitable (to the point of being a *fait accompli*)
whilst the left equivalent, with the exception of the *Daily Worker,*
tended to admit the understandable inadequacies and heroic
failures of its defenders. Press attitudes demonstrate that the
Republic was now seen as the doomed underdog of the contest.
The impression was of a desperately uneven fight, and the British
public reacted accordingly. This image was, of course, dramatically enhanced by the role being played by Germany and Italy in
the Republic's impending fate, a role adopted in cynical defiance
of the international community as represented by the Non-
Intervention Committee. And then the bombs began to fall, in
the popular imagination fertilized by front pages and whirring
cameras, they fell as regularly as the autumn rain on the hospitals,
on the working-class ghettoes, on the upturned, terrified faces of
women and children. In early November, the official Republican
daily made the satisfied observation that 'the air raids on Madrid
have produced a very bad impression in London'.[8] The world had
entered a new phase of danger, 'a new kind of war', a new species
of global contest.[9]

Six months after the end of the Spanish war, and shortly after
Britain's declaration of war against Germany, Graham Greene
gave voice to what many, even amongst his admirers, must have
regarded as a world-weary, even unpatriotic attitude. Writing
about cinema newsreels, Greene warned readers of *The Spectator*
that as a result of the Spanish Civil War, and films like Ernest
Hemingway's *Spanish Earth*, 'surely by now we should realize that
art has a place in propaganda'. He added with knowing insight
that

> There was much that Hemingway had to slur over in his
> commentary: his cause was far more dubious than ours, but the
> language was far more effective. Let us hope that Germany is not
> employing a commentator of his standard, for I cannot believe that
> neutral opinion – or home opinion if it comes to that – will be
> impressed by the kind of words we listen to – shoulder to shoulder,
> liberty, *baby-killers* . . . [10]

Baby-killers in Spain had been at the forefront of many British
minds three years earlier, in the autumn of 1936. In Wales, where

this book began, communists, liberals and many ministers of religion appeared at public meetings (at times on the same platform) to protest the bombing of Madrid. The Welsh Baptist newspaper referred to 'Franco's inhuman rage' as the main impulse behind the assault. A speaker invited from Barcelona told audiences in the south Wales valleys not only about the bombed children, but also about other children whose hands the fascists cut off for giving the Popular Front salute.[11] As we have seen, the Welsh Nationalist party was the first to organize a popular protest campaign that condemned any policy of aerial bombardment, indicting the British government as accessories before the (potential) fact of massacre from the air.[12] In November 1936, the chief constable of Glamorgan attended 'a course of instruction' on civil defence against bombing. Not long afterwards, Cardiff City Council sent employees of its public library service to attend similar classes. In January 1937, funds were aside 'to cover necessary expenditure to be incurred in respect of air-raid precautions'. A few weeks later, the Council set up a sub-committee for civil defence.[13] Not long after, a Liberal Party activist from Anglesey who had driven a 'Welsh Ambulance' to Republican Spain sent back newspaper articles about fascist 'bombing of open towns', and suggested that orphaned Spanish children might be brought to Wales for rehabilitation.[14]

Even before the Madrid raid of 30 October, Emma Goldman, the tireless and influential American anarchist, addressed a letter to the *Manchester Guardian* in which she alleged that 'it is with neutrality as it is with people who can stand by a burning building with *women and children calling for help*'.[15] In subsequent weeks what had been a persistent and irritating whine in the left press grew to a tremendous roar as, regardless of party allegiance, every editorial throat in Fleet Street opened wide.[16] This culminated on 17 November, when the *Daily Telegraph* published the Madrid intellectuals' pronouncement which had appeared in *Claridad* on 31 October: 'we must protest before the conscience of the world against the barbarism underlying the aerial bombardment of our city'.[17] In the absence of any lead from Whitehall, and unable any longer in conscience to 'tolerate this', an *ad hoc* cross-party group of backbench MPs responded by organizing six of their number to go to Spain. This independent deputation (having been duly 'invited' by the Republican government) arrived in Madrid on 25

November. Buildings were still burning, since this was only forty-eight hours after Franco had called a halt to his 'final offensive' on the capital. The deputation itself was bombarded merely with attention and information by the Ministry of State. Nevertheless, given the problems of language, the exigencies of war, and (above all) the emotional context of their work, a remarkably even-handed report was produced. The MPs had given themselves the brief of investigating 'the condition of the civilian population, the prisoners, and of the sick and wounded'. At least to some extent – despite official 'supervision' – the first of these objectives could be authenticated via simple observation. Scenes in the sector of Madrid that lay immediately athwart the Nationalists' offensive provided in itself a shocking (because unprecedented) experience. Once informed that the district had been the main working-class quarter, and that 'between one third and a quarter of the houses of Madrid were estimated to have been destroyed', the response of horror and outrage was automatically constructed. Over the second objective, however, the deputation was not deterred by official ministerial 'explanation' of the 'excesses which have admittedly occurred' earlier in the war. On the contrary, its fears that civilian deaths through bombardment might trigger off reprisals against political prisoners were by no means allayed. In this area, they remained unsatisfied that matters had improved. They confirmed the sad fact already well known in Whitehall that 'it is seldom that either side takes prisoners of war' in the first place. The MPs were prepared to accept that Nationalist atrocities, such as the murders of wounded militiamen in their hospital beds at Toledo, rendered desperate acts on the part of Madrid's defenders at least understandable.[18] But they also acutely noted that a large number of right-wing inmates who had been moved from Madrid's main prisons during the enemy onslaught 'have never arrived at their destination, nor been heard of since'. Not surprisingly, the Spanish embassy in London deferred publication of the report for some months.[19]

Yet this document was still rejected by one of the deputation, who left Madrid on his own initiative before his colleagues signed and presented the report to their hosts. Perhaps Crawford Greene (Conservative, no relation) demurred perhaps as much because of the 'supervision' to which the group had been subjected in its investigations as over the fanciful suggestions the report made for practical solutions to the problem.[20] The latter included proposals ranging from the immediate supply of gas-masks for the whole population of Madrid (over a million) to an idea for the RAC and AA, in conjunction with their French equivalents, to organize thousands of volunteers 'driving their own cars fully supplied with reserve petrol and ample food organized in columns to come to Madrid to assist evacuation'. Foreign Secretary Antony Eden was the dubiously appreciative recipient of a telegram outlining the latter of these schemes that the delegation sent prior to leaving.[21] At the time, Eden was being assailed by public and private protests about events in Spain.[22] But he was also a key member of a government that by the day was becoming more nervously preoccupied by domestic events: a wave of protests against the means test, hunger marches on London, Edward VIII's unwelcome intervention in social policy issues during a visit to depression-stricken south Wales: not to mention (and no public medium yet did) the looming crisis over the king's own private life. Shortly before the unfolding of the Spanish events being examined here, Eden was granted an official meeting with his chief, Stanley Baldwin – the first time in three months he had gained such an audience. But nothing the Foreign Secretary struggled to bring to his attention seemed to make any impression on a distracted Prime Minister. Once Eden had finished his briefing, Baldwin made a vague reference to the King's Great Matter – helpfully adding 'I hope you will try not to trouble me too much with foreign affairs just now'.[23]

For his part, however, the Foreign Secretary had barely noticed the palace crisis. Although thirty years later Eden's memories of Madrid had lost everything but their bare outline definition, there is evidence to suggest that at the time he had a real concern with, even involvement in, the emotions caused by 'suffering Madrid'. During the summer, reports from agents in several parts of Republican Spain had sharpened his concerns over thousands of political prisoners. Aware of the murderous incidents which had already occurred in various towns, he and his officials now firmly linked the Francoist bombing offensive with the danger of reprisals. Ogilvie-Forbes, *chargé d'affaires* in Madrid, was (not unreasonably) motivated as much by this secondary effect as by the bomber's primary casualties. As air raids increased in frequency, he recommended that the government issue an open condemnation of indiscriminate air raids.[24] On or about Wednesday 28 October, in conjunction with a similar *démarche* to Madrid about prisoner reprisals, Eden sent a note to Burgos protesting the bombing of civilians.[25] His staff were awaiting a response from Franco when, that Friday night, Ogilvie-Forbes sent a dramatic telegram:

> Rebels have been heavily counter-attacking Government lines and bombed Madrid this afternoon in several places. Fifteen people were killed and about seventy injured. *In Getafe about thirty small children were killed or horribly maimed* . . . Today the Press advocates proper treatment of prisoners and [although] I have no doubt that [the] official answer to the note on this subject was disappointing your remarks have gone home. But if the rebels continue killing innocent people especially children as above popular indignation cannot be contained.

In what was surely a moment of sheer horror and exasperation at the news about Getafe, Eden scrawled with his fountain-pen on the document containing the decoded message. He wrote: 'Can we do anything now with Franco's people? – AE'.[26] Whilst Ogilvie-Forbes hurried to convey commiserations to Alvarez del Vayo, Sir George Mounsey, assistant permanent under-secretary, kept a stiff upper lip. Evidently responding to *viva voce* points made by Eden, he insisted that further protests to Burgos would do no good even if accompanied by references to the safety of pro-rebel hostages. Moreoever, 'I hardly feel that in the face of such a position it is advisable for foreign powers to make any move or show of partiality for either side *even on humanitarian grounds.*'[27] In the end, given the inflexible dictates of Non-Intervention, Eden was persuaded that any further action might weaken the effect of moral pressure in future contingencies. Nevertheless, under the headline 'Eden makes final effort to prevent massacre in Madrid' the *Daily Express* reported him as urging the Republic to reach some kind of deal with Franco.[28] In fact, the predominant feeling amongst Eden's subordinates was even less positive, if brutally realistic. One of them minuted that 'the best chance [of saving lives] is a sudden collapse of the defenders' morale' – referring (we may charitably assume) to an early victory for Franco rather than the actual objective sometimes presumed to lie behind 'terror raids'.[29]

Not long afterwards, the Abdication Crisis, so long held in
check, inundated government, press, nation and all. Around the
middle of November, the first whispers of the royal constitutional
crisis began to creep into the corners of certain society pages in
the London press. By early December, news from Spain had been
driven pell-mell from the sites of primary public attention in press
placard and cinema newsreel. As Louis Delaprée complained, Mrs
Simpson's smile led to the spiking of many a Spanish story. For
the tragic refugees of Spain's capital it was like a second evacuation: its ubiquitous victims in food queues sometimes had diffi-
culty even rating the British news pages at all. In the gloom of
what was effectively a black-out of foreign news, the Foreign
Office conceded to the Air Ministry's demand for information
that might be useful for strategic planning. Accordingly, Ogilvie-
Forbes was ordered to spend less time worrying about victims and
more reporting on the material effectiveness of bombing for
future reference. How many aircraft took part in raids?; what was
the graduated level of material destruction and the effect on
morale?; what were the differential effects of high explosive and
incendiary bombs. . . ?[30] It was a reversion to a similar scale of
priorities as had been on display at an earlier point, before the
Getafe story, when Ogilvie-Forbes 'was instructed to bring officially to the notice of the Spanish Government the deep concern
felt in the United Kingdom for the safety of artistic works.'[31]

For the whole of 1937, what we might term the 'Mounsey
Doctrine' remained the uncontested basis of British policy. Even
following the destruction of Gernika, no official and/or public
protests were made to Burgos 'on humanitarian grounds'.[32]
Indeed, whilst popular opinion in Britain and France fell into a
state of intense apprehension in the wake of this event, Whitehall
seemed to remain unmoved. Behind the scenes, however, efforts
were made to ascertain 'the facts' about strategic bombing, by
commissioning visits to Spain by military experts and interviewing
airmen who had returned from service with the Republican air
forces.[33] Consistent with Britain's own ('imperial') practice, as
well as its approach to the subject at various international disar-
mament conferences held down to 1933, the government clearly
accepted the principle that air attacks on specific military targets
should be legally permissible.[34] In effect, this allowed the whole
issue of 'bombing of open towns' to fall into a grey area. For who

was to decide exactly *what* were, and exactly *where* were, these 'military targets', and on what basis of evidence?

The complex of diplomatic cross-hatching was material as well as moral. Not just the British, but the whole international approach to the war was characterized by the paralysing indecision this engendered. Indeed, for all its efforts in Geneva to put an official end to non-intervention, the Republican government itself was for some time in a quandary on seeking publicity over the issue of aerial bombardment. This problem was, however, resolved for them by two events broadly coincident in time. The first was Gernika (26 April 1937) and its ever-widening global impact; the second, the Republic's steady but definitive loss of air superiority during the campaigns of the following summer and autumn. In May 1937 the League of Nations Council passed an initial (if anodyne) resolution condemning the bombing of open towns in Spain. Yet not until over a year later, in September 1938, did Negrín's government feel confident enough in its own clear conscience to place the specific issue before the General Assembly of the League. Though there was no serious negative backfire in terms of propaganda, this too failed to produce the unequivocal condemnation of Germany and Italy so craved after in Barcelona.[35]

In Spain as elsewhere, factories and dockyards existed cheek-by-jowl with the crowded residential districts of their workers. In Spain particularly, military barracks were numerous and almost always situated in town centres. Basil Liddell-Hart, military correspondent of *The Times*, concluded from the record of the siege of Madrid that even from less than 1,000 feet, successfully targeting an average-sized industrial plant or railway station was largely a matter of chance. Attempts to bomb the bridges across the Manzanares or to silence enemy gun batteries by air attack had been remarkably fruitless. At the same time, he argued, it was impossible physically to destroy large areas of cities through air attacks alone.[36] These conclusions were soon used to excuse the actions of the Condor Legion at Gernika, but this was not Liddell-Hart's intention.[37] He continued throughout the war, despite the embarrassment caused to *The Times*'s editorial office, to argue that a Republican victory was preferable to the alternative.[38] Though he made clear that his professional opinion derived primarily from assessment of the security needs of Britain

and the Empire, Liddell-Hart was a committed liberal and demo-
crat as well as journalist, teacher and adviser to the War Office.[39]
Almost simultaneously with his opinions, another informed study
returned similar conclusions, in particular that 'it is wholly incor-
rect to assume that bombs can always be dropped with mathemat-
ical precision on their objectives'.[40] In contrast to Liddell-Hart,
General J. C. F. Fuller, who was sponsored by the War Office for
two reconnaissance trips to the Nationalist zone in 1937, was at
the time a prominent member of the British Union of Fascists.
For Fuller, concern for the humanitarian rights of foreigners was
simply irrelevant to British interests. He reported, in awkward
contradistinction to Liddell-Hart, that no defence of ground
troops, vehicles or installations was viable in the face of skilled air
attack, and that only one in twenty planes downed in action had
been hit by anti-aircraft fire.[41]

As the year 1937 progressed, the Nationalists steadily over-
hauled what had at its outset been a clear Republican superiority
in the air. A series of bitterly contested offensives in Aragon
(August to October) cost the latter huge losses in terms of planes
and pilots, whilst on the other side reserves of operational
aircraft, especially of German machines, steadily augmented.
Following the successful defence of Zaragoza – yet another of the
war's sanguinary stalemates – the Nationalists were able to mount
a major air raid on Lérida (Lleída) which, despite the Catalan
city's military importance, was virtually unopposed by 'La Gloriosa'.[42] By the following spring, Franco's airmen were *blasé* about
the future possibility of 'collateral damage' inflicted on their own
cities by the enemy.[43] Nonetheless, such raids – later to be
categorized as 'tit for tat' – were still carried out. Furthermore, on
occasion they were announced in detail by Valencia (later, Barcelona) sources as taking place in reprisal for the killing of its
citizens during specific enemy attacks. In January 1938, however,
another phase in the war had opened. Following minimal consul-
tation with his allies in Burgos and Berlin, Mussolini took it upon
himself to win the war from the air. His plan was to pulverize the
coastal cities of Catalonia, destroying the Republic's industrial
and maritime infrastructure. Thus both the material capacity and
the collective will to resist would vanish from the equation.[44]

The campaign, mounted by the 'Italian Air Legion' from its
bases in Majorca, opened on 19 January with a death toll of 138
civilians in the Catalan capital. By the end of the month (it was

claimed) a total of eighty-eight raids had produced 'at least 1,349 mortalities'. Sticking to its regular policy, the Republic unhesitatingly struck back at the enemy:

> The Defence Ministry states that the Republican air raid on Salamanca on Friday was in retaliation for the attacks on Barcelona, Valencia and other towns. Twenty aeroplanes dropped about seven tons of bombs on the city.
>
> . . . Continuing the policy of reprisals enforced by the rebel air raids, 15 government bombers today raided Valladolid . . .[45]

Indalecio Prieto, Republican war minister, also made it public that the cities – in effect, *the citizens* – of Salamanca, Valladolid and Seville had been raided by 'La Gloriosa' in reprisal.[46] In early February, Eden, apparently influenced by the Republic's London ambassador, Pablo Azcárate, told Parliament that he had appealed to Franco to desist.[47] Simultaneously, as one source reported, Barcelona

> on its own initiative . . . decided to abstain from all air raids of a general character and stopped the elaborate preparations being made to bomb Franco territory. One cannot but admire the dignity and self-restraint of such a decision in a moment of extreme provocation.[48]

There followed a pause, perhaps occasioned by Franco's backstairs protests to Mussolini.[49] But in March the Italian air offensive was renewed. Since this move coincided with the large-scale offensive of Franco's forces in Aragon, Burgos's protests to Rome were likely to have been even more muted. After all, on the last day of March, the Condor Legion, with whose commanders the *Caudillo* had a better relationship, again plastered Lérida, this time with a raid lasting three hours and involving forty machines. With its garrison and a fair proportion of its population in flight, the city fell to the Nationalist army within forty-eight hours. The next phase of the Italian air offensive followed in June. This was not as costly in casualties as earlier attacks. But this was a blessing more due to improvements in civil defence on the ground than to the instructive effect upon Italian airmen of their accumulated experience in missing the docks of Barcelona and Tarragona. By now, indeed, co-ordinated anti-aircraft barrages helped to keep the assailants high and often wide of the big cities.[50]

In Britain, meanwhile, the humanitarian issue had taken an important twist: bombing came (at least in one sense) closer to home. On 26 June a large crowd gathered in Manchester's Stevenson Square in a protest demonstration that linked the bombing of Spanish civilians with similar attacks on British ships engaged in legitimate food and fuel supply to Catalonia.[51] For the first time, British citizens being killed in Spain were not merely the political subversives or social misfits of the communist-run International Brigades, but respectable, hard-working employees of British commercial enterprises. In this period, the BBC normally steered firmly and scrupulously clear of any 'political involvement'. The level of interest in the general issue stimulated by these fresh outrages may thus be gauged from the Corporation's decision to broadcast 'eye-witness accounts of the bombing of Barcelona, based on the official diary of the Barcelona Air Raid Precautions authorities [and] including the personal stories of about thirty people'.[52] Once again, the government was minded to a stronger intervention, in part responding to pressure from Commons backbenchers over the mounting casualty list of British seamen, but also inspired by renewed fears of large-scale Republican reprisal. On 24 June, Lord Halifax (Eden's replacement as Foreign Secretary) held a long conference with Azcárate. The latter apparently revealed the desire of Juan Negrín and others to hit back against the Italians. Talk in Whitehall (*The Times* alleged) was not just of Barcelona taking action *within Spain*, but of launching revenge operations against cities in Italy itself.[53] This was probably an elaborate ruse intended to threaten London and Paris with the spectacle of an international escalation of the war, accompanied by a descent into wholesale barbarism in its conduct: in other words, a grandiose version of 'If You Tolerate This'. At any rate, the Barcelona government immediately dismissed these stories as rumours, asserted that they 'could not bring themselves to reply to the death of women and children with the killing of more women and children'.[54]

During this, the last and most desperate phase of the war, public opinion in Britain had veered round to overwhelming support for the Republic. In November 1938, in the aftermath of Munich, the British Institute of Public Opinion found that 76% of National Government supporters in the general election of 1935 – that is, voters of a conservative inclination – hoped that the Republic would survive its enemy's onslaughts.[55] There seems little doubt that the issue of 'bombing of open towns' had been mainly responsible for the sea-change. Fatally wounded, awaiting Franco's final *estocada,* Barcelona played this propaganda card for all it was worth. In a note to Whitehall, the Republic emphasized that

> it proclaims with pride its 'helplessness' to protect the civilian population of its towns and countryside against the aerial bombardment by the application of the one effective method – reprisals . . . This helplessness arises not from any insufficiency of technical means but from the firm decision of the Spanish government not to commit the monstrous action of taking reprisals against people innocent of the crime.[56]

NOTES

1   Orwell (1938 & 1943/1966), 226.
2   Warner Brothers (1945); directed by H. Shumlin, written by R. Buckner, starring Charles Boyer, Lauren Bacall, and Peter Lorre. See International Movie Database, *http://www.imdb.com/title/ tt0037610.*
3   Greene (1939/1958). Ethical equivocation in treatment of character and cause is widely accepted as a dynamic feature of Greene's work. After all, he was both Catholic and Communist. He was alerted to the Spanish context by stories of the wholesale murders of priests *in Mexico* – one of the Spanish Republic's strongest supporters – encountered during an extended visit in 1938.
4   *Parliamentary Debates Official Report* [Hansard], Commons 1936–7 (HMSO, 1936), col. 10.
5   Noted in Ogilvie-Forbes to FO, 3 November 1936, BNA FO/371/ 20545/W14909.
6   For an instructive revision of conventional views on British diplomatic attitudes, see Buchanan (2003).
7   Buchanan (1992), p. 63ff.
8   *El Socialista,* 6 November 1936.
9   A useful conspectus is in Brothers (1996), pp. 102–45. The author comments (pp. 60–1) that as early as November 1936, *Nationalist* propaganda also began to emphasize violent effects of the war on children. The phrase 'a new kind of war' was coined later, by George Steer, in connection with the bombing of Gernika: see below p. 217 *et seq.* and esp. p. 219 and n. 17.
10   Q. by Cunningham (1986), pp. 211–12 (my emphasis). Greene was emulating Orwell in his eagerness to 'face unpleasant facts' – and threw in a prophecy of William Joyce ('Lord Haw Haw') for good measure.
11   Cf. Merin (1938), p. 315. See also the photograph of a group of

children allegedly hanged by Nationalist soldiery in Badajoz in [?] 1937;   WPP@URL   *http//www.photos1.blogger.com/blogger/615/1914/1600/IMG_8240.jpg.* (Accessed summer 2006.)

12   See above, pp. 18–20.

13   *Proceedings of Cardiff City Council,* November 1936–November 1937, pp. 14, 107, 253, 306.

14   For background and further references relevant to this paragraph, see Stradling (2004), esp. pp. 31–45 & 119–22.

15   Published on 18 October 1936, Haigh (1986), 51. (My emphasis.) Given anarchist torching of churches and convents, especially evident in Barcelona, Goldman's choice of simile was unfortunate.

16   See assorted press cuttings from November 1936 in *Madrid* (1937), pp. 10–13.

17   *Madrid* (1937), p. 11.

18   Before leaving London, the delegation leader told Eden that 'one or two of us are quite prepared to sit, for example, in a hospital, unarmed of course, & to say to any invaders that if they want to kill the wounded patients they can only do it over our dead bodies': BNA FO 371/20549/W16397.

19   Report (1937), pp. 6–18, *passim.* The fate of political prisoners, at least 1,500 of whom were massacred during the weekend of 7 November, is examined by Gibson (1983) and Fernández (also 1983). The MPs were alerted to this by British and American journalists, but Ogilvie-Forbes had reported the salient facts on 16 November; see BNA FO 371/20548/W15817.

20   The other members were S. Cocks (Chair, Labour) and D. Grenfell (Labour); A. W. James and J. R. MacNamara (Conservative); W. Roberts (Liberal); and Labour peer Lord Kinnoul.

21   Report (1937), pp. 20–1.

22   See (e.g.) protest to Eden about bombing of Madrid by the Women's International League, 18 November 1936, BNA FO 371/20549/W16138, and typed *resumé* of earlier 'Humanitarian Appeals in the Spanish Civil War', 27 October 1936, ibid. 20545/W14573

23   Eden (1962), p. 410. The scene is reminiscent of the Marx Brothers' skit on the European pickle – *Duck Soup* (1933).

24   On the reprisal murders of prisoners, see below, pp. 256–60.

25   BNA FO 371/20545/W14589.

26   Telegram No. 430, BNA FO 371/20545/W14737 (my emphasis in quotation from Ogilvie-Forbes).

27   Minute by Mounsey dated 5 November on wireless report from Madrid, 4 November, BNA FO 371/20546/W15040 (my emphasis).

28   *Daily Express,* 6 November 1936.

29   Minute by Shuckburgh, 2 November, BNA FO 20545/W14737.

30   F. O. to Ogilvie-Forbes, 18 November 1936, BNA FO 371/20550/W16575.

31   'Humanitarian Appeals' [!]; see above n. 22. However, Ogilvie-Forbes and other diplomats joined forces to continue pressure over the bombing 'crisis'; see BNA FO 20547/15610 (12 November 1936). For

a detailed account of Ogilvie-Forbes's time at the Madrid embassy, see Buchanan (2003).

32 To pursue this course, HMG would have needed to assure itself beyond reasonable doubt of Franco's government's responsibility – an exercise which would still present difficulties today. For general treatment, see Avilés Farré (1991), pp. 45–9, Buchanan (2003); and Alpert (1984), pp. 425–6, who comments acidly (but disingenuously) that 'the Foreign Office appears ... to have perceived the needs of the situation on a different plane from that reflected by the energetic humanitarian effort' allegedly under way amongst the nation at large.

33 The first alleged 'expert' was sent to Madrid as early as October, 1936; see Buchanan (2003), p. 287.

34 See Linqvist (2001), section 115 *et seq.*

35 Veatch (1990), pp. 192–202 *passim.*

36 Liddell-Hart also believed anti-aircraft fire could have a deterrent effect: see Bond (1977), pp. 109–10.

37 *The Times*, 21 May 1937. These views were sound when published: but things changed so quickly as to annihilate the shelf-life of prognostic assessments. For example, Nazi supply to Franco of the Ju 87 dive-bomber and Me 109B fighter took place in the weeks (respectively) before and after Liddell-Hart's article and rendered some of its conclusions obsolete. To the author's chagrin, a German expert plagiarized his piece: see cutting from *Daily Telegraph*, 24 July 1937, in LHC 390.

38 According to the *History of The Times* (IV,2, 906), the paper was – in the partisan sense – 'completely disinterested in the Spanish Civil War'. This could be taken as an honouring of non-intervention as well as the personal views of Baldwin and Chamberlain. However, it is also implied that the policy may have been different had Liddell-Hart been appointed earlier. See also ibid., pp. 924 and 1141–2.

39 Bond (1977), esp. pp. 101–2. Buchanan (1996), p. 32, points up his support for the Duchess of Atholl, the Republic's leading propagandist in Britain. See also a letter (8 February 1938) drafted following a visit to Barcelona. Here, he asserted that in the broad humanitarian area the Republic's behaviour – in contrast to that of its enemies – had become consistently more moderate: LHC 390. This has not protected him from indictment by one writer who regards any justification of urban bombing as criminal, *tout court*; Lindqvist (2001), p. 124.

40 Hyde & Nutall (1937), p. 39. For expert modern confirmation of the consistent failure of bomb-sighting experiments in this epoch, see McFarland (1995), especially pp. 44 and 103.

41 Report dated 28 October 1937, BNA WO 106/1579.

42 This was on 3 November, 1937; see Solé & Villaroya (2003), pp. 120–2 and 164.

43 See above, p. 68.

[44] For exhaustive statistical detail on the bombing of Spain's Mediterranean communities during the war, see Infiesta Perez (2001–2), *passim.*

[45] *The Times*, 24 January 1938; *News Chronicle*, 27 January 1938.

[46] Avilés Farré (1994), p. 157.

[47] See Avilés Farré (1994), pp. 157–9. Eden was fortified by rising indignation in Paris. The same day as his Commons statement, French Premier Chautemps announced that France could not tolerate 'these massacres of old men, women and children'; *The Times*, 3 February 1938. See also *La Depêche de Toulouse*, 31 January 1936 (copy in LHC 391).

[48] *The War in Spain – A Weekly Summary* (No. 4, 12 February 1938), 13. 'Of a general character' was presumably a euphemism.

[49] Above, p. 69.

[50] See (e.g.) *Spanish News*, No. 9 (15 March 1938). However, the Barcelona raids of 16–19 March resulted in casualty lists approaching Second World War levels; whilst bomber crews frightened away from big cities sometimes compensated themselves by attacking 'softer' targets, as in the appalling raid on the small market town of Granollers in early June; see *The Times*, 8 June 1938; Solé & Villaroya (2003), pp. 194–7.

[51] *Manchester Guardian*, 27 July 1938; see also *The War in Spain* No. 22 (18 June 1938), LHC 391. (Vol. 394 has a large selection of cuttings covering the latter issue.) For the public campaign, Fyrth (1986), p. 256.

[52] *The War in Spain*, No. 23 (25 June 1938), 92.

[53] *The Times*, 25 June 1938.

[54] *The Times*, 28 June 1938, see also *The Sunday Times*, 26 June 1938.

[55] *News Chronicle*, 28 November 1938.

[56] *Daily Telegraph*, 10 December 1938, but the same source had earlier reported a greater than 5–1 Nationalist advantage in planes; 5 September 1938.

Part Four

Aspects of an Imaginary Tragedy

Chapter 13

Guilty By Authorship?

I

The epoch-making bombing raid on Madrid, which changed the course of the war in Spain and war in general, took place – if indeed it took place at all – on 30 October 1936. The next day, the Socialist Party newspaper, now (in effect) the official government mouthpiece, spoke for the first time of enemy bombs falling on civilian districts. The attack was, they announced, 'an indescribable crime'.[1] On another page, they called for the author of a book published several years earlier to admit his personal responsibility. The book in question, which appeared in 1931, carried the apparently prophetic and specifically threatening title *Madrid bajo las bombas* ('Madrid Under the Bombs'). 'Let the author stand forth!' proclaimed *El Socialista*:

> In the name of Madrid, bombarded yesterday by the enemy's aviation, we cry out for the indictment of the author of this aggression. We believe that perhaps the exemplary instructor knows his own name, but history will turn its back on this hero . . . He was the man who once abortively attempted to bomb our city and wrote a book about it. Now, we have the bombs all right, and we hope to hear no more of the book . . . How valid are our suspicions about this person? It's a difficult judgement. . . At the moment we must speak of him anonymously, but sooner or later we will uncover his name and those of his guilty collaborators.[2]

The peculiar equivocations of this indictment reflect the government's many-sided dilemmas. In general terms, they wanted the world to know about the 'indescribable crimes' of bombing, but wished at the same time to avoid causing mass panic amongst the population. Likewise, in this particular, they were sorely tempted to name the guilty man, and the second sentence quoted above shows how close they came to doing so. But they hesitated, not because of any legal nicety, but because to print the name might offer some positive publicity not only to the Franco side but actually to the name of Franco himself. For the ironic 'hero' whom *El Socialista* wanted to be blasted as a criminal by history was not Generalísimo Franco, supreme commander of the forces ranged against the Republic, but his younger brother, Ramón.

In a decade when aviation exploits attracted as much public attention as the doings of Hollywood, and famous flyers adulation akin to that of film stars, not only was Ramón Franco y Bahamonde a heavenly body of the flying firmament, but he was also the most laureated hero of the Spanish Republic. His career epitomized the forward-looking, modernist image in which the Republic liked to portray itself. In the early 1930s, 'Spain's great aviator' enjoyed considerably more fame than his well-known sibling, 'the youngest general in Europe'. Ramón Franco sprang to prominence in 1926, when he and a colleague became the first team to pilot an aeroplane non-stop from Europe to South America.[3] The achievement brought him widespread attention, and made him a household name in the Hispanic world.[4] Ramón exploited his fame to launch a political career, and became active in pro-Republican circles even before the fall of the monarchy. During the closing years of Primo de Rivera's military dictatorship, he gained a reputation as a vigorous advocate of social revolution.[5] In the course of 1930, Primo resigned, and with anti-monarchical fever growing apace, a succession of weak, oligarchic governments supervened.

Before that year was out, Ramón intervened to help a military rebellion launched by a small group of 'progressive' army officers stationed in Jaca, a remote Pyrenean town near the Aragonese border with France. As this bizarre geographical detail suggests, the whole context of *Madrid Under the Bombs* resembled a comic-opera in a Brechtian setting.[6] Supported by a motley gang that included Gonzalo Queipo de Llano (future *Francoist* general and so-called 'Viceroy of Andalusia'), Ignacio Hidalgo de Cisneros (later to be commander of the *Republican* air force and prominent communist), along with other radical officers from army and aviation units, Ramón was determined to 'bring Madrid onto the streets' for the revolution.[7] With the famous flyer at its head, a convoy of private cars and taxis drove out before dawn on 15 December to the Madrid airfield of Cuatro Vientos. Displaying the histrionic adventurism to be expected from film stars and aviators, they disarmed the guards and took over the base. Several planes then took off to drop revolutionary leaflets, whilst Ramón and a friend got airborne last of all, determined to bomb the Royal Palace (Palacio de Oriente) in the city centre. It was to be the ultimate modernist, anti-feudal statement, the Spanish equivalent of Louis XVI at the guillotine. As Ramón later described in *Madrid bajo las bombas*:

> I'm at the controls whilst my assistant, Rada, takes charge of the bombs. We arrive over the Palace. Two cars are stopped outside the Palace gates. *Lots of children are playing* in the public promenades of the Plaza de Oriente. The streets are just as busy as usual. As we pull slowly across the main tower of the Palace, ready to drop our bombs, I recognize the impossibility of doing so without producing innocent victims ... Thus, *the fear of killing one poor mother and half-a-dozen of her offspring* made us desist from our plans.[8]

Even before taking off, the conspirators were aware of the failure of the *pronunciamiento* in Aragon, where the leaders had already been shot. It had also become evident that the call for a general strike in the capital had been met with indifference by the workers themselves. After landing to refuel at Cuatro Vientos, they flew on to Portugal and into exile.

Ramón was living in Paris the following spring, when the mundane event of general elections in Spain led to the king's actual overthrow. He immediately left for Madrid, arriving by train to a tumultuous popular welcome. Already hours late for a reception dinner organized by prominent Republicans in the intellectuals' club (Ateneo), Ramón's car was held up so often by well-wishers that he eventually attempted to walk – only to find himself being carried to his destination in triumph through the streets. It seemed to many a jealous rival that the diminutive flyer was the unique and beloved champion of the newly-born Republic. The proto-Fascist writer, Ramiro Ledesma Ramos, commented that 'in the last ten years Franco has carved out a more amazing career than could ever have been imagined amongst our people ... and has shown himself to be one of the most capable revolutionaries of our nation.'[9]

In the provisional elections held that summer Ramón was elected as a Cortes delegate for the Catalan Left Party, and was soon appointed head of aviation under Minister of War, Manuel Azaña. The latter was quickly to become Prime Minister and dynamic leader of Republican reform. Ramón proved to be a fervent *Azañista*. Not only was he wholly in agreement with Azaña's radical programme of army reforms, but he also fully shared his exemplar's determination to abrogate the political role of the Catholic Church, which both men regarded as little more than institutionalized hypocrisy. In the 'Epilogue' to *Madrid bajo las bombas*, Ramón had referred to the need to combat Spain's 'reactionary elements' and bring about 'a profound social trans-formation'.[10] Though few details are extant on this aspect of his career, it seems Ramón used his influence to expand the air department of the Republican army at a time when more trad-itional branches of the armed services were being lopped away. Subsequent Republican governments used his name and fame in order to point up the positive aspects of their commitment to reform and modernity in the armed services. Franco was a symbol of the Republic's apparent identification with the pioneering, the up to date, the technological: a dimension of national defence that was hazardous and expensive, perhaps, but thereby all the more glamorous. The Republic – as some of its leaders realized – certainly needed a touch of glamour.[11]

In an era when, regardless of a nation's broad political make-up, air forces were usually associated with the extreme right wing, the Spanish exception would seem perverse were it not for the historian's awareness of the indigenous claim that 'Spain is differ-ent'. Of course, however abnormal a rule, there are always exceptions to it. Juan Ansaldo, Comandante Franco's co-pilot during the long hours over the freezing and furious Atlantic in 1926, had an equally fervent commitment to anti-establishment radicalism, which led to his helping to found the Falange, Spain's fascist party, in 1933.[12] But the majority opinion of the military air arm retained firmly Republican sentiments. Its pilot officers tended to join the pro-Republican association (UMRA, partly founded by Ramón Franco) and not the right-wing grouping (UME) to which most army officers belonged.[13] The split was accentuated by the jealousy and resentment felt towards airmen by the earth-bound majority of the armed forces. The latter nurtured strongly contrary emotions in everything to do with government policy and priorities. They skulked and sulked over postponed promotions, forced retirements and reduced procurement budgets. Feelings of national humiliation degenerated into overt disgrace after the failure of General Sanjurjo's easily suppressed *golpe de estado* in August, 1932. Meanwhile, in contrast, Ramón Franco became the government's chief consultant on aviation affairs. As we have seen, in 1934, he took part along with other senior officials at a ceremony marking the beginning of work on a new state-of-the-art military aerodrome just outside the township of Getafe.[14]

In 1935, Ramón resigned his political post and accepted a job as aviation *attaché* in Washington. Just as sexual scandal had surrounded his years as a Madrid politician, now rumours of nest-feathering in aircraft procurement contracts filtered back to Spain.[15] At the outbreak of the civil war Francisco Franco's role in the military uprising rendered Ramón's diplomatic position untenable. To the intense embarrassment of both parties, he was obliged to seek his brother's protection. In October a loyalist newspaper noted that Ramón Franco had been dishonourably discharged from the Republican air force, 'with loss of all employments, prerogatives, salaries, perquisites, pensions, honours, decorations and anything else pertaining to him'.[16] Following the failure of a Republican attempt to recapture Mallorca, Ramón was appointed to command the Nationalist air base on the island. So unpopular was he among ex-colleagues in the military that this attempt to find him dignified exile in an obscure corner of the war provoked considerable recrimination within the Nationalist leadership.[17]

As seen in the last chapter, at sporadic intervals throughout the year 1938, the Italian 'Legionary' air unit, based in Mallorca, was engaged in bombing operations against the port towns of Catalonia and Valencia. One of his biographers assumes (with no positive evidence) that Ramón was involved in these sorties. Garriga notes that his subject's earlier scruples about the killing of innocent children had now evaporated. The hero of aviation had descended from moral heights to become a typically murderous Nationalist pilot.[18] If this were indeed so, then *El Socialista*'s indictment of the guilty author may be regarded as justified, if premature. In any case, the accused did not live to tell his side of the story. In October 1938, whilst he was commanding a hydroplane squadron, Ramón's plane crashed into the sea, apparently during an attack against Republican supply-lines from France. Much of the circumstantial evidence seems to exonerate Ramón from Garriga's charge. His latest biographers clear him of any complicity in policies adopted by the Italian governors of Mallorca, either in the civil or military spheres.[19] In the end, it seems, *Madrid bajo las bombas* was neither prescription for nor ominous warning of 'Getafe', but merely a fascinating cultural document of its era and genre.

II

André Malraux was the twentieth century's Renaissance Man – *l'uomo universale,* if there ever was one. The areas of his achievement are surely unparalleled in width, if not in depth: explorer, revolutionary, orientalist scholar, journalist, novelist, film-maker, resistance fighter *par excellence,* politician, statesman. (That's nearly two lines of print.) Malraux was instilled with the spiritual mission of a modernist *noblesse de l'epée.* To put this another way, his life was stamped by a sense of adventure which was essentially amateur, even dilettantish. But although jealous professionals scowled and scoffed, only one of Malraux's glittering aspirations proved, in practice, beyond his grasp: to fly. As Jean-François Lyotard puts it:

> Constant is his desire to fly – the desire of Icarus. To fly as a member of a group – a team – with bombs and machine-guns on board and with enemy fighters hurtling down out of the clouds: paradise! His dream is of a winged antifascist platform . . .[20]

Spain was the theatre of Malraux's dream, the stage for his new Song of Roland. In the summer of 1936, like his Spanish coeval Ramón Franco, he was already widely admired as writer and man of action. Whereas at this stage both French and Soviet governments were obliged to resist – or at least to bridle – their instinctual desire to send aid to the Spanish Republic, it was André Malraux ('Man's Hope') who intervened. Almost entirely owing to his efforts, what was in effect a completely new air force was placed at the disposal of the Madrid government during the month of August. As General Franco's Army of Africa advanced from the south, the 'escuadrilla de España', under Malraux's command and staffed overwhelmingly by Frenchmen, was at the forefront of attempts to halt its progress. So intense was their activity that by the time the crisis of Madrid reached its climax at the end of October almost all the sixty-odd planes brought from France had been lost and most of their pilots were dead.[21] Ironically, therefore, the squadron took virtually no part in the defence of the capital against the 'iron eagles' of fascism. Whilst Malraux and his surviving paladins retreated and regrouped, it was the Soviets who arrived to succour the hapless women and children of Madrid.[22]

In this period it seems doubtful that Malraux ever slept. Not only was he the indispensable operational commander who planned and supervised every sortie. He had also become in his own right a minor power, or at least a warlord, in constant negotiation with arms suppliers and munitions agents, with army corps commanders, and with the French, Belgian, Spanish and (indirectly) Soviet governments. A significant fraction of his time was spent in the air, not only in combat operations, but also in shuttling, like some chief of a modern multinational conglomerate, between Madrid, Valencia, Albacete, Toulouse and Paris. Moreover, in the midst of all this, he was writing a partly autobiographical novel about events, virtually as they unfolded. Before he finally quit the main stage in May 1937, Malraux was well advanced with this book and had also drafted the screenplay for a documentary film in which the exploits of his team, above all their moving and mutual empathy with the suffering Spanish people, would become both universalized and immortalized. The book was *L'Espoir,* known in its English version as *Man's Hope:* the film, *Sierra de Teruel.*

But in one essential *unlike* Ramón Franco, Malraux was not really a famous aviator, and certainly not a famous pilot: in fact, he was not a pilot at all.[23] Though use of air machines had been central to the epic adventures which had captured the imagination of France, in this unique but basic capability zone he remained in the shade of another French champion of word and deed, Antoine de Saint-Exupéry. In Spanish skies (it was said) Malraux's occasional offers to take the controls were strenuously rejected by colleagues.[24] The Republic lost far too many planes, in any case, as a result of their being entrusted to *poseurs* and cranks of all kinds, who volunteered to join the highly paid and even higher-living ranks of the aviators.[25] Instead of pilot, therefore,

Malraux acted as assistant to better-qualified subordinates, variously in the roles of navigator, gunner – and bombardier. It is the last of these three activities that elementally interests us here. Very little is known for certain about the sorties in which the *comandante* himself took part.[26] Nevertheless, according to a veteran's testimony, on one occasion he and a young apprentice pilot took off to attack the city of Zaragoza:

> Malraux and his novice flew off in the night to carry out their mission. The colonel dropped his bombs by sight – the plane had lost its bombsight – and somehow or other they managed to head back to the [landing] field, where I was anxiously waiting to see the outcome of the mad escapade of a pilot who could hardly fly and a flight commander who knew nothing at all about piloting an aircraft.[27]

Late in 1936, in what was effectively the squadron's last campaign, they were assigned the task of bombing the city of Teruel to 'soften it up' for a major ground attack.[28] These sorties, like others undertaken by Malraux's men, were mostly flown at night. Especially after France closed down munitions supplies in conformity with the Non-Intervention Agreements, every plane was precious to the Republic. Until the arrival of Soviet aid in late October, the venerable chargers of 'La Gloriosa' had little or no fighter protection, and needed to avoid the attentions of anti-aircraft guns as well as enemy fighters that were often of superior speed and manouevrability. Since, even in broad daylight, accurately targeting anything smaller than a football field was a matter of chance, it follows that night-time bombing in or near urban concentrations meant (let us say) a degree of acceptance by plane crews of the risk of civilian casualties.[29] For a period of two or three months, the *Escuadrilla Española* bore a sensible fraction of the total burden during Republican air operations which (as we have seen) included hundreds of raids on Nationalist-held towns and cities. Even if we allow charity to conquer reason, in assuming that Malraux was never personally involved in 'the bombing of open towns', he certainly brought to Spain in abundance the guilty men and their weapons.[30] In sum, it should come as little surprise that (as one associate put it) 'after it was over, Malraux was inclined to keep quiet about this episode of his life.'[31]

But in one sense, at least, he was anything but quiet. Malraux's
novel *L'Espoir* returns time and again to the issue of bombing, like
a barking dog to its vomit. One of the early scenes is set in a
Madrid airbase, some weeks before the Nationalist air onslaught
on the capital. Squadron commander 'Magnin' (= Malraux) has
appointed an exiled Russian as pilot training officer. 'Sibirsky'
had fought in the Russian civil war *against* the Bolsheviks but now
professes complete conversion to the democratic way of life. He
tells Magnin: 'I don't want to have to bomb objectives within a city
– not under any circumstances.' Magnin's reply, repeating the
official Republican propaganda line, is that 'the Spanish government doesn't countenance bombing of open towns'. This seems
not to satisfy Sibirsky: 'You see, I was detailed once to bomb the
enemies' headquarters. *The bombs fell on a school.*'[32] This obvious
reference to the alleged site of the Getafe massacre is followed up
by a careful documentary investigation of nice issues concerning
effective targeting from the air. In the wake of the first big raids
on Madrid, the Republican intelligence chief in Madrid ('Garcia')
is interviewing Magnin's most experienced pilot, 'Scali'.

> Scali sat down, while Garcia opened an untitled file of papers. The
> fascist advance, it seemed, was being held up at Carabanchel.
>
> 'You know Madrid well, Scali, don't you?'
> 'Pretty well.'
> 'You know the Plaza del Progreso?'
> 'Yes.'
> 'And of course you know the Calle de Luna, the Plaza de la Puerta
> de Toledo, the Calle Fuencarral, and the Plaza del Callao?'
> 'I used to live on the Plaza del Callao.'
> 'And the Calle del Nuncio, the Calle de los Bordadores, and the
> Calle de Segovia?'
> 'Not the second street you named.'
> 'All right. I'm going to ask you a question; think it over before
> answering. Is it possible for an exceptionally skilful pilot to hit just
> those five [sic] places' – he repeated the names 'which I've
> mentioned?'
> 'To hit them? What do you mean? To hit the houses along those
> streets?'
> 'No, to drop bombs on the streets and open places beside the
> houses, but without touching any of the roofs. Only the streets
> themselves. And always at crowded spots. A tram on the Plaza del
> Callao, for instance.'

'A tram?' That would obviously be a matter of luck.'
'Quite so. And the other places?'

Scali ran his hand through his hair; behind the glasses his eyes looked thoughtful.

'How many bombs?'
'A dozen.'
'That would be extraordinary luck. What about the other bombs?'
'There aren't any others. Twelve bombs – and a direct hit with each. On women in front of the grocer's shops, children at the Puerta de Toledo.'
'I'm trying to find an answer. But my first reaction, let me tell you, is to say all that's beyond the bounds of possibility. Even if the plane flew very low.'
'Well, this particular plane was flying high – so high nobody heard it.'

The more fantastic Garcia's questions were, the more uncomfortable Scali grew; for he knew Garcia's scrupulous regard for accuracy.

'Look here – the whole idea's too grotesque for words . . . Look here, why not issue orders and let's go up together tomorrow? I'll fly you over the Calle de la Luna at whatever height you wish. You'll find your theory hasn't a leg to stand on. . . [If] there's a high wind, then pilot won't even be able to keep his course above the street.'
'Even if the pilot's Ramon Franco?'
'Even if it's Lindbergh!'

. . . The mention of Ramon Franco's name had made Scali suspect that Garcia was referring to the bombardment of October 30 . . .[33]

This dialogue of the author with himself is nothing other than a searching of the soul. Malraux is pleading with his readers to accept that no pilot, not even if he were Ramón Franco, and whatever his actual intentions, was in practice able to carry out acts of first-degree murder from the air. The author's plea is surely a plausible one. But more apposite here is the question of why he should need to entreat the understanding of his readers at all. The answer is obvious. Malraux felt a sense of guilt about his actions during the Spanish war, and needed to appeal to the judgement of history. In an almost palpable sense his book is a statement for the defence before us, the jury. Though he evidently wished to clear Ramón Franco of the suspicions articulated by *El Socialista,* it is not Franco, but Malraux who is really in the dock. Various episodes of his novel which return to the theme of bombing represent the accused calling up his witnesses, testimonials of character and good faith. In a later episode of the novel, 'Garcia' reappears, this time as the bland spokesman of Republican propaganda. He tells us, as if in response to examining counsel, that

> It is, of course, easier to bomb Seville than it is to bomb the Seville aerodrome. Now, if it has happened that some of our bombs have missed their military objectives and wounded civilians, at least we can assert that never has a Spanish town been systematically bombed by us.[34]

As *my* readers will already appreciate, Garcia's assertions are not the whole truth; rather, they could be called *anything but the truth.* But although the general charge of Republican guilt over bombing of civilians may be held as proven, this is only to establish a circumstantial context. We must proceed to the specific (if theoretical) charge against the individual accused: *the murder of children.* As it happens, the novel includes some harrowing passages in which the indiscriminate killing of mothers and children in Madrid by Nationalist bombardment is described at repetitive length.[35] In a piece of reportage frankly propagandistic in tone, and published some time before *L'Espoir,* Malraux told the following story:

> In Madrid on the first day of January toys which had been sent from every country in the world were distributed to the children. The distribution took place at the center of the great bull ring; the toys were heaped up in little piles, each like a tangled mass of insects. For an hour the children passed in silence among these little piles of toys; and it seemed as if the generosity of all the world was also accumulated there. Then came the sound of the first bomb. A squadron of Junkers was bombarding the city. The bombs fell six hundred meters away; the attack was very short, and the bull ring is very large. By the time the children had reached the gates, the Junkers had departed, and the children turned back to get the last toys.
>
> When it was all over, there remained in the immense empty space one little heap, untouched. I approached to examine it; it was a pile of toy aeroplanes. It lay there in the deserted bull ring, where any child could have helped himself. The little boys had preferred

anything, even dolls, and had kept away from the pile of toy aeroplanes, not with fear, but with a sort of mysterious horror. That scene has stayed in my memory. We and the Fascists are forever separated by that little heap of abandoned playthings.[36]

By the time he reached the end of his work on *L'Espoir*, Malraux's feelings about this ethical separation at the bar of history had altered somewhat. For example, the novel's later chapters contain the admission that even heroic leaders of the Popular Army were forced by the ruthless exigencies of battle to 'execute' some of their own men, *volunteers* who had tried to desert; possibly too, some enemy prisoners of war.[37] Was all war atrocity indistinguishable, then? Since the virtuous Republic performed the same deeds as its evil enemy, are we obliged to plead that in the extenuating circumstances of war there are no war crimes?

III

'Il y avait politique – et il y avait la morale', asserts 'Magnin', again as if in response to cross-examining counsel. To be a better commander, one must be a worse human being. 'We are populated with bodies, all along the road leading from ethics to politics'.[38] Exactly these considerations, it seems, explain why Antoine de Saint-Exupéry refused to fly for either side in Spain. In character the complete opposite of Malraux and Ramón Franco, a loner, with a temperamental *sang-froid* almost amounting to misanthropy, Saint-Exupéry visited Spain twice to carry out journalistic commissions. The results were some of the most objective and balanced contemporary findings ever to come out of the Spanish Civil War.[39] Saint-Exupéry believed the conflict to be an epiphenomenal struggle between two equally valid but irreconcilable faiths. In his view, *the ethical equivalence of the two sides was absolute*. Whilst admiring the resolution, fraternity and self-sacrifice of the combatants, he reported frankly on the war's horrors:

I am not going to discuss ideology. Franco bombards Barcelona because in Barcelona (according to him) they have massacred the priests. Therefore, Franco is protecting Christian values. But also

therefore, Christian aviators, in the name of these values, turn
Barcelona into a bonfire in which women and children burn.[40]

In another place, his sense of ethical abstraction is encapsulated
in a philosophical question:

> Spain. A child is playing. From exactly what moment will he
> develop opinions which may cost him his life?[41]

Let me glance over my shoulder, momentarily, at Malraux and
his alter ego, Magnin. The most thoroughgoing study of Malraux's encounter with 'Spain' also considers the ethical questions
so frequently asked in his writings. Thornberry presents his
subject as seeing in Spain a terrifying vision of the greater war to
come, a precognition that explains his eventual disillusionment.
His exhaustive descriptions of atrocity, including 'the systematic
bombardment of open towns and the use of incendiary bombs
where no-one would be spared . . . the nocturnal gunfire lit up by
the searchlights; the civilian hostages', are in this assessment,
proof that 'Malraux had been one of those rare men – the
organisers apart – not to have been specially surprised by [the war
of 1939]'. Thus 'this war novel is really more of an anti-war
novel'.[42] However, although Malraux may not have been one of
the 'organisers' of the Second World War, he was irremediably
one of those responsible for the conduct of the war in Spain. This
seems to place him in a more equivocal moral category than
other protagonists discussed in this chapter.

Indeed, at the time in question Malraux was arguably a more
important player on the Spanish stage than his fellow-novelist, the
President of the Republic himself. A week before the events of 30
October 1936, and two weeks before his government adopted a
similar course of action, President Manuel Azaña decided that a
visit to Barcelona would be relaxing, now that the rigorous
Madrid winter was coming on. That the season would be particularly uncomfortable this year could be foretold from the sounds of
distant enemy gunfire which might be heard from his west-facing
apartment in the main ex-royal residence, the sumptuous Palacio
de Oriente; once the abortive target of Ramón Franco, now soon
to be in the sights of the aviator's brother. Barcelona was a city
where Azaña was personally very popular, and moreover the
Catalan President, Luis Companys, was a good friend. Once
arrived, to a welcome rather more polite than enthusiastic, he

found the weather was not as clement as expected, so he announced that Barcelona was to be the first stop on a extensive lecture tour of friendly Latin American states, raising support for the Republic.[43] As things turned out, the depressed and frustrated head of state was to spend most of what remained of the war in splendid isolation in a well-guarded Catalan retreat, agonizing over the war that he had done more than most Spaniards – and certainly more than General Franco – to bring about.[44] In January 1937 he addressed the Cortes in Valencia, pledging his readiness to fight as 'a soldier in the ranks', and rousing delegates' enthusiasm by his encomium to Madrid:

> Madrid, her sons slain, her monuments destroyed, her works of art in flames! The sublimity of her martyrdom raises the drama of Madrid to a moral height such as no Spanish town ever knew till now.[45]

A few months later, Azaña completed a treatise on the war, written in the traditional literary form of a dialogue between stereotype protagonists. Their meeting is set in a hotel at the Mediterranean seaside. During a discussion of ultimate responsibility for the atrocities, one disputant claims that most of them are carried out by foreign mercenaries. Others point out that this is disingenuous, since the Spaniards themselves have hired these executioners. The author's own mouthpiece, 'Garcés', adds that 'when the foreigners bomb, burn, and machine-gun, and our compatriots succumb in their thousands, the hirers applaud in the name of the Fatherland'. Garcés's indictment – notably – does not single out the Nationalist enemy alone for this accusation. Like others (we have noticed some) Azaña's self-confession is disguised in fictive garments. The tired and emotional disputants, like any satiated group of holidaymakers or conference delegates, retire to bed as dawn is breaking. Suddenly, the sound of aircraft is heard. The idyllic little fishing village of Benicarló is under attack:

> The planes are already overhead. Deafening bangs, chain explosions reverberate. Great crashes, subsidence, dust, flames. Where did such creatures come from? Another wave of planes. More explosions. Blasts of machine-guns. The people scatter, screaming and bleeding. The village is burning. Nothing is left of the hotel except a mountain of bricks, which give off black smoke,

as if they are being re-fired. The planes fly off to the east, brilliantly reflecting the rays of the rising sun.[46]

Azaña, like a true artist, believed that art was there to make things better. Through its spiritual balm, Spain, transfixed by tragedy, was enabled to transmute wounds into words. In the compassionate cause of art, which was to replace religion as sublime dispensatrix of consolation, but more importantly in order to reduce his sense of personal responsibility for the tragedy which had engulfed Spain, Azaña transmuted a real horror into something fictional, almost beautiful.[47] For this purpose, Benicarlò stood in for Gernika – or for Getafe.

NOTES

[1] *El Socialista*, Saturday 31 October 1936.
[2] *El Socialista*, 31 October 1936. Its use of the demand ('¡Qué salga el autor!') shouted by Madrid playgoers after a successful theatrical debut, was an early expression of Michel Foucault's theory about the 'authorship of crime'.
[3] Franco later wrote about the feat in an autobiographical memoir, *Desde Palmos hasta La Plata* (1926).
[4] 'Ramón Franco, a quién el pueblo español quiere como a su ídolo'; Guzmán (1973), p. 274.
[5] Guzmán (1973), pp. 127–8. See also Cortada (1982), pp. 226–7.
[6] For a detailed narrative, Guzmán (1973), pp. 429–510 (see especially p. 473). An account by a frustrated participant – blaming Ramón for the coup's failure – is Díaz Sandino (1990), 51ff.
[7] All three of these notables later wrote books about their exploits.
[8] Q. in Garriga (1979), pp. 202–3, from *Madrid bajo las bombas*. (My emphases.) Hidalgo de Cisneros confirmed that Franco gave him this explanation on the day itself; q. Guzmán (1973), p. 482.
[9] From 'Un Libro del Comandante Franco', a review of *Madrid bajo las bombas* in Ledesma's 'weekly paper of struggle', *La Conquista del Estado*, No. 10, May 1931; WPP@URL *http://www.ramiroledesma. com/nrevolucion/lcden10a2.html*. (Accessed 30 December 2003.) Ledesma's encomium illustrates how the objectives of fascists and socialists overlapped in some countries – Britain and Spain, for example – in the crisis years around 1930.
[10] The memoir was largely 'ghosted' by the Marxist writer Julián Gorkín. Ramón (who needed to support an expensive Parisian exile) gave interviews to Gorkín, who wrote up the results in autobiographical mode: see Leguina & Nuñez (2002), pp. 149 and 162–5. The Epilogue, however, was Ramón's unaided production.
[11] Leguina & Nuñez (2002), p. 167ff. Ramón further opined that

savings on the armed services might be devoted to providing free secular education for Spain's children. He was also one of the first to take advantage of the Republic's *Ley de Divorcio*. Thus readers will appreciate that a full house of commitments divided Ramón from Francisco. To his elder brother's particular dismay, Ramón's influence was mainly exercized through Masonic circles; see the pen-picture posted at *http://www.fuenterrebollo.com/Masoneria/ramon-franco.html*.

[12] Like the disparate future careers of republican conspirators of 1930, this illustrates the lack of ideological coherence (endowed to us by hindsight) amongst Spaniards who supported a radical socio-political agenda. The situation was resolved by the razor-edged 'moment of truth' in July 1936, in which many were to perish.

[13] Vilar (1986), p. 59, states that more than one-third of flyers were active in the former organization in 1936.

[14] Above, p. 80.

[15] For details, Howson (1998), p. 32.

[16] *Claridad* (Barcelona), 14 October 1936.

[17] Alfredo Kindelán, now head of the Nationalist air force, but who had been passed over by the Republic in favour of Ramón in 1931, protested volubly to the Generalísimo about his act of nepotism.

[18] Garriga (1979), pp. 203 and 290–2.

[19] Leguina & Nuñez (2002), pp. 232–4.

[20] Lyotard (1999), p. 178.

[21] For a dedicated study of Malraux's involvement with the Spanish War, see Thornberry (1977).

[22] Thornberry (1977), p. 42ff.

[23] See Cate (1995), p. 234.

[24] Galante (1971), pp. 113–14.

[25] For example: two men, entranced by tales of get-rich-quick aviators, stole a plane from Portsmouth airport and attempted to fly it to Spain. With no experience of flying, they crashed and one of them was killed; TNL Archive, unused item from 'Contributors' Marked Copy' of *The Times* for 23 October 1936.

[26] In the nature of air operations during this epoch, record of any given sortie can be provided only by participants; detail can easily be either embellished or obscured by them. My estimates are therefore based on a consensus of expert Malrucian opinion.

[27] Recollections of an anonymous veteran of Malraux squadron; q. in Galante (1971), pp. 113–14.

[28] Thornberry (1977), p. 51. Teruel was bombed every day for over a week, as part of a campaign intended primarily to divert the enemy from his intention to capture Madrid.

[29] See various remarks in the testimony of veteran Paul Nothomb, in Levy (1991), pp. 215–24.

[30] According to his close friend, André Gide, during a visit to France in September 1936, Malraux mentioned a plan to organize a big raid on Oviedo, then besieged by Republican forces: Thornberry (1977), p. 47, and see above, pp. 64–6.

[31] Nothomb, q. Lévy (1991), p. 217.

[32] Malraux (1938/1979), p. 71 (my emphasis).

[33] Malraux (1938/1979), pp. 302–3. It seems that Malraux, in addition to pursuing his own enquiries *en haut*, kept copies of Madrid newspapers – including *El Socialista* of 31 October which linked Ramón Franco with the previous day's atrocity: see above, pp. 197–8. The places named by 'Garcia' (a character probably modelled on Mikhail Koltsov) were allegedly hit by bombs on that day. For example, Carmén García Cisneros (aka 99–22–38) one of the children featured in the 'Getafe' photo dossier, lived in the Calle del Nuncio. The interrogator is clearly sceptical about 'official' reports. The results of the interview confirm his suspicion that it was the 'fifth column', and not enemy aircraft, which did the damage. For the significance of this theory, see below, pp. 233–4.

[34] Malraux (1938/1979), p. 377.

[35] Malraux (1938/1979), pp. 374–6 – which refer to the results of artillery fire, not to air raids.

[36] From *The Nation*, 20 March 1937, quoted by Thornberry (1977), p. 147.

[37] Malraux (1938/1979), e.g. pp. 402–6 and 504 and cf. Thornberry (1977), p. 149.

[38] See Harris (1997), p. 324. This hypothesis allows (without proposing) the view that one of the reasons why Malraux emphasized the role of the communists in running the war was to help shuffle off his own feelings of responsibility.

[39] His political sympathies were progressive but 'with certain leanings towards the right, and no excessive repugnance towards aspects of fascism'; Matamoro (1979), p. 81. See also ibid., pp. 7–16.

[40] Q. Matamoro (1979), p. 84 *et seq.* This excellent study is supported by extracts from its subject's Spanish writings, originally published in *L'Intransigéant* and *Paris Soir.*

[41] Q. Matamoro (1979), p. 86, see also p. 99.

[42] Thornberry (1977), p. 150.

[43] *Claridad*, 20 October 1936.

[44] See, for example, the case argued in Stradling (1997).

[45] Azaña (1937), pp. 23–5.

[46] Azaña (1937/1981), pp. 120 and 154.

[47] Cf. the lines from Pemán q. above, p. 87.

Chapter 14

Gernika – The True Getafe?

One of the most blatant acts of unmitigated cruelty in the history of mankind.[1]

Similar sentiments to these can be found in almost any educational course textbook about the Spanish Civil War. *Mutatis mutandis*, they turn up in newspaper supplements and voice-overs of TV documentaries. They represent the mind-set of media-mediated comment not only about the atrocity of Gernika itself, but about the war as a whole. They form an eternal mantra of anti-fascism, a definitive word-byte, a hand-me-down encapsulation of history. This litany touches every part of our collective lives on an almost daily basis. The single event of Gernika, ubiquitously recycled in the full range of discourses from pop-up press presentations, readers' digests, and broadcasts on the one hand to the canon of scholarly writing on the other, suffices to keep the public eye fixed on a monoscopic history. Its cyclopean hegemony predetermines judgement – and precludes rational debate – on all the issues of the Spanish Civil War which might otherwise demand considered and mature thought. Above all, it blasts the Spanish Nationalists, in their irremediable but erroneous characterization as 'fascists', to a dark place far beyond any possibility of redemption. In the incendiary furnace of the burning town, all the ideals of the Nationalist cause are rendered to ashes and dispersed by the four winds. As a result, no pretension to legitimacy of law or ethics can be admitted on behalf of any of its legatees.[2]

The quotation given above is from a work of art history. This is surely appropriate, since the historical event of Gernika, a town in Vizcaya, was immortalized by 'Guernica', a painting by Pablo

Picasso. The Spanish artist Picasso is regarded as the last century's most important (that is, in every sense, 'valuable') painter.[3] 'Guernica', almost beyond argument, is the most significant and symbolic image we possess of the universally terrible twentieth century. Painting followed event by a matter of weeks, so that an irrefutable claim to veracity of detail, emotion and interpretation was stamped on its narratology from the moment it was unveiled. Thus, when we think of Gernika we visualize the painting, 'Guernica'; when we think of war, we visualize the painting; when we think of bombing, and of 'collateral damage', we visualize the painting. Because of its ubiquitous use in schools and universities across the globe, for many, *when they think of history itself*, they visualize the painting. Apparently, even when we think about football, our involuntary subconscious summons up the painting.[4] Most remarkably, it seems that when the painting is deliberately blacked out in order to preclude our thinking about the message it conveys (which notoriously occurred at the United Nations in February 2003, during the making of the case by the US-led 'coalition' for the invasion of Iraq) we *still* obstinately visualize the painting.[5] As I have argued elsewhere, there is no atrocity like *artrocity*.[6] Art, even where it blatantly purveys a propaganda point, lies beyond political impeachment. Attempts at censorship have the counter-productive effect of re-confirming its reified status. Despite what all the black crafts of modern manipulation can achieve, the *Pietà* remains: at the painting's doorway, the mother still stands screaming with the dead child in her arms.[7]

Picasso established his eternal influence on the twentieth century with a calculated restraint. There is no blood – unlike the poets' suppurating verse – even from the soldier's severed arm which lies on the floor of the bombed house, grasping its shattered sword. Unlike the propaganda products of the poster studios, there are no explosions, no planes, no swastikas, no anti-fascist rants. Yet the artist's apostrophe to the Popular Front and the cause of the Republic is unmistakable and overwhelming. When the painting was first displayed, in the Spanish Republic's pavilion at the Paris Exhibition in the spring of 1937, the camp of the war criminals themselves, surmounted by appropriate eagle and swastika, was only a hand-grenade's throw away. Few visitors to Paris, during what proved to be a hugely successful tourist and propaganda occasion, could have doubted the national identity or ideology of the men guilty of Gernika. But, in any case, this identity had been revealed from the start by *The Times* reporter George Steer. The American expert, Herbert Southworth, regards Steer and his press colleagues, rather than Picasso, as the creators of 'Guernica'. Without them, he believed, 'there would not have been *the event of Guernica* as we know it today'.[8] Indeed, Picasso himself deliberately acknowledged this precedent by shrouding his dismembered martyrs not in the banners of party or cause but with torn shreds of newsprint. Based on their own observation in the town's vicinity at the time, together with reports of direct eyewitnesses in the immediate aftermath, Steer and two other English-speaking journalists presented the fundamental documentary testament of the case to the public within forty-eight hours, and whilst the ruins were still smouldering.[9]

The fundamental facts in these despatches have resisted challenge through decades of unremitting controversy and historical investigation. In the late afternoon of 26 April 1937, the Condor Legion and some Italian auxiliary planes, about forty aircraft in all, operating in groups, made a series of four bombing runs against specified targets in and around Gernika. The town had no civil defence capacity, and it was a busy market day. Since sorties took place over a period of more than three hours, they were certainly sustained (if you like, systematic), though in the nature of such operations at the time, each separate attack lasted only a matter of a few minutes. Nonetheless, incendiary explosives set several streets on fire almost at once. A blanket of smoke quickly covered the town so that, by the time of the second attack, air crews were unable to identify their targets. Gernika contained various sites (a river bridge, a railway station, and two small arms factories) which were legitimately subject to military action, but were not, in the event, damaged. Nevertheless, it was not merely in frustration that escorting fighters swooped down to strafe people attempting to flee into the hills. The facts laid out by Steer and company demonstrated beyond doubt that the raid had other priority objectives. It was a conscious and determined experiment in 'a new method of warfare' using a new generation of weapon technology, and a terror tactic intended to engender panic behind the lines and to undermine the determination of the Basques (above all, citizens of Bilbao) to resist the Nationalist offensive.[10]

The planners of this cold-blooded operation relied on the cutting-edge technology of advanced weaponry both to achieve their objectives and to escape scot-free. They did not, however, reckon on the parallel development of modern telecommunications, which sparked a resistance that was, in the end, far more potent than anti-aircraft batteries or protective fighter air cover. The international effect of Steer's intervention was unprecedented. In many of the world's newspaper offices, editors and/or proprietors changed their minds on Spain overnight. As it were in one fell scoop, victory in the propaganda war was handed to the Republic: an advantage which, immortalized in the arena of history, has never been relinquished.[11] If anything, the bumbling miscalculations of Franco's publicity advisers in response to press revelations did more to alienate conservative cohorts of capitalism from his cause than the atrocity itself. In this context, at least, it was an early example of the now familiar media-world nostrum that cover-up rather than crime can often do the more serious damage. As far as the lasting reputation of the Nationalist cause was concerned, the attempts of Burgos not only to deny the involvement of its allies, but to counter-accuse the Basque army of Gernika's destruction, was a palpable case of suicide by propaganda.[12] Meanwhile, the abundant atrocity material presented tendentiously to the world six months earlier by the designers and disseminators of 'Getafe' (and similar 'events') became by osmosis a post-validated species of truth. The destruction of Gernika was rapidly characterized as deliberate murder of women and children.

During this latter process, corroborative detail was introduced which was often by no means endorsed by the original press reports. Only days after Steer's dispatch, an American foreign affairs expert used it as the starting point of a story titled 'Women and Children First' in the *New York Herald Tribune*.[13] Then, a week later, the Senator for Idaho made what Southworth calls 'the most vigorous denunciation of the destroyers of Guernica delivered before a parliamentary body at any time'. More significant (but a feature Southworth did not notice) was that Senator Borah's discourse seemed in almost telepathic contact with the main elements of Spanish Republican propaganda:

> Here Fascism presents its masterpiece. It has hung upon the wall of civilization a painting that will never come down – never fade out of the memories of man. [The history of atrocity] will linger longest and with the greatest horror over the savage story of the

Fascist war in Spain [but] it remained for Fascist warfare to show to the world how thorough and effective [modern] weapons are when used for *the destruction of women and children* ... how airplanes, swooping low like winged monsters, *can massacre thousands of innocent children* without endangering in the slightest the lives of the brave assailants ... Fascism boasts of courage ... and now doubtless will take pride in the *successful slaughter of women and children* throughout Spain.[14]

Senator Borah was probably not a crypto-communist. The alternative explanation of his amazing precognition is surely that behind the breaking news from the Basque country he figured out the bombing of Madrid and in particular the story of Getafe and its dramatic poster. Via a perfectly natural subliminal process this imagery was now grafted onto the fresh growth of 'Guernica'. As it happens, Steer (like Picasso) resorted only cautiously to the common discourse when describing the human consequences of the Nazi raid. He states, for example, that 'I saw a place where fifty people, *nearly all women and children, are said to have been trapped* in an air raid refuge under a mass of burning wreckage.'[15]

In a best-selling book which he published some time later, Steer largely ignored the theoretical issue of the 'bombing of open towns', and the empirical history of its practice down to 26 April 1937. However, he made an exception over the previous month's raids on Durango, which received full treatment from his incisive descriptive style. In the four weeks since arriving in Bilbao, Steer had become deeply implicated with the Basques and their cause. (Before that again he had been expelled from a similar posting by the Franco side.) His book – as George Orwell remarked – was written from a perspective of resonant empathy with Basque, history, culture and political aspirations.[16] To Steer, General Mola's campaign against *Euskadi* represented a foreign invasion. It was prosecuted by means of 'a new method of war, more terrible than any practised against Madrid'; whilst the air raid carried out against Durango on 31 March was 'the most terrible bombardment of a civil population in the history of the world'.[17] And indeed, the killing of civilians during this savage twenty-minute attack, at least in terms of an indisputable casualty toll, was more terrible than at Gernika. Over 300 people, including the denizens of a convent, the congregation of a church, and their parish priest in the act of distributing the Eucharist, were casually slaughtered by forces acting on behalf of a so-called

'Christian Crusade'. In contrast to his original Gernika files, Steer's description of the Durango atrocity was also subject to the osmosis mentioned above. He paid particular attention to the spectacle of dismembered children which (though he makes no relevant reference) he surely must have seen as reminiscent of 'Getafe'. 'Slowly', he tells us. 'the bodies were lugged out of the masonry and *laid on slabs in the cemetery of Durango and ticketed, 1 to 127.*'[18] Yet in Bilbao, as in Durango and Gernika, even George Steer, for all his cold fury, accepted that the killing of children was not deliberate, if only because he knew that murder could not, in practice, be carried out in this way:

> I neither desire nor intend to make any claim that the German aircraft which made its daily mess of industrial Bilbao were out to kill civilians. They wanted to hit factories: and, more often than not, they missed.[19]

Within weeks thousands of children, mainly from Bilbao and other Basque communities, but also including refugees from the wider non-Basque hinterland, were being evacuated to France, Belgium, Holland, Great Britain, Russia and Mexico in order to escape the expected aerial holocaust.[20] These 'orphans of the war' were assembled day after day on the quaysides, where preparations for departure included their being labelled – *again, like the dead children of Getafe* – with a number encoding personal details.[21] In the circumstances it seems hardly surprising that instructions issued to British naval vessels in the vicinity seemed to be based on the assumption that the Francoist fleet would set out to drown as many children as possible.[22] In fact, the refugees arrived without enemy intervention at various destinations, and immediately impressed their hosts as a dire warning of some approaching Armageddon. There could hardly have been a more plangent advertisement for the indiscriminate barbarity of fascism than these lively little portents of devastation, innocent evacuees wrenched from homes and families, and now distributed for the world's succour. The children's chaperones, along with hundreds of Basque seamen who sought shelter in Britain's ports, were welcome for reasons as much selfish as altruistic. They knew about bombing and could share their experiences with pressmen and politicians. Public opinion had suddenly become desperate for specialist knowledge on 'civil defence'.[23]

Whilst its extension in terms of meaning and judgement over the Spanish Civil War is effectively limitless, the universal scandal over Gernika did little to alter the pattern of Nationalist air campaigns. It is true that for some months after the fall of Bilbao in June 1937, the Condor Legion limited itself to strictly battle-field operations. But on 2 November, nine Junkers 52 attacked the Catalan provincial capital of Lérida. According to official reports, they hit a school: the corpses of fifty children were dug out; civilians were strafed by fighters; the death-toll was put at 150. It was the Feast of All Souls.[24] Here, even if no propaganda exaggeration was involved, we might invoke Steer's reservation just quoted. Lérida was the focal point of the Republican war effort in Aragon, tightly packed with military installations, material and personnel. However, once the land offensive against the Mediterranean provinces began, in the wake of the watershed Republican defeat at Teruel (March, 1938), the common discourse of extenuation appears increasingly threadbare. All that remains to any commentator is the reductive and subjective criterion of 'military targets'; a thing as ethically indeterminate today as it was then. On 27 March, Lérida was subject to a fresh onslaught by planes of the Nationalist air force. Amongst an alleged 400 civilian casualties were a number of teenage children.[25] Two months later, on 31 May, the small Catalan town of Granollers, near Barcelona, was blasted by five Junkers. Reports claimed that it was market day, and that over 100 women and children were killed in the town square alone, with a total loss of 350 lives. British reporters wrote of 'massacres' where 'some houses have been bespattered with blood up to the second storey'. Others wrote of 'fearful execution amongst shoppers' and (in one headline) of a 'Bomb on Food Queue'.[26] Even the *Daily Telegraph* expressed shock and horror.[27] After visiting the scene, the British *chargé d'affaires* in Barcelona could find no military justification for the attack.[28] In the meantime, an apparently autonomous Italian campaign against the main Mediterranean dockyards had begun. After a raid on Barcelona of 30 January, it was reported that 'in one place, 120 children, war refugees from Bilbao and Madrid, were buried [underneath rubble]. It is feared all are dead.'[29] In a later raid, almost inevitably, 'another bomb fell on a queue of men and women waiting to buy food'.[30] Throughout the year, city authorities in Barcelona and Valencia (*inter alia*) continued on a regular basis to issue inflated statistics of the human damage to foreign pressmen and/or to official British investigators – when, in all conscience, the true figures were surely unprecedented and horrific enough.[31]

Thus, the doom-laden events of 1938 included atrocities at least as awful as those of Gernika and Durango. In history textbooks, however, the killings at Lérida, Granollers, Alicante and several other places are rarely mentioned, even *en passant*. A similar observation might be made about the self-consciously brutalist actions of Italian airmen in carrying out the destruction of over 1,000 civilian lives during the course of 1938. At least as much as the German action at Gernika, this anticipated the routine massacres of the Second World War – in a campaign which was entered upon with little more than a craving for cheap military glory, but has yet to evoke the research interest of a professional scholar. Perhaps the academic community is reluctant to transpose reified tales of fascist barbarity out of the realm of meta-narrative and into that of empirical examination. Perhaps the empirical resources for research do not exist. In any case, it seems that 'Gernika/Guernica' *is sufficient on its own* to carry the full burden of memory, of accusation, process and sentence.[32] For this reason, the singular events of 26 April 1937 continue to attract attention from a variety of media sources as well as the interest of scholars in a range of disciplines. For the same reason, pre-committed commentators on both sides still quarrel over the Gernika event as bitterly and as tendentiously as they did when the polemic first began. By now the subject has hardened into a touchstone of world opinion on the Spanish Civil War *as a whole*. The underlying reason is obvious. The representational twinning of Gernika and 'Guernica' fixes in all minds, dramatically and irrefutably, the alliance between Franco and Hitler, the indelible link between Nationalists and Nazis.[33] Once this link is recognized, it stimulates for most observers the mental process of guilt by association. At the logical conclusion of this process, part of the blame for the Jewish Holocaust and other Nazi war crimes rubs off onto the Nationalist cause.

In 1974 an English edition of the first general history of civil war air campaigns appeared. It dealt with the subject of bombing on the one hand by *ignoring* all the controversial issues and on the other by *praising* the Condor Legion for its demonstration of military expertise during 'the famous attack on Guernica'! Though this version of General Salas's book also presented a

blank aspect to the issue of 'bombing of open towns', in the
original Spanish edition *only the Republican air force* is listed
(statistically) as having bombarded civilians and caused 'great
carnage'. In contrast, the Nationalist side, the general asserted,
always bombed strictly military targets.[34] The breathtaking pirou-
ette of the Gernika raid from being 'notorious' to becoming
'famous', even when most of them remained unaware of the
precisely contrary motion attributed to 'La Gloriosa', must have
represented to readers outside Spain a vertiginous reversal of
normative assumptions. It was a novelty that precipitated the
publication (in 1977) of Southworth's meticulous exposé of the
shabby history of Nationalist attempts to shake off the succubus of
world condemnation.[35]

Southworth's determined dialectic settled for good and all
many of the details over Gernika that had been so long disputed.
It did so emphatically in the Republic's favour. One bone of
contention, however, was not effectively buried, and that the most
critical in terms of ethical judgement: *the casualty figures*. On this
subject Southworth is not only equivocal and self-contradictory,
but also irrational. At the time, official sources in Bilbao set the
number of deaths in the town at 1,654, along with 889 wounded,
giving a total of 2,543. These figures were set out in a best-selling
contemporary book by the British pro-Republican publicist, the
Duchess of Atholl, and thereafter became common currency.[36] In
contrast to ruling passions in the Spanish Republic *per se*, estimates seem to have been arrived at honestly. Gernika had been
crowded with people and much of the town was on fire, but it had
fallen into Nationalist hands before bodies could be recovered. In
any case, it seems that a majority of victims were cremated in the
intense heat of fires started by incendiary bombs.[37] Basque officials proceeded by interviews with refugee survivors (including
wounded) in Bilbao. In addition, an obvious benchmark of
comparison was available in the case of Durango. Here, a full
month elapsed between the raid and the place's capture, allowing
time for the compilation of provisional lists. Since some 240
citizens died in this town as result of an attack by far fewer
machines than had been used against Gernika, and lasting less
than half an hour, it seemed (at the time) reasonable to apply a
coefficient of seven to the Durango statistics.

The resulting totals were accepted in the pioneering English-
language textbook on the Spanish Civil War, by Hugh Thomas,

published in 1961. But four years later, in the second edition (as Southworth puts it) the author 'for some whimsical reason reneged on these figures and wrote in a footnote that it was impossible to establish the number of persons killed; "Estimates vary from 1,600 to 100. The lower estimate is likely" '.[38] Like any historian, Thomas was entitled to change his mind without being accused of 'reneging' (and whimsically so!) on some sacred commitment fancied by others to reside in his heart.[39] Yet Southworth's criticism seems to have helped Thomas to change his mind again: or perhaps – to imitate Southworth's pejorative language – 'stung him into retraction'. In the third edition of *The Spanish Civil War* that appeared shortly thereafter (1977), Thomas wrote that 'the number [of victims] is extremely difficult to establish . . . perhaps 1,000 died.'[40] All this would be less bewildering were it not for the fact that Southworth was performing competitive statistical somersaults. He, too, concluded that 'nobody knows how many died', thus himself reneging on the personal commitment to the Republican cause which he had absurdly transferred onto Thomas.[41] Furthermore, although demanding that 'neo-Franquista historians' should not haggle over figures, Southworth arrived at this point after a good deal of haggling over figures. This curious procedure included his offering the opinion that the original figure of 1,654 dead was 'far nearer the truth' than lower estimates made by (for example) the prominent Francoist historian, Ricardo de la Cierva.[42] It seems difficult to square this assertion of Southworth's with the other (just quoted) that 'nobody knows' the truth on this issue.

Since the publication of Southworth's book, whilst the temperature of debate over Gernika has hardly diminished, the median figure of its casualties has steadily fallen to nearer Thomas's 1965 guesstimate.[43] Indeed, it now seems that rather than acting 'for some whimsical reason', Thomas, on the contrary, had reconsidered this thorny issue with due professional care and attention.[44] If anything, it is his second change of tack that now seems 'whimsical'. As we have seen, Thomas carried out a similar exercise with respect to 'Getafe'. At first recording the original propaganda story, he later dropped any reference to dead children *and* made clear that the object of attack was the Getafe air base, not the civilian districts. In this case, Thomas's change of mind has survived into the latest edition.[45] Gernika's ghosts are more resilient, if only because they need to be. In 1998, following an official apology made by Chancellor Helmut Kohl, on behalf of the Federal Republic of Germany, for the atrocity carried out by the Condor Legion, Spanish newspapers were agitated by a German TV programme purporting to 'unmask the truth' about Gernika. In the words of one reporter, it suggested that the event 'was an invention of Republican propaganda' and that only 126 people had been killed.[46]

The present author is convinced that reliable statistics on the wider subject of bombing during the Spanish Civil War can never be faithfully reconstituted. This seems demonstrably justified in the specific cases of Getafe and Gernika. At the same time, he considers it likely that if not the actual data, at least the proportions indicated by the other of the Salas Larrazábal brothers (Colonel Ramón) are acceptable in broad terms.[47] However, as a more recent study correctly explains, Ramón Salas's figures of 4,000 nationalist mortalities compared to 11,000 Republicans were meant to include *victims of artillery along with aerial bombardment*.[48] Thus, the overall total attributed to the latter action can confidently be reduced by one-third, to 10,000 rather than 15,000. At the same time the differential between the two sides' records must be increased in the Republic's favour, since no city – not even Oviedo – was shelled by Republican forces with the same intensity or for the same physical duration as the Nationalists shelled Madrid. Finally, two other quantitative factors must be reckoned in the account. First, for much the greater fraction of the war's chronological length, the Republic was endowed with markedly less capacity for either category of bombardment than its enemy. Second, up to the juncture when the war's military outcome had effectively been decided (that is, by early 1938) all the densest centres of Spain's urban population, vastly engorged with refugee masses, were to be found in the Republican zone.[49] Common sense alone inclines me to believe that Nationalist operations caused at least three times more casualties overall as those brought about by the Republic.

NOTES

[1]   Fisch (1988), p. 18.
[2]   See Stradling (2007B).
[3]   Notably enough, the painting adorned the most expensive postage

stamp (200 pesetas) ever issued by the wartime Republic; see Carulla & Carulla (1999), p. 64.

4   E.g. in a TV documentary about 'Fascism and Football' Picasso and his painting are sent on to the pitch (as it were) at half-time in order to remind the fans what 'fascism' meant; BBC 4, 6 October 2003, produced by S. Hughes. More recently, flashes of detail from the painting decorated the narrative sequence of a TV interview with Wales's football coach John Toshack, presumably intended to illustrate his *afición* to the Basque people; 'Tosh – A Portrait', produced by G. Rowlands, BBC 1 Wales, 23 March 2005.

5   See 'Powell Without Picasso' by Maureen Dowd, *New York Times*, 5 February, 2003.

6   Stradling (1989).

7   Just as The Poster is Getafe, Picasso's painting is Guernica. The difference is that hardly anybody today has ever heard of Getafe.

8   Southworth (1977), p. 11 (my emphasis).

9   The story of the story is told by Rankin (2003), p. 114 *et seq.*

10   Still the most useful general treatment is in Thomas and Morgan-Witts (1975). The revised version (1992) has some pejorative changes in approach and tone, adumbrated in its subtitle.

11   See, for example, Johnson (1992), pp. 335–6. This author also suggests that the Comintern exploited the opportunity offered by Gernika in order to divert attention from the brutal suppression of the POUM and other dissident groups, happening at exactly the same time.

12   This is both proposition and project of Southworth's book; (1977), *passim.*

13   Southworth (1977), p. 182. Steer's report also appeared in the *New York Times* on 28 April.

14   Q. Southworth (1977), pp. 186–7. (My emphases added.) Picasso was approached for a commission linked to the Paris Exhibition in January, 1937 – but not until *c.*4 May did he announce that he had chosen the event of Gernika as his subject; Martin (2002), pp. 1–3. The life-size reproduction of 'Guernica' in the lobby of the UNO building (referred to above) can surely be said to occupy 'the wall of civilization'.

15   Southworth (1977), p. 15, quoting *The Times* report filed on 27 April 1937 (my emphasis). Cf. Noel Monks in the *Daily Express*: 'A sight that haunted me for weeks was the charred bodies of several women and children huddled together in what had been the cellar of a house'; q. in Lewis (1998), p. 391.

16   See Orwell's review of Steer, *Time and Tide*, February 1938; also Rankin (2003), p. 87.

17   Steer (1938), p. 161. It seems the author had not heard about, or chose to discredit, the deliberate bombing of women and children in food queues, the destruction of whole blocks of workers flats, the targeting of ambulances, hospitals and schools, all of which – *according to Republican sources* – were common events during the siege of Madrid.

18 Steer (1938), p. 167. (My emphasis.)
19 Steer (1938), p. 178. Before completing his book, Steer had probably become conscious of the Republic's own dubious record in the bombing war.
20 However, it is notable that official Republican operations to persuade parents to send children abroad began before the end of 1936. In particular, strong pressure was put on Bilbao families from as early as January 1937, long before the Nationalist offensive against the Basques had started; Legarreta (1984), pp. 34–40.
21 Newsreel clip used in 'The Spanish Civil War' (Granada/TVE production first broadcast 1983), episode 3. In close-up, a girl of about the same age as Getafe victim 4–21–35 is being labelled 'A Inglaterra 4121' – a remarkably similar enumeration.
22 My inference from Cable (1979), pp. 8–14.
23 See, for example, Stradling (1996), p. 5 & *passim*. For a general study of the evacuation, Lagarreta (1984); for the British experience, Bell (1996). It would be interesting to examine the connections between the bombing of the Basques and British civil defence preparations for the war of 1939.
24 This follows Solé & Villaroya (2003), pp. 120–2 and 164.
25 Data here are highly unreliable. If reports that forty planes were involved are correct, the Condor Legion must have participated: see *Daily Telegraph*, 29 March 1938. As in the cases of Getafe and Gernika, the town fell almost immediately. The victors destroyed municipal records of the raid; Solé & Villaroya (2003), pp. 164–5.
26 *The Times*, 31 May and 1 June; *Manchester Guardian*, 2 June 1938. I write this on the day after a lone suicide bomber killed 125 people in Hillah (Iraq); TV news coverage included images of blood spattered against a wall to a height of 10 feet or more.
27 *Daily Telegraph*, 2 June 1938.
28 *The Times*, 8 June 1938. But another correspondent pointed out that 'figures are sometimes quoted high on account of their propaganda value abroad'; *Sunday Times*, 27 June 1938. Witnesses at Granollers reported that forty bombs were dropped, destroying eighty houses, *and that the attack was made from a height of 15,000 feet*. It is sometimes hard not to suspect that quantity and volume, rather than accuracy or consistency, were of the narrative essence: see Solé & Villaroya (2003), pp. 194–7.
29 *The Times*, 31 January 1938. On this occasion, the bombers flew at an estimated 9,000 feet
30 *The Times*, 18 March 1938.
31 See above, pp. 73–5. For some discussion of statistics, below, pp. 242–3 and 255–6.
32 In stark contrast to the case of Gernika neither of the Lérida (Lleida) raids is mentioned *in any English-language textbook* of the Spanish Civil War that I have seen, unless one counts captions to a photograph (by A. Centenelles) reproduced in Mitchell (1982), p. 155 and Carr (1986), also p. 155. The Granollers raid is ignored by all except

Thomas: (1965), p. 678 and (1977), p. 826. A much earlier account by Allison Peers (1943) pp. 62–3 relied on newspaper reports such as those cited above.

[33] To cite one amongst countless potential examples, the voice-over introduction to a 1986 TV documentary entitled 'Picasso' tells the viewer that 'Nazi bombers called in by the fascist general Franco bomb Gernika'; script W. Janusczak, director D. Baissy (RM Arts), broadcast on Artsworld Channel 157 on 20 October 2005.

[34] Salas (1974), p. 137, see also p. 105. This version rates Durango as unworthy of mention. Cf. *idem* (1969), pp. 485–6. English translation of indigenous publications on the Spanish Civil War was even rarer in 1974 than it is today. This illustrates the importance of the topic and indicates some material support for the publication from Francoist sources.

[35] It should be said that (in his turn) Southworth disdained the subject of *Republican* bombing except in one place where he effectively refuted Nationalist claims of a raid on Valladolid in which 83 children allegedly died; (1977), p. 148.

[36] Atholl (1938), p. 189.

[37] Despite this, an Australian Catholic (and pro-Basque) reporter, Noel Monks, who found himself in the vicinity of Gernika on 26 April, was able not only to count 600 bodies but also to identify them as 'nurses, children, farmers, old women, girls, old men, babies'; q. from the *Scottish Daily Express*, 11 May 1937, by Atholl (1938), p. 189.

[38] Southworth (1977), p. 362.

[39] Moreover, Thomas (1965), p. 537 had actually written 'it has not been possible' rather than the abstract assertion attributed to him by Southworth.

[40] Thomas (1977), p. 624, n2. This compromise knocks off 600 bodies or piles on 900, depending on one's point of view.

[41] Southworth (1977), p. 370.

[42] Southworth (1977), p. 362.

[43] The completely discredited official figures were recently repeated by an American writer; see Kurlansky (2001), p. 200. (This will not be the last example, a prediction I make despite any publication due to appear in the year 2007, which marked the 70th anniversary of Gernika.) Cf. Vidal (1997), p. 101 who gives 'between 250 and 300'. Steer's biographer suggests that 'by the soberest reckoning today, at least 300 died': Rankin (1997). The latest Spanish treatment I could find, by Basque historian Fusi Aizpurua (2002), p. 254 gives a figure of 237. The most widely-read study has 248: Thomas & Morgan-Witts (1991), p. 44.

[44] Given 6,000 people present in Gernika on 26 April 1937 the original estimates would yield a casualty rate of 42.38%, higher than those registered in the fire-storms of Hamburg (August 1943) or Dresden (February 1945). During the first-ever '1,000 bomber raid', on Cologne in May 1942, 469 citizens (less than 0.01% of the population) were killed.

[45] Thomas (1977), p. 470 & (2001), p. 456, and see above p. 107, n. 4.

[46] 'La TV pública alemana reduce a 126 las víctimas del bombardeo de Gernika. Sostiene que las imagenes de época eran ruinas pertene-cientes a Madrid'; *El Mundo,* 21 April 1998. Public outrage took account of a compensation package currently being offered by Germany to Gernika and its citizens. However, even a Condor Legion pilot and firm Nazi believed at the time that 'there are certainly thousands more dead beneath the rubble', whilst admitting that 'it was a rotten trick to destroy such a militarily unimportant city'; see Ries & Ring (1992), pp. 62–4.

[47] R. Salas (1980), p. 310.

[48] Solé & Villaroya (2003), p. 315, in a summary which also confronts the difficulties of establishing global figures.

[49] Cf. the three biggest cities on either side: Madrid, Barcelona and Valencia, with a peacetime total of 2,277,000, and Seville, Saragossa and Granada, with 520,000; R. Salas (1980), p. 277.

Chapter 15

Getafe Airbrushed Out

More than any other British newspaper, the *Daily Worker* never missed an opportunity to keep the topic of air bombardments in its headlines. For its editors, and for many of the British public, bombing of civilians had become at once the paradigm perennial of 'fascist atrocities' and the most disturbing 'story' of the Spanish war. For example, an interview with Franco was published in the Tory press, apparently by coincidence, just as his troops began their offensive in the Jarama valley in February 1937. The *generalísimo* was quoted as boasting 'you have seen our army at work and you know what it's capable of.' The *Worker* referred scathingly to this remark, illustrating it with clever and bitter irony by reprinting photographs of three 'Getafe' children – grisly examples of 'fascist' military efficiency.[1] This time, however, the actual word '*Getafe*', so sharply profiled in the newspaper's earlier stories, *was not mentioned*. The elision was not accidental.

Over a year after the October 1936 raids on Madrid, the *Volunteer for Liberty*, in a typical feature, stoked up the fighting morale of International Brigaders with the news that the 'Fascists close down more schools as loyal Spain opens new ones'. The accompanying picture showed a group of smiling schoolgirls – but its caption conditioned reader response by adding: 'there's no need to describe what fascism does to these smiles. You've seen the shrapnel-torn faces'.[2] Of course, even this anonymous profile kept images and thoughts of 'Getafe' alive in many minds; but now, reference to the original crime scene is absent. As it happens, 'Getafe' was by no means the only attempt made by the Republican propaganda machine to project a location-specific story about bombing of children onto the screen of universal awareness. As we have seen, Ogilvie-Forbes of the British embassy was taken to see children allegedly killed by bombing in Leganés, not far from Getafe.[3] In January 1937, Arturo Barea devoted one of his radio broadcasts ('La Voz de Madrid') to a similar outrage at Vallecas, a village on the capital's south-eastern periphery. Around this time, too, publicity was given to an alleged airborne massacre of schoolchildren, near a military hospital in Tarancón, a logistically important town on the Madrid–Valencia road. All these incidents (and a similar one at Lérida later in 1937) were allowed to drop out of the record – along with propaganda claims made about them.[4]

In November 1936, with the exception of the Nationalist slaughter of militia prisoners at Badajoz, 'Getafe' was the biggest single atrocity story of the war. But within months, if not weeks, it began to dissolve into the ether. From the end of 1936 until the end of the war itself, the name of Getafe crops up with extreme rarity in the whole gigantic literature of Republican propaganda. Even in the large sub-section of this genre dedicated to 'the bombing of open towns', compilers of flysheets and pamphlets almost unanimously refrained from recalling the dastardly murder of sixty or more schoolchildren in an obscure little settlement near Madrid. When the Republican government came (at the invitation of the League of Nations) to publish official figures for civilian casualties incurred over the first twenty months of the war, *no reference to the Getafe victims appeared* in the detailed narrative that reckoned up a total of 10,699 dead children, and no example amongst dozens of demonstrative photographs was selected from the Koltsov picture dossier.[5] Early in 1937, the poet Antonio Machado compiled an elegiac evocation of heroic Madrid in verse, prose and pictures. Evidently (but curiously) 'Getafe' had made no lasting impression on any contributor.[6] Equally Getafe-free is an extended catalogue of 'fascist barbarism' first issued in Catalan. In this submission, the strafing of refugees fleeing the fallen city of Málaga is described as an atrocity worthy of Attila the Hun, whilst Gernika is destroyed as though by a band of ravaging apemen. Enemy aviation, it asserts, makes a speciality of killing women and children. The cover of a modern facsimile edition shows a doll-like baby superimposed upon a bomb-ruined street.[7] In spring 1937, the British Foreign Office compiled its own photographic dossier of bomb-damage in Spain. When filed, it was accompanied by a fly-sheet (probably provided by the Spanish embassy to the Non-Intervention Committee) on 'The Deplorable

Role of the Germans' in the killing of women and children by 'bombs thrown from their Junker and Heinkel planes'. Despite the concerns over 'Getafe' demonstrated originally by Ogilvie-Forbes and his boss, Eden, no illustration of this particular atrocity found a place in the folder.[8]

Meanwhile, the efforts of the *Daily Worker* staff never slackened. Not long after the Foreign Office picture dossier was filed, a one-off magazine dedicated largely to atrocity and resistance in Spain was issued by the CPGB publishing house of Lawrence and Wishart. An anonymous article titled 'The Massacre of the Innocents' concentrated upon fascist baby-killing. It *disincluded* mention of Getafe but *did* include a curious gloss on the Madrid events of 30 October 1936:

> On October 30, bombs were thrown from buildings on to women queuing for milk at the end of the Gran Via. It was thought at first that these bombs came from rebel planes, but, upon investigation, it was found that *no-one had seen or heard a single plane over Madrid at the time* . . . [9]

The writer clearly meant to implicate members of the so-called 'Fascist Fifth Column', a nebulous civilian army allegedly summoned up by General Mola to spread sabotage and fear behind Madrid's defence lines at the critical moment of his army's onslaught. But these words have considerably greater significance for the report that this book presents. If only by implication, *as early as July 1937 readers were being asked to accept that on 30 October there had been no aerial bombing of Madrid at all!*

The Republic's propaganda machine was, it seemed, more proficient at looping the loop than any Chato or Mosca in the ranks of La Gloriosa. Around the same time as this unexploded 'factual' bombshell was unearthed – as if by faceless agents of some Orwellian 'Ministry of Truth' – André Malraux was apprised by his communist contacts of a similar re-arrangement of the past. Thus, in Malraux's novel, his character 'Garcia', chief intelligence officer and propaganda guru of the Madrid junta, concludes his enquiry (presumably, that referred to by the anonymous pen quoted above) into the events of 30 October:

> No aeroplane, no field-gun was responsible; the so-called Fifth Column had been at work ... Each man before launching his bomb had looked down on the line of women queued up outside a grocery, had seen the old men and children in the square. The

women had been slaughtered without a qualm . . . But what about the children? Garcia had seen the photographs taken immediately after the explosion. . . [10]

This *volte face* has a particular and widely-known background explanation. It was connected to a renewed intensification of Republican propaganda against alleged internal subversives, in the wake of the anti-communist 'insurrection' in Barcelona (3–6 May 1937) and subsequent purges. The urgent priority now was to present enemy-inspired terrorist elements as a real and continuing threat to the people and to the war effort. In turn, this threw into relief the vicious treason of the POUM and other anti-Stalinist organizations – the 'Trotsky-Fascists' who had (it was proclaimed) made common cause with Franco in their hatred of the Soviet Union and Spanish democracy. It was especially important for British supporters of the Republic to appreciate why stern action had to be taken against these 'vipers'. But a side-effect of this campaign was, in effect, to deny the version of events over the bombing of Madrid initially disseminated by the Comintern, and which today forms the received wisdom of historians.

The previous two paragraphs expose an operation carried out in the interests of the Comintern (that is to say, Stalin) in order to hit a temporary political target. Indeed it is a paradigm instance of the tactical truth patented by Stalinism. In so doing, Moscow was happy for the world to believe that that native Spaniards, not (after all) German or Italian 'Fascist mercenaries', had been responsible for the massacre of Madrid's mothers and children in the autumn of 1936. But even this treasonous tergiversation pales beside the sordid possibility, mooted by *The Times*'s Madrid correspondent: 'the rumour arose that a government aeroplane had been told to commit an act of frightfulness . . .'[11] Surely, the question must at least be posed: *where would the grand narrative of 'Fascist Barbarism' stand – not to mention the portentous history of 'Fascist Intervention in Spain' – were either of these 'explanations' of 30 October to have substance?*

In recent decades hundreds of survivors and other witnesses of aerial bombardment on the Republican side have been interviewed in the course of various historical investigations into daily life behind the lines. None has ever recalled 30 October as having any special – let alone apocalyptic – significance. None has remembered anything relating to 'Getafe'.[12] It may be argued that bombing atrocity was *mainly* a thematic package meant for export and not for domestic consumption. No photographs of the Koltsov dossier variety ever appeared in the contemporary Spanish press, any more than its reporters described scenes of carnage and destruction or provided lists of victims. In this, at least, 'Getafe' was no different from any other bombing incident. But it remains a matter for puzzlement that news of its extraordinary horror apparently did not travel into the streets (and hotels) of nearby Madrid via the bush-telegraph of refugees or retreating combatants.[13]

Thus the time has come to ask another, less rhetorical but equally vital question about 'Getafe'. It is the same question we find pre-echoed by Malraux's fictional hero (quoted above) and by William Soutar's poems in 1937. *What about the children? Who were these children?* From the 'Koltsov Dossier' of at least eighteen individual photo portraits, nine specimens of contemporary provenance are extant in the archive of the International Brigade British Battalion, housed in the Marx Memorial Library (London).[14] Each is captioned with the information that the photograph was taken in the 'depositario judicial' (police mortuary) of Madrid on 31 October 1936, and portrays a victim killed by aerial bombing on 30 October. Each carries a name and (with one exception) address.

The sequence is as follows (the tag number appears first):

Tag Number	Name	Address
4–21–35	María Santiago Robert	Calle de la Paloma, No. 6
46–21–89	José Pomar Montes	address unknown
7–21–30	Blas Forte Blanco	Calle de Humilladero, No. 26
29	Juana Blanco de Castro	Plaza del Marqués de Comillas, No. 5
73–22–11	Pedro Carrascal Puertobarrero	Calle de Amparo, No. 12
53–21–96	Josefa Sánchez Pastor	Calle de Amparo, No. 27
75–22–13	Francisco Chamorro Pastor	Calle de Amparo, No. 13
95–21–136	Teodoro Fort Blanco	Calle de Humilladero, No. 26
99–22–38	Carmén García Cisneros	Calle de Nuncio, No. 9

Without exception, the addresses correspond to central Madrid, and to various *barrios* immediately to the south of the seventeenth-century Plaza Mayor. Housing in these narrow, warren-like streets is also of considerable antiquity. In October 1936, their apartments had few facilities and were desperately overcrowded. The children were nearly all wearing coats or warm clothing, and had obviously been playing in the street. Bombs fell in at least four streets. Victims evidently included siblings, cousins and/or neighbours. But none of them was killed in Getafe.[15] From this, it seems reasonable (though not definitive) to suppose there were no *Getafeños* amongst nine other children, those whose pictures are absent from the IBA collection.

For some time the secret of 'Getafe' remained within a relatively small circle of initiates – Alvarez del Vayo and some assistants, certain members of Madrid's *Junta de Defensa*, and Soviet advisers.[16] Meanwhile 'Getafe' was, in so far as practically feasible, withdrawn from circulation.[17] The Junkers, which had been quite literally inked in to some other photographs of the kind which provided 'evidence' of military intervention by the Fascist powers, now had to be – in this case metaphorically – airbrushed out of the scene.[18] The message never got through to some corners of the Comintern network, two salient cases being the publicist Peter Merin, who operated on behalf of the German communist resistance, and the British–Czech reporter Frank Jellinek, who worked for the *Manchester Guardian*.[19] But in terms of the subsequent history of the Spanish Civil War, the Getafe story was stillborn (or rather, aborted) and the foetus buried at night in a shallow grave. As we have seen, the abstracted details themselves remained in circulation to provide a 'bombing thesaurus' of propaganda effusion in picture, poetry and prose. Following 26 April 1937, these tropes were usefully re-absorbed into the Gernika campaign, to become part of a reified litany of fascist barbarism. Of course, it was more difficult to withdraw The Poster, copies of which had been distributed worldwide (though perhaps not in any great profusion).[20] But here, too, the scene depicted proved readily adaptable to the circumstances of Gernika/Guernica – event *and* painting – which was now the central mediator in the minds of observers.

The most extravagant of all these depictions was that given by the Aragonese writer, Ramón Sender. Before the war a mordant critic of the Republic from the left-wing perspective, Sender volunteered for militia service in 1936 and was stationed near Getafe in the hours immediately following the alleged incident. He later published an autobiographical, 'factional' account of this period, devoting a chapter to a heart-rending evocation of 'Aeroplanes Over Madrid':

> Sometimes they threw bombs on a 'school group'. The little shelters in gardens could not be mistaken for arsenals, workshops or barracks, and then seventy, eighty, a hundred, in one case three hundred and nine children were killed, which filled the suburb, the city and loyal Spain with the deepest mourning and an infinite grief. Why children? Why these lives of five or six years and of unlimited hopes? The metal, even the smallest fragment, was monstrously too large for their small breasts ... By their blood, their tender arms broken, and their eyes which passed from astonishment at life to astonishment at death before having seen anything ...[21]

Sender's fellow warrior, author of a generically identical novel, André Malraux, ended his book by speculating on the nature of sacrificial commitment. Why do men and women decide voluntarily to place their bodies and their lives between a perceived aggressor and his potential victim? 'Garcia' arrives at some startling conclusions:

> After eight months of war there's something that still remains a mystery to me – the exact moment when a man decides to pick up a rifle? ... What interests me is the actual spark that sets them off. It seems as if fighting, the apocalypse, and hope, are baits used by war to catch men. After all, syphilis starts with love. Pugnacity forms part of the play-acting in which almost every man indulges in, and it leads men into war just as every sort of play-acting leads us right into life.[22]

'Getafe' seems precisely the kind of spark Garcia is talking about. Many Spanish Civil War posters warned soldiers against the dangers of venereal disease, and there were times in which contraction thereof was regarded as a self-inflicted wound and punished appropriately. In a scenario which might push Malraux's fancy to its logical conclusion, The Poster becomes a work of pornography – 'the pornography of violence' as Gamel Woolsey called it – and child 4–21–35 a sort of prostitute. One relevant echo of 'Getafe' came from the pen of the American communist and celebrated commander of the Lincoln Battalion

in Spain, Milt Wolff, who in his autobiographical novel describes a
victim of an air raid in Barcelona:

> a young girl, a kid with her dress pulled slantingly up across her
> waist, white and hairless in the grey gloom, smooth, rounded,
> unwrinkled, innocent. The attendant who brought her out yanked
> the girl's dress down. Making her, Leo mused, decently dead . . . yet
> by death deflowered.[23]

In one of the rare exceptions to the effective ban on use of the
Koltsov dossier, a poster issued in Valencia in late 1936 utilized
eight of its portraits. The grim gallery is headed by the symbolic
victim María Santiago (aka '4–21–35'), a girl whose very names
are suffused with the aura of the Spanish Christian Virgin and her
traditional warrior-saint champion, the killer of Moors. The poster's legend reads: 'Murderers! Which of you on seeing this would
not take up a gun in order to crush Fascism, the destroyer?'[24]
Another poster with the same import shows two children hiding
in a sewer, anxiously looking up at the sky: they accuse the
observer – 'are you doing anything to prevent this?'[25] In this
sense, the central propaganda artefact and stimulus of the present
book represents a classic genre, the recruiting poster; María
Santiago being (as it were) lineally descended from Lord Kitchener. It cannot be doubted that thousands responded in the
desired spirit, enlisting to fight and die in the 'struggle against
Fascism'. Thus The Poster is not the only memorial to the Getafe
incident, since it might be argued that its legacy lays claim to a
share of the willing self-sacrifice of volunteer combatants –
whether Spaniards or not – who came to the defence of the
Republican cause. It seems not by mere happenstance that the
end cover of the official book dedicated to International Brigade
Memorials in the United Kingdom and Ireland should consist of a
reproduction of The Poster.[26]

However, the question of which story we can now accept in the
empirical world simply does not arise: all the versions emanating
from contemporary Republican and pro-Republican sources are
equally fictional. In broad ethical terms, the self-contradictory,
self-negating web of lies presented and analysed in the broad body
of this book almost succeeds in achieving the exact opposite of
what it intended – and which, for seventy years, it brought about.
Its mock atrocity vitiates the truth of real atrocity, almost deflecting blame from the Junkers and their masters over the

events of a day which has been dubiously presented as a watershed in the history of war and war crime. Both the doom-laden skies of 30 October and the Getafe children who died under them have become irremediably part of a tableau of dramatic deceit. Of course, it would be wrong to assert that there was nothing more to it than that, to claim that the children were nothing more than puppet propaganda tragedians. The real tragedy remains that Koltsov's children were killed, probably on 30 October, *almost* certainly by enemy bombs, which were very likely dropped from Junker aircraft crewed by German or Spanish Nationalist personnel.

This leaves to be considered the mundane, in some ways almost immaterial, question of *what actually happened at Getafe*. Despite its apparent absurdity, we can only begin to construct an answer with a deductive summary of *what did not happen*, those features of the story which are definitively or very strongly contra-indicated by what has gone before in this book. First and foremost, we believe this material justifies the following conclusions. That (on this occasion) no children were deliberately murdered by 'fascists'; no Junkers plane swooped low to drop its bombs on specific civilians; no squadron of bombers circled over the town targeting residential areas; no photographs of dead children were consequently taken. Thus far, we can assert that the details provided initially by the Republican Ministry of State to George Ogilvie-Forbes; subsequently propagated by various agencies of the Comintern outside Spain – in particular by the *Daily Worker*, Peter Merin, and Frank Jellinek; and later recapitulated in the published recollections of Arturo Barea, are without empirical foundation.

On the other hand, common sense suggests the unlikelihood of pure, unalloyed invention. María Santiago was certainly a virgin, but was not the result of some parthenogenesis. After all, Getafe airbase had been the objective of sporadic air raids ever since August. Post-war judicial proceedings of the victorious regime in the town indicate strongly (if indirectly) that, in the course of such attacks, civilians had been killed and injured. Thus, some 'collateral damage' was a fact.[27] Furthermore, in the days immediately before and after 30 October, Getafe (airfield and town) formed the epicentre of the war's headline military exchanges.[28] The decisive repulse of the Seseña offensive enabled Varela's Nationalist column quickly to advance within artillery

range of the town, but this situation was not effective until some
forty-eight hours after the alleged atrocity. Meanwhile, Getafe was
crammed with defeated and/or desperate soldiery of all descriptions. These included aviators, who were taking off from the
airstrip, either in attempts to delay the enemy advance or (more
likely) to save themselves and their machines from capture or
destruction. Nationalist operational reports for 30 October
describe the shooting down in flames of three Republican Potez
bombers, one of which fell 'on enemy lines close to Getafe'.[29]
One week later, a British reporter 'embedded' with the Nationalist army reported *en passant* that 'Red' planes that were shot
down, allegedly in large numbers, often crashed directly onto
houses and streets below.[30]

If there was a deadly explosion in the streets of Getafe on that
day, it might (alternatively) have been the result of an accident
involving a 'friendly' sortie. As historians of the Spanish war have
pointed out, losses of planes on both sides were frequently due to
accidents.[31] In the Republic's case the promiscuous mix of
machine types, along with lack of experience and expertise,
meant that downings were as much the result of shortcomings of
supply and incompetence of personnel as to its adversary's attentions. Even when ground staff were not under the kind of
pressure present at Getafe on 30 October, machines sometimes
took to the air after incomplete or inadequate repair, and/or with
incomplete or inadequate equipment, often with disastrous
results. Contraptions fitted to antiquated biplanes for the manipulation and sighting of bombs were notoriously crude and unreliable. A plane, or even one bomb, falling out of the sky because of
hasty and faulty maintenance work could have had dreadful
consequences for innocent bystanders in the vicinity of the run-
way.[32] And what of the victims? Though attempts had been made
to evacuate non-combatants, more than one eyewitness speaks of
children still being present in Getafe on 30 October. However, in
the chaotic and dangerous circumstances obtaining, they were
surely not playing in groups on the streets, far less calmly attend-
ing classes at school.[33]

As we have seen from material reviewed at various points
above, all these doubts and queries may well be applied to the
'siege of Madrid' itself, and perhaps to the whole issue of the
'bombing of open towns'. Most of the specialist monographs
agree that a sustained air campaign against the capital city took

place over a period of about three weeks, between *c.*30 October and *c.*23 November 1936.[34] Even experts not well-disposed towards the Republican cause tend to accept (in the words of a recent example) that the air bombardment of Madrid was 'basically criminal'.[35] It is generally stated that on a regular (some give, daily) basis during this campaign planes deliberately dropped bombs on residential areas, and/or that air crews sent to hit military objectives were wholly indifferent to the plight of non-combatant citizens living adjacent to their targets. But when these studies are analysed, it can only be concluded that the great bulk of relevant detail originates from (mainly foreign) newspaper reports, or the published memoirs of Republican-based fighters and journalists, and that these in turn were based to a crucial extent on information provided by Republican ministerial sources. Geoffrey Cox, who was present in Madrid, and later published a detailed narrative of this period and subject, though stoutly denying that he was 'spoonfed' information, as good as admitted that the Austrian socialist, Ilsa Kulcsar, who worked alongside Barea in the Telefónica censorship office, was the main source of his 'human interest' stories. Cox's book recapitulates all the details by now familiar to readers, but only once does he (vaguely) intimate personal witness of the human consequences of an air raid.[36] Another reporter, who described scenes of chaos and carnage as a result of one 'ruthless bombardment' which accounted for 'wives in shopping queues [and] children playing in the streets' admitted that 'I watched the whole raid from the comparative safety of north Madrid'.[37] As Emile Témime has pointed out, 'quand on cherche des articles de première main sur les épisodes importants de cette première partie de la guerre, on s'aperçoit qu'ils sont singulièrement rares.'[38] And even if we did not know about control of the press by the *Junta de Defensa,* the sheer amount and stark profile of the detail shared between and constantly recycled by war correspondents in Madrid would surely give cause for scepticism.

Another factor on which the experts widely concur is also anomalous in one key respect. Bombing damage is seen as reaching its greatest intensity at exactly the time (following 2–3 November) that Soviet 'Chato' and 'Mosca' fighters appeared in numbers over Madrid, decisively restoring command of its air space to the defenders. Thus, without benefit of the Condor Legion, and with fewer than thirty machines operational in this period – fewer still available for any given day's sorties – the Francoists were apparently able to reduce one-third of Madrid to ruins *at exactly the time that Republican sources claimed that they were being driven from the skies!* Little wonder that one historian refers to 'the bombardment of propaganda' as being more important than, and bearing little empirical relationship to, the bombardments themselves: or that (at the time) the pro-Republican US ambassador in Madrid assured his president that 'nine-tenths of the press reports are false. I have not seen, even during the World War, such persistent and outrageous propaganda'.[39] As a French (Marxist) expert, a strong advocate of the Republican cause, has concluded, censorship was 'almost total' on both sides, and was used to create misinformation as much as to stifle information.[40]

It remains the case – something which would be a matter for amazement in any other country but Spain – that no historian has yet been able to mount a sustained search of sources which may still be found in the municipal and state archives at Madrid, and among the State Administration Archives in Alcalá de Henares. As long ago as the 1960s, Gabriel Jackson gained access to some Madrid police records concerning bomb damage. Collating the data thus gained with a range of published sources, he concluded that

> Acting on German theories of war, Mola attempted to terrorize the city into surrender by indiscriminate bombing. But he did not have an airforce comparable to those which flattened English and German cities during the Second World War, and his raids, made by about a dozen planes each day, killed less than 50 persons on each occasion.

In relevant footnotes, Jackson added that (1) 'on November 2 Russian fighters appeared for the first time, and on the fifth, they forced the Junker bombers to turn back, so that in fact these raids reinforced the fighting morale of Madrid...'; and that (2) 'figures vary very widely for the air-raid casualties in October and November. My "less than fifty" is based upon municipal police reports of Madrid which I had occasion to examine for the period October 20–November 20.'[41]

If we accept that at least one raid was made every day, and fixing Jackson's viscous coefficient at fifty (rather than 'less') deaths per day over thirty-one days, a maximum death toll of 1,550 would result. If there were two raids every three days – a

figure which seems inherently more likely – this maximum would
be 1,000. As it happens, the latter total accords quite closely with
contemporary official Republican claims. But such figures are
inconsistent with the comparative example cited by Jackson. In
March 1941, at the height of the Blitz, with nightly raids involving
not eight or a dozen but hundreds of much heavier bombers,
hugely greater explosive power and numbers of projectiles, 4,300
Londoners were killed at a daily average of 139.[42] In other words,
the official figures for Madrid represent a considerable exaggeration: if you like, propaganda. We should not be surprised that
women and children in food queues gave little evidence of being
terrorized by Mola's bombers, any more than they were by the
teams of 'fascist snipers' that the same general allegedly summoned to his aid.

Yet even as I write (winter 2004–05) the Municipality of Madrid
is lobbying the national Cortes for the removal of General
Franco's statue from its position outside government buildings,
on the grounds that he 'betrayed his military oath' in ordering
the indiscriminate bombing of the city and its population.[43] Six
years ago, the Cortes, then dominated by a centre-right party,
passed a resolution asking the government to proclaim as an
official principle of state that Franco directly ordered the destruction of Gernika carried out by the Condor Legion. This would
have established an unproven allegation of mass murder against a
deceased head of state as an item of constitutional law, with a
corresponding sanction upon Spanish nationals analogous to that
incumbent upon Germans in respect of the Jewish Holocaust.[44]
Yet thousands of Spaniards refuse to accept Francoist responsibility for the atrocity of Gernika. Although I do not agree with
their reasons, it would be unreasonable to assume their dishonesty, and criminal to assert their criminality. Not too long ago,
renewed assertions that Gernika was razed by the Basque militia
and not by German incendiary bombs (as Nationalist sources
claimed) were not uncommon. This may be no more than
obstinate recalcitrance, but even this is understandable when we
recall the rankling inspiration to disbelief caused by certain
counter-productive excesses of Republican propaganda. One that
springs to mind in this context is the story from September 1936
that claimed that the town of Irún was destroyed by German
planes, and its maternity hospital 'full of mothers and new-born
babies' burned to the ground. In fact, as shortly became well

established, the burning of the town was carried out by retreating Republican militia units.[45]

NOTES

1 *Daily Worker*, 5 February 1937, p. 4.
2 *The Volunteer for Liberty*, 8 November 1937, p. 3.
3 See above, p. 100.
4 On Vallecas, Barea (1946/1984), p. 284 and Appendix A, below p. 273–9. On Tarancón, Jellinek (1938), p. 597; Fyrth (1986), pp. 76–7.
5 *Bombardements* (1938), especially p. 52. The figure for deaths included 879 in Madrid alone. The total given for injuries was 15,320.
6 Machado (1937).
7 Vinyes (1937/1978), esp. pp. 13–20, 31–2.
8 'El Triste Papel de los Alemanes'; BNA FO 371/21287/W5173.
9 *Spain Illustrated – A Year's Defence of Democracy* (July, 1937) unpaginated. This item was also probably contributed by the Spanish embassy.
10 Malraux (1938/1979), p. 305. See also above, p. 205–7. 'Garcia' is a conflation of two Soviet intelligence chiefs, Mikhail Koltsov and Vladmir Goriev: see Jato Miranda (1976), 323. A scholarly study of the Madrid 'Fifth Column' is sceptical that sabotage operations were either conducted or co-ordinated on a large scale: Cervera (1998), especially 257ff.
11 'The Bombing of Madrid – An Uncensored Account', *The Times*, 23 January 1937; for context, see above, pp. 55–6 and 93ff.
12 For Madrid, see esp. Vidal (1996); for Barcelona, Serra & Serra (2003), both *passim*.
13 With the exceptions made in ch. 6 above, no foreign visitor to Madrid at the time evinced any awareness of 'Getafe'. In late 1936, the Republic published a pamphlet incorporating photographic material presented to the British parliamentary delegation in November (see above, pp. 181–3). The 'Getafe' children were not included; *Documento* (1936). Similar negative evidence applies to (e.g.) *Ayuda* (1937); *Agressions* (1938) and *El Fascismo* (1937). Although these examples were published in Spanish, they were probably aimed at mobilizing support for the Republic in Hispanic America.
14 IBA Box A-2, photographs D55–63. These probably reached the CPGB via the Spanish embassy.
15 Of course, it is not beyond the bounds of possibility that some victims may have been recently evacuated to Madrid from that *pueblo*.
16 These categories are not mutually exclusive.
17 Barea himself saw examples of the photo dossier used as part of a propaganda exhibition about 'suffering Madrid' put on in Barcelona in the last days of 1938: Barea (1946/1984), p. 377.

18 See *Bombardements* (1938), p. 12, where dozens of extra plane silhou-
    ettes have been crudely drawn onto the original in order to show an
    overhead sky black with 'Junkers', creating a 'spot the real bomber'
    conundrum.

19 See Merin (1938), pp. 217, 315 and picture captions, and also the
    anonymous pamphlet *Erlebnisse* (1938); and Jellinek (1938), p. 511.
    (Merin's real name was perhaps Pedro Merino.)

20 Only two extant examples are known to me in the UK; at the
    Imperial War Museum (London) and the Museum of Labour History
    (Manchester).

21 Sender (1937), pp. 203–12, especially 205. The 'suburb' here evid-
    ently intends the town of Getafe.

22 Malraux (1938/1979), p. 503.

23 Wolff (1994), p. 281.

24 'Niños muertos en Madrid por las bombas facciosas', Carulla &
    Carulla (1997) No. 1245, p. 376. This is certainly the poster seen by
    Barea in Valencia in December 1936; Barea (1946/1984), p. 255. Cf.
    similar contemporary use of the photo dossier, Carulla & Carulla,
    nos 717–8, p. 228.

25 See Anderson (2003), between pp. 98 and 99. Similar posters were
    used to whip up hatred for the 'fifth column'. One showed bombs
    falling from a Nazi plane onto a screaming mother and child. 'We
    accuse the enemy of murder – children and women innocent victims.
    Free men repudiate all those who help fascism from behind our
    lines'; Van Hensbergen (2004), 34.

26 C. Williams *et al.* (1996).

27 See above, pp. 82–3.

28 For full narrative material and references on this point, see ch. 6,
    above.

29 Gárate Córdoba (1977–78), I, p. 61.

30 H. Cardozo in the *Daily Mail*, 6 November 1936, p. 15.

31 For example, Beevor (2006), p. 235.

32 A further consideration for which little space is available here is that
    of anti-aircraft fire. Getafe airfield was defended by artillery batteries.
    Such units often fired far more than was necessary or wise. Faulty
    rounds which failed to explode in the air were likely to do so when
    hitting the ground. Even shrapnel falling from such heights could
    kill and maim. See Knoblaugh (1937), p. 100ff.; Spender (1978), p.
    74.

33 On 31 October, one school was being used as a dressing-station; Cox
    (1937), p. 13.

34 Montoliú Camps (1999), I, p. 170ff.; Reig Tapia (1999), pp. 216–22;
    Romero (2001), pp. 144–50; Reverte (2004), p. 142ff. All these give
    slightly differing dates and other details.

35 Moa (2002), pp. 336–7. Also broadly unsubscribing of the 'myth of
    Madrid' is Jato Miranda (1976), p. 367ff.

36 Cox (1937), *passim* but esp. pp. 73–4 and 195.

37 *Daily Herald*, 9 and 10 November 1936. J. Stubbs Walker wrote at first
    that 'the real force of the raid was directed on the government forces

246 *Your Children Will Be Next*

in the Carabanchel area', but changed this opinion the following day. Carabanchel, at the city's southern tip, was the only residential *barrio* to be (partly) occupied by the Nationalists during the siege – a permanent battleground, completely cleared of non-combatants.

[38] Témime (1986), p. 65.
[39] Rey García (1997), pp. 191–2.
[40] Témime (1986), p. 66.
[41] Jackson (1965), pp. 320–1. Unfortunately, Professor Jackson did not specify the place where he consulted these documents; nor the substantive data on which his estimates were based; nor the statistical method he utilized in arriving at them.
[42] Gilbert (1989), pp. 148 and 167.
[43] *El País*, 6 November 2004. (I owe this snippet to Dr J. Ruiz.) The deed was duly done under cover of darkness and official subterfuge in the early morning of 17 March 2005; see *The Guardian*, 18 March. For discussion of Franco's culpability, above pp. 51–2.
[44] 'Verdad Oficial' by J. García Añoveros, *El País*, 8 July 1999.
[45] Brothers (1997), p. 112, and sources cited. See also the recent equivocation in Hensbergen (2005), pp. 36 and 42.

Chapter 16

Journey to Getafe

It is important to emphasize in advance that my treatment does not mean to suggest that air raids mounted by either side during the war were part of *a deliberate operational policy of attacking civilian populations*, or that relevant casualties resulted from specific orders given to the flying personnel involved in a particular sortie.

I

After one of many robust bouts of debate with my alter ego, I deleted the above sentence from a draft of Chapter 3 – which is printed above as thus shorn. But now, as its restoration here suggests, neither of us feels quite comfortable with this decision. Congenital uncertainty and occasional discomfort are characteristics of study of the Spanish Civil War: and perhaps they should be more characteristic than they have traditionally been of the study of history as a whole. A prominent protagonist of this book, because one of the most proficient contemporary disseminators of the Getafe story, is Arthur Koestler. An extravagantly gifted polymath, a writer who could seamlessly combine intensity of political dialectic with personal psychology and narrative imagination, a man endowed with both moral and physical courage, in later years Koestler became as strongly committed to the anti-communist camp as he previously had been to the Bolshevik cause itself. In the 1950s, morosely reflecting on the war in Spain, he admitted 'we know now that out truth was a half-truth, our fight a battle in the mist, and that those who suffered and died in it were pawns in a complicated game between two totalitarian pretenders for world domination'.[1]

The unexpectedly extended journey towards producing this book has given me plenty of time to reconsider its arguments and conclusions. It has brought me to the conclusion that the immediate context of the Getafe atrocity as conveyed in many textbooks and specialist studies of the war (particularly published material concerned with 'the siege of Madrid') has something like the status of a half-truth, whilst the atrocity itself has no essential (as opposed to accidental) truth in it. Having once again re-read all that is written above, I consider it more than likely that on 30 October 1936 there was no massed-bomber raid (involving, say, more than six units) on Madrid:[2] that there was no deliberate attack on the residential areas of Getafe; that the children featured in 'the Koltsov Dossier' were not killed there; and that they were not killed in a school. Of course, absence of evidence should not be given equal status with evidence of absence. This professional cliché has become a truism, and might soon be needed as a motto. Moreover, on the balance of probabilities, it seems very likely that children were killed in Getafe during the course of the war – even, perhaps, by Republican air attacks, which naturally began once the town and its air base passed into Nationalist hands. This chapter might not be the end; rather than the terminus, it could be merely another station on the line. In any event, for the time being, since a book insists on being completed and granted rest, I too will go to rest my head in some *posada* near the railway line and in sight of the horizon, and sleep with one eye open for breaking news.

Quite a few stops back down the line, in June 2001, I paid a visit to Getafe. It seems that nothing has ever been heard in the town concerning María Santiago Robert and her playtime companions. Even at that stage of my work, having surveyed various Getafe community websites, boasting history pages that shimmied smoothly around the years 1936–9, I had no expectations of finding a public memorial to the alleged tragedy of 30 October 1936. Neither was I surprised that no reference to them could be found in the Municipal Archive. This latter lacuna would be credibly explained by the violent circumstances of Getafe's war experience, and especially of its capture by Varela's command on 4 November 1936. Even if not accounted for by the random destruction of combat, both sides had both reason and opportunity to destroy or remove compromising documentary materials. What gave me more pause for thought, as I ordered up (as they proved, deceptively) relevant-looking files was that the duty archivist had not the least cognisance of the event I hoped to research. Thereafter, evidence of a wider absence of local memory accreted quickly. The curator of a local art gallery had likewise never heard of 'Getafe'. In one of the oldest buildings still standing in the town, the Hospital de San José (1502), founded by the Church as a refuge for the relief of the poor and sick, now a day-centre for senior citizens, I accosted the janitor, who it turned out was born in Getafe in 1937. He remembered his place of employment being used as a school for war orphans in the 1940s, but insisted firmly that no bombing of children had happened in Getafe. 'Why don't you try Griñón?' he suggested.[3] As we were talking, the institution's young chaplain joined us, and confirmed his colleague's remarks. As I later discovered, a retired Spanish academic with family antecedents in the town has also attempted to follow up the story of Getafe's children, with similarly negative results. His son wrote to me on his behalf that 'like you, he has found no-one who remembers anything about the event [of 30 October 1936] and little or nothing is recorded in local chronicles.'[4]

Present-day denials ought not to be regarded as deliberately evasive. Unlike a thousand other cases scattered all over Spain, they are nothing to do with 'collective amnesia', or with residual anxiety about summoning up avenging spirits. Given the horrendous events of October–November, the headlong flight and dispersal of Getafe's population, the obliteration of its physical structure during the battle for its capture, and the climate of fear and persecution existing both before and after its fall, it seems unlikely that many pre-war denizens would ever have returned to resume their previous lives in the town. Even if some tragic event involving the deaths of children had occurred, the chances of finding any drops of recollection in the swirling seas of modern *urbanización* would have been remote. Meanwhile the community has achieved an entirely new character, and one which in the new millennium both reflects local prosperity and indicates maturity of aspiration and identity. In 2004 Getafe's football club achieved promotion to the *Primera Liga* for the first time, and in March 2005 scored its first victory over Real Madrid.

But exactly twelve months before this landmark, in a manner impossible to foresee, Getafe had been caught up in another tragic bombing incident. It was a terrorist atrocity in the full sense

of the term, intended to inspire panic fear in the people of
Madrid and of Spain. On 11 March 2004, nearly 200 people,
including several children, were murdered when bombs placed in
commuter trains heading into Madrid's Atocha Station were
detonated by members of a radical Islamic cell. During the
ensuing emergency operation, wounded victims were taken to
hospitals in various outlying centres, including Getafe.[5] For me,
this particular news item brought to mind the hurried removal of
the inmates of that same hospital in the opposite direction, from
the pathway of Varela's all-conquering column towards the comparative safety of Madrid's urban mass. In the immediate aftermath of the 2004 outrage, images of the civil war and the siege of
Madrid returned likewise to many minds in Spain. The day after
the bombs, *El País*, Spain's leading left-liberal newspaper, carried
many pages of extended comment by political writers and others.
Although responsibility for the murders had not yet been claimed
or (officially) attributed, contributors made ominous connections
with the events of autumn 1936:

> Once again, as in the Civil War, Madrid is the capital of suffering,
> the crucified city, the city martyred for democracy. Time flies and
> banners change, but fanaticism remains. Then Fascism bombarded
> Madrid, and now it is bombarded by fanatics who emerge from the
> darkest corners ... The cold cruelty of the torturer, the precise
> calculations of the sadist, the blindness of absolute evil, have, it
> seems, fallen on Madrid. *Franco acted in the same way. Cold, implacable
> and unbiddable, he preyed upon the heroic people of Madrid during our
> Civil War.* Some military historians explain that Franco had more
> than enough resources to beat down the capital's defences and
> quickly to make himself its master. But he preferred to bleed it
> slowly, and in this manner to destroy not only the Republic but also
> the civic values on which it was founded, robbing the population of
> any hope that democracy would one day be restored. He promoted
> mutilation, he favoured death, he spread humiliation, he carved
> the memory of pain on the hearts of survivors. This was the tactic
> of the dictator during the siege of Madrid ...[6]

Another contributor, like the majority of Spaniards more in
bemusement than self-righteous certainty, but still assuming the
horror was the handiwork of the Basque terrorist organization
ETA, pointed out that

> Under Franco, Madrid suffered the same oppression as the Basque
> Country or any other region of Spain – perhaps more, given that

the central government was situated here, able to control and repress with greater ease 'in its own backyard'. Today it has again been visited with maximum oppression. It could have happened anywhere else, except that only here live numbers of people sufficient to guarantee the greater harvest of victims.[7]

The mayor of Barcelona wrote to offer his city's solidarity with Madrid, just as in the crisis of 1936 thousands of Catalan militiamen had come to its defence against Franco:

> In the face of such monstrosities as these, in which innocent lives are claimed – like those endured by Barcelona and Madrid under the indiscriminate bombing of the civil war – in these sad hours, our citizens feel a fraternal sense of unity.[8]

A well-established columnist, Antonio Múñoz Molina, readily agreed that

> Today Madrid has suffered a calamity just as criminal as those provoked by bombardments of the fascist airforce during the war. Some bombs touch us all, and these examples are just like those which fell on the poor districts of Madrid, on the working people, on the most innocent. **In November 1936, according to Antonio Machado, Madrid was smiling 'with lead in its guts',** and in the middle of suffering erected a popular fortress which gallantly resisted fascist aggression.

However, this particular observer marked himself off from the rest. He warned in solemn and striking terms against the atavistic passions which extravagant writing might awake:

> After all, Madrid is the seat of a government against which any insult, it seems, can be legitimately made, which is presented to us not as a government of the right – which it is – but as if it were a prolongation of the Francoist dictatorship. Reading the papers, listening to various radio talks, or to certain artists or writers who have elected themselves as champions of a popular rebellion, one might think that it was not in power as a result of free elections, but because of a *coup d'état*. It has been said and written that our governing party is identical to the terrorists in its extremism and unwillingness to compromise; that it represents those who murdered García Lorca; or even those who used to sing 'Cara al Sol'. These things have been said and written, and repeated many times, mixing truth with lies, mixing justified criticism and rejection with the most insensate accusations. The result has been a rupture of the most primordial elements of civil concord, a

bastardization of the state which does not undermine the present
government so much as democracy itself. . . [9]

Despite – indeed partly because of – the fact that within a few
days a majority of Spaniards became convinced that ETA was
guiltless of the events of 11 March, this has proved an accurate
prediction. For developing events brought about not only the
unexpected defeat of the Conservative (Partido Popular) government at the impending elections – generally agreed to be the
terrorist's main objective – but also in subsequent months a new
and more frenetic outburst of media-inspired anti-Francoism. The
latter phenomenon, which had been smouldering since the mid-
1990s, is focussed on the campaign to exhume, document and
memorialize the many thousands of victims of Nationalist repression both during and after the war.[10] The feelings involved had
already led (inter alia) to the banning of academics wishing to
pour the oils of tolerance and compromise on troubled waters
from speaking at universities; and the outright rejection by prominent experts as not worthy of serious attention of a new and
scholarly four-volume study of the civil war which challenged the
commandments of the orthodox majority.[11] Since 11 March,
however, campaigners have gone much further, adopting not just
the positive principle of restitution for one side but adding its
negative, deprivation for the other. This takes them into the very
realms of censorship and repression of history which, up till now,
has been the campaign's main point of condemnation. The
campaign now demands the final and official destruction of all
'fascist' monuments, the changing of street names that com-
memorate prominent Francoist generals, and the removal of
Madrid's last statue of Franco – as the man who ordered the
bombing of the capital in 1936.[12]

As I write, a year after the awful murders of March 2004, Sñr
Múñoz Molina's words are acquiring an ever more prophetic
force. The division of Spain over the origins, motives and consequences of the atrocity continues to deepen. Indeed, these
fractures in the nation's body politic seem more fundamental –
even disturbing – than at any other time since the death of the
dictator and the beginning of Spain's miraculous transition to
democracy. There are virulent disputes over responsibility for
11-M, over the circumstances in which the PSOE came to power,
over the proceedings of the Cortes Committee of Investigation.

The vindictive clashes of the main party protagonists are being fuelled almost to a point of combustion by outrageous media manoeuvring.

II

On the eve of these convulsions, the first attempt at a serious revaluation of the air war in Spain was published by two Catalan scholars.[13] It marked a partial departure from previous habits. For the first time, not only did professional historians face up to the uncomfortable reality of Republican participation in the 'bombing of open towns', but they also provided some narrative detail of these events. On the face of things, this seemed encouraging. However, in practice a total of just twenty pages in a text of over 300 suffices to establish both the fact itself, and – much more importantly for the authors – its comparative material and moral insignificance alongside the similar actions of the other side.[14] (For example, the new monograph also devoted twenty pages to the bombing of Madrid alone.) Though giving a new lease of life to the claim that sixty children died in Getafe on 30 October, its authors also argue that it was not until the last week of Franco's onslaught that the capital city was subjected to 'the methodical killing of its civil population'.[15] Despite this conclusion, in most relevant areas of probability, the evidence seems weighted against the belief that any sustained and systematic aerial campaign aimed at the working-class inhabitants of Madrid ever happened; against the occurrence of massive civilian mortality, either of children, or of any other category of humanity, during Franco's assault on the capital;[16] and against any deliberate air attack on the residential districts of Getafe during defence of its air base against the Nationalists. In the last of these cases, therefore, this book has been dealing with an imaginary tragedy; but one whose morbid influence has helped inspire, over several generations, the monstrous anger of many guns and words.[17]

We cannot escape treating the matter of responsibility. So far (and despite the exposition with which I opened this final chapter) I have drawn back from asserting an opinion that *any given air raid, mounted by either side, was the result of a deliberate operational policy of attacking civilian populations.* Equally, I have refrained from implying that relevant casualties *resulted from specific orders* given to the flying personnel involved in a particular sortie. Of course, the *possibility* remains that such orders were issued, along with the *probability* that air crews did at times, and with calculated indifference, release bombs above urban areas of no military significance. Such action might have occurred for various reasons. These include self-preservation, when pursued by fighters or threatened by flak, perhaps when also needing to save fuel in order to recover their bases; or for personal reasons of bravado, vengeance, vindictiveness or mere caprice. Yet a well-known veteran of the Spanish War, following experiences which famously led him to expose and condemn the communist propaganda machine in Spain, and even after some years of reflection, *still wanted others to believe that the Franco war effort had been essentially rather than accidentally barbaric.* In a BBC radio broadcast in May 1942, George Orwell remarked on 'the Nazi airmen serving with General Franco [who] deliberately carried out wherever they went the most atrocious raids on open towns, *deliberately aiming their bombs on residential working-class districts,* with the idea of terrorising the people into surrender.'[18]

Throughout the recent Spanish monograph already mentioned, a double standard of ethical assessment is presented in appropriate language: emotive and detailed about Nationalist raids, abstract and vague when it comes to those of the Republic. In their conclusion, the authors consider that the ultimate distinction lies in the area of intention. The Francoists, they assert, *frequently* attacked urban targets lacking any military significance; the corollary negative and opposite about the Republic wisely is left unstated, *but nonetheless voluble.*[19] Such misleading conclusions, presented by expert authors, led inevitably to renewed assertions by lesser authorities like the British academic Helen Graham, whose recent popular introduction to the war alleges that

> Franco had no doubt that he was justified in using terror against the civilian population. He opened cities and towns to mass aerial bombing . . . What has remained particularly shocking about the air raids to outside observers is that . . . Franco was doing it to his 'own' people . . .[20]

But as we have seen at various points above, contemporary evidence suggests that the number of such 'terror raids' can be pinned down with relative confidence to little more than a handful. And the final ethical balance is worse still for the

Republic. It is not just that their side started the 'terror raids' and showed the way to their enemies during the opening campaigns of the war. But also, acting on the basis of its own propaganda, for much of the war (in practice, for as long as it was physically able) the Republican air force carried on explicit 'reprisals' for civilian casualties caused by enemy air raids. In many histories of the Civil War, the figure of Francoist leader Queipo de Llano, the oft-intoxicated 'radio general' of Seville, is cited as the acme of the Nationalist spirit of revenge. As it happens, Queipo, on at least one occasion, ordered an air attack – against (Republican) Jaén – in reprisal for a similar operation against (Nationalist) Córdoba.[21] But such actions became, for the Republic, a matter of policy, not of instinct. Another veteran of the war who is lately becoming almost as celebrated as Orwell – above all, because of his experience of bombing atrocities – greeted this policy with approval. 'It was good to hear [wrote George Steer] that they had raided Salamanca at last – unpleasant though it is, reprisal is the only sound method in war.'[22] But surely, it follows both logically and inevitably that in so doing Republican pilots attacked Nationalist towns and cities with the express purpose of killing civilians. Which side, therefore, was demonstrably guilty of this headline war crime during the Spanish Civil War? One way of deflecting this indictment is to sustain and persist with the article of faith that it was the Nationalists who mounted a systematic campaign of murder from the air (with regular readings of the litany: Madrid, Gernika, Barcelona). At any rate, the modern historical interpretation of the issue turns out to be hardly less partisan than the systematic and obdurate denials of the Francoist version it was designed to replace.[23]

Some years ago (as already noted) Ramón Salas Larrazábal made estimates of the total numbers of civilians killed by military action. These figures – 11,000 in Republican Spain and 4,000 in the Nationalist zone – are useful as far as they go. Salas's table appears as the last lines of his book, and carries no explanation or gloss of any kind either there or in the body of his text.[24] However, logic indicates that by 'military action', in addition to small numbers of unfortunates caught in the crossfires of street fighting, Ramón Salas meant to convey *not only aerial bombardment but also artillery fire*. It is beyond doubt that large numbers of the latter category must be accounted for: in Madrid and Oviedo, in contrast (say) to Barcelona and Granada, the majority of casualties were caused by shellfire. Reservations over Salas's statistical procedure compromise his estimates to an awkward degree. In my view there can never be a way, either of unscrambling these confused data, or of replacing them with something more specific and reliable.[25]

This uncertain conclusion merely reflects the obtaining situation over the death toll of the war as a whole, in every category. Even today, it is not possible to estimate this with any confidence, to the extent that it would be an act of bravura to enumerate any figure between 350,000 and 550,000 other than as a provisional working median. On the other hand, I have no disagreement *with the rough proportions* indicated by Salas's figures. Common sense suggests a larger casualty rate in the Republican zone. For one thing, during much of the war the Republic controlled Spain's most populous cities. Before July 1936, Barcelona, Madrid, Valencia and Málaga had 2.5 million denizens between them. Once hostilities began, these cities were continually and hugely augmented by refugee influx. In contrast, the two major Nationalist cities, Seville and Saragossa, boasted an aggregate population of only 400,000.[26] For another, the much greater intensity of bombing operations on the Nationalist side can hardly be doubted from cognisance of the Italian campaign against Catalonia and Valencia in 1938 alone. Despite important improvements in civil defence techniques made in the course of the war, at least in its big cities, the Republic was always the more vulnerable target. An important factor here is that from the initial stages of Stalin's aid programme (October 1936) the urgent needs of Madrid set a default agenda. To the end, the overall supply of warplanes to the Republic from the USSR was heavily slanted in favour of fighters.[27] The Republican platform on the whole issue of civilian bombing may have been riddled with wormwood; but it can hardly be doubted that in this sector of the war effort – as in most others – its resources for an offensive strategy were at no time better than severely limited.

III

Whatever the final statistical reckoning, the air war in Spain has a
further dimension which has been almost overlooked by historians. I refer again to non-combatant civilians, and to 'reprisals',
but not in either case to *the direct victims* of the bomber. At various
earlier points I have mentioned acts of vengeance carried out by
'the people', usually (though not invariably) in a frenzy of hatred,
in retaliation for the deaths of local citizens in air raids. Usually,
the victims were prisoners, overwhelmingly adult males, perceived
as political enemies of whichever side had prevailed in the locality,
and rounded up in the weeks following 18 July. Their persons
were easily available to hand as a source of propitiatory and
cathartic action by determined individuals, or by mobs made up
(let us charitably assume) of relatives and friends of people whose
lives had been suddenly ended by shockwave and shrapnel.
Indeed, we might go a small step further. At least in the period
before the Republican government regained control over
so-called 'uncontrollable elements' in many officially 'loyalist'
regions (a complicated process taking place in stages over the first
twelve months of the war), these prisoners were *in effect hostages*,
liable at any moment to be held to account for the perceived
misdeeds of the rebels. Next-to-nothing about this subject is to be
found in general textbooks of the Spanish Civil War. Indeed, until
the recent appearance of a comprehensive survey of 'víctimas de
la guerra civil', the subject had remained virtually untouched.
Now, in some path-finding pages, Julián Casanovas has argued
that reprisals taken in the wake of air raids were *the dominant
category of civilian atrocities* during the last three months of 1936.
Such casualties were caused by the 'bombing of open towns' as
surely as if they had been the direct victims of the bombing
itself.[28]

Most of the following material refers to events in the Republican zone. However, the circumstances of incidents described
means that, in most cases, it would be unreasonable to ascribe
moral responsibility to the Republican government. The guilt for
these murders lies with their actual perpetrators, above all with
local militia warlords who encouraged and often directed them.
Of course, such men were (if only 'objectively') pro-Republican
agents, and frequently members of one of the governing (Popular
Front) parties.[29] On the other hand, the responsibility of the

Nationalist authorities for these crimes, if certainly indirect, and ethically complicated, is not easy to dismiss *tout court*. Evidence suggests that the effect of air raids in producing deadly reprisals against political prisoners was brought to Franco's attention at an early stage.[30] Nothing in the records suggests that awareness of it affected his strategic decision-making. At the same time, because references to similar reprisals on the Nationalist side are rare, it certainly does not mean that criminal acts motivated by revenge did not happen there.[31] True, the Francoist zone contained fewer and much less troublesome 'incontrolables', if only because it was more fearsomely policed. The culture of the Nationalist zone suggests that acts of 'spontaneous' popular feeling in any direction or cause were severely discouraged. Censorship and secrecy were also (arguably) more ubiquitous characteristics of life in rebel territory, especially at a local level. In many parts of 'National Spain' political prisoners were spared the firing squad, only to be kept in custody and in a state of suspended mortification for months and even years. It seems beyond reasonable doubt that numbers of these prisoners were finally hauled to their deaths as part of some (admittedly hypothetical) conjuncture involving Republican atrocities – often an air raid.[32]

A remarkable testimony concerning this subject was left by Gamel Woolsey, an American writer living in Andalusia with her husband, Gerald Brenan. It was in her memoir of the war that Woolsey coined the famous phrase describing press atrocity stories as 'the pornography of violence'.[33] Though evacuation from Spain by the Royal Navy was available to them, Gamel and Gerald elected to stay put in their adopted village of Churriana during the war's early weeks. Of course, they 'did not then know the horrors which were going to take place ... the cruel murders by the terrorists among the parties on the left, the brutal massacres by the extremists on the other side'.[34] In the first days, they had no news of any 'horrors' that might have happened in nearby Málaga. But then the air raids began and Churriana itself became a prime target. One night the village was reported hit by over seventy bombs.[35] This had an understandably traumatic effect on its inhabitants, but Woolsey understood the reason for the raid: the village was adjacent to a small airfield.[36] When Málaga itself came under attack from the air, the atmosphere turned menacing and 'a veritable reign of terror' was unleashed. In a café, the couple noticed a young Englishman who turned out ('to our surprise') to be a war correspondent. 'He was practically a child, had never seen a shot fired in anger . . . He had not managed to see any atrocities as yet, though that, we gathered, was what was chiefly expected of him.' During their conversation an air raid began. Gamel and Gerald, fluent in Spanish and having a certain local influence, got their new friend attached to a patrol assigned to the recovery of victims' bodies. But there was a bonus, for later on he saw armed gangs 'dragging people on the Right out of their houses'. The next morning, he told them he had seen the bodies of forty reprisal victims piled in a trench in the cemetery. Gamel comforted herself, in a revealing remark, maybe inspired by recent experience in Churriana, that such incidents 'will happen in any city where there are air-raids'. She also noticed that 'by an ingenious system known to atrocity collectors [the reporter] seemed to have multiplied the number [of victims] by four in his story which he showed us.'[37]

Similar reactions were to be observed in Madrid during this period. Here, quasi-autonomous police sections run by political parties and trades unions (known collectively as the 'checas') went into overdrive in the wake of air raids. On one such occasion, hundreds were arrested and shot overnight, bodies being dumped at dawn for public viewing along the banks of the Manzanares. A communist contact of Arturo Barea's told him: 'On the day of the bombing, they didn't bother with holding tribunals, they just shot anyone who was hauled in.'[38] Some months later, George Ogilvie-Forbes, senior British diplomat in Madrid, became deeply disturbed about reprisals against political prisoners.[39] In London, under-secretary Sir George Mounsey was sceptical about his colleagues' suggestion that, if nothing else, concern about such bloodletting might influence General Franco against further use of this tactic.[40]

The story of Málaga and Madrid was replicated many times all over Spain, and in places which before the war seemed idyllic, remote and untouchable. On 13 September 1936, for example, the loyalist port of Ibiza was bombed by planes operating from rebel-held Mallorca. It was a Sunday and the promenade was crowded. According to an American writer resident nearby, who went into the town early the next day, fifty-five people were killed, 'forty-two of whom were women and children'. Militiamen guarding the jail turned on the 'fascists' who had been rounded up after the events of 18 July. Out of 239 detainees, only one boy escaped the carnage.[41] In the same month, after a single plane had attacked Albacete, killing two citizens, a mob entered the prison, dragged out 'a certain number' of inmates and murdered them.[42] At Jaén, in western Andalusia, 260 prisoners were 'executed' systematically in reprisal for a single Nationalist raid.[43]

In November, passengers on a commercial flight that called at Alicante as part of a trip from Toulouse to Casablanca claimed that local anarchists had 'killed hostages' after just one civilian died in an air raid.[44] On Spain's northern coast, in the last days of the year, 276 inmates of prison ships anchored in the bay of Santander were massacred following an air raid in which eighteen enemy aircraft took part.[45] In Bilbao, where there had been no 'revolutionary justice' and comparatively few arrests, the first air raids (January 1937) inspired a popular invasion of a prison where political prisoners were being held. In this case, the police arrived to interrupt the slaughter, though not before the mob had put 224 helpless scapegoats to death.[46] And even in nearby Durango – the small town that German and Italian air legions later came virtually to use as target practice – a speculative initial attack in September 1936 provoked local vigilantes to murder twenty-one political prisoners in revenge for the enemy's toll of twelve equally innocent citizens.[47]

The Condor Legion carried out its pioneering operations (November 1936) against one of the Republic's leading ports, Cartagena, which was also its main naval base. Indeed, Franco's air force had first targeted this site some weeks earlier, when it became known that it was being used as the principal reception centre for Soviet arms supplies to the Republic. Ogilvie-Forbes informed the Foreign Office that fifty prisoners had been murdered in Cartagena 'about three weeks ago, after the first air raids'.[48] Six months later, in the spring of 1937, the British consul in Cartagena reported that 'there are still about 200 political suspects and hostages in San Anton prison, 60 of whom are on the list to be killed as a reprisal if there is another air-raid'.[49]

The consul's implication was that something might be done in London to prevent the organized murders which these *matanzas* represented. There was, of course, a causal – not a casual – connection between the categories of crime that is our subject here. In December 1936, almost 300 political prisoners were

massacred in Guadalajara. According to the *Pravda*-trained propagandist Mikhail Koltsov, enemy bombers had destroyed a hospital,
killing and maiming its patients. But also,

> more bombs have fallen on an orphanage, creating a mountain of
> little corpses ... an infuriated crowd surged to the jail, disarmed
> the guards and took out a hundred fascists, who were duly shot.
> The same day, the local militia rounded up a group of suspicious
> elements, who soon refilled the jail's empty cells. These are to be
> held as hostages 'in case there should be another bombardment' –
> as the people in Guadalajara darkly put it.[50]

NOTES

[1] Koestler (1954), p. 325.
[2] The term 'massed' is, of course, relative. Within seven years of 1936,
     Bomber Command sent over 1,000 planes to bomb Berlin.
[3] The village of Griñón lies some 30 km to the south of Getafe.
[4] E-mail from Xosé Manuel Domínguez Prieto to author, 19 December
     2004. José Manuel Domínguez Rodríguez was formerly a Professor of
     Philosophy at Madrid's Universidad Complutense.
[5] WPP@URL   *http://www.madrid112.org/not00.asp?id=212.*   (Accessed
     March 2004.)
[6] 'Madrileños' by Antoni Puigverd, *El Pais*, 12 March 2004. (My
     emphasis.)
[7] 'De Buena Mañana' by Javier Marías, ibid.
[8] 'Barcelona, con Madrid' by Joan Clos, ibid.
[9] 'Con plomo en las entrañas', ibid. It seems from the first extract
     quoted that even this irenic authority accepted propaganda myths
     about the bombardment of Madrid. ('Cara al Sol' was the hymn of
     the Falange.) On Monday 15 March, four days after the bombing,
     BBC TV's 'Newsnight' programme also made the connection with
     the Spanish Civil War, informing viewers that 'as usual' the Guernica
     Gallery at Madrid's main art museum was crowded with people
     reflecting on Picasso's depiction of an earlier species of terrorism.
[10] The *Guardian* and its Madrid correspondent, Giles Tremlett, consist-
     ently devotes space to this campaign, dubbed the 'Recovery of
     Historical Memory', seemingly at the expense of other aspects of
     contemporary Spanish life.
[11] See Stradling (2007A).
[12] See above, pp. 51–2 and 243–4.
[13] Solé & Villaroya (2003).
[14] Solé & Villaroya (2003), especially pp. 25–34, 133–8 and 230–1.
[15] Solé & Villaroya (2003), pp. 46–7.
[16] J. Salas Larrazábal, using captured Republican reports found in the
     archives of the Nationalist army, calculated that 312 civilians were

killed in Madrid during November, 1936 – easily the most intense period of bombing: (1969), pp. 214–15.

17 None of this is intended to apply to the analogous context of Barcelona and (e.g.) the atrocity of Granollers in 1938.

18 Q. from a script of May 1942, by West (1986), p. 95 (my emphasis).

19 Solé & Villaroya (2003), pp. 313–16.

20 Graham (2005), pp. 71–3.

21 Hidalgo Luque (2006), 8. See also above, p. 30.

22 Letter of January, 1938, q. in Buchanan (2007), p. 41.

23 In an earlier study, the same writers estimated that only 20 civilians were killed in Catalonia by Republican bombing, compared with 5,000 deaths caused by Nationalist action; Solé & Villaroya (1986), p. 83.

24 'Civiles muertos en acción bélica', Cuadro 57; R. Salas (1986), p. 310.

25 However, Salas's estimates find broad approbation in Solé & Villaroya (2003), especially pp. 313–14.

26 Salas (1980), p. 277.

27 See Howson (1998), especially pp. 302–3.

28 Juliá (1999), pp. 29 and 141–51. The latter pages cite examples on the Republican side, some of which overlap with cases which are described below directly from sometimes differing sources.

29 This was more true after the political directorate of the anarchists (FAI) joined the Madrid government in September 1936. It must also be said that many of the guilty paid for their crimes with their own lives after the Republic's defeat.

30 See above, pp. 183–4 and below, p. 260.

31 As one scholar has shown, reprisal shootings of political prisoners certainly took place in Nationalist-held towns like Córdoba (and some other places in Andalusia). Moreover, these were carried out in cold blood by the military authorities: Hidalgo Luque (2006), 3–4.

32 In Granada, 'each time the Republicans bombed the town a batch of prisoners was shot in reprisal': Gibson (1973/1979), p. 90.

33 Woolsey (1988), p. 126.

34 Woolsey (1988), pp. 51–2.

35 Gathorne-Hardy (1992/1994), p. 310. The figure seems excessive, especially since the author mentions no casualties.

36 Woolsey (1988), pp. 83, 187. See also Gathorne-Hardy (1992/1994), pp. 304–5 ('In retaliation the Málaga air force – four tiny droning passenger planes – took off and threw their little bombs out by hand over Granada'.) In the 1960s, Churriana was chosen as the site of Málaga's international airport.

37 Woolsey (1937), pp. 134–40; Gathorne-Hardy (1992/1994), pp. 307–8. Seidman (2002), p. 76 describes this category of prisoners as 'hostages', but this status was generally *ex post facto*.

38 Barea (1946/1984), pp. 156–7 and 161.

39 On 21 October 1936, *The Times* carried a relevant 'uncensored' warning from a 'special correspondent' in Madrid, which probably originated inside the British embassy.

40 Holograph note by 'G.M.', 5 November 1936, on BNA F0 371/

20546/W15040. Fraser (1979), p. 175 seems to endorse a Nationalist claim that a massacre of prisoners in Madrid's Modelo prison on 23–4 August was inspired by this motive. Another expert suggests that Republican Spain's biggest single war crime, the mass 'execution' of nearly 2,000 'fascist' prisoners on 7–8 November 1936, was also a relevant act of reprisal. He offers the opinion by way of moral extenuation for the atrocity: Reig Tapía (1990), p. 97.

[41] Paul (1937), pp. 415–19.

[42] Martínez Amutio (1974), pp. 159–60. (The author was civil governor of the city.)

[43] Hermet (1989), p. 136; Hidalgo Luque (2006), 8. It was estimated that 155 citizens died in the raid – which (as we have seen) was itself a reprisal attack for one on Córdoba.

[44] *The Times*, 7 November 1936, p. 12.

[45] Here, hand-grenades were thrown into the holds of a prison-ship (SS *Cantabria*). As survivors tried to escape, they were shot on the decks. Kangaroo courts subsequently condemned many other political prisoners to death: Casanova (1999), p. 148; see also González Echegaray (1977), p. 175.

[46] Kurlansky (1999), p. 208.

[47] Irazabal (2001), pp. 27–8.

[48] 11 November 1936, BNA FO 371/20547/W15486.

[49] 'Information from Mr Leverkus', 17 March 1937, ibid. 21289/107.

[50] Koltsov (1963), pp. 269–70; see also Casanova (1999), p. 148. As one scholar points out (and as he suspects was the case in Córdoba) it is likely that on these occasions some victims of reprisals were themselves relatives or friends of victims of the raids: Hidalgo Luque (2006), 17.

Part Five

Postlude

Chapter 17

Return to Wales

The last chapter ended with horrific stories of stolid indifference to civilian casualties, mainly by one side, and of apparently cold-blooded reprisals in kind, largely by the other. The context and detail of all this was little known or reported outside Spain at the time. By 1937, with the world's emotions of horror and empathy newly and more spectacularly engaged with the Japanese aerial assault on Chinese cities, bombing was at the forefront of common concern. What continued to inspire the daily efforts of interested parties, the 'popular front' organizers of aid and commitment, was the primary victims of indiscriminate air raiding, and above all the children. In contrast to the minimal coverage of one indirect consequence, the reprisal murder of hostages, publicity given to the actual dropping of bombs on mothers and children was in inverse proportion to its authentic magnitude. Here, it was an increasingly desperate Republic that believed that 'something might be done in London'. As some British well-wishers suggested, why not extricate children from the furnace of hatred and violence altogether: or rather, as it was usually expressed, 'rescue them from Fascist barbarism'. For example – amongst other ideas – Sir Richard Rees and John Williams-Hughes, two Welshmen involved in relief work in Valencia (temporary capital of the Republic), put forward a plan for taking Spanish children evacuated from war zones for a healing holiday in the peace and tranquillity of rural Wales.[1] As it happened, the Republic's own advisers had been aware for some time of the manifold advantages of an operation involving the shipping of children abroad. In autumn 1936, the project emerged (originating most likely from Koltsov or his team) of evacuating children *en masse* not just from Madrid, but from all of

Republican Spain. It was an extension of the type of proposals for (strictly) humanitarian assistance which had appealed to international observers like the Seymour Cocks delegation.[2]

In succeeding months, the idea was pursued by the Valencia authorities, who over the next two years were to send many thousands of children, mainly to the friendly Republic of Mexico. However, it was taken up even more energetically by the autonomous Basque government in the north of Spain. Bilbao was swamped by refugees, especially hundreds of families from San Sebastián who swarmed west after the fall of Guipúzcoa in September 1936. Food supplies soon became critical. In the winter of 1936–7, Basque president José María Aguirre negotiated with Church leaders, union activists and various international aid organizations. Households were alerted to the option of sending their children out of harm's way. A campaign was mounted via radio, press, poster and pamphlet to persuade parents that this (only temporary) sacrifice was a duty to themselves, to their children, and to Euskadi. Though at this point Bilbao itself had suffered only light and sporadic air attacks – the rest of urban Vizcaya was still almost unscarred by the bomber – huge emphasis was placed on the aerial factor and its alleged threat to children.[3] Here, as in other parts of Spain, much use was made of images and statistics from 'suffering Madrid'. By December, the embarkation of Guipuzcoan refugee children to France, a traffic sponsored by Popular Front organizations and the similarly-constituted government in Paris, was under way. Once ensconced in French camps and homes, these groups were mobilized for public fund- and awareness-raising for the cause of Republican Spain.[4] Through choral and dancing performances, drama and poetry readings, sporting competitions and magazines, Basque refugee children were to become known in many parts of western Europe as an infallible focus of anti-fascist sentiment and fund-raising.

All these activities had a profound impact upon foreign observers: maritime and commercial personnel, aid workers, journalists and junior diplomatic officers from various western European nations were all present in numbers in the Basque capital. In short, the evacuation policy was dictated, if not wholly motivated, by short-term considerations of politics and propaganda. The whole operation was dramatically disproportionate to any danger ostensibly justifying or necessitating it: but the key *desideratum* was that it should be dramatic, attracting the maximum attention.

The rescue ships carrying their infant cargoes were to set sail, above all, in order to make waves. The primary objective, which needs a final reiteration, was to move the democracies out of the crippled zone of non-intervention. The process might begin with a show of 'international solidarity' over the child-victims, but would end – hopefully – with lifting the ban on munitions supply, or even outright military intervention in favour of the Republic. As the Burgos press vociferously but ineffectively proclaimed, the children were exploited as ideal representatives of the (alleged) victimization of innocents.

By the spring of 1937, little response to the pressure for evacuation had been noted among Vizcayan families. But the opening of Mola's offensive in March 1937 soon altered perspectives. His campaign was spearheaded by the air arm, mostly by German and Italian squadrons. The raids on Durango and Gernika, accompanied as they were by fresh refugee influxes from neighbourhood towns and villages, caused panic in Bilbao. In between these two atrocities, a Welsh sea captain reported rumours that 450 child refugees recently arrived in St Jean de Luz were bound for the Soviet Union.[5] In May, the Soviet camera team headed by the brilliant cinematographer Karmen was sent from Madrid to Bilbao in order to record the evacuation operation on film. Koltsov, senior editor of *Pravda,* Stalin's personal emissary and propaganda overlord in Spain, also arrived in person at the Basque capital. He interviewed Aguirre, who dutifully sent thanks to Stalin for offering to care for nearly 2,000 infant 'refugees'.[6]

Meanwhile, the British consul and the ex-MP Leah Manning, the latter frequently present in Bilbao on behalf of the National Spanish Aid Committee, worked together to facilitate matters. Their efforts resulted in Eden's message to Aguirre that the Royal Navy would guarantee safe passage of refugee ships through any Nationalist warship cordon in place as part of Franco's (partly fictional) 'blockade' of Basque ports.[7] From this it was a modest step to the government's agreement that Britain would take its share of evacuees.[8] Prominent in supply of Vizcaya with munitions, fuel and food during the winter, Welsh skippers and merchantmen came to the fore during events surrounding the 'breaking of Franco's blockade' in the spring of 1937. There was also an older sense of fraternity in Wales, stemming from long-cherished commercial links with the Basque region, and (more fanciful) feelings of ethnic kinship. In the immediate aftermath of

Gernika, Wales's greatest living person, ex-prime minister Lloyd
George, turned up at Immingham Docks, where

> the little freighter Backworth last week loaded $10,000 worth of
> sugar, flour, fruit and dried salt fish for starving Basques in Spain's
> besieged Bilbao. More than one-tenth of the cargo was paid for by
> David Lloyd George who seldom misses a chance to make political
> capital of anything. Down to the dock hurried Britain's Wartime
> Prime Minister to wring Captain Russell of the Backworth by the
> hand. 'I too am a Basque!' cried he, shaking his white mane.
> 'Marshal Foch was a Basque! The Welsh and the Basques are the
> same . . .'[9]

In similar phrases, some of which percolated down to J. F.
Kennedy's 'ich bin ein Berliner' speech of 1961, Lloyd George
later exhorted Parliament not to desert the Basques, whom he
credited with helping to sustain Britain during the German
U-boat offensive of 1917–18.[10] Lloyd George's example may have
enhanced the international dimension of the Welsh role in saving
the Basques, but in any case the enthusiasm for the 'orphans of
war' that swept Wales now took on a life of its own.[11] During the
second half of 1937, the campaign to welcome and succour the
400 children allocated to Wales became an authentic 'popular
front', a common cause of all its peoples regardless of class,
region, politics or religion. The doings of Cambria House in the
little town of Caerleon, where the 'orphans of war' took up
residence, attracted the beneficent interest of thousands. In the
children's carefully managed exploits in sport, literature and the
performing arts, in their appearances at fund-raising festivals all
over the country, the aspirations of many protagonists, individual
and collective, were realized. The children themselves were a
veritable powerhouse of persuasion. As Cyril Cule, their English-
language tutor noted (with affected ingenuosity)

> some of them were very clever at drawing, and when left to
> themselves with a pencil and paper, the result was always some such
> picture as that of an aeroplane dropping bombs on an ambulance.
> The ambulance would be clearly marked with a red cross, and the
> aeroplane with a swastika.[12]

For the Communist Party, Cambria House was an example of
how local and communal cooperation could counter the horrors
of international fascism. For Saunders Lewis and company, it was
graphic demonstration and justification of their prophecies of

'baby-murdering' and their pacifist stand over the Bombing School. For commercial patriarchs and leading elements of the centre-right, it offered a chance to demonstrate their anti-fascism and general public-spiritedness. In the middle of a decade when Wales had never been so divided, for six months the nation was more united than it had ever been.

A passing attempt has already been made to place The Poster in the broad context of other world-famous examples of its genre.[13] The comparison perhaps needs further pursuit, for in more specific terms, like General Kitchener and Ché Guevara, it was a recruiting advertisement. The Great War poster says 'Join up and save your Country'; Ché and his beret are saying 'The Revolution is Cool – get with it!' María Santiago cries 'Help! Please save the Spanish Republic!' In one dimension, the intentions of its creators are hardly subject to reproach. Though the Republican government was acting quite differently on other media fronts, in none of its three versions does The Poster itself claim any connection between victim No. 4–21–35 and Getafe. Moreover, its subject was (almost) certainly killed by a Nationalist bomb. The Poster's prophecy – the title of this book – that a similar fate would soon happen to the children of many who looked upon its image of María Santiago proved correct. Even its crucial conditional ('If You Tolerate This') is a 'fact' widely accepted today by those who believe that the Second World War and all its horrors could have been averted by international commitment to the Spanish Republic.

To these extents, upon investigation, some notional 'Propaganda Standards Authority', a standing committee of philosophers, jurists and historians established by the International Court of Human Justice might declare itself satisfied. Yet to my mind, residual ethical distinctions remain. For one thing, when María Santiago was reborn in The Poster, Spanish children were also being bombed from the air by the very side which was demanding salvation. For another, whilst few today would register any meaningful response to Kitchener, and Ché has become little more than radical chic, as I write this there are still people all over the world – perhaps to be numbered in millions rather than thousands – whose heart's desire is to save the Spanish Republic. They strive to achieve this posthumous miracle by preserving its memory as an object of eternal veneration. For this reason, it seems a poignant parable of the last century that through the

medium of a propaganda poster, the angelic spirit of a little
Madrileña, María Santiago, No. 4–21–35, victim of the Spanish
Civil War, killed in Calle Paloma ('street of the dove') in October
1936, adaptive child of Koltsov and Koestler, Katz and Kulcsar, was
wafted down the decades to Blackwood in Gwent, and thereby
rose again to No. 1 in the charts.

NOTES

[1] Reuter report in *South Wales Weekly Argus*, 3 July 1937.
[2] See above, pp. 182–3.
[3] It should be recorded that air forces under Basque command also engaged in offensive sorties. Vitoria, capital of the nationalist-held Basque province of Alava, was raided several times, and one sortie even reached Pamplona, HQ both of Mola and the fearsome Carlist militia, the Requetés; Talon (1980), III, pp. 713–14.
[4] Legarreta (1984), p. 34ff.
[5] Jones (2002), p. 82.
[6] Karmen filmed the departure of the SS *Havana* for Southampton, and later left Spain on the same vessel with a party of children bound for Russia; Talon (1980), I, p. 177; Koltsov (1963), pp. 402–6; Legarreta (1984), p. 156ff. Despite the tergivisations of the last source, it seems incredible that fiercely Catholic Basque mothers would have agreed to their children being taken to the USSR, or that priests and bishops would have connived at the operation. At any rate, with or without parental permission, some 3,000 were eventually sent into a new life as subjects of Stalin. It proved tragic for most, and events soon placed them beyond any possibility of return to their families. See 'Los Juguetes rotos de Stalin: Un historiador revela la trágica verdad de los niños de la guerra en la URSS', La Vanguardia Electronica 14 June 1998, *http://www.guerracivil.org/Diaris/980614vang.html* (accessed 6 January 2004).
[7] Talon (1980), I, pp. 172–3. For Manning's opportunistic interest in propaganda see Stradling (2004), pp. 140–1.
[8] See above, p. 220.
[9] *Time Magazine*, 3 May 1937: WPP@URL *http://www.jcgi.pathfinder.com/time/archive/preview/0,10987,931579,00.html*. (Accessed December 2006.)
[10] In a speech subsequently published as *Spain and Britain* (1937).
[11] See Stradling (2004), pp. 41–5 and esp. Francis (1984), pp. 123–35.
[12] C. Cule, 'The Spanish Civil War: A Personal Account', SUCC Ms. SC158. Cf. the remarkably congruent testimony of an English teacher at the Cambridge 'colony', given in 'The Guernica Children', TV documentary produced by Eyewitness Productions for BBC 4, 2005.
[13] Above, pp. 147–9.

Appendix A

Arturo Barea –
a Censor Obsessed

The memoirs of Arturo Barea appeared in three volumes between 1941 and 1946, after he had settled in Britain as a refugee. Though composed in Spanish, they were published (by Faber & Faber) in English translations made by Barea's wife, Ilsa Kulcsar. Spanish-language editions were issued by Hispanic–American publishers, but the book was not published in Spain itself until the Franco dictatorship had ended. In recent decades the memoirs have gained an important place in the academic curriculum inside and outside Spain. It is now commonplace for them to figure in syllabuses and on reading lists for university degrees not only in History but also in Hispanic Literature and Politics courses.[1] More particularly, the third and last episode, *La Llama* (*The Clash*), constitutes the most sustained and significant personal testimony to the central events dealt with in this book. Though any conclusions should be limited to the case in point, it seems necessary to conduct an abstract, and abstracted, examination of its trustworthiness as history.

Barea's overall reputation as a witness resembles that of his admirer, George Orwell.[2] It arises from the fact that he was a committed supporter of the Republic, yet one who honestly reported what he saw and disliked about 'the cause'. Barea's candour was stimulated by a dilemma over his personal political identity: in turn, this dilemma had two contrasting chronological phases. Before the military uprising of July 1936, he was acutely conscious of his transition from the lower depths of Madrileño society – a street-urchin of Lavapies – to the ranks of the central bureaucracy, and the middle-class status of two homes and a secretarial mistress. Determined never to renounce his class origins and allegiances, yet from a necessarily privileged technocratic standpoint, he clinically observed the shortcomings of the 'reforming Republic'. The obstinate survival of an old, corrupt Spain, of vested interests, rampant opportunism and routine oppression both in town and countryside disturbed him deeply. After the coming of a centre-right government in 1933, he was disgusted by the increasing degree of business cooperation between Spain and (Nazi) Germany. For these and other reasons, in the crisis of 1936 he rallied to the Republic. However, the chaotic and bloodthirsty social revolution which ensued in Madrid alarmed his sensibilities, in effect alienating him from its support, and from many former working-class friends. Paradoxically, he came both to dislike the arbitrary persecution and violence of life in wartime Madrid, yet also to distrust the main agency attempting to restore 'bourgeois' standards of authority and discipline, the Communist Party – which finally hounded him out of both his job and his homeland.

One of the bourgeois habits Barea acquired was a love of Spanish literature, and during the war he began to write fiction. Ilsa Kulcsar, a highly-educated Austrian socialist, proficient in languages and techniques of critical appraisal, became Barea's lover, political mainstay and literary mentor. In exile, they decided that his memoirs should be written as a first-person psychological narrative, recording not only private feelings and reactions, but also the public domain of events and conversations. It is the latter feature, in particular, which because of its intimate relationship to fictional genres (above all, the novel) often arouses suspicion in historians. Barea makes clear that he writes purely from memory (in practice this means Ilsa's as well as his own). He brought no documents or contemporary diaries with him to England. Yet he writes with confident recall of a myriad details: the sight, sound, smell, colour and texture of his material environment; the physical appearance, comportment, and dress of others, even in the most fugitive encounters. But also – crucially – he reconstructs the spoken words that articulated all these elements.

The novelistic resort to direct speech, at best only a vague approximation of reality, inevitably complicates our attitude to the truth-claims inherent in any 'documentary' testament. It seems to me palpable that Don Arturo's book was intended as a work of art, a contribution to 'The Literature of the Spanish People' – to quote his friend, Gerald Brenan. Notably, George Orwell greeted its author as 'one of the most valuable of *the literary acquisitions* that England has made as a result of Fascist persecution', whilst *The Times*'s reviewer (seemingly with a phrase of Orwell's in mind) referred to 'that rare quality, *partisanship* without intellectual dishonesty or the distortion of the truth'.[3] Another friend, Helen Grant, a Cambridge academic, rationalized his technique as 'a vivid sense of life experienced at first hand and *recreated through the imagination*'. His own explanation was 'I have tried to present [these events] as they were, uncoloured by the glasses through which I see things today, as I might wish to write the truth about somebody other than myself'.[4] The present writer finds all this to be a less than ideal reassurance when it comes to assessment of the issues examined in this book.

Two basic features of Barea's wartime experience put me further on my guard. The overarching narrative of *The Clash* reveals its author's personal obsession with bombing, to the point of paranoia. It's little surprise to find that the cover artwork of the modern English edition displays a fleet of B52-size bombers unloading sticks of bombs on a ruined city littered with bodies.[5] In addition to many pages devoted to objective descriptions of raids on Madrid, Barea repeatedly describes subjective symptoms of paralysing fear and nausea which grip him during air raids – ultimately, at the mere threat of an air raid. As we read on, the bombs seem to drop more and more thickly, getting closer and closer to the panic-stricken narrator. They follow him to Valencia, then to a remote Mediterranean beach, then to his Barcelona hotel, and finally – at least in terms of public apprehension – even to Paris, where fear of the Luftwaffe is already looming. There's no escape, not even in England.[6] The distorting effects of his book's morbidly intense concentration upon bombing and his fear of it tends to place a question mark against Don Arturo's reliability as witness on the subject.

In addition it cannot be overlooked that for a crucial period of the war, Barea was deeply involved in both censorship and propaganda. The further one reads into *La Llama*, the more he seems to be acting as a source of misinformation. He makes no secret of his increasing involvement in the 'creative' aspect of propaganda, stimulated as he was by Ilsa's 'revelation' to him of his true calling as a writer. At the same time, they both became chiefly responsible to, and dependent for protection upon, General Vladimir Goriev, head of Soviet intelligence in Spain and *eminence grise* to the Madrid Junta. By early 1937 the couple were intimate with senior power-brokers in both Junta and War Commissariat (including International Brigade luminaries in Madrid). Goriev was anxious to win over moderate and conservative elements among the foreign press gang. Though Barea had an undisguised contempt for certain individuals, he and Ilsa had gradually gained the confidence of the press corps as a whole. Goriev expected this relationship to pay dividends. Naturally, 'human interest' stories assumed top priority.[7] The genre, examples of which Barea was already developing in his own fiction, tended to obtrude into the radio broadcasts he made as 'La Voz de Madrid' during the spring of 1937.[8]

In this connection, likewise, it is notable that on no fewer than three occasions Barea tells an almost identical story about a lone bomber that deliberately seeks out packed civilian streets. He presents each event in unmistakably discrete contexts. In chronological sequence, these were the (inaugural) attack on Madrid, which Barea carefully dates as 7 August 1936, and which is not convincingly corroborated by any other source. The second was the alleged bombing of Getafe on 30 October.[9] The third incident is related by Barea as taking place in Vallecas, a *barrio* located in the south-east of Madrid's urban mass. In the second case – the core 'event' of this book – Barea was unable to speak from the perspective of personal witness. In the first, he had been present when the bombs fell. In the third,

> I went to investigate the damage done by a single three-engined Junkers which had swooped low and slow over the Vallecas hovels on the afternoon of 20th January [1937], dropping a rosary of bombs on a little square. Women were sewing in the sunshine, with their kids playing nearby. Having met the father of three children murdered there, I thought to do what the professional journalists would not, because minor raids were no longer a good story for them. The man's house – he was a fish-seller – had been destroyed by seven small bombs. His wife had died on her own doorstep, a baby in her arms. Two older girls had been killed. A four-year-old boy had one of his legs amputated in hospital. His little body was covered with more than a hundred scratches and abrasions from pulverized shrapnel. The eldest boy, eardrums bleeding, carried

> him to a medical post on his shoulders. I visited the one-legged boy
> in the main Hospital and heard his father, Raimundo Mallanda
> Ruiz, tell the story, while the boy *watched us with staring, misty eyes.*

> I had imagined this was a good story with which to illustrate the
> consequences of non-intervention, but it seems I entirely failed to
> grasp what might be sold on this market, or what foreign public
> opinion really wanted to know. . . '

Did Barea, with his technical interest in aviation, really think a
bomber could swoop 'low and slow'? How could he for even a
moment have believed the manifest absurdity of seven bombs
falling on one minuscule dwelling? Did he actually count the
children's wounds? Were the mother and baby killed on the
doorstep possibly reflected onto his imagination by Picasso's
'Guernica'? Why has none of the survivors of this, nor for that
matter all the other bombing horrors, ever spoken publicly of
their suffering?[10]

Is it possible that Barea had also 'failed to grasp what might be
sold' in the case of Getafe? In the light of the above, it hardly
seems excessive to regard Barea as *an important part of the
Republican propaganda machine*, rather than as one who, in the
impression constantly conveyed, stood conscientiously aloof. On
several occasions *The Clash* refers to the Getafe bombing as
unquestioned fact.[11] Barea repeatedly asserts the connection
between the photographic dossier and Getafe. Could he have
been 'guilty by authorship' of the alleged crime of Getafe? Be this
as it may, it seems that when Don Arturo came to write his
memoirs, a certain atrocity story was fixed in his mind with
absolute clarity of detail and equally absolute vagueness of circumstance, a story that cannot be corroborated from any extant
source in any of the three locations and dates in which he sets it.[12]

One final consideration. On several occasions Barea refers to
himself as having 'saved the children' from a metaphysical species
of second death. Until a late stage in writing, it never occurred to
me to question this claim, or the intensely dramatic narrative with
which he presents it to the reader. But even though his account of
the night of 6–7 November may be true in its essentials, I am now
less sure about its central significance. According to the authoritative source on the poster production of the war, The Poster
originated as early as 5 November 1936, which suggests that
Koltsov and his staff acted in aid of its production with urgent

immediacy after he received the dossier.[13] Moreover, even assuming access to the latest technology, could the example of the dossier (plus negatives) which Barea took to the PCE offices – on 9 November *at the earliest* – have reached London in time for the CPGB politburo *and* the editorial committee to discuss and decide on its use: *and then* for pictures to be set up by the *Daily Worker*'s compositors, *all by the night of 10–11 November?* From all this it seems clear that more than one set of the pictures had been printed by Ministry of State agents before Barea acted, and that the resulting propaganda exercise was already under way. Indeed, the generic physical appearance of the (incomplete) set extant in London's International Brigade archive, presumably sent to the CPGB/*Daily Worker* by the Spanish embassy, suggests that the photos were printed off in magazine format and on appropriate newsprint.[14] It may be speculated that copies of the file received by Koltsov on the night of 4 November, or some other set, reached London without Barea's intervention.[15]

NOTES

[1]   See, for example, a compendium including several Barea gobbets, which has become standard issue in Hispanic Studies courses: Kenwood (1993), p. 30 and *passim*. Here, the author is described as one 'who reported [his] personal experiences with remarkable honesty'.

[2]   On which see Stradling (2003), pp. 48–73.

[3]   These encomia are printed on the back cover of the English version; Barea (1946/1984A).

[4]   Barea (1943/1984), p. 12. Grant is quoted from her introduction to the first volume. (My emphases in all this paragraph's quotations.)

[5]   Barea (1946/1984A).

[6]   Barea (1946/1984), for example, pp. 361–2, 375–82, 397–8.

[7]   Barea (1946/1984), pp. 270–2. In corroboration, see (e.g.) the highly relevant remarks by Cox (1937), p. 195.

[8]   Although some of the stories fail to foreground the topic, a majority at least make some reference to the bombing of Madrid. They were published in Valencia in 1938; Barea (1938/1980).

[9]   For *La Llama*'s treatment of these two incidents, see above, pp. 43–4 and 105–6.

[10] Barea (1946/1984), p. 284. This 'autobiographical' account differs in no important respect from the 'fictional' version. Cf. 'Proeza', in Barea (1938/1980), pp. 23–4. The only other mention of a raid on Vallecas I have found dates it to 8 or 9 November, 1936 – ten weeks earlier than Barea's date; see [New York] *Daily Worker*, 10 November

1936. The front page column heading ('School Bombed') precedes description of a raid on Vallecas lasting for two hours, 'with high explosive and incendiary bombs' in which ' women and children were blown to pieces'. Hardly a 'minor raid'.

11 Barea (1946/84), pp. 192 and 199.
12 The 'single bomber' story was also used by *El Socialista* about the Madrid raid of 30 October; see above, p. 95.
13 Carulla & Carulla (1997), p. 379.
14 IBA Box A2/D55–63. It was presumably in this format that the dossier was sent to various prominent individuals, such as Virginia Woolf (see above, p. 171)
15 See, for example, the evidence from the *Daily Herald* for early November, commented above, p. 158.

Appendix B

The Albrighton Diary

James Albrighton, who claimed to have witnessed the deliberate massacre of Getafe's children by German airmen in October 1936, was born in Salisbury in 1917 and died in Swansea in 1984. Two years before his death he wrote to Bill Alexander, one-time commander of the British (57th) Battalion of the XV International Brigade concerning a TV documentary in which the latter had appeared. (At the time, also, Alexander's history of the British in Spain was about to be published.) Albrighton took the author to task on various points, citing his personal experiences and a handwritten diary he had kept at the time. Claiming to have fought with a Spanish anarchist militia company throughout the battles for Madrid (from October 1936 onwards), he challenged Alexander's account of the period prior to that in which the British Battalion was first formed (in December). Our knowledge of volunteer involvement in Spain before the Comintern took over its organization derives entirely from published accounts, letters and other memorabilia of the volunteers themselves. Alexander himself did not join the battalion until May 1937. During a correspondence lasting through most of the year 1982, Albrighton, despite increasing complaints of serious infirmity and pain, typed out a set of substantial extracts from his diary for Bill Alexander's benefit.[1] Partly for reasons given above, but mostly because he found them so convincing *sui generis*, Alexander – rarely inclined to persuasion, far less gullibility in such matters – came to accept Albrighton's diary as genuine, and in 1987 included information from it in the revised edition of his book.[2]

Among the extracts copied by Albrighton is one carefully headed in underlined type as 'The bombing of Getafe.'

I have started this account by copying out the extract for the previous day to show why we happened to be in Getafe on that particular day.

Thursday 29th October. After two days of advancing in which we covered about five miles the first day, and one mile the second day, we were ordered to withdraw back to our reserve positions outside Getafe. Evidently the orders for our moving out were mistakenly given and our presence was not needed . . . The U. G. T. and the Communist units are able to continue without our support . . . We have spent most of the day sleeping, making up for the last two nights . . .

Friday, 30th October. Today is a day that I think will live for ever in my memory. I had read before coming to Spain, the atrocities committed by the Nazis and the Fascists. I have listened to Alfred about their actions. I have heard from Nikki of his experiences under them. (note: these two comrades escaped from the Gestapo) From many others who have escaped from Germany and Italy, I have heard tales of barbarism, but I have taken them all with the proverbial grain of salt, believing most of them to be basically propaganda . . . Today, I now know different . . . We were entrenched well outside the town of Getafe, and everything has been fairly quiet except for the air raids upon our positions . . . Today I was detailed to go to the intendencia[3] which was on the other side of Getafe. We were just entering [this particular part of] Getafe when we heard the Fascist planes . . . According to his orders the driver stopped the lorry [in the shadow of an old building on the outskirts] this was done so that we would not attract the attention of the planes.

It was a sunny morning, and from our vantage point we could see and hear the many young children playing in a large open space to the rear of the houses . . . We could hear their shouts and laughter as these care free and innocent little children played their make believe games in the clear open space.

The Fascist bombers instead of passing over, started to circle Getafe . . . They flew so low that their black shadows swept the ground . . . The children had stopped their playing and appeared to be more fascinated than frightened by these circling, mechanical, harbingers of death . . . Slowly the planes circled overhead . . . There can be no excuse for the pilots that flew so slowly, and without hindrance, that they could not see their targets or distinguish them.

The children stood as if spell bound by some irresistible power that these strange machines held over them . . . They may have glimpsed with out understanding the metallic glint of the bombs as they hurled earthwards . . . Fascination was soon turned to terror and fear, as the sounds of the explosions shattered the silence of that sunny morning. The screams of little children, many of them under nursery school age, rent the air, screaming for their parents, or just screaming with fear . . .

The pilots continued to circle, no doubt looking down with great satisfaction at the degree of accuracy, and the precision with which they had placed their bombs . . . Again and again their target was the open space where many children still remained, motionless, transfixed by the paralysis brought on by their apparent state of terror. As we raced forwards to reach these little ones, parents, women, men, both the young and the old, grandparents and other relatives also came streaming from their homes towards the children, activated by the sounds of screams they raced on heedless of their own danger . . . We were now within a few, (may be one hundred yards) of the children when these inhuman fiends jettisoned the remainder of their bombs, raining down more death and destruction upon these innocent none combatants whose only crime was the thought of saving the children.

As a final example of their callous disregard that these Fascist barbarians have for humanity, one of the planes that up till then only circled the town, flew higher and while circling released his bombs indiscriminately on the homes of the victims . . .

I consider this scene as one of wholesale carnage that exceeds any other act of barbarism that history has recorded over the centuries . . . This is indeed a modern version of the slaughter of the innocents.

I find it very distressing to try and even describe the picture that I saw . . . The remnants of limbs, the particles of flesh and blood spattered against the white washed walls, fragments of all that remained of what only minutes before had been innocent, care free, joyful toddlers playing in the morning sun . . .

The wounded, some limbless, all mutilated, many dying in our arms as we attempted to comfort them . . . I realised that there was no longer the sounds of planes, or any more screams . . . The silence caused by shock had taken hold . . . To these people, a carnage of such catastrophic proportions was unbelievable . . . There was no need for them to speak with their lips, their eyes told it all, their expressions spoke louder than words.

> This action taken by the murderous scum will for ever disgrace the name of man. It should be sufficient in itself to show the free world what the future holds in store for all humanity under a Fascist regime.

> I met again later in the day the members of the Scottish Ambulance unit . . . They have done great work with the best amount of equipment . . . I wonder if the so called press who stay in Madrid will give full coverage to this day's work, I have my doubts if any of them will publish a true account of this outrage.

Considerations of space preclude anything more than a cursory examination of the Albrighton case, and the following brief remarks will have to suffice for present purposes. Taken as a whole, and on first reading, the texts sent to Alexander have the ring of authenticity even to the expert reader. There is no obvious sense of plagiarism in respect of other familiar accounts. The style is vivid – if not always convincingly immediate – and the historical reality of many events described can be corroborated from extant sources. Albrighton recounts them with a convincing plausibility of context, for example over the circumstances in which he encountered several (later legendary) figures who were fighting alongside his own unit as members of the XI and XII International Brigades: men like John Cornford, Bernard Knox, Esmond Romilly and Bill Scott. Indeed hardly any prominent figure from these two discrete groups is missing from the story. A sense of verisimilitude is deepened by the inclusion of muster lists from the militia company in which he served, and which (as acting company secretary) he personally compiled at the time. These reveal a mixture of Spanish fighters with dozens of surnames of French, German and east European origin, as well as several Britons. Indeed, if these lists were authentic, Albrighton's anarchist unit was more thoroughly 'international' than any of those organized by the Comintern. However, when examined with expert attention, none of these names can be corroborated from other contemporary sources, no-one Albrighton met seems to have remembered him, and even the alleged title of his militia unit – 'Muerte es Maestro (sic)' (Death is the Master) – cannot be identified.[4]

Furthermore, none of the original papers from which Albrighton claimed to have transcribed his extracts is extant. Despite several promises to make photocopies, and even to send

Alexander some of the original materials, in practice Albrighton never seems to have provided examples. The only original artefact we can be certain he had preserved was an identity card (apparently also no longer extant) adorned with a photograph of the author as a 'Voluntario Extranjero', made in October 1936. Following his death, a son and daughter of Albrighton – the former stated to me that his father never talked about Spain – believed that he had sent his original papers to the Imperial War Museum. But I have ascertained that no-one at the written archives of the IMW has ever seen them.

My scepticism about his evidence was increased upon discovery of Albrighton's personal file amongst the official records of the XV International Brigade in Moscow. Here, his date of arrival in Spain is entered as 'May 1937'.[5] A passport-type photograph appended to pro-forma materials displays no resemblance to the portrait made for similar purposes eight months earlier (a photocopy of which was sent to Alexander): likewise, the autograph signature is radically unlike that to be found on the identity card mentioned above. The subject's holograph autobiographical statement in the Moscow file makes only one indication of previous service in Spain, the uncanny and mysterious inclusion of 'Cordoba' (December 1936) amongst the places where he claimed experience of battle. But according to various Brigade officials, as a member of the British Battalion he consistently avoided being sent to the front! He was in effect dismissed the service and repatriated as 'demoralized' and 'weak' in September 1938.[6]

If Albrighton was the anonymous 'Englishman fighting with the militia' who spoke to Geoffrey Cox of the *News Chronicle* in Getafe on Saturday 31 October – the day after the alleged massacre, when the dying children's bloodstains must still have been visible on his clothing – it seems strange that he did not think it worthwhile to mention the incident.[7] On the other hand, if his diary were an authentic record, it would prove its author to have been by far the most courageous, accomplished and experienced British warrior to have fought in Spain. As things stand, nevertheless – a judgement which might be thought mundane were it not for the extraordinary circumstances of the case – it must be regarded as a bizarre and elaborate forgery, the result of many years of obscure but painstaking research and imaginative reconstruction, intended by its author to efface a besetting and shameful memory of actual non-achievement, even malingering, in the service of democracy in Spain.[8] Finally, it can be stated that even were all other doubts about his claims to be resolved by miraculous revelations at present beyond our ken, the details Albrighton gives of the alleged 'Bombing of Getafe' (as I hope the content of my book has demonstrated) will remain the stuff of fiction.

NOTES

[1] Correspondence and Diary extracts are in MML, IBA Box 50/AL.
[2] Alexander (1987), pp. 52–4.
[3] Quartermaster's Stores.
[4] Negative evidence comes from ANGC, Sección Militar, legajo 324 (rosters) and legajos 4623–24 (personal files). These cover militia units present in Madrid's defence army in November 1936. (However, these are only three bundles amongst several dozen which seem relevant.) One company, raised and commanded by Juan Perea Capulino, ex-army officer turned CNT commander, was titled 'Legionarios de la Muerte', but had no foreign component. It was later attached to Líster's Brigade: PCE, Microfilm Roll 28, f. 58. Much evidence suggests that foreigners who enlisted before the Madrid campaign were transferred to the International Brigades by November at the latest.
[5] Moreover, a muster roll of the British Battalion in May 1938 recorded Albrighton's date of arrival in Albacete as '30–7–37'; MML IBA Box D7/A1.
[6] RAPH, 545/6/101. On his pro-forma 'Biografia de Militantes' (a questionnaire required of all volunteers present in Spain after April 1938) Albrighton claimed to have served as a medical orderly during the battles of Córdoba, Teruel and Gandesa, being wounded in each of them. But the official Comintern report states that he 'did not see action. He dodged it. He twisted an ankle and said he would only have an operation in England'; ibid., ff. 6–9.
[7] See above, p. 84.
[8] The case may be one of personation. It may be conjectured that Albrighton befriended a veteran of 'Madrid, 1936' during his hospital service, later expropriating and embellishing the stories he was told.

Appendix C

Tabularized Data from 'Getafe' References

Source & Date	No. of Victims	Getafe Specified	Site of Bombs	No. of Bombs	No. of Planes	Comment
A Immediate						
Albrighton*		yes	street	many	6+	*?eyewitness diary
Ogilvie-Forbes	c 40*	yes	street			*inc. wounded + adults
Koltsov	20*	no				*no. of pictures
Pitcairn		no	school			
D. Worker	72	yes	street	1	3	
The Times		yes	street	several		
Daily Mail	70	yes	street		1	
News Chronicle	20*	yes				*inc wounded + adults
L'Humanité	70	yes	school	many		
B Contemporary						
CP Pamphlet 1937	71	yes	school		1	
LP Pamphlet 1937	40*	yes	street			*inc wounded + adults
Koestler 1937	60			6		

Source & Date	No. of Victims	Getafe Specified	Site of Bombs	No. of Bombs	No. of Planes	Comment
Jellinek 1937		yes				
F. Ryan 1937		no	School yard			
Katz 1937	100	yes	school			
Merin 1938	63	yes	near school			
Erlebnisse 1938	63	yes	school			
Bombarde- ments 1938	125	yes				
Sender 1939	363	no*				*'in one case'
Monserrat 1939		yes				
Del Vayo 1940		yes	hospital			
Barea 1944	50	yes	school	1	1	
C Subsequent						
Thomas 1961*	60	yes				*amended 1977
Hills 1976	60	yes	school			
Jato Miranda 1976	50*	yes				* inc wounded + adults
Kurzman 1980	70	yes				
Reig Tapia 1990*	60	yes		Many	6	*repeated 1999
Montoliú Camps 2000	60	yes	School- children			
Solé / Villaroya 2003	60	yes				

Source & Date	No. of Victims	Getafe Specified	Site of Bombs	No. of Bombs	No. of Planes	Comment
AirWar Website 2004	60	yes	School-children			

Bibliography

1. Primary Source Collections

AGMA – Archivo General Militar, Avila
AHMG – Archivo Histórico Municipal de Getafe
ANGC – Archivo Nacional de la Guerra Civil, Salamanca
BNA – British National Archives, Kew, London
FO – Foreign Office Files
WO – War Office Files
IBA – International Brigade Memorial Trust Archive, Marx Memorial Library, London
IWM – Imperial War Museum, London, Written Archives Section
LHC – Liddell-Hart Collection, King's College, London
NMLH – National Museum of Labour History, Manchester
MAE – Archivo del Ministerio de Asuntos Exteriores, Madrid
Archivo de Burgos – Nationalist Documents
Archivo de Barcelona – Republican Documents
PCE – Archive of the Spanish Communist Party, Madrid
RAPH – Russian Archive of Political & Social History, Moscow
SUCC – Coalfield Collection, University College of Wales, Swansea
TNL – The Times Newspaper Archive, International House, London

2. Secondary Sources

NB Here and in the footnotes to the text, I have inserted 'WWP@URL' (= Website Previously Present') before those sites which are no longer accessible, or from which material once available has since disappeared. Place of publication is London unless otherwise entered.

Abella, R. (1973) *La vida cotidiana durante la guerra civil* (2 vols, Barcelona, Planeta)
Abrahamson, A. (1994) *Mosaico Roto* (Madrid, Compañía Literária)
Abrosov, S. (2003) *V Nebe Ispanii*; translated and abstracted as *In the Skies of Spain* by I. Gordelianow (made available to members of Spanish Civil War list group: *spanish_civil_war@yahoogroups.com*)

Acier, M. (ed.) (1937) *From Spanish Trenches: Recent Letters from Spain* (New York, Modern Age Books)

Ades, D. *et al.* (eds) (1995) *Art & Power: Europe under the Dictators, 1930–1945* (Hayward Gallery for XXIII Council of Europe Exhibition)

Alcocer Badenas, S. (1978) *Fusilado en las tapias del cementario* (Barcelona, Plaza y Janes)

Alcofar Nassaes, J. (1971) *Los asesores soviéticos [los 'mejicanos'] en la guerra civil española* (Barcelona, Dopesa)

Aldgate, A. (1979) *Cinema and History: British Newsreels and the Spanish Civil War* (Scolar Press)

Alexander, B. (1982/1987) *British Volunteers for Liberty: Spain, 1936–39* (Lawrence & Wishart)

—— *et al.* (1996) *Memorials of the Spanish Civil War: The Official Publication of the International Brigade Association* (Stroud, Sutton)

Allison Peers, E. (1943) *Spain in Eclipse, 1937–1943* (Methuen)

Alpert, M. (1977) *El ejército republicano en la guerra civil* (Barcelona, Ruedo Ibérico)

—— (1984) 'Humanitarianism and Politics in the British Response to the Spanish Civil War, 1936–9', *European History Quarterly*, 14 (1), 423–40

Alvarez del Vayo, J. (1940/1971) *Freedom's Battle* (Heinemann)

Alvarez Lopera, J. (1982) *La política de bienes culturales del gobierno republicano durante la guerra civil española* (2 vols, Madrid, Ministerio de Cultura)

Alvarez Rodríguez, R. & López Ortega, R. (eds) (1986) *Poesía Anglo-NorteAmericana de la Guerra Civil Española: antología bilingüe* (Salamanca, Junta de Castilla-León)

Ambler, E. (1939/1966) *The Mask of Dimitrios* (Fontana/Collins)

Anderson, J. M. (2003) *The Spanish Civil War – A History and Reference Guide* (Westport, Conn., Greenwood Press)

Andrés-Gallego, J. & Pazos, A. M. (eds) (2002) *Archivo Gomá: Documentos de la Guerra Civil,* Vol. 2 (Madrid, CSIC)

Armero, J.-M. (1976) *España fué noticia; Corresponsales extranjeros en la Guerra Civil Española* (Madrid, Sedmay)

Arxer i Bussalleu, J. & Torres, E. (1999) *La guerra civil en Arenys de Mar* (Barcelona, Abadía de Montserrat)

Ashford-Hodges, G. (2000) *Franco – A Concise Biography* (Wiedenfield & Nicolson)

Ataques Aéreos (1937) *Ataques aéreos a poblaciones civiles* (Salamanca, Imprenta Nacional)

Avilés Farré, J. (1994) *Pasión y Farsa: Franceses y Británicos ante la Guerra Civil Española* (Madrid, Eudema)

Ayuda (1937) *Ayuda a Madrid* (Valencia, Ministerio de Propaganda)

Azaña, M. (1937/1981) *La Velada en Benicarló* (Madrid, Espasa Calpe)

—— (1937) *Speech by His Excellency the President of the Spanish Republic* (Spanish Embassy)

Aznar, M. (1958) *Historia Militar de la Guerra de España,* (3 vols, 3rd edn, Madrid, Editorial Nacional)

Baquero Gil, G. (1997) *Laboratorio de Retaguardia: Diario de la guerra en Madrid, 1936–39* (Madrid, La Palma)

Barea, A. (1938/1980) *Valor y Miedo* (Madrid, Esteban Editor)

—— (1943/1984) *The Forging of a Rebel: The Forge* (Flamingo)

—— (1946/1984) *La forja de un rebelde, 3: La llama* (Madrid, Turner)

—— (1946/1984A) *The Forging of a Rebel: The Clash* (Flamingo)

Barta, P. (1990) 'The Writing of History: Authors Meet on the Soviet–Spanish border', in M. Perez & W. Aycock (eds), *The Spanish Civil War in Literature* (Lubbock, Texas Technical University Press), pp. 75–86

Becker L. & Caiger Smith M. (eds) (1995) *Art & Power: Images of the 1930s* (Hayward Gallery)

Beckett, F. (1995) *Enemy Within: The Rise and Fall of the British Communist Party* (Merlin)

Beevor, A. (1982/1999) *The Spanish Civil War* (Cassell)

—— (2006) *The Battle for Spain: The Spanish Civil War 1936–1939* (Weidenfeld & Nicolson)

Bell, A. (1996) *Only For Three Months: The Basque Children in Exile* (Norwich, Mousehold Press)

Bennassar, B. (2005) *El infierno fuimos nosotros: la guerra civil española (1936–1942. . .)* (Madrid, Taurus)

Black, J. (2000) *A New History of Wales* (Stroud, Sutton)

Bombardements (1938) *Bombardements et Agressions en Espagne, Juillet 1936–Juillet 1938* (Paris, Comité Mondial contre la guerre et le fascisme)

Bombardeos (? 1939) *Bombardeos de la aviación nacional a la retaguardia republicana* (Barcelona, Seix y Barral)

Bombing (n.d.) *The Bombing of Guernica – Exhibition* (Gernika-Lumo, Gernikazarra Historia Taldea)

Bond, B. (1977) *Basil Liddell-Hart: A Study of his Military Thought* (Cassell)

Borkenau, F. (1937/1986) *The Spanish Cockpit* (Pluto Press)

Borrás y Bermejo, T (ed.) (1962) *Madrid, teñido de rojo [the diary of A. Ramos Martín]* (Madrid, Sección de Cultura)

Bradshaw, D. (1997–8) 'British Writers and Anti-Fascism in the 1930s', *Woolf Studies Annual* (New York, Pace University Press) 3, 1–27 and 4, 41–66

Bradshaw, S. (1982) 'Spain – Six Years after Franco', *The Listener*, 14 January

Bridgeman, B.(1989) *The Flyers: The Untold Story of British and Commonwealth Airmen in the Spanish Civil War and Other Air Wars from 1919 to 1940* (Swindon, privately published)

Bronowski, J. (1939) *Spain 1939: Four Poems* (Hull, Andrew Marvell Press)

Brothers, C. (1997) *War and Photography: A Cultural History* (Routledge)

Buchanan, T. (1992) *The British Labour Movement and the Spanish Civil War* (Cambridge, C.U.P)

—— (1993) ' "A Far Away Country of Which We Know Nothing"? Perceptions of Spain and its Civil War in Britain, 1931–39', *Twentieth Century British History*, 4 (1), 1–24

—— (1997) *Britain and the Spanish Civil War* (Cambridge, C.U.P.)

Buchanan, (2003) 'Edge of Darkness: British "Front-line" Diplomacy in the Spanish Civil War, 1936–1937', *Contemporary European History,* 12 (3), 279–303

—— (2007) *The Impact of the Spanish Civil War on Britain: War, Loss and Memory* (Eastbourne, Sussex Academic Press)

Bullón de Mendoza, A. & de Diego, A. (2000) *Historias orales de la Guerra Civil* (Barcelona, Ariel)

Cabezas, J. A. (1984) *Morir en Oviedo* (Madrid, Editorial San Martín)

Cable, J. (1979) *The Royal Navy and the Siege of Bilbao* (Cambridge, Cambridge University Press)

Candela, A (1989) *Adventures of an Innocent in the Spanish Civil War* (Cornwall, United Writers)

Cañete, A. (1975) *El Sitio de Oviedo* (Madrid, Editorial San Martín)

Caparros Lera, J. M. (1981) *Arte y política en el cine de la República (1931–1939)* (Barcelona, Ediciones Universidad de Barcelona)

Carey, J. (1987) 'When the Lying Wouldn't Stop' *The Sunday Times,* 24 May, 48

Carr, R. (ed.) (1971) *The Republic and the Civil War in Spain* (Macmillan)

—— (1986) *Images of the Spanish Civil War* (Allen & Unwin)

Carulla, J. & Carulla, A. (1997) *La guerra civil en 2000 carteles. República. Guerra Civil. Posguerra* (3 vols, Barcelona, Postermil)

Casanova, J. (1999) 'Rebelión y Revolución', in S. Juliá, pp. 57–185

Casas de la Vega, R. (1994) *El Terror – Madrid 1936: Investigacion histórica y catálogo de vícimas identificadas* (Madridejos, Editorial Fénix)

Cate, C. (1995) *Andre Malraux: A Biography* (Hutchinson)

Causa (1944) *Causa General de la Dominación Roja en España. Avance de la información instruida por el Ministerio Público* (Madrid, Ministerio de Justicia)

Cervera, J. (1998) *Madrid en guerra: la ciudad clandestina* (Madrid, Alianza)

Cid i Mulet, J. (2001) *La guerra civil i la revolució en Tortosa (1936–1939)* (Barcelona, Abadía de Montserrat)

Cobo Romero, F. (1990) 'La Junta Provincial de Defensa Pasiva contra aeronaves de Jaén', in O. Ruiz-Monjón & M. Gómez Oliver (eds), *Los nuevos historiadores ante la Guerra Civil española* (2 vols, Granada, Diputación Provincial)

Cochrane, A. (with Blyth, M.) (1989) *One Man's Medicine* (British Medical Journal, The Memoir Club)

Cockburn, C. (1936) *Reporter in Spain* (Lawrence & Wishart)

—— (1967) *I, Claud . . . The Autobiography of Claud Cockburn* (Harmondsworth, Penguin)

—— (ed. Pettifer, J.) *Cockburn in Spain: Dispatches from the Spanish Civil War* (Lawrence and Wishart, 1986)

Colodny, R. (1958) *The Struggle for Madrid: the Central Epic of the Spanish Conflict, 1936–1937* (New York, Paine-Whitman)

Coma, J. (2002) *La Brigada Hollywood: Guerra Española y cine americano* (Barcelona, Ediciones Flor del Viento)

Cook, J. (1979), *Apprentices of Freedom* (Quartet Books)

Cope, P. (2007) *Wise and Foolish Dreamers: Wales and the Spanish Civil War* (Cardiff, Welsh Centre for International Affairs)

Copeman, F. (1948) *Reason in Revolt* (Blandford)

Cortada, J. (ed.) (1982) *Historical Dictionary of the Spanish Civil War* (Westport, Conn., Greenwood Press)

Coverdale, J. F. (1975) *Italian Intervention in the Spanish Civil War* (Princeton, Princeton University Press)

Cowles, V. (1941) *Looking for Trouble* (Hamish Hamilton)

Cox, G. (1937) *Defence of Madrid* (Gollancz)

Cunningham, V. (ed.) (1980) *The Penguin Book of Spanish Civil War Verse* (Harmondsworth, Penguin)

—— (ed.) (1986) *Spanish Front: Writers on the Civil War* (Oxford, Oxford University Press)

Davies, D. H. (1983) *The Welsh Nationalist Party, 1925–1945: A Call to Nationhood* (Cardiff, University of Wales Press)

Delaprée, L. (1936) *The Martyrdom of Madrid* (Madrid, Ministry of State)

Desmond, R. (1984) *The Tides of War: World News Reporting, 1931–1945* (Iowa, University of Iowa Press)

Díaz-Plaja, F. (ed.) (1994) *La vida cotidiana en la España de la guerra civil* (Madrid, Edaf)

—— (ed.) (1972) *La Guerra de España en sus Documentos* (Barcelona, Plaza y Janés)

Díaz Sandino, F. (1990) *De la Conspiración a la Revolución, 1929–1937* (Madrid, Libertarias)

Documento (1936) *Documento lo que han visto en Madrid los parliamentarios ingleses* (Valencia, Ministerio de Estado)

Documentos (1992) *Documentos Inéditos para la Historia del General Franco*, Vol. I (Madrid, Azar)

Dollard, J. (1944) *Fear in Battle* (Washington DC, The Infantry Journal)

Durango (1937) *Durango 1937* (Bilbao, Basque Department of Justice)

Dutt, R. P. (1936) *World Politics, 1918–1936* (Gollancz)

Eden, Anthony [Lord Avon] (1962) *Facing the Dictators* (Cassell)

Edwards, J. (1979) *The British Government and the Spanish Civil War, 1936–1939* (Macmillan)

Ehrenburg, I. (1979) *Corresponsal en la Guerra Civil Española* (Madrid, Ediciones Júcar)

El Fascismo (1937) *El Fascismo al desnudo* (Madrid–Valencia, Ediciones Españoles)

Elstob, P. (1973/1980) *La Legión Condor: España, 1936–39* (Madrid, San Martín)

Entrala, J. L. (1996) *Granada Sitiada, 1936–1939* (Granada, Ediciones Comares)

Episode (?1938) *Un episode de la lutte fratricide: deux mois de bombardement* (Paris, Editions des Archives Espagnols)

Erlebnisse (1938) see Merin, P

Eaude, M. (1996) 'Arturo Barea: The Unflinching Eye' (unpublished Ph.D thesis, University of Bristol)

Fegan, T. (2002) *The 'Baby Killers': German Air Raids on Britain in the First World War* (Barnsley, Leo Cooper)

296   *Your Children Will Be Next*

Fernández, C. (1983) *Paracuellos de Jarama – Carillo culpable?* (Barcelona, Argos Vergara)

Fernán-Gómez, F. (1986) 'Octubre del 1936' and 'La guerra y la vida', *El País Semanal,* 12 and 19 October

Figueres, J. M. (ed.) (2004) *Madrid en Guerra: Crónica de la batalla de Madrid, 1936–1939* (Barcelona, Destino)

Fisch, E. (1988) *Guernica by Picasso: A Study of the Picture and its Context* (2nd edn, Lewisburg, Bucknell University Press)

Fischer, L. (1941) *Men and Politics* (Cape)

Fisera, J. (?1937) 'The Bombardment of Madrid', in *Spain Assailed – Student Delegates to Spain Report* (c/o Student Forum, WC 1), 41–2

Foss, W. & Gerahty, C. (n.d ?1939) *The Spanish Arena* (Right Book Club)

Francis, H. (1984) *Miners Against Fascism: Wales and the Spanish Civil War* (Lawrence & Wishart)

Fraser, R. (1979) *Blood of Spain* (New York, Pantheon Books)

Fusi Aizpuru, J. P. (2002) *El País Vasco, 1931–1937: Autonomía, Revolución, Guerra Civil* (Madrid, Bibloteca Nueva)

Fyrth, J. (1986) *The Signal Was Spain: The Aid Spain Movement in Britain, 1936–1939* (Lawrence & Wishart)

Galante, P. (1971) *Malraux* (New York, Cowles Book Co.)

Gárate Córdoba, J. M. (ed.) (1977–78) *Partes oficiales de la guerra* (2 vols, Madrid, San Martín)

García Suárez, A., see Pérez Couto, A.

García Volta, G. (1975) *La Campaña del Norte* (Barcelona, Ediciones Bruguera)

Garriga, R. (1978) *La Legión Condor* (Barcelona, Plaza y Janes)

—— (1979) *Ramón Franco: el hermano maldito* (2nd edn, Barcelona, Planeta, 1979)

Gathorne-Hardy, J. (1992/1994) *Gerald Brenan – The Interior Castle* (Sinclair Stevenson)

Geist, A. L. & Carroll, P. (2001) *They Still Draw Pictures: Children's Art in Wartime from the Spanish Civil War to Kosovo* (Urbana, University of Illinois Press)

Gellhorn, M. (1959/1986) *The Face of War* (Virago)

—— (1989) *The View from the Ground* (Granta)

General Cause (1946) *The General Cause. The Red Domination in Spain. Preliminary Information drawn up by the Ministry of Justice* (Madrid, Tribunal Supremo del Ministerio Fiscal)

Gibson, I. (1973/1983) *The Assassination of Federico García Lorca* (Harmondsworth, Penguin)

—— (1983) *Paracuellos – Como Fué* (Barcelona, Vergara)

Gilbert, M. (1989) *The Second World War* (Fontana/Collins)

Gillan, P. (1937) *The Defence of Madrid* (Young Communist League)

Goñi Galarraga, J. M. (1989) *La guerra civil en el Pais Vasco: Una guerra entre católicos* (Vitoria, ESET)

González Betes, A. (1987) *Franco y el Dragon Rapide* (Madrid, Rialp)

González Echegaray, R. (1977) *La marina mercante y el tráfico marítimo en la guerra civil, 1936–1939* (Madrid, San Martín)

González Portilla, M. & Garmendía, J. M. (1988) *La guerra civil en el País Vasco: política y economía* (Leioa, Universidad del País Vasco)

Graham, H. (2002) *The Spanish Republic at War, 1936–39* (Cambridge, Cambridge University Press)

—— (2005) *The Spanish Civil War: A Very Short Introduction* (Oxford, Oxford University Press)

Greene, G. (1939/1958) *The Confidential Agent* (New York, Bantam)

Griffin, F. (1937) 'The Tragedy of Spain', 25 March 1937. Full text printed in *The Empire Club of Canada Speeches, 1936–37* (Toronto, Empire Club of Canada, 1937), pp. 289–307; *http://www.empireclubfoundation.com*

Grimau, G. (1979) *El cartel republicano en la Guerra Civil* (Madrid, Cátedra)

Gualtieri, E. (1998) 'Three Guineas and the Photograph: The Art of Propaganda', in M. Joannou (ed.), *Women Writers of the 1930s: Gender, Politics, History* (Edinburgh, Edinburgh University Press)

Guttmann, A. (1962) *The Wound in the Heart: America and the Spanish Civil War* (New York, Free Press of Glencoe)

Guzmán, E. de (1973) *1930: Historia política de un año decisivo* (Madrid, Tebas)

Haigh, R. H. *et al.* (eds) (1986) *The Guardian Book of the Spanish Civil War* (Aldershot, Wilwood House)

Harding, J. (1998) 'No One Leaves Her Place in Line', *London Review of Books*, 7 May, 26–7 and 30–1

Harris, G. (1997) 'Malraux, Myth, Political Commitment and the Spanish Civil War', *Modern and Contemporary France*, 5 (3), 319–28

Hensbergen, G. van (2004/05) *Guernica – The Biography of a Twentieth-Century Icon* (Bloomsbury)

Hermann, D. (2002) '*The Devil's Backbone* and the Phantoms of the Spanish Civil War', in *The Volunteer* (March), pp. 18–19

Hermet, G. (1989) *La guerre d'Espagne* (Paris, Editions du Seuil)

Hidalgo de Cisneros, I. (1986) 'Through the Eyes of a Spanish Patriot', in *Fighting side by side with Spanish Patriots against Fascism: Recollection of Soviet citizens who took part in the Spanish Civil War* (Moscow, Novosti), pp. 70–6

Hidalgo Luque, P. (2006) 'Los bombardeos aéreos republicanos sobre la retaguardia nacional durante la Guerra Civil Española: Aproximación al caso de Córdoba'. (Paper read to the Civil War Conference of the Spanish Catholic University Organisation [CEU], Madrid)

Hills, G. (1976) *The Battle for Madrid* (Vantage Books)

Hopkins, J. (1998) *Into the Heart of the Fire: The British in the Spanish Civil War* (Stanford, Stanford University Press)

Howarth, T. E. B. (1978) *Cambridge Between Two Wars* (Collins)

Howson, G. (1992) *Aircraft of the Spanish Civil War* (Putnam)

—— (1998) *Arms for Spain: The Untold Story of the Spanish Civil War* (John Murray)

Huxley, A. (intro.) (1938) *They Still Draw Pictures! A Collection of 60 Drawings Made by Spanish Children During the War* (New York, The Spanish Child Welfare Association of America)

Hyde, H. Montgomery & Nutall, G.R.F (1937) *Air Defence and the Civil Population* (The Cresset Press)

Ibárurri, D. (1976) *They Shall Not Pass: The Autobiography of La Pasionaria* (New York, International Press)

Infiesta Pérez, J. L. (2000–1) *Bombardeos del litoral Mediterráneo durante la guerra civil* (2 vols [Vol. II with J. Coll Pujol], Barcelona, Editorial Quirón) [N. B. I have relied on extensive abstracts of this work provided to members of the internet list, spanish_civil_ war@yahoogroups.com, by Sñr Julián Oller, Barcelona.]

Ingram, K. (1985) *Rebel: The Short Life of Esmond Romilly* (Weidenfeld & Nicolson)

Irazabal Agirre, J. (2001) *Durango: 31 de Marzo de 1937* (Durango, Fundación Sabino Arana)

Jackson, G. (1965) *The Spanish Republic and the Civil War, 1931–39* (New Jersey, Princeton University Press)

—— (ed.) (1972) *The Spanish Civil War* (Chicago, Quadrangle)

Jato Miranda, D. (1976) *Madrid: Capital Republicana* (Barcelona, Acervo)

Jellinek, F. (1938) *The Civil War in Spain* (Gollancz)

Jenkins, D. (ed. Davies, J.) (1998) *A Nation on Trial: Penyberth 1936* (Cardiff, Welsh Academic Press)

Johnson K. *et al.* (eds) (1996) *The Spanish Civil War Collection: Sound Archive Oral History Recordings* (Imperial War Museum)

Johnson, P. (1992) *Modern Times: A History of the World from the 1920s to the 1990s* (Phoenix)

Jones, R. (2002) 'Running Franco's Blockade: Captain John Jones, Aberarth and the S. S. Sarastone', *Ceredigion*, XIV (2), 79–88

'Journalist, A.' (1936) *Foreign Journalists Under Franco's Terror* (United Editorial)

Juliá, S. (ed.) (1999) *Víctimas de la guerra civil* (Madrid, Temas de Hoy)

[Katz, O.] (1937) *Nazi Conspiracy in Spain* (Gollancz)

Kenwood, A. (ed.) (1993) *The Spanish Civil War: A Cultural and Historical Reader* (Oxford, Berg)

King, J. (1990) *The Last Modern: A Life of Herbert Read* (Weidenfeld & Nicolson)

Knoblaugh, H. E. (1937) *Correspondent in Spain* (Sheed & Ward)

Knell, H. (2003) *To Bomb a City: Strategic Bombing and its Human Consequences in World War Two* (Cambridge MA, Da Capo Press)

Knightley, P. (1975/2000) *The First Casualty: The War Correspondent as Hero and Myth-Maker from the Crimea to Kosovo* (Prion Books)

Koestler, A. (1937) *Spanish Testament* (Gollancz)

—— (1954) *The Invisible Writing: Being the second volume of Arrow in the Blue, An Autobiography* (Hamish Hamilton)

Koltsov, M. (1963) *Diario de la Guerra de España* (Paris, Ruedo Ibérico)

Kowalsky, D. (2006) 'The Soviet Cinematic Offensive in the Spanish Civil War' (Paper read at Bristol University Conference on 'War Without Limits', 17 July)

Kurlansky, M. (1999) *The Basque History of the World* (Cape)

Kurzman, D. (1980) *Miracle of November: Madrid's Epic Stand 1936* (New York, Putnam's Sons)

Langdon-Davies, J. (1937) *Behind the Spanish Barricades* (Secker & Warburg)

Lannon, F. (2002) *The Spanish Civil War, 1936–1939* (Oxford, Osprey)

Larios, J. (1966) *Combat Over Spain* (New York, Macmillan)

Last, J. (1939) *The Spanish Tragedy* (Routledge)

Legarreta, D. (1984) *The Guernica Generation: Basque Refugee Children of the Spanish Civil War* (Reno, Nevada University Press)

Leguina, J. & Núñez, A. (2002) *Ramón Franco: El hermano olvidado del dictador* (Madrid, Temas de Hoy)

Lévy, B.-H. (1995) *Adventures on the Freedom Road: The French Intellectuals in the 20th Century* (The Harvill Press)

Lewis, G (2006) *A Bullet Saved My Life. The Remarkable Adventures of Bob Peters. An Untold Story of the Spanish Civil War* (Abersychan, Warren & Pell)

Lewis, J. E. (1998) *The Mammoth Book of How it Happened* (Robinson)

Lewis, W. & Davies, R. (2005) *In the Footsteps of the Spanish Civil War: A Guide to South Wales Monuments to the International Brigades* (International Brigade Memorial Trust)

Lindqvist, S. (2001) *A History of Bombing* (Granta)

Líster, E. (1977) *Memorias de un luchador: I. Los primeros combates* (Madrid, Del Toro)

Llarch, J. (1978) *Cantos y Poemas de la Guerra Civil Española* (Barcelona, Producciones Editoriales)

London, A. (1965) *España, España* (Prague, Artia)

Low, R. (1992) *La Pasionaria – The Spanish Firebrand* (Hutchinson)

Lunn, A. (1937/74) *Spanish Rehearsal for World War: An Eyewitness in Spain During the Civil War (1936–1939)* (Old Greenwich, Conn., The Devin-Adair Company)

Lyotard, J.-F. (1999) *signed, Malraux,* trans. R. Harvey (Minneapolis, University of Minnesota Press)

McFarland, S. L. (1995) *America's Pursuit of Precision Bombing, 1910–1945* (Washington, Smithsonian Institution)

Machado, A. (ed.) (1937) *Madrid – Baluarte de nuestra guerra de independencia* (Barcelona, Servicio de Información)

Madrid (1937) *Madrid – The Military Atrocities of the Rebels: A Record of Massacre, Murder, Mutilation* (The Labour Party)

Madrid 1937 (1996) *Madrid 1937: Letters of the Abraham Lincoln Brigade from the Spanish Civil War* (New York, Routledge)

Maisky, I. (1966) *Spanish Notebooks* (Hutchinson)

Malraux, A. (1938/1979) *Man's Hope [L'Espoir]* (New York, Grove Press)

Manuela de Cora, M. (1984) *Retaguardia Enemiga* (Madrid, Altalena)

Marques, P. (2000) *La Croix-Rouge pendant la guerre d'Espagne* (Paris, privately published)

Martin, R. (2002) *Picasso's War: The Destruction of Guernica and the Masterpiece That Changed the World* (Dutton)

Martín Jiménez, I. (2000) *La guerra civil en Valladolid: amaneceres ensangrentados* (Valladolid, Ambito)

Martín Rubio, A. (2005) *Los mitos de la represión en la guerra civil* (Madrid, Grafite Ediciones)

Martínez Amutio, J. (1974) *Chantaje a un pueblo* (Madrid, del Toro)

Martínez Bande, J. (1972) *La ofensiva de Segovia y batalla de Brunete* (Madrid, San Martín)

—— (1974) *La batalla de Teruel* (Madrid, San Martín)

—— (1976) *Frente de Madrid* (Barcelona, Caralt)

—— (1982) *La marcha sobre Madrid* (Madrid, San Martín)

—— (1984) *La lucha en torno a Madrid* (Madrid, San Martín)

—— (1988) *La batalla del Ebro* (Madrid, San Martín)

Massot i Muntaner, J. (1976) *La guerra civil a Mallorca* (Barcelona, Abadía de Monstserrat)

Masters, J. (1983) *Man of War* (Sphere)

Matthews, H. (1938) *Two Wars and More to Come* (New York, Carrick & Evans)

—— (1957) *The Yoke and the Arrows: A Report on Spain* (Heinemann)

Mendez Luengo, E. (1977) *Tempestad al amanecer: la epopeya de Madrid* (Madrid, del Toro)

Merin, P. (1938) *Spain between Death and Birth* (New York, Dodge)

—— [anon but idem] *Erlebnisse in Spanien* (n.p. 1938), WWP@URL *http://felix2.2v.net/english/spain/sp3e.html*

Middles, M. (1999) *Manic Street Preachers* (Omnibus)

Miller, W. (?1937) *I Found No Peace: The Journal of a Foreign Correspondent* (The Book Club)

Mitchell, D. (1982) *The Spanish Civil War: Based on the Television Series* (Granada)

Mitchell, D. & Reed P. (1991) *Letters from a Life: Selected Letters and Diaries of Benjamin Britten* (2 vols, Faber)

Moa, P. (1999) *Los orígenes de la Guerra Civil Española* (Madrid, Ediciones Encuentro)

—— (2001) *El derrumbe de la segunda república* (Madrid, Ediciones Encuentro)

—— (2003) *Los mitos de la guerra civil* (Madrid, Esfera)

—— (2003A) *Contra las mentiras: Guerra Civil, izquierda, nacionalistas y jacobinismo* (Madrid, Libros Libres)

Moloney, T. (1985) *Westminster, Whitehall and the Vatican: The Role of Cardinal Hinsley 1935–43* (Burns & Oates)

Monserrat, N. (1939) *This is the Schoolroom* (Cassell)

Monteath, P. (1994) *Writing the Good Fight: Political Commitment in the International Literature of the Spanish Civil War* (Westport, Conn., Greenwood Press)

Montero García, M. *et al.* (1994) *Pais Vasco* (Bilbao, Diputación Foral de Bizkaia)

Montoliú Camps, P. (1999) *Madrid en la guerra civil* (2 vols, Madrid, Silex)

Moradiellos, E. (1990) *Neutralidad benévola: El gobierno británico y la insurrección militar española de 1936* (Oviedo, Ediciones Pentalfa)

—— (1996) *La perfidia de Albión: El Gobierno Británico y la guerra civil española* (Madrid, Siglo XXI)

Moreno Gómez, F. (1985) *Córdoba en la guerra civil (1936–1939)* (Madrid, Alpuerto)

Morris, F. (ed.) (1986) *No Pasaran! Photographs and Posters of the Spanish Civil War* (Bristol, Arnolfini Gallery)

Muñiz Martín, O. (1976) *Asturias en la Guerra Civil* (Salinas, Ediciones Ayalga)

Nenni, P. (1977) *España* (Barcelona, Plaza y Janés)

Orwell, G. (ed. Davison, P.) (1998) *The Complete Works of George Orwell*, Vols 11 (*Facing Unpleasant Facts, 1937–1939*) & 13 (*All Propaganda is Lies, 1941–42*) (Secker & Warburg)

—— (1938 & 1943/1966) *Homage to Catalonia and Looking Back on the Spanish War* (Harmondsworth, Penguin)

Palacio Atard, V. (1973) *Cinco historias de la República y de la guerra* (Madrid, Editora Nacional)

Payne, S. (2004), *The Spanish Civil War, The Soviet Union, and Communism* (Yale University Press)

Paul, E. (1937) *The Life and Death of a Spanish Town* (New York, Random House)

Pérez Couto, A. [ed. García Suárez, A.] (1988) *Yo viví el drama de la guerra civil española* (La Habana, Editorial Pablo de Torriente)

Pérez Solís, O. (1937) *Sitio y defensa de Oviedo* (Valladolid, Palencia)

Piqué Padró, J. & Sánchez Cervelló, J. (2000) *Guerra civil a les comarques Tarragonines (1936–1939)* (Tarragona, Cercle d'estudis històrics i socials Guillem Oliver del Camp)

Preston, P. (1993) *Franco – A Biography* (Collins)

Proctor, R (1983) *Hitler's Luftwaffe in the Spanish Civil War* (Westport, Conn., Greenwood Press)

Pujadas, X. (1988) *Tortosa, 1936–1939: Mentalitats, revolució i guerra civil* (Tortosa, Ediciones Dertota)

Radosh, R. & Habeck, M. R. (eds) (2001), *Spain Betrayed: The Soviet Union in the Spanish Civil War* (Yale University Press)

Raguer, H (1980) 'La Santa Sede y los bombardeos de Barcelona', *Historia y Vida* No. 145 (April), 22–35

—— (2001) *La pólvora y el incienso: La Iglesia y la Guerra Civil española (1936–1939)* (Barcelona, Ediciones Península)

Rankin, N. (1997) 'Bombs, What Bombs? Guernica Revisited', *Times Literary Supplement*, 2 May

—— (2003) *Telegram from Guernica: The Extraordinary Life of George Steer, War Correspondent* (Faber & Faber)

Read, D. (1999) *The Power of News: The History of Reuters* (Oxford, Oxford University Press)

Reig Tapía, A. (1990) *Violencia y Terror: estudios sobre la Guerra Civil Española* (Madrid, AKAL)

—— (1999) *Memoria de la guerra civil española: Los mitos del tribu* (Madrid, Alianza)

Report (1937) *Report of a Delegation of Members of Parliament to Republican Spain* (Press Department, Spanish Embassy)

Reverte, J. (2004) *La batalla de Madrid* (Barcelona, Crítica)

Rey García A. (1997) *Stars for Spain: La Guerra Civil Española en los Estados Unidos* (La Coruña, Edicios do Castro)

Ries, K. & Ring, H. (1992) *The Legion Condor: A History of the Luftwaffe in the Spanish Civil War* (West Chester PA, Schiffer)

Rilova Pérez, (2001) *Guerra civil y violencia política en Burgos (1936–1943)* (Burgos, Editorial Dossoles)

Romancero (1937) *Romancero General de la Guerra de España* (Madrid-Valencia, Ediciones Españolas)

Romero, E. (2001) *Itinerarios de la guerra civil española: Guía del viajero curioso* (Barcelona, Laertes)

Romilly, E. (1937/1971) *Boadilla: A Personal Account of a Battle in Spain* (Macdonald)

Rosenthal, M. (1975) *Poetry of the Spanish Civil War* (New York, New York U.P.)

Rossif, F. and Chapsal, M. (1963) *Mourir a Madrid: L'Historie vecue de la guerre de l'Espagne* (Paris, Editions Seghers)

Sagués San José, J. (2003) *Una ciutat en guerra: Lleida en la guerra civil espanyola (1936–1939)* (Barcelona, Abadía de Montserat)

Salas Larrazábal, J. (1969) *La guerra civil española desde el aire: dos ejércitos y sus cazas frente a frente* (2 vols, Barcelona, Ariel)

—— (1974) *The Spanish Civil War in the Air* (Ian Allen)

Salas Larrazábal, R. (1977) *Pérdidas de la guerra de Espana* (Barcelona, Planeta)

—— (1980) *Los datos exactos de la guerra civil española* (Madrid, Drácena)

Schneider, S. (1992) 'Manipulating Images: Photojournalism from the Spanish Civil War', in L. Costa *et al.* (eds), *German and International Perspectives on the Spanish Civil War: The Aesthetics of Partisanship* (Columbia S.C., Camden House)

Schwarz, F. (1971/1999) *La internacionalizacion de la guerra civil española: julio de 1936-marzo de 1937* (Barcelona, Planeta)

Scott-Ellis, P. (ed. Carr, R.) (1995) *The Chances of Death: A Diary of the Spanish Civil War* (Norwich, Michael Russell)

Seidman, M. (1990) 'The Unorwellian Barcelona', *European History Quarterly* 20 (April), 163–80

—— (2002) *The Republic of Egos: A Social History of the Spanish Civil War* (Madison, University of Wisconsin Press)

Sender, R. (1937) *Counter-Attack in Spain* (Boston, Houghton Mifflin)

Serra, D. & Serra, J. (2003) *Testimonis d'una ciutat en guerra (Barcelona 1936–1939)* (Barcelona, Textos Columna)

Serrano, C. (ed.) (1991) *Madrid, 1936–1939: Un peuple en résistance ou l'epopée ambigue* (Paris, Autrement)

—— (ed.) [1989] 'El "informe" de Vital Gayman sobre "La base de las Brigadas Internacionales" [July 1937]', *Estudios de Historia Social*, 315–459

Sloan, P. (ed.) (1938) *John Cornford – A Memoir* (Cape)

Solé i Sabaté, J. & Villaroya i Font, J. (1986) *Catalunya sota les bombes (1936–1939)* (Barcelona, Abadía de Montserrat)

—— (2003) *España en llamas: La guerra civil española desde el aire* (Madrid, Temas de Hoy)

Southworth, H. (1977) *Guernica! Guernica! A Study of Journalism, Diplomacy, Propaganda and History* (Berkeley, University of California Press)

Spain (1938) *Spain Against the Invaders – Napoleon 1808 – Hitler and Mussolini 1936* (United Editorial)

Spain Assailed (?1937) *Spain Assailed – Student Delegates to Spain Report* (c/o Student Forum, WC 1)

Spain Illustrated (1937) *Spain Illustrated – A Year's Defence of Democracy* (Lawrence & Wishart)

Spanish (2001) *The Spanish Civil War: Dreams and Nightmares* (Imperial War Museum)

Speaight, R. (1966) *The Life of Eric Gill* (Methuen)

Spender, S. (1951) *World Within World* (Hamish Hamilton)

—— (1978) *The Thirties and After: Poetry, Politics, People* (Fontana)

Sperber, M. (ed.) (1974) *And I Remember Spain: A Spanish Civil War Anthology* (Hart-Davis, McGibbon)

Stansky, P. & Abrahams, W. (1966/1986) *Journey to the Frontier: Two Roads to the Spanish Civil War* (Constable)

Steer, G. (1938) *The Tree of Guernica: A Field Study of Modern War* (Hodder & Stoughton)

Stradling, R. (1989) 'The Propaganda of the Deed: History, Hemingway and Spain' *Textual Practice* 3(1), 15–35

—— (1996) *Cardiff and the Spanish Civil War* (Cardiff, Butetown History & Arts Centre)

—— (1997) 'History and the Triumph of Art: Manuel Azaña's Vision of Spanish Democracy' in idem, D. R. Bates & S. C. Newton (eds), *Conflict & Coexistence: Nationalism and Democracy in Modern Europe* (Cardiff, University of Wales Press)

—— Ed. (1998) *Brother against Brother: Experiences of a British Volunteer in the Spanish Civil War* (Stroud, Sutton Publishing, 1998)

—— (1999) *The Irish and the Spanish Civil War, 1936–1939: Crusades in Conflict* (Manchester, Manchester University Press)

—— (2003) *History and Legend: Writing the International Brigades* (Cardiff, University of Wales Press)

—— (2004) *Wales and the Spanish Civil War: The Dragon's Dearest Cause?* (Cardiff, University of Wales Press)

—— (2007A) 'Moaist Revolution and the Spanish Civil War: "Revisionist" History and Historical Politics', *English Historical Review* CXXII No. 496, 442–57

—— (2007B) 'Guernica in Context', unpublished article commissioned by *History Today* but subsequently rejected in favour of an alternative offered by Prof. P. Preston

Strong, A. L. (1937) *Spain in Arms 1937* (New York, Henry Holt & Co.)

Tagüeña, M. (1978) *Testimonio de dos guerras* (Barcelona, Planeta)

Talon, V. (1980) *Memoria de la Guerra de Euzkadi de 1936* (3 vols, Barcelona, Plaza y Janes)

Taylor, A. J. P. (1972/1974) *Beaverbrook* (Harmondsworth, Penguin)

Témime, E. (1986) *La Guerre d'Espagne Commence* (Brussels, Editions Complexe)
Thomas, F. [see Stradling, R. (1998)]
Thomas, G. & Morgan-Witts, M. (1975) *The Day Guernica Died* (Hodder & Stoughton)
—— & – (1991) *Guernica: How Hitler's Air Force Destroyed a Spanish City for Franco in Practice for World War II* (Chelsea, Minn., Scarborough House)
Thomas, H. (1961) *The Spanish Civil War* (Eyre & Spottiswoode)
—— (1965) 2nd edn (Harmondsworth, Penguin)
—— (1977) 3rd edn (Harmondsworth, Penguin)
—— (2004) 4th edn (Harmondsworth, Penguin)
Thornberry, R. S. (1977) *André Malraux et l'Espagne* (Geneva, Droz)
Tierney, D. (2004) 'Franklin D. Roosevelt and Covert Aid to the Loyalists in the Spanish Civil War, 1936–39', *Journal of Contemporary History*, 39 (3), pp. 299–313
Times (1952) *The History of The Times, Vol. 4: The 150th Anniversary and Beyond, 1912–1948* (The Times)
Torriente Brau, Pablo de la (1938) *Peleando con los milicianos* (Mexico City, Editorial México Nuevo)
Toynbee, P. (ed.) (1976) *The Distant Drum: Reflections on the Spanish Civil War* (Sidgwick & Jackson)
Trythall, J. (1970) *El Caudillo – The Political Biography of Franco* (New York, McGraw-Hill)
Valleau, M. (1982) *The Spanish Civil War in American and European Films* (Ann Arbor, UMI Research Press)
Van de Esch, P. A. M. (1951) *Prelude to War: The International Repercussions of the Spanish Civil War (1936–1939)* (The Hague, Martinus Nijhoff)
Vázquez, M. & Valero, J. (1978) *La guerra civil en Madrid* (Madrid, Tebas)
Veatch, R. (1984) 'The League of Nations and the Spanish Civil War, 1936–9', *European History Quarterly*, 20 (2), 181–207
Vera Deleito, A. & J. (2000) *Defensa Antiaéria Republicana (1936–1939): Artillería y Refugios (Algo de Valor)* (Requena, Privately Published)
Vergara, A. (2001) 'Images of Revolution and War', being the Introduction to the website archive of the H. R. Southworth Poster Collection, *http://orpheus.ucsd.edu/speccoll/visfront*
Vidal, C. (ed.) (1996) *Recuerdo mil novecientos treinta y seis. Una historia oral de la guerra civil* (Madrid, Amaya)
—— (1997) *La destrucción de Guernica: Un balance sesenta años después* (Madrid, Espasa)
Vilar, P. (1986) *La Guerra Civil Española* (Barcelona, Crítica)
Villaroya i Font, J. (1981) *Els Bombardeigs de Barcelona durant la guerra civil, 1936–1939* (Barcelona, Abadía de Monserrat)
Vinyes, R. (ed.) (1937/1978) *La ideologia i la barbarie dels Rebels Espanyols* (Barcelona, Grafiques Avia)
West, W. J. (ed.) (1986) *Orwell: The War Commentaries* (New York, Schocken Books)
Whiston, J. (1996) *Antonio Machado's Writings and the Spanish Civil War* (Liverpool, Liverpool University Press)

Williams, C., Alexander, B. & Gorman, J. (1996) *Memorials of the Spanish Civil War* (Stroud, Alan Sutton)

Willis, J. (?1938) *Restless Quest: An Odyssey of War's Aftermath* (Hurst & Blackett)

Woodward, E. L. & Butler, R. (eds) (1950) *Documents on British Foreign Policy (1919–1939)*, Third Series, Vol. II (HMSO)

Wolff, M. (1994) *Another Hill* (Chicago, University of Illinois Press)

Woolf, V. (2001) *Three Guineas* (Shakespeare Head Press)

—— (1980) *Letters of Virginia Woolf, Vol. 6* (Hogarth Press)

Woolsey, G. (1936/1988) *Death's Other Kingdom* (Virago)

Worsley T. C. (1939) *Behind the Battle* (Robert Hale)

—— (1971) *Fellow Travellers: A Memoir of the Thirties* (London Magazine Editions)

Wyden, P. (1983) *The Passionate War: The Narrative History of the Spanish Civil War* (New York, Simon & Schuster)

Yakushin, M. (1986) 'En la primera batalla contra el fascismo', in *Bajo la bandera de la República Española: Recuerdan los voluntarios soviéticos participantes en la guerra nacional-revolucionaria en España* (Moscow, Progress Publishers), pp. 343–63

Zavala, J. (2004) *Los horrores de la guerra civil* (2nd. edn, Madrid, Random House-Mondadori)

Zugazagoitia, A. (1940) *Guerra y visicitudes de los españoles* (Buenos Aires, Vanguardia)

Index